THE
BIRTH
OF
SHYLOCK
AND THE
DEATH
OF
ZERO MOSTEL

diary of a play 1973 to 1980

Arnold WESKER

Quartet Books

First published in Great Britain by Quartet Books Limited in 1997
A member of the Namara Group
27 Goodge Street
London W1P 2LD

Copyright © by Arnold Wesker 1997

The moral right of the author has been asserted

A catalogue record for this book is available from the British Library

ISBN 0 7043 8063 3

Phototypeset by F.S.H. Ltd
Printed and bound in Great Britain by C.P.D. Wales Ltd

'I think that what the Venetians in this play
have done to Shylock is turn him into the
Shylock of the other play'

John Dexter

to whom I dedicate this book
despite some things
but
because of most things

Shylock is meant to be a villain. There can be arguments about his motives and his personality, but there can be no serious argument about his behaviour. Given the opportunity — an opportunity which he himself has created — he attempts to commit legalized murder. He is also a Jewish villain. He did not have to be: Christians were moneylenders too, and the story would have worked perfectly well with a Christian villain... He belongs, inescapably, to the history of anti-Semitism... At no point does anyone (any other character) suggest that there might be a distinction to be drawn between his being a Jew and his being an obnoxious individual. The result is ugly... The ground for the Holocaust was well prepared...

John Gross, *Shylock — Four Hundred Years in the Life of a Legend*, 1992

Contents

A New York Cast

SHYLOCK KOLNER	Joseph Leon
JESSICA	Julie Garfield
RIVKA	Marian Seldes
TUBAL DI PONTI	John Seitz
ANTONIO QUERINI	John Clements
BASSANIO VISCONTI	Nicholas Surovy
LORENZO PISANI	Everett McGill
GRAZIANO SANUDO	Riggs O'Hara
PORTIA CONTARINI	Roberta Maxwell
NERISSA	Gloria Gifford
SOLOMON USQUE	Jeffrey Horowitz
REBECCA DA MENDES	Angela Wood
MOSES OF CASTALAZZO	Leib Lensky
GIROLAMO PRIULI (DOGE)	William Roerick
ABTALION DA MODENA	Boris Tumarin
MAID/SINGER	Rebecca Malka
SERVANTS/SENATORS	Russ Banham
ANDROIDS	Mark Blum
	Philip Carrol
	James David Cromar
	Brian Meister
	John Tyrell
DIRECTED BY	John Dexter
DESIGNED BY	Jocelyn Herbert
LIGHTING BY	Andy Philips

Preamble

On 7 February 1975 I began writing a play I hoped would be my best – first named *The Merchant*, subsequently entitled *Shylock*. Its history has been dramatic and fraught with a bewildering resistance which is on-going. To fully comprehend the effect of the play's misfortune, an earlier history is necessary.

I was blessed to have emerged as a playwright in 1958 when, following in the wake of John Osborne's *Look Back in Anger*, my first five plays – though not without initial rejections and stumbles – earned generous critical acclaim if not riches. The eyes of the international theatre world were focused on British theatre; many of us were made international playwrights overnight.

My sixth play, *The Four Seasons*, a love story for two actors, received mixed reviews as did the next two: an epic about the conflict between the dream and reality, *Their Very Own And Golden City*, and a highly stylised play about facing death, *The Friends*. Out of eight plays only one – *Chips With Everything* – had been a commercial success. I was an established playwright but still somehow a peripheral one.

Then came the promise of those accolades all playwrights strive for – two new plays were contracted to be performed each by the two major theatres of the realm. Rights to *The Old Ones* were bought by the National Theatre, John Dexter directing; rights to *The Journalists* were bought by the Royal Shakespeare Company, David Jones directing. My career was to be consolidated. And the age was right – I was forty.

Within months of each other, both projects collapsed. While Dexter was abroad, Ken Tynan, the National's literary manager, threw *The Old Ones* out of the scheduled programme due, I think, to an internal quarrel between the two men.[1] I made representations to the National's board of trustees, and subsequently received a letter from Sir Laurence Olivier, then artistic director, saying the play had been reinstated. By this time a very hurt and angry John Dexter had been invited to direct the play at our old home, the Royal Court Theatre, and John asked me to follow him there. Though the National was a prize I'd long waited for, I felt strong loyalty to John and agreed to let the Court have the rights.

Meanwhile, back at the RSC, after casting *The Journalists* from the resident company, David Jones went on holiday. He returned to discover most of the actors had refused to perform the play. An unprecedented act and one not heard of since. Perhaps we'll never know why the actors took against it; my suspicions are that the 1971/2 company were strongly under the influence of the Workers' Revolutionary Party, and *The Journalists* contained portrayals of four Tory cabinet ministers who were highly intelligent – we're talking of days when the Labour Party was in power and Margaret Thatcher was undreamt of as leader of the Conservative Party. Actors can have hearts of gold and heads of wool when it comes to the subtleties of politics. I believe they misread the play. The artistic direction of the RSC sided with the actors, the play was dropped – an early victim of political correctness. I sued for loss of earnings. The legal wrangling went on for eight years. I settled out of court. My reputation was not enhanced.

It is against this background that I set to work on *Shylock*, the play I believed would crown the others. It was not an easy ride –

---

1 Though Tynan later told me he didn't think the play could be cast out of the company, not a decision he was in authority to make. Casting was the director's responsibility.

neither to write nor to market. Like much earlier work, it earned initial rejection. While trying to sell the play there came another roller-coaster episode – a brilliant production of a new play mounted by John Harrison of the Leeds Playhouse, *The Wedding Feast*, which earned me the best reviews since *Chips With Everything* some ten years earlier. Despite all previous vicissitudes my luck seemed about to change – with such reviews the play could transfer to London. My agent found an ingenuous producer who bungled the arrangements. The transfer never happened.

Shylock was finally bought, initially by Eddie Kulukundis who showed it to John Dexter who brought in the famed Shuberts of Broadway. On 2 September 1977 it had its first English-language preview in the Forrest Theatre, Philadelphia, USA.

The star of the play was Zero Mostel, probably best known for his performance alongside Gene Wilder in Mel Brooks' classic comedy film *The Producers*. Due to his fame and the affection he inspired as a son of New York, the advance bookings in the scheduled Broadway theatre were reported to have amounted to $2,000,000. Zero had hoped in this role to make his mark in theatre as a serious actor. He gave one preview performance in the Forrest Theatre, fell ill, and six days later, at 7.47 in the evening, died of an aneurysm of the heart.

The play was rerehearsed in New York with the understudy, Joseph Leon, taking over the role of Shylock. It ran five weeks at Washington's Kennedy Centre. After five previews, mixed reviews, and four further performances it folded in Broadway's Plymouth Theatre.

This diary charts the play's birth from an idea, through its development, drafts, rejections, acceptance and rehearsals, up to the opening in New York on 16 November 1977. I have culled most of it from my personal diary which, because it is a rushed hotchpotch of records and impressions, I have tidied up without, I trust, distorting or disturbing the sense of 'news from the front', thus saving the reader from the offence of shabby prose. And since the play is now known as *Shylock* I have referred to it as such from the beginning, even though it means slightly falsifying what people have written or said when referring to it as *The Merchant*.

One final word of thanks to Riggs O'Hara, John Dexter's

companion and literary executor, for permission to print John's letters. Riggs may not enjoy the picture of himself that emerges from this angst-ridden period but he has generously said, 'It's another time, we were other people, we must all live for the future.' He is now artistic director of the Post Office Theatre Company in London, a performing space he has taken over, converted and runs with infectious enthusiasm.

ARNOLD WESKER
June 1997

Introduction

Shakespeare wove his play *The Merchant of Venice* out of three extant sources. John Russell Brown, in a scholarly edition of the play, reveals them. First, a story written in Italian at the end of the fourteenth century about a rich merchant of Venice called Ansalado who borrows money against a pound of flesh from a Jew so that his godson, Ciannetto, can seek his fortune. The second, a story about wooing which involves having to chose the right casket out of three in order to secure the woman for a wife. And the third, probably a fifteenth century story by Masuccio di Salerno about a daughter escaping with her miserly (not Jewish) father's jewels to her lover, aided by a slave.

In 1973 I watched Sir Laurence Olivier perform the role of Shylock, the Jewish money lender, in Jonathan Miller's Victorian production at the National Theatre. Disappointingly the great actor offered an 'oi-yoi-yoi' Jew, a racial caricature, and I was powerfully reminded of the play's irredeemably anti-Semitic impact. Miller's production, setting the play at the height of Victorian capitalism, attempted to create sympathy for Shylock by showing him to be a banker like any other. Even omitting his opening speech about Antonio, '*I hate him for he is a Christian ...*', didn't help. Here was a play which, despite the poetic genius of its author – or, who knows, perhaps because of it – could emerge as nothing other than anti-Semitic. It was not that Shakespeare's *intentions* were anti-Semitic. Not at all. His genius is a generous one. But the *effects* were anti-Semitic. Worse, the so-called 'defence of Shylock' speech – *Hath not a Jew eyes? ... If you prick him doth he not bleed?* – was so powerful a piece of special pleading that it dignified the anti-Semitism. An audience, it seemed to me on that night, could come away with its prejudices about the Jew confirmed but held with an easy conscience because a noble plea for extenuating circumstances had been made. Forgive the poor Jew! See how human he really is, *doth he not bleed?* And if you spit on him of course he will murder. Not quite an eye for an eye, but flesh for phlegm. Perfectly understandable.

I recognised no Jew I knew. Shylock was revengeful and, against all humanity and reason, had insisted on his pound of flesh. Something was wrong. Then came the moment when Portia announced that Shylock couldn't have his pound of flesh because it would involve spilling blood which was not called for in the contract, and I was struck with what I felt to be an insight. The real Shylock would not have torn his hair and raged for being denied his gruesome prize but would have said, 'Thank God!' Thank God to have been relieved of the burden of taking life. The problem of writing a play in which Shylock uttered this cry of profound relief could only be resolved if it could be explained how Shylock committed himself to such a bond in the first place. This is what I set out to do. Borrowing Shakespeare's names and half a dozen of his lines, I began in 1974 to think about a play that has engaged me on and off for nearly twenty years. Shakespeare plundered three stories to write one play, I was repeating the plunder to write another.

In June 1974 I was in Boulder conducting, among other courses, one on the history of contemporary British drama for a five-week summer school at the University of Colorado. In the evenings, so my plan went, I would begin to think about and make notes for the new play. After two weeks of teaching I came to a halt realising how little I knew about contemporary British drama and, more distracting, desperately wanting to concentrate on the new play for which I'd made only three pages of notes. What could I do? Poor students! Lumbered with an inadequate teacher! An idea excited me: what better way of giving my students an insight into contemporary drama than for a contemporary dramatist to begin thinking with them about his new play?

I confessed to them the bad news of my shortcomings followed by the good news of my proposal. They were immediately enthusiastic, and I set to work at once outlining the approach I was taking: my Shylock and Antonio were going to be friends – the former an ebullient bibliophile, the latter a world-weary merchant. Shylock was going to lend his friend the money with no bond attached, but Antonio was going to insist upon one. Shylock, the foreigner, was going to be romantic about friendship; Antonio, the Venetian, was to be more practical. I planned Portia as an energetic and highly educated young woman of the Renaissance who was inheriting ruins from a father full of foolish philosophical theories. Not only had his theories led to those ruins, but also to a curious belief that whoever chose lead from one out of three caskets – the other two being reprehensible gold and silver – would make the best husband for his daughter. My students and I went on from there.

I divided the class into three parts, asked each to tackle a third of Shakespeare's play, break it down, comment on it. I urged them to think about my approach and see if it was both plausible and justified. I led them in discussion and invited essays. One, a postgraduate student, quite outstanding from the rest, excitedly set to work and presented me with three papers. She used scholarship to vindicate and encourage what was initially only an instinctive approach, and assembled for me the first stage of my reading. Her most decisive discovery was a fact about Venetian society and its relationship with Jews which gave the play's structure its key pillar, namely: Venetian law demanded that no citizen could have dealings with a Jew unless a contract existed. Gentlemen's agreements were unacceptable – the Jew was no gentleman.

Lois Bueler is the student's name. I dedicated the play to her.

ARNOLD WESKER
Blaendigeddi, 3 May 1997

THE WRITING OF IT

1974

28 October, Blaendigeddi, Wales

... Have been here twelve days reading and researching for *Shylock*. I'm almost too frightened to acknowledge it but already feel the play tumbling and trembling about inside me, the scenes, the rhythm, the mood. Think I know how it will begin. I've known from the start that the first scene would be with Shylock and Antonio in Shylock's house, Shylock exploding forth on his love of books and showing his collection to his friend, Antonio:

> SHYLOCK   Here, my little treasure, from the very first Hebrew printing press, the code *Arba 'a Turim* of Jacob ben Asher of Toledo. Look. The date — 1475, in a place you've never heard of I'm sure, Piove di Sacco, near Padua.
>
> ANTONIO   Only twenty-one years after Gutenberg.
>
> SHYLOCK   Pah! Gutenberg! I have here some sheets of printing in Hebrew which go back ten years before Gutenberg. And not in Germany, but in France! Avignon! Very clumsy work. Can't even make out what it is. Book of psalms, I think. Looks like sample sheets.[2]

The truth is I didn't know what that first printing press produced and had romantically decided it was *Song of Songs* until I looked into Roth's *Jews in the Renaissance* and discovered the first press had turned out 'the code'. Roth also reveals that another press existed at the same time in the south. He tells the remarkable story of the Jewish dyer, Davin of Calarousse, and the Prague

---

[2] The final version begins:

> SHYLOCK   (*Reading*) *Guide to the Perplexed.* Author, Maimonides, Ram-bam, known as the Great Eagle. Cairo. Twelfth century. (ANTONIO *writes*) *Hebrew/Hebrew Dictionary.* Author, R. David Kimhi. England. Twelfth century. Not too fast for you, Antonio?
>
> ANTONIO   It's not the most elegant script, but I'm speedy.
>
> SHYLOCK   And I'm eager. I know it. But here, the last of the manuscripts and then we'll begin cataloguing my printed books. Such treasures to show you, you'll be thrilled, thrrrrrilled! You'll be... I can't wait ... just one more ...
>
> ANTONIO   Do I complain?

goldsmith, Procopius Waldvugel. Waldvugel seems to have heard about, even seen, the Avignon press in its early stages and described it to Davin. They had both set to and tried experimenting with this 'art of artificial writing'. Their partnership failed and it's not known whether they ever got around to printing anything. I'm assuming they did! ...

It rains here most of the time but I'm getting great pleasure from reading. And I have this growing sense of responsibility towards the image of the Jew. Shakespeare's Shylock has contributed such an ugly image to the world that my play must be massive enough to lift that caricature out by its four-hundred-and-fifty-year-old roots.

1975

3 January, London

... Am raring to get into *Shylock*. Will have to get back to Wales, though, to start. Need quiet to break the back of the play ...

7 January, London

... Have got back into research for *Shylock*. Educating myself, at last! Would like to go deeper into the history of the Renaissance. Into all history, in fact. Can see myself drifting more towards learning and study, away from creativity. The history of printing is fascinating ...

11 January, London

... Have reached that stage in the reading and research where I fear I've done enough and now will have to face writing the play. Got enormous pleasure reading about the Renaissance and the development of printing, especially to have discovered the role of the Italian publisher, Aldus Manutius.

Perhaps a little more research – on coffee. Was coffee drunk in Italy in 1560? Can it be a speciality which Shylock has brought back from the East – if coffee came from the East. I'd like to have a coffee-making scene to interweave with Shylock's story that I plan to have him tell about the Aldine Press ...

2 February, Blaendigeddi

... Read aloud to friends Vera and John excerpts from the notes I'd made for *Shylock*. It worked. 'It will be your best,' they said. They were thrilled. I know I'm right about that play ...

8 February, Blaendigeddi

... I start this new [note] book with a calamitous entry: Yesterday, having anxiously inched my way these months towards beginning *Shylock* – I began. A day to celebrate. Was thrilled and tense, but confident. Could feel it all in me. It would be a bold, stunning new work. The peak of my dramatic skills. Giddy thoughts! The first day went well. Two and a half pages. Most of it from notes I'd already made. Then today, it still read well, and I found more to add to what was there before continuing. Continued. Stopped to go shopping in Hay-on-Wye. Returned to read what I'd written this morning. Still good. Then wrote more. And added. Then broke for dinner, which Paul [local farmer's son] joined me in.

'Are you working?' he asked. I explained the process, being full of it, and – as always – curious about myself, about the way it happened.

'The real terror,' I told him, 'is to start at all. Because when you start you either don't put it down quite how it's in you or you do – *exactly* how it's in you. And both can be bad. But the first is not *so* bad, because if you can see you haven't put it down quite as you *felt* it then there's hope you can change. But to get it down exactly as you imagined it, to make your hand follow your head and heart and *then* find it's no good – *that's* the nightmare.'

After dinner returned to the study, wrote a little, then became stuck. Sat and sat in front of the book but couldn't think how best to go on. Read through the original breakdown I'd made of the Shakespeare plot to see if his structure could point a way forward. In the first scene Bassanio asks for the loan, in the second, Portia reveals her obligation to her father and the caskets, by the third the bond is made with Shylock. Master craftsman – the main ingredients and characters of his plot laid out at once. *I'd* reached Scene 3 and the only element revealed of my plot was related to Portia and the caskets.

Decided to go back to the beginning, read what I'd written and see if I could tighten up. Fatal! By the time I'd read the second page it seemed I had no play to write after all. This work, which was to have been the most 'brilliant' of them all, now read like a flabby, wordy, historical bore. Even more disturbing it seemed racially self-conscious. A phantom pregnancy!

And here I am, in the middle of the Black Mountains, isolated and alone with this dreadful discovery, this unbearable knowledge, and not even a vehicle into which I can throw my bags and leave.

Think I must get out of this study for a start. And yet feel I ought to force myself to look at the script again. To start savagely cutting and rewriting, to go back and look as I might at a dead body just in case I've panicked too soon and it's really still breathing. Leave it now, and by morning it might *really* be dead.

My God! How did I write all those other plays?

Later – 11.30 p.m.

I've brought sanity and order to the first scene. Will leave the second till tomorrow when it will seem either lost or redeemable. Too tired to fight any more. When I was young I wrote best at this time of night. What lunacy to take on Shakespeare.

10 February, Blaendigeddi

... God knows how I recovered. Went back at it and cut again and again and then went on with the fingers of my heart crossed. Wrote a lot yesterday and even more today. Too much in fact. It worries me. But much of it is work already written in the book called 'Notes'. What I'm doing is just creating a structure in which those notes can sit. Still, it's going to be long. After only three days writing I'm at page 22 – about sixty minutes of playing time.[3]

---

[3] A miscalculation. I'd calculated three minutes per page. More like one and a half minutes – thirty-five rather than sixty minutes in all.

Ideally I want to make the first act ninety minutes and the second seventy-five minutes long. That's not too long for a work that aspires to sit beside the Master's. No, not sit *beside*, more as an appendage to.

The fear remains, however, the panicky feeling lurks constantly. The play is too facile! The language can't make up its mind whether to be fifteenth or twentieth century, prose or iambic pentameter. Shakespearean rhythms creep in. The imagery is impoverished, non existent ... so many fears.

John [Allin][4] has arrived. Won't do much more on it before leaving for London, I suppose.

16 February, London

... Needless to say I've touched nothing of *Shylock*, hardly dare look at what *is* written. Not that I've had time ...

29 March, Blaendigeddi

Haven't touched *Shylock* but, with trepidation, began reading over what I'd written till now. Not too bad. Could be ... could be ...

3 April, London

... And then news like this comes through my post: a magazine collating press references to Jews and the Israeli problem, organised by the Campaign Against Hate Propaganda, writes: 'Dear Mr Wesker, Throughout Britain an anti-Israeli and anti-Semitic propaganda campaign is gathering momentum ... !' Read in the *Sunday Times* (23 February, page 6) of recent attempts to deny six million Jews were slaughtered in the gas chambers. Feel even more driven ...

13 April, London

... *Shylock* continues. Grows rich and succulent in arias, argument

---

[4] John Allin, primitive painter (born 1934, died 1991). He painted, I edited: *Say Goodbye You May Never See Them Again*.

and historical colouring. But over-ripe, I fear. The first draft looks like running for four hours! Will have to be cut. But a shape goes down, it does! And part of me is excited while part of me is filled with despair, feeling that it will not merely be hated in this country but ignored.

Times headline: ARAB BOYCOTT STARTS TO HURT THE ISRAELIS ...

14 April, London

... Asked the Kustows and Appignanesis[5] if they'd listen to what I'd written of the dinner scene which includes Shylock's long Renaissance speech (Act I, Scene 7) and about which I had been worried, feeling it was overloaded with information – all history and no drama. Silly, really, since history is very dramatic. They were a generous and receptive audience ... Mike was a little hesitant and later I'll push him further to say why. But it was reassuring. Thank God for friends. Orna was very alert and said she's a good test because she usually gets quickly bored if a play becomes too intellectually heavy. It was alive, they said ... Still, there's a long way to go and much honing to do.

16 April, London

... Further evidence of the mess the theatre is in – Mike [Kustow] tells me there are now strong fears that the RSC will have to abandon its London home at the Aldwych for lack of funds. He also related how the stage hands at the National, now numbering in their ranks those arch-reactionaries of Vanessa Redgrave's Workers' Revolutionary Party, refused to move the Beckett play on tour because it didn't involve any set changes – only two characters stuck in the sand – which meant they couldn't earn their £175 a week. I think they've stated they'll only tour it if those salaries are paid. Which makes the tour difficult. Irony, irony – the 'workers' party refuses to allow theatre out of the metropolis to the workers! ...

I write my *Shylock* and fear for it so much ...

---

[5] Michael Kustow, writer, TV producer, translator; Richard and Lisa Appignanesi (divorced), both novelists.

8

25 April, London

... Read out excerpts from *Shylock* to American students from Lisa's college in Arundel who came for tea. They responded warmly, but a couple of acquaintances present (Ulle Pegler, a German agent from Munich, and Jenny Sheridan from my agent's office) remained stonily unresponsive, which made me at once feel that the play was wooden, long, a failure of language, totally unplayable ...

Think I must not read to anyone again. This crazed hunger for feedback is a writer's curse. Two scenes remain to be written: the court scene and the return to Belmont. I approach them slowly though it seems I know what they must do: carefully structured, not a speech too much, not a word out of place.

If this play fails to take wing then it will be a sign: that I can make no claim to being a playwright ...

26 April, London

... Haven't been able to touch *Shylock*. Lost appetite for it. Well, well! The artist really does need feedback, nothing crazed about it at all ...

2 May, London

... Still haven't been able to touch *Shylock*. Wasted the week away with domestic chores ...

10 May, London

... Asked bank manager to lend me £6000 to go into partnership with the printer, John Gorman, to print a limited edition of silk-screen prints of John Allin's paintings – to be called 'Stepney Streets'. He listened to the project, immediately saw its virtues, said he trusted me, and agreed. Gratifying to experience faith in one. But how time-consuming it is setting up a business venture. I'm determined to see it through, however – panic preparations for supplementing the drop that must one day hit my theatre royalties. Unless *Shylock* works ...

Finished the court scene. Am now working on the last scene. Short but difficult to construct because it must draw together delicate endings ...

Between 19 and 30 May the first typed draft was completed, i.e. the second draft. I write in long hand, correct, cut and change copiously until the script is unreadable at which point I need to type it.

2 July, London

... Should have rushed to write about everything that's happening in my life and the world: overwhelming vote to stay in Europe – good for the English. Seems they don't mind mixing with foreigners after all. My three days in Warsaw, and my week in Venice with Nina[6] which was lovely and almost silent, just full of walking the streets, drinking espressos, a little sunning, and blocks of conversation between long pauses. She was a great help during our discussions, though I think she partially disapproves of my motives for writing *Shylock* since she does not see the original as having an anti-Semitic impact ...

30 August, London

Nearly two months later. Diary entries made less and less frequently. Why? Because I can't be bothered, mainly. Also because I've been so absorbed writing *Shylock*, which I've now finished, second typed draft, two weeks in Wales typing the bloody thing. Also, perhaps, because I think it of diminishing importance to record the bits and pieces of my life. Perhaps another reason is because I'm – kind of – happy! *Shylock* works, may even prove to be my best play ... Certainly responses from friends are good ...

Robin wants to give it to P. Hall at the National. I suppose it *is* the only place for it but I flinch. The climate is so, so aggressively

---

[6] Nina Adler, 1927–1991. Daughter of painter Jankel Adler, dear friend and German translator of *Shylock* and other of my plays. It was she who, from the beginning, thought the play should be called *Shylock* rather than *The Merchant*. I wish I had listened to her.

infantile in the theatre ... I feel raw. I don't want to offer it to them. Send it round the world, yes, but here – ach! here the theatre is run down like everything else – industry, services, politics. The little bombs have started again in the West End, laid down by a splinter of a splinter of the IRA. And the sectarian killings in Northern Ireland go on and on. Men picked up and killed at random. I shall never forget reading about a social worker who, before he was killed in Belfast, described the violence as 'The beery hatred that is handed down from father to son.' *The Journalists* looks like happening in Cardiff, followed by a ten-week tour, maybe ending up in the Edinburgh Festival. That'd be nice.

9 September, London

... Reports of and responses to *Shylock* are still warm. Though I can't see how it can hope for life in the present theatrical climate ...

14 September, London

...Responses to *Shylock* coming in are gratifying. Richard [Appignanesi] says, 'It's a masterpiece! You made it!' Ron[7] came round to tell me specially: 'It's a level you've not touched before.' Beryl[8] said it was so 'assured'. All talk about it in a special way, as though they'd read something really unprecedented.

Can I have made it work? What will P. Hall say? And Papp[9] in New York? Ian McKellen[10] wrote: '... it's better than Will's one!' I feel so full of confidence for it that I'm tempted to buy myself a new typewriter, or gramophone!

---

7 Ron Groom, writer, teacher – long-standing friend, now dead.

8 Beryl Ruehl – long-standing friend.

9 Joseph Papp – creator and artistic director of the New York's Theatre in the Park, now dead.

10 Ian McKellen – actor. Now Sir Ian McKellen.

THE MARKETING OF IT

1975 *continued*

18 October, London

... How much can I take I wonder? [Lord] Michael Birkett rang from the National Theatre.

'We're all very despondent here about the Shylock play, we just can't fit it in and I'd like to talk about it.'

'Why are you despondent,' I asked, 'because you all like it and can't fit it in, or because you don't like it and therefore it won't fit in?'

'The latter,' he said.

'You're all potty,' I exploded. 'Absolutely potty'[11]

'I wish I could slide out of it and say I didn't agree with them but I'm afraid I do. And we all have warm feelings for you and feel we should be doing you here and so let's talk.'

I've made a date for next Thursday, breakfast, for him to come here. But I'm wondering: shouldn't I cancel it? What's the point? What can he say? It will be profoundly depressing for us both. Can I be so wrong? Are all those friends and colleagues so wrong? I knew, I just *knew* this would happen. I so wish I'd not given it to them ... I recall an interview with *Women's Journal* saying how full of trepidation I felt, like casting pearls before swine.

We gave a farewell dinner to Mike and Orna last night, they're going to Israel for two months. Kirsten Sorlie (assistant artistic director of National Theatre, Oslo), here for six months study at our National, had told me she'd heard from Peter Hall's assistant that they were buying the rights to *Shylock*. I mentioned this over the dinner table. Mike paled a little and said it ought to be checked. He must have known but lacked the courage to tell me.

... Dusty was very distressed. She feels I shouldn't meet with Birkett, said she too had feared this might happen ...

Dear God, I need strength. And I thought I'd written a masterpiece! What now?

---

[11] Could I really have said that? I suppose so. I'd not be so indelicate these days and can only explain – not excuse – such an expostulation as sheer frustration with the earlier behaviour of the National and the RSC (see Preamble). My nerves must have been frayed. Lord Birkett's response was controlled and sympathetic.

23 October, London

Michael Birkett came for early morning coffee.

I'd been for my swim, returned and made some good double roast. Prepared matzos, some with sardines, some with blackcurrant jam. Came up to the study to read and answer mail. Put on Shusha's[12] new record, and at 10 a.m. he arrived. He seemed different, larger than I remembered him from our last meeting over *The Wedding Feast*. He was dressed in a dark blue suit and waistcoat, very elegant, with a black and white striped tie, his slim metal case at his side.

I left him in the study and went down to reheat and collect the coffee. He'd declined my matzos, only wanted coffee. No toast. Nothing. Just coffee.

When I returned I asked him did he know Shusha's music. He said no – he had great difficulty listening to folk or pop music. He was very much a classics man. I told him Shusha was more a *chansonnière*, of which there's no tradition in this country, and so she has a hard time. Then *I* began *for* him.

'Now,' I said, 'you've got a very difficult task, haven't you?'

'Yes, indeed I have.'

'I'll try and make it easy for you.'

'It's awfully difficult to know how to begin and how to say what it is we *all* felt. In a way we all found it too much, too big. I suppose we were overwhelmed by it.'

'You can't really be meaning that,' I suggested. 'It would be an awful comment if the National Theatre of Great Britain was saying it couldn't do a play because the work was too big for it. You must mean something else.'

'Yes, of course, not big in the sense that we're incapable of doing something big, because after all we're doing the huge *Tamberlaine*. No, I mean we felt there was too much in it, everything was there, too well worked out, too packed, too neat. There was a reply for everything.'

'No, you can't mean that either. You can't be complaining because the play was too well made, or too well researched, that

---

12 Shusha Guppy – writer, journalist, singer and friend.

would also be a strange confession. You must be trying to say something else.'

'Yes, indeed. It's very difficult to articulate for a group of others and not let it seem it's only one's own opinions. No, of course it's not that we reacted against the structure or the research. It's that it was big in the sense that it would really be more of a thirteen-part serial for TV, or a six-part, you know what I mean. A study of Shylock, then of Renaissance Venice, then the state of the Jews. It would be too much for an audience to take. And it was all so contemporary. You felt as though nothing had changed.'[13]

I think he was trying to tell me the play strove too *hard* to be contemporary. The joints were showing!

'Look,' I said, 'it's difficult to say exactly what one means. And of course if one went through a work and said, yes − that's well done, and I see what you mean by that, and you've succeeded in that aspect, or that − one might still have to say that somehow the sum total doesn't touch one. "I simply don't like it!"'

'Of course, and that's what we finally mean, we don't like it. But one wants to be more helpful than that. I felt, in a strange way, that it was too − naïve. Too simple. Yes, yes I know − it's a strange word to use when there's so much apparent richness in the play, and when it's so full ... '

'But those are interesting words to use,' I said 'I'm not sure I know what you mean but they sound as though they're beginning to say what you mean.'

'Everything is too answered, too neat.'

'Let's be systematic. You could be saying the history has overwhelmed the characterisation − it's possible . . .'

'No, no. Not that. The characterisation is there, and the history, in the right proportions. . . '

'Or you could be saying there's no drama, the conflict is gone ... '

'No, not that either. The conflict and the drama are still there ... '

'Or perhaps − and this was my own fear − you could be feeling the language is all wrong. I mean I'd decided from the start not to go into competition with Shakespeare the poet, so there's no

---

13 When I encounter such a comment I immediately imagine a scene in a pub between Shakespeare and, say, Kitt Marlowe who's telling him that 'the problem with your *Julius Caesar* or *Anthony and Cleopatra*, Will, is that it's too contemporary, too Elizabethan, it doesn't feel Roman enough!'

poetry in the work. And I'm not an Arden[14] so I couldn't invent an archaic language. Though I did think I had succeeded in creating a strong modern language that still had rhythms and a tone belonging to the period. But you might not agree.'

'No. I don't think any of us felt that the Renaissance was missing from the language. I mean we didn't read and say, "But what's happened to medieval Italy?" No, it wasn't language.'

'Well then, here's a last thing, which perhaps none of you were consciously aware of, and if you were then none of you could articulate it: you might have felt an insistent Jewishness about the play.'

Here he hesitated, not necessarily because I'd hit the truth, but because it was a genuinely new thought which had – it certainly couldn't be denied – a distinct *possibility* of truth.

'Well, maybe, it could be that you were pursuing your theme too heavily. But perhaps no more than someone rewriting *Julius Caesar* from the Roman point of view would be too Roman.'

'Then, with none of those things worrying you, I can't really understand your reactions.'

And then he came out with something perfectly valid.

'I feel as though everyone is saying exactly what they mean. No one holds back. Everyone has a position and states it. In relationship to Venice, its politics, to each other, to their situation. Everyone is being too open and honest. No one is being devious, saying what they don't mean, or not saying what they do mean. That's what I mean by simple.'

'Ah, now that's something tangible,' I told him. 'That at least is something I understand and which is possible. Perhaps that's really hit our difference. You used the word "simple" in a critical sense, but I'd accept it and use it in a "right" sense. I mean I'm an old-fashioned artist and believe that life is so complex and full of contradictions, and we're all so fallible, weak, that art mustn't compound all that by being itself obtuse and over-complex. It has to be clear and simple and all the complexities and contradictions of life must be left to filter through, surface by themselves. So I'd be glad to think the work "simple" in that sense.'

---

[14] John Arden – playwright *Sergeant Musgrave's Dance*, etc. A playwright I admired enormously for his ability to invent rich, original dialogue.

He accepted this statement of our two positions though I suspect he would like to have said not 'simple' but 'simple-minded'. Or perhaps 'unsubtle'.

Anyway, part of me is appalled that they feel the work lacks subtlety, while another part of me pauses and wonders: are they right? Can I be *so* wrong?

We went on to discuss the hazardous problem of selection. I think that throughout I was quite cool, even aloof, certainly courteous and friendly, but I had to let him know that I felt my authority matched theirs at the National, and that it was frustrating that they held the power. He defended their group, felt it was well balanced, reiterated the affection felt for me at the theatre and the genuine hope that we'd one day work together. I suggested that as long as that regime remained it was unlikely, since we must conclude that having rejected *The Journalists*, *The Wedding Feast* and *Shylock*, we were out of tune and sympathy with each other.

One strange moment. I asked who the group consisted of. He said there was P. Hall, himself, Peter Stevens the administrator – though of course he and Stevens would have a less influential view – John Schlesinger, who was hardly there because he was always away making films. It was Pinter and the directors Michael Blakemore and Bill Bryden who, with Peter, would have the strongest voice. Oh, and there's also John Bury, designer, and Harrison Birtwhistle the composer – but they too would carry little weight. And of course Mike Kustow who, he said, feeling in a difficult position as a close friend and therefore unable to be objective about the work, held back. 'Though,' added Birkett not without a hint of mischief, 'he didn't seem wildly enthusiastic about the play.'

I made no sudden response but had the feeling he was watching to see what effect this information about a close friend would have on me. I revealed nothing ...

So, he left after about an hour and a half. I think it was brave and gracious of him to come, even though I'm stunned at his (their) inability to see the play's merits. And there is nowhere else. My law suit is still on with the RSC – not that *they'd* do it. Robin is going all out to commercial managements, but it's bound to be too expensive for them. We're sending it abroad. To everyone. Especially in the States. To Zeffirelli - for a film. To Dexter!

Henrik[15] has just written to confirm they're doing it in Aarhus. But I still feel gloomy. What, now, financially?

24 October, London

I've sent the 'dialogue' from the diary entry to Birkett at the National to check. Plus a letter.

DEAR MICHAEL

Thank you for coming to give the National's reasons for rejecting *Shylock*. It was brave and gracious.

I keep a diary – a bad habit – and of course had to record our meeting. But I want to make absolutely certain I got it right – not word for word, but in spirit. Would you mind glancing over this copy I've made of the relevant part of the entry and correcting any injustice I've done to your case.

The more I think about what you said the more accurate it sounds as a reflection of the corporate feeling: '*Your characters all say what they mean.*' It's a curious criticism and one that I fear betrays fashion. It's a very limited – and I think sterile – expectation of art that it should present people who don't say what they mean (or who say what they don't mean). When I create a character who's devious – like Bassanio or Graziano, even Lorenzo to a certain extent – then I have them say what they don't mean. But for the rest, yes, you're right, I am more interested in people who struggle to explain themselves or communicate ideas. There are people who do that, the world's full of them. Certainly Shakespeare's world is full of them.

But there was one final aspect which I forgot to suggest might be behind your reservations, and which I suspect must have been as strong a contribution to the general response, and one the most impossible to say: the presumption of writing those monologues, which couldn't help but echo the grand style; and the way they were written (not talking of the

---

[15] Henrik Bering-Lisberg, then head of Aarhus Theatre, Denmark. Subsequently ran Danish Royal Opera, Ballet and Theatre. Currently with the Danish Ministry of Culture.

Renaissance tone now). I guess you must all have not liked the writing. Simply that. And that of course you couldn't say. It would have sounded too awful.

But in a strange way – the need to survive aside – I'm not hurt. (And I *have* screamed inwardly in pain before). I'm not hurt because I do so strongly feel in tune with a main stream, and suspect that you are all victims of transient climates. It's not unknown in the history of the arts and its managers.

Still, that's easy to hurl, difficult to prove. Time, time!

I'm just sad that the creative artist is trusted less than the interpretive one. The British theatre is not scintillating these days, as my friends from abroad keep telling me. Perhaps that's why!

Kind regards ...

1 November, London

... On my return from Wales, these letters: from Birkett to me, and from Peter to Robin. They have such well intentioned tones I must accept that their conclusions are deeply felt and carefully thought-out. Oh, how awful! It makes me feel even clumsier, heavier. And – wrong! Is eighteen months' work *so* wasted?

And yet I must have faith in my intuition. Problem is – that intuition is now confused. Beginning to think I too had always secretly shared their thoughts about the work. If people don't like you, you have to begin thinking maybe something about you is not likeable.

And yet, and yet ...

From Michael Birkett, the National Theatre:

28 October 1975

DEAR ARNOLD

Thank you for such a long and considerate letter. I don't think keeping a diary's such a bad thing at all – I'm just too lazy for it, and too self-conscious, but I'm sure yours will be a marvellous document. I am, of course, rather appalled to find myself in it in such a state of inarticulate dismay. I'm even more appalled to acknowledge that the description is by and large true. All the same, it's difficult to express accurately an opinion which is partly one's own and partly a corporate view, especially when that corporate view is made up not merely of stated opinions, but of intangible ones which one has to sense as much as listen to.

The only part really where I would take issue with your recollections for the diary is in the last paragraphs of page two. The point I was trying to make, and thought that I had finally succeeded in making, was not that the characters were too true, that they expressed themselves too truthfully, but simply that they expressed too much, that every character was articulate and expressive of every single point of view that he might take about every aspect of the situation – the characters in fact were too encyclopaedic – and that you had taken pains to see that they embodied all the arguments you wanted to introduce about every aspect of Venice, of usury, and every other theme in the piece – too exhaustive is perhaps the word that I'm looking for. This you may not find a valuable criticism in itself, but it is, I think, different from the rather simplistic view that I and my colleagues only like oblique characters, as if in fact we only liked Harold Pinter's plays!

The most important thing about all this is that you did sense that I was trying to be helpful, to make criticisms, not that would change your mind or alter your play but would show you that a whole lot of people who care about the theatre had thought seriously and deeply about your work, even if, in the long run, they had to admit they didn't like it. As you say in your letter, in the last resort it's inescapable that we didn't really like the writing because otherwise our reactions must have been different, but again I don't believe it's the presumption of writing such monologues, it's the effect of the whole; that, as you rightly say, is all it can ultimately come down to.

I make the point about what sort of exhaustiveness and completeness on the part of the characters I meant in order to rebut the charge that we are somehow in the grip of fashion. This I really believe is not the case. We are doing or planning an enormously varied collection of plays, old and new. I don 't believe there is a common factor to be found in them, except that of quality. In other words I don't believe we like one sort of play and not another. I really believe our taste is Catholic, almost to the point of being dangerous – I say dangerous in the sense that the coherence of a season, or of a repertoire, is something that is expected of the National Theatre and is difficult to achieve. Sooner or later, I suppose, our tastes will be obvious in the choice of plays, but I think it will be very difficult to analyse what it is that we do and what it is that we don't like, except in terms of each individual play. I don 't even believe that it'll be possible to work it out in terms of authors. I am in fact most keen to deny any element of the fashionable in our judgement.

Once again though, I appreciate your giving up so much time to what must have been a fairly distressing experience for you, as it was for me. We must somehow make sure that our next meeting is happier, though I'm bound to say it could scarcely have been friendlier.

Yours sincerely,

MICHAEL

To Michael Birkett:

1 November 1975

DEAR MICHAEL

No, not a long correspondence. But one of us is mad.

You see, I agree again with what you say about the characters knowing what they're talking about. But I feel that's the play's strength.

I really don't see what else is expected. Shylock is a bibliophile. He must be knowledgeable. Antonio is a lapsed patrician. It's not surprising that he's aware of why he's lapsed. Lorenzo is supposed to be an up-and-coming politician, articulate therefore, and caught up in what the young Venetians were caught up in – the vote, usury, power. Portia is a perfectly recognisable lady of the Renaissance, of whom many such did exist, in England also. The daughters of More to name only a few!

Who else is knowledgeable? Graziano possesses schoolboy knowledge. Bassanio excels not in knowledge but cunning. Had I written these characters without giving them intellect and an awareness of their times that would surely have been a fault.

I think there *is* an excess of information, but nothing that a good rehearsal period wouldn't point to.

Maybe we mix in different worlds. I meet characters like these constantly. People I know are in there somewhere. People who are articulate, knowledgeable, hold definite views on this and that.

It's a very Jewish play, perhaps!

And, by the way, the state of being in the grip of fashion involves not being aware of the condition at all. It's only years later that one realises . . . Your letter takes its place in my diary. So your correction is registered.

Thank you.

Regards.

ARNOLD.

From Peter Hall to Robin Dalton:

24 October 1975

DEAR ROBIN

I'm sorry it's taken me so long to get back to you about Arnold Wesker's play, *Shylock*, which you kindly sent me some time ago. I've been deep in rehearsals for *Hamlet* for some weeks now, but more than that, I was anxious that my colleagues should read and discuss the play before we came to any decision.

They have now done so, and I am very much afraid that our decision is that it's not a play we want to do. Michael Birkett is seeing Arnold this week to discuss the whole thing in detail, but broadly I think it's fair to say that we found the play too dense and too heavy. Everybody has an affection for Arnold and a great desire to present the best of his work, but this play doesn't seem to be that. In some ways, it's too naïve, as if Arnold were really so fond of his subject that he couldn't bear to leave out anything that occurred to him. You will know that I don't mean any of these things unkindly, but my views are shared by so many of my colleagues that the conclusion is inescapable.

I'm sorry we shan't be doing *Shylock*, because we do want to work with Arnold. Indeed, we've asked him if he would do a one-act play for us as a kind of celebration of the Olivier Theatre (we have sent a similar invitation to a few other distinguished playwrights in the hope of putting together a programme or two). I believe Arnold is not much attracted to one-act plays, but he says that if an idea should occur to him, he will send it to us forthwith.

Very many thanks for sending *Shylock* in the first place.

Best wishes.

Yours ever,

PETER

From me to Peter Hall:

12 November 1975

DEAR PETER

Robin read me your letter. No, I do not think you're 'prejudiced'.[16] Here's what I think.

That twenty years in the theatre as actor, writer, director, essayist and audience – with my plays in constant performance somewhere or other, covering fifty countries, and translated into thirteen languages – gives me an authority equal to anyone of you sitting on the artistic direction of the National.

And I'm bewildered to find myself still having to fight for my plays as I've been doing since *The Kitchen*, *Chicken Soup*, and *Roots* which Devine and Richardson[17] at the Royal Court said couldn't work, and wanted me to change, and I *knew* they worked and didn't change them, and so they were launched at the Belgrade[18] instead. (Not *The Kitchen*, the Court actually

---

[16] Robin told me over the phone that Peter had said he hoped I wouldn't think he was 'prejudiced'. I thought it a strange word to use at the time, being slow to understand that he feared being thought prejudiced against Jews. The notion that an antipathetic response to the play could be rooted in 'closet anti-Semitism' had not occurred to me then.

[17] George Devine and Tony Richardson, artistic directors of the Royal Court Theatre (1955–1965).

[18] The Belgrade Theatre, Coventry, one of the newest theatres in England, built in that city devastated during the war as part of its resurgence programme. The director was Brian Bailey and it was he who enthusiastically gave John Dexter the opportunity to direct my first two plays, *Chicken Soup With Barley* and *Roots*.

dared hazard that for a Sunday night experiment *after* the success of *Roots!*)

Time and time again I've been vindicated, and still I'm not trusted. When does trust in me begin to operate instead of trust in you? Your record is as pitted or glittering as mine. Dexter, though perceptive about *The Kitchen* and *The Trilogy* and *Chips* when the Court were wrong (yes, they also turned down *Chips* at first) was himself wrong in his advice to Bill Gaskill over *The Golden City*.[19] I've made that work. Just as perhaps you were wrong about *The Wedding Feast* – I've seen that work in two cities now – and perhaps wrong about *The Journalists* which, after that reading[20] I *know* works. Why is it that it takes so long for experienced theatre people to – I don't know what – to *hear* the plays? I hear them. Clearly. Sharply. And they're vibrant while most theatre here is efficiently lifeless.

Here's what I think.

That having written two books of prose, thirteen plays – six of which I've directed – I *know* what I'm doing by now. I write little, and carefully and with great thought, but when they're done I hear them working – with an energy that may be foreign to this country just now, but working. And I bitterly resent being at the mercy of a composer, or having judgement passed on me by a young Bryden. I'd never presume to sit in judgement on Birtwhistle's music. Shouldn't you protect me from that? Besides, I too can produce the comments of a composer, ecstatic ones, and of other artists – an architect, painter, actor, writer, all eminent and all of whom have gasped at the play.

Can't you understand how I, we, resent no machinery existing through which our authority can operate? Still, *still* the

---

[19] *Their Very Own And Golden City*, winner of the Italian Marzotta Prize in 1964, was directed by William Gaskill at the Royal Court Theatre in May 1966. The play was originally scored for two sets of actors to play the main roles: one set to be ageing into the future while another set remained young in the present. Gaskill called Dexter in to an early run-through for advice. Dexter advised that one set of actors should play the characters both young and ageing. I can't for the life of me recall why I agreed to this. The result was disastrous. I later directed the play in Danish in the city of Aarhus, Denmark, in 1974, using two sets of actors as I'd originally intended. The play seemed to make a great impression.

[20] *The Journalists* was given two readings – 13 July 1975 – with actors from the RSC and the National Theatre at Jackson's Lane Community Centre in Highgate, London, as a fund-raising event for that Centre's theatre.

creative artist (as opposed to the interpretative one) is made to feel the outsider, the intruder, the irritant in his own home. The theatre is our domain as much as the director's and the actor's. We give it life blood, and yet we still have humbly to knock at the door, wait outside for answers, and suffer the humiliation of being told, by those who nearly always fail to hear and see what is being offered, No! not today, thank you.

I don't think you're prejudiced but something *is* wrong in the theatre. Desperately wrong. I get reports from all over the world. There is a death about. A blindness. A peak has been passed.

And yet there is no other way for the National to be run. I see that. Tradition has it that power is best left in the hands of the director, even though the great and lasting moments of the history of theatre seem only to have centred around writers, never directors. Still, I can't challenge that power, but you must understand the resentment that no alternative machinery exists where I and others like me can exercise our indisputable authority. In our own theatres, for example. A writers' theatre. Where we would direct or learn to direct our own plays. Four writers to a theatre. Our plays not subject to one another's decisions, but performed simply because <u>we'd earned the right</u>.

Here's what I think:

That there operates a tyranny of directors that is unhealthy for the creative life of the theatre in this country, and the director who understands that, will be the one who will trust the writer again, even against his own judgement.

Yours ever,

ARNOLD.

From Peter Hall to me:

17 November 1975

My dear Arnold,

I have considerable sympathy with your letter. What you're really saying is that the achievements of your talent so far give you the right to put your plays on, even if people whose job it is to select plays have reservations about them.

I think there's a lot to be said for this theory when we're dealing with a proven talent like yours.

But what happens if nobody comes to see the play? Do you still expect to be able to do your next play without question?

I think you only put a foot wrong once in your letter. You say about your own plays 'and they're vibrant while most theatre here is efficiently lifeless'.

By making that remark aren't you making yourself into precisely the kind of judge that you object to having? Aren't you in fact making yourself a kind of me?

We either live in a dramatists' paradise in which anything written by anybody can be put on. Or we have to have directors − who are not prejudiced and not (I hope) stupid, whose job it is to select and evaluate priorities. Otherwise you're going to demand a situation in which publishers are to publish everything that's written, or editors print anything in newspapers.

I think you have earned performance of your work. And I find it difficult to believe that if we turn your play down, you won't get it done somewhere else.

But, as I said at the beginning of the letter, I have considerable sympathy with your position and would really like to talk it out with you further. You're full of contradictions. But then so am I. Different ones, though. There is not a tyranny of directors in this country. And if we gave total freedom to all the writers, there would be anarchy. But more when we meet ...

Yours ever,

PETER

From me to Peter Hall:

22 November 1975

MY DEAR PETER,

I won't take up too much time answering your letter, which when you reread it, I'm sure you'll find is hastily thrown together and little to do with what I wrote.

Firstly you confuse my 'opinion' about 'the efficient lifelessness of most theatre' with my 'judgements'[21] about it. You're entitled to your opinion about *Shylock* as I am about, say, Pinter; my point was that you should not be in a position to pass judgements about my play appearing or not, any more than I should be in a position to make judgements about Pinter's work appearing or not. He has proven himself sufficiently to be beyond our judgement just as I feel I've proven myself sufficiently to be beyond yours.

I did not, as you well know, talk about any 'dramatists' paradise in which anything written by anybody can be put on', or about 'total freedom to all writers'. You've carelessly given me arguments which are easier for you to knock down.

I was very specific and careful and gave an example of a writers' theatre consisting of four writers whose plays were 'not subject to one another's decision, but performed simply because <u>we'd earned the right</u>'. And I underlined those words in my original letter to you.

I don't understand your question about do I expect my next play to be done without question if nobody comes to see a current one. Are you suggesting that people didn't come to see my last plays? In numbers it's simply not true. If anything — with the exception of *Chips* which ran for a year — *The Four Seasons* and *The Friends* had bigger audiences than the earlier plays (which only ever had short six week runs at the Court anyway) because they were performed outside the Royal Court for longer periods.

Nevertheless, yes! If a writer, with a certain level of achievement, has a play that fails, I do expect his next one to be done. Why not? You expect people to trust you with the leadership of the National Theatre even though you've had failures as a director in the theatre and cinema ... don't you? And rightly so, for you've also had sufficient successes.

But more when we meet ... Regards.

ARNOLD.

---

21 On reflection I see that what I really meant was 'judgements carrying sentences'. My opinion does not result in a play not being performed, his did!

From Peter Hall to me:

25 November 1975

MY DEAR ARNOLD,

You mustn't stoop to being abusive. It's boring and will get a very important conversation nowhere.

If you think my letter was hastily thrown together, I think it would be better for you to keep your criticisms to yourself and read what I wrote rather than what you'd like to think I wrote.

I wasn't talking about your plays in the past being failures or successes – they are relative journalistic terms anyway. I was posing a situation in which a theatre didn't like your play but felt that your talent deserved offering you the opportunity of putting it on. Suppose then the public did not come – that there were very small audiences. Would you think the theatre had the duty to go on offering this facility to your next play?[22]

I look forward to our meeting. But please don't expect it until I've finished *Hamlet*. We shall need time ...
Best wishes.

Yours ever,

PETER

From me to Peter Hall – postcard sent from Charing Cross Hospital:

27 November 1975

MY DEAR PETER If you think my observation that your letter was hastily thrown together was an abusive comment then we're going to have a tense conversation. Imagine what it's like being told that your play isn't good enough! But Dusty will feed you well – and I'm not really an abusive person. But you are rather school-masterish, aren't you? Good luck with *Hamlet*.
ARNOLD

PS I'm here having a prostrate scraped away. Most unromantic!

---

[22] Interesting statistic from *25 Years of the English Stage Company at the Royal Court* (published Amber Lane Press, 1981): John Arden's play *Live Like Pigs* played in 1959 to a 34% audience. His second play *Sergeant Musgrave's Dance* played in 1960 to a 30% audience. The English Stage Company maintaining its faith in Arden – whose work has since become recognised as major in the English contemporary theatre – presented his next play *The Happy Haven* which played to 18%. When *Sergeant Musgrave's Dance* was revived in 1965 it played to 61%.

28 December, London

... Two months have passed since I could bring myself to write anything. Soon it will be 1976. Though we are in the middle of filming *Love Letters On Blue Paper* for BBC TV, and there's some pleasure in that, yet I feel generally flat and untalented and frightened. Three plays unperformed. The fear is creeping upon me, despite defiant hisses at the state of affairs, that my gifts were only ever thin and that now they are being seen through. We are hugely overdrawn at the bank, and though quite a bit of money is in the pipeline it comes slowly, indifferently, and in small amounts, signifying nothing much achieved. I may be directing *The Friends* in Paris this year, a distraction (though one Dusty is already dreading), but I can't bring myself to care about it as much as I care for the future of these three other works.

If I hadn't been working hard I wouldn't feel I'd earned the right to rage so much.

Perhaps it's all childish, the rage. A bad period. Everyone is cutting down, not only in the theatre but in the drama departments of the BBC. Perhaps one should just wait for -what? North Sea oil and better times? ...

There are faint stirrings. Eddie Kulukundis[23] has shown interest in *Shylock*. People in his office have read it and urged him to produce it. He's sent a copy to John Dexter. I vowed I'd never let John direct another of my plays,[24] yet I suspect the young John could have made a fine production of this one. Mort Gottlieb[25] rang from New York to say how tremendous he thought the play was, but he didn't want to do it. Didn't feel it was for him. Felt it

---

[23] Eddie Kulukundis – theatre producer. He travelled to Stockholm to see my production of the première of *The Friends* and was sufficiently impressed to invite me to direct it in London which I accepted. My first production in this country, ill-fated – it opened at The Roundhouse in May 1970 to mixed reviews.

[24] Ten years after directing *Chips With Everything*, John directed *The Old Ones* at the Royal Court. Rehearsals did not get off to a good start because he'd agreed on the design without consulting me – a design which finally destroyed the play's rhythms. However, rehearsals themselves were exciting and I owe to John an important change in the play's structure. We quarrelled over the ending. Difficult to explain here but he wanted a kind of *Fiddler On The Roof* finale which I considered sentimental and against the play's intention. After promising me he would not pursue his ending I arrived on the first night to discover that he'd lied. The sentimental ending had been retained!

[25] Mort Gottlieb – Broadway producer of *Chips With Everything*.

ought to be done by an institutional theatre, with a company and a subsidy ...

30 December, London

... I feel panic setting in ...

These things loom: my law suit against the RSC over *The Journalists*; the failure of the John Allin folio of prints, 'Stepney Streets', to sell in sufficient numbers; and the gloomy prospects for *Shylock*. Despite an initially encouraging response from the 'big names' to my personal appeal to buy the folio at 25% discount in return for using their name, and having sent out seven hundred and fifty brochures, and taken a full page advert in *The Jewish Chronicle*, yet only about thirty-two folios are sold. The response to the *JC* advert has shocked me. Four people sent in the full amount, two sent in deposits, and only four made enquiries. The *JC* claim sales of 70,000 with a readership of 200,000 out of which we attracted only six sales and four who were curious! Does it signify a dull economic climate, or a philistine Jewish community? (I'm inclined to think the latter. On another occasion an impressive editorial in the *Chronicle* appealed for subscribers to the *Jewish Quarterly* – the only Jewish literary magazine in the UK. One response was received!)

Shylock – the play I believed my 'best' work! No one is biting. Vivica[26] and/or her theatre have decided not to present it in Stockholm. It is planned only for Aarhus. Nowhere else. Have I written a dud? Am I blind about it? God help me! Five years' work, three plays unperformed. We will have to sell Blaendigeddi. I see nothing ahead. Not even the inspiration for further work.

And yet tomorrow could bring a cable from somewhere to change it all. Possible, but unlikely. We will have to live through dark and lean times. Somehow ... Let me, by way of consoling myself, list what is happening. We are in the middle of filming *Love Letters On Blue Paper* for BBC TV. The collected plays are being printed in the States in two volumes, and a third volume of

---

[26] Vivica Bandler – ex-artistic director of the Staatstheatre, Stockholm, who invited me to direct the world première of *The Friends* in 1970 and who later produced the world première of *The Wedding Feast*.

the stories by Harper and Row. Munich TV has bought *Love Letters*. Madrid is rehearsing *The Four Seasons*. Athens is about to rehearse *The Kitchen*. Our West German publisher – Fischer Verlag – has bought the rights of *Shylock* and Nina is translating it. Our East German publisher – Henschel Verlag – will publish an edition comprising *The Wedding Feast*, the television version of *Love Letters On Blue Paper* and *Shylock*. *The Kitchen* is still running in Buenos Aires,[27] though money from there is infinitesimal and frozen! The Flemish theatre in Brussels have applied for the rights of *The Wedding Feast*. There's a small amount of money due in from Tokyo for *Their Very Own And Golden City*. French radio is transmitting *The Old Ones*, and it looks as if *The Friends* is really going to happen in Paris, with me co-directing, perhaps fully directing, for both stage and television.

That's all lovely, and they may be life-savers, just, but there are still three new plays crying out for London productions. My own country, dammit!

31 December, London

... The year ends with the news that the Arts Council touring board have turned down Cardiff's application for a grant to tour *The Journalists*. That means it can't be mounted in Cardiff. Or anywhere?

1976

2 January, London

... And a dream: that I was in New York with John Dexter casting the production of *Shylock* which in the dream he'd agreed to direct. He was thin (not, as reputed in waking life, fat), and his old self – sweet and attentive.

'I see the production,' he was telling me, 'in simple block movements, nothing elaborate.' I agreed but added that although the settings should be uncluttered yet each item must be rich or

---

[27] This production finally ran for over a thousand performances.

else it would look like a production of Shakespeare which they couldn't really afford.

'Ah yes,' he said. It was a lovely dream, full of a promise of friendship and co-operation for the future.

10 January, London

Following the National's comment '*your characters say what they mean*', a letter came from Shaiyke[28] in Israel:

> ... if one conceives of the play mainly as an instrument to convey an apologetic Jewish message to a Gentile world ... it is really questionable whether the message would carry in Israel the same meaning as in Europe...

and from Poland, a friend wrote:

> ... Much as I am impressed ... may not be possible to publish or perform here ... If I may travestize the absurd excuse given to you by the National Theatre people − the characters say what very many people think and feel here, much of which should never be said loudly ...

Accepted neither here, nor in a 'socialist' country, nor in Israel ... Where *do* I belong?

30 January, London

Read the Court scene night before last at the *Jewish Quarterly* fund-raising gathering. Alan Sillitoe[29] wanted to leap into my arms he was so touched. It was held in the private house of the Littmans.[30] Collete Littman, the hostess, a demure little Egyptian Jewess, shy and − she confessed to me − terrified of such large gatherings, stood up at the end, her pale blue eyes moist and intensely shining, and

---

[28] Shaiyke Weinberg − head of the Cameri Theatre in Tel Aviv.

[29] Alan Sillitoe, novelist.

[30] Louis Littman − industrialist and founder of the Littmnan Library, a publishing house devoted to books of Jewish interest.

said, 'Thank you, thank you, that was so moving.' She seemed transported. So much so that *she* moved *me*. Felix Scharf[31] who had first urged me to help the Quarterly, and to whom I'd given a copy of the play about which he'd not written a word to me because, I'd imagined, he'd not liked it, came up and said how he'd been moved and how different it was to *hear* it ... and Michael Church[32] was cautious, a very English reaction, though I was grateful to hear him comment on the success of the language which he thought spanned time – '*muscular and Victorian*', he said.

Anyway, I'm at work honing down the play. The Danish première is on October 23rd and Henrik has urged me to scrutinise the text for cuts.

May end up with a longer published version than the one used for performance, though I *am* finding many things to cut from both versions. Not without anxiety, though. A neglected work creates around itself a kind of vacuum of fears in which is seeded that poisonous flower – The Panic Cutter. Rhythms are scuttled, the play's arguments debilitated, structure cracks. But there are gains of course: clarity, lightness, improved rhythms. If only I could *hear* it in rehearsal, watch it, I'd be certain then.

13 February, London

Yesterday evening John Russell Brown came for dinner to discuss our correspondence over his book,[33] his views on *Shylock*, and the National Theatre's invitation to me to direct *Love Letters On Blue Paper* at the Cottesloe. Dusty did him proud. Baked grapefruit, beef stroganoff on a cabbage base, salad, and summer lemon cake ... I began to understand his response to *Shylock*, his reasons for not warming to it. He'd edited the Methuen 'Arden' edition and so knew both the Shakespeare and its background better than I did. He couldn't see the landscape of my play because of the bard's mountainous shadow which fell over it. He seemed surprised to hear me violently declare the *Merchant of Venice* a hateful play. He

---

[31] Felix Scharf, businessman with a passion for literature.

[32] Michael Church – then literary editor of the *Times Educational Supplement*, now a freelance arts journalist.

[33] John Russell Brown – author of *Theatre Language: a Study of Arden, Osborne, Pinter and Wesker*.

really *does* believe the defence speech given to *Shylock* by Shakespeare to be vindication of the play and evidence of its integrity.

I repeated all my arguments and asked him did *he* know a Jew who would insist on a pound of flesh against all reason and humanity? I think he considered that irrelevant. One of his criticisms was that all my characters talked alike. I attempted to delineate the differences in their personalities. As I described the ebullience of Shylock, the acerbity of Antonio, the intellectual vigour of Portia, I noticed his eyes cloud over as though it was occurring to him that he may have misread the play.

'I hated Portia. Very tinny she seemed to me, brittle!' Tinny? I redescribed her as I imagined I'd written her. Robust! Intellectually and emotionally juicy! But *tinny*?

Then he complained that there was no action in the play. People simply debated in each scene. I asked him what action he saw in the Shakespeare. He listed: people borrowing money, people insulting each other, escaping in masks, dressing up ... I listed similar 'actions' in *Shylock*: people cataloguing books, borrowing money, running away, being painted, on trial ...

Finally I told him: 'I know the National's decision is irrevocable, but I'm telling you all this because you're a man of the theatre who writes about it and lectures on it and may one day be doing more writing on me and so I'd say this: after Shakespeare's *Merchant of Venice* being around for five hundred years I suggest that it's the National's responsibility to present an alternative version, especially now when the Shakespeare play is once again required reading in schools.' I don't think he'd ever contemplated it in those terms.

17 February, London

It's taken me two days to prepare a press statement announcing the world première of *Shylock* in Denmark – type envelopes, fold, stick stamps. I'm slightly embarrassed to be doing it. My agent's office should have initiated it but – no flare, no sense of occasion. On the other hand it could be seen as evidence of anxiety. Which could also be true. I do fear that vicious circle in which a play is attacked, fails, the next one isn't done, nor the next, silence; Wesker isn't being produced therefore what he next writes can't be any good, so *that* play is not done, and the silence grows ...[34] I feel this need to make sure they know I'm alive, working, being performed *some*where. Don't suppose I'll ever get over that extraordinary *Guardian* review that began: 'There's a plot to rehabilitate Arnold Wesker ...' Good grief!

The more I contemplate Russell Brown's statement about *Shylock* fading in the shadow of Shakespeare's play, the more I realise that I've launched a conflict more complex than ever I could have gauged. Of course I knew some would say, 'How dare he presume ...' but I'm absolutely convinced that once the play is performed it will creep out from the shadow of WS, take on its own life, speak with its own voice. Problem is who will unlock that life, allow that voice to speak?

19 February, London

Last night dreamt I was going to a concert and on my way met Arthur Miller, Saul Bellow and Neil Simon, and we all went to what I imagined was Simon's rented house where I told them how lucky they were to be Jews born in the States.

Phone call from Eva Tisel, my Scandinavian agent, in Stockholm. Great news! The Royal Dramaten, Bergman's theatre in Stockholm, is going to present *Shylock*. Before Henrik in Aarhus. This September. They wanted to know if there were any conditions about London doing it first. I said, 'Never! Not again!' The RSC had demanded that their production of *The Journalists* should be the world première and I'd had to ask Stockholm, Brussels and a theatre in Germany – all of whom had bought the rights – to hold back their productions. Because the RSC reneged on their contract I lost productions in, and important income from, those countries. Now – first come first served.

And the day before yesterday heard that West Berlin TV and two West German theatres are going to present *The Wedding Feast*. We will have bread.

---

[34] And soon people ask that question for which you want to murder them: 'Are you still writing?' On occasions I've replied: 'No, gave up all that nonsense long ago. I've gone into property. Made millions. Haven't you heard?'

6 March, London

The two German theatres are not going to present *The Wedding Feast*.[35] German TV will, however ...

Well, the television production of *Love Letters On Blue Paper* went out on Tuesday. *The Times* ignored it, as they did the television production of *Chips*, my collection of stories,[36] and the published version of *The Journalists*. The remaining reviews, so far, are tawdry, silly – mean with their tears, tatty in thought. And this morning I went to see Robin to discuss productions of plays in France. In passing, she brought home the degree of hostility towards me that exists in Fleet Street – she'd been speaking to journalists, they'd told her something, she didn't say what ...

7 March, London

... And the other night I'd dreamt two vivid dreams. In one I was sitting at a long trestle table eating with 'others'. Who – I don't know. But there was to be a 'performance' in between the tables. I can't remember the performance but it ended with a bad actor crying out, in the tone of voice usually reserved for the declaration 'I'm dying', 'I'm sixty, sixty! I'm sixty, I'm sixty. SIXTY! SIXTY!' Everyone except me was moved by this melodrama. I declared how awful it was. So *what* if he was sixty. His humbug enraged me. Rage seems to recur in my dreams. The other was about a man who was telling people how he'd visited me and I'd told him off for being late. I corrected him, and told him I hadn't really told him off, and besides even if I had there was a good reason because Dusty had prepared the meal at such and such a time, and the children were hungry. The dream contained echoes of the exchange Shylock has with his daughter, Jessica, who turns up late for a portrait sitting.

---

[35] One did perform it subsequently.

[36] *Love Letters On Blue Paper*, a hardback volume, published by Cape, including 'The Man Who Became Afraid' and 'A Time Of Dying'.

12 March, London

... Arden, Osborne and myself described by Anne McSomebody or other as 'menopausal playwrights' in the new issue of *Time Out*. They do go on, don't they.

Nice letter from Peter Hall.

National Theatre – 9 March 1976

MY DEAR ARNOLD

Thank you for your letter. I apologise for the delay in answering it – but I am working night and day trying to get this building open. Forgive the brevity, therefore. And the tardiness.

I'd love to hear *Shylock* read by you.[37] But if I still don't like it by the end, your opinion of me as an arrogant schoolmasterly fellow who is refusing you the right to fail (!) is going to increase. And you'll probably accuse me of being prejudiced about your reading as well ...

If you promise me that you will respect my opinion as something which is as objective and unprejudiced as I am capable of making it, I'd be delighted to come. But not until we've got this building open. I hardly have time at the moment to come home to sleep for a few hours.

Incidentally: warmest congratulations on your television play.

I had it taped and played the tape yesterday (Sunday) at an unlikely hour. There's devotion for you ... but I was richly rewarded. I thought it an extremely moving and powerful piece of work. I was very affected.

Best wishes.

Yours ever,

PETER

From me to Peter Hall.

---

[37] The reading never took place.

11 March 1976

MY DEAR PETER,

Robin says the fault lies in my letters. So I won't write saying how you've managed to misunderstand me, simply that I'm delighted you like my suggestion. Whenever you're ready.

Particularly, though, I was touched with your response, to *Love Letters*. It's been a rewarding experience. No work of mine has ever brought me in so much – and such extraordinary – fan mail.

Now, I had a dream about you some nights ago. There was a press conference in the National. The area seemed divided between audience and them. I was sitting in the audience. You were sitting next to me. You stood up to face the first question. A red-faced, middle-aged, grey-haired lady, with glasses and a constant smile began. 'I saw your Hamlet and it was' – smiling all the while – 'disgusting! Disgusting!'

Which was the cue for a concerted attack from them all. You were shaken and had to leave to recover. When you were gone I stood up to take over. A journalist said: 'Oh, there's Wesker, showing off again!' And I began. I can 't remember what I said, but one sentence rings. I seemed to be yelling at them: 'Say something serious about the theatre. Say something SERIOUS about the theatre!'

See how my nights are taken up? There's devotion for you ...
Good luck with the beginnings.

ARNOLD

ENTER JOHN DEXTER

[1976 *continued*]

20 March, London

...Have just returned from the National ...momentous encounter ...
It was while talking to Peter [Hall] – Dusty had slipped away to look around the new building – that I turned and saw a beaming John Dexter. He opened his arms and we embraced. Damn him, he's irresistible for me I suppose. Surely I've said this before – he's like a first love, inevitably! He had directed my first five plays, and they were *his* first five as a director.

Within seconds he was saying: 'I've read *Shylock* and isn't it good. It's very good indeed.' My heart leapt. It was like that moment when he was living with us in Clapton Common.[38] I'd gone to work[39] and left him to read *Roots*, the play the Royal Court had turned down after I'd refused to make a major change. Returning from work he'd leapt to hug me and had cried out: 'Of course it doesn't need changing, it works, and I know exactly how to do it.'

It didn't take long for us to be talking about where, who, when. I said I'd like *Shylock* to be done here, in the National. He winced and said, never! that it was a terrible regime. I said that of course there are people walking on the streets of New York each one of whom could play Shylock and so New York was my next thought. He talked immediately about Zero Mostel. It was my turn to wince and tell him that I'd thought of Zero as soon as I'd finished writing the play but wasn't he an unpredictable actor? Didn't he ad-lib and invent? John asked when had I last seen Zero perform, adding that despite his and my talent we'd need a star ... I argued that we just needed the right actor...Anyway we babbled and bubbled, confused and excited, but I know, I *know* he's smelt the gunpowder in that play. We made a tentative date to meet on Wednesday and talk.

It's like old times. I go to bed happy.

---

[38] Having successfully directed *Chicken Soup With Barley*, John foolishly made advances to a young boy in a play he was directing. The boy told his parents who told the police. After a six-month prison sentence John lived with us until his life came together again with his production of *Roots*.

[39] I was working for my brother-in-law, Ralph Saltiel, helping him in his small furniture-making basement in Swiss Cottage.

26 March, Blaendigeddi

... arrived here today to work ... to go over *Shylock* ... John Dexter
came to Bishops Road for dinner last night ... Told him how I'd
first thought of the play but, partly because I was tired from some
late nights and partly because he was full of energetic
observations, I didn't tell him all I had wanted to. It was an
exciting reunion. He'd been comparing different drafts of the play
and said I'd made ridiculous cuts – such as Shylock's story of how
the Jews had invented God; such as Antonio's big speech at the
beginning of Act 2 Scene 4. He loved all the history. It was his 'big
passion now' (whereas almost everyone else had been worried by
too much history). He thinks Bassanio's caskets speech ought to
go, and Nerissa's speech on Bassanio, and that something is
missing from the court scene and from the last Belmont scene.
'Up till then there's great muscle in the writing, but it thins out
at the end.'

I warned him that to bring back the Antonio speech would
detract from the Renaissance story. Perhaps, I suggested, I could
incorporate it in the court scene at the end, perhaps that would
give to it what he thought was missing. Nothing more could be
added to the Belmont scene, I said, as the last one it had to be
short – the play was long and couldn't sustain a lingering end. I
pointed out that the scene had greater tension now that I'd
rethought the character of Lorenzo. Nor did I feel we could lose
Nerissa on Bassanio, or Bassanio on the caskets. I wanted Nerissa
to have flesh, not be a cipher, an unthought-through character;
and we needed the fun of Bassanio's speech in which he mocks
the absurd notion that a true husband could be found through a
love of 'lead'. He had ideas for the sets: three huge old maps, one
to the back of the stage, the other two down the sides on which
would be shown the trade routes of Venice. All other settings
would be dropped in and out. I like the three maps idea but if he
blocks out his wing space he's going to give the production a see-
saw look – sets would have to be dropped in, none could come
from the wings. But, it's early days.

We talked about where to open it. Eddie [Kulukundis] was
juggling with the idea of opening it at the National (Hall would

let Dexter direct it), or at the RSC if they agreed, and then transfer it to the West End; or simply mount it commercially straight away. We decided it couldn't be the RSC because I was suing them! And John hates the regime at the National – it's a personality conflict between him and Peter Hall.

'I used to think those university boys were right and we were wrong. Don't now. They want to make everything fit a scheme.' He was incredulous when I told him they'd already turned the play down.

'Though of course they'd do it if you wanted to direct it,' I added.

We talked about whether it should be London or New York. I warned him of the hostility towards me in this country. My head was really on the block with this play.

He knew it and said, curiously: 'Your lot aren't going to like it either are they!'

He meant the Jewish community. I was surprised. Why not? I'd always expected the Jewish community would rally round. On the other hand I suppose there will always be those full of fear and caution. As the sentenced Jew in the joke warned the other sentenced Jew who was trying to think what he'd like as a last request before they were executed: 'Ssh! Don't make trouble!'

Well, I don't enjoy making trouble but it does seem that I can't avoid writing that which makes certain people feel uncomfortable.

On balance, I concluded, I'd like to open in New York and cock a snoot at the English. But in that city if 'the one newspaper' – the *New York Times* – panned the play we'll have had it; whereas in London the papers could be divided in their opinions and we could survive. John seemed to think there was no chance of the play not succeeding. 'Besides, in New York with Zero Mostel you'd be three months booked in advance.'

'You've smelt gunpowder between the pages, then,' I said. He had! He had!

We chatted like old times. Dusty made us supper but discreetly stayed away till the end when she sat with us at the table, sewing the turn-ups to my new jeans on the outside of the leg instead of the inside – she was so excited that John and I were coming together again. On leaving we embraced warmly, and kissed – almost on the lips. Both said how thrilled we were, and looking forward to everything.

Can't resist feeling vindicated. How absurd that the fortune of a play turns upon one man liking or not liking it. John's reputation is so high that the play will now appear in a new light to many who before had doubts. It will even be easier to sell abroad. Though it didn't need a Dexter to persuade Al Levinson, or Nina, or Henrik, or Vera, or John, or Pat Tarn, or the Appignanesis, or the Josephs ...

And so I come to the end of another [note] book. It's a high note on which to end but oh! I have been here before. A lot can go wrong between now and October.

1 August, Ritz Hotel, Aarhus, Denmark.[40]

Nothing momentous to report from the read-through of *Shylock*. The actors laughed at the funny lines, and those playing the major roles seemed impressed by them and the weightiness of the play. Warned them they should be prepared for a long haul; each scene had to be carved out and laid alongside the others like pieces of sculpture adding up to a whole. Can't feel involved with this production. I'm here out of loyalty,[41] to spur them on their way, give them hints about character, and I'll return for the last ten days of rehearsal. But I'm not directing, it's out of my control, and never having seen a production of the play, I feel limited about what to advise.

A message comes through from London to ring John Dexter in New York which I do from the theatre. He seemed on top form. Said he was now as familiar with the play as he'd ever be, and he wanted me to consider one thing before coming to meet them for talks. In view of my relationship with the critics in London and the eighty per cent possibility that they'll damn the play with faint praise (when they're not being downright vindictive!), which would kill the chances of a production in New York, wouldn't I

---

[40] On holiday with the family, driving around Europe. We stopped in Denmark to enable me to attend the beginning of rehearsals for *Shylock*.

[41] I'd directed *Their Very Own And Golden City* there some years previously.

like to consider once again opening in New York before London? I reminded him that this had been my first thought but we'd talked ourselves out of it fearing to be at the mercy of the one newspaper – the *New York Times* – which decided the fate of a play. It was a lot of money to put in the hands of one man. He said he remembered, and realised all that but – it was also a fact that the largest part of the theatre-going public in New York was Jewish, and they guaranteed the success of the play in a way which London Jewry did not.

'Golders Green does not get off its arse in quite the same way as Brooklyn.' Of course this could be true, but only could be. I reminded him that Hobson was leaving the *Sunday Times*, and Bernard Levin was taking over.

'Don't rely on old allies,' he said. He was right. Levin was just the kind of English Jew to delight in showing how 'objective' he could be about his roots – non-partisan, unintimidated by his talented *luntzman*,[42] loyal to the bard (just as Jews, at bar mitzvahs and weddings, like the strangers and guests they feel themselves to be, pay homage to their 'hostess' and drink toasts of loyalty to the Queen). So Levin is quite capable of showing his debt to England by paying homage to the bard rather than taking off time to give detailed and serious consideration to my play. On the other hand it's also true that he's unpredictable – even if in a predictable way.

What, I asked John, if it was such a success in NY that the English critics in their mean, spiteful, tight-lipped way were tempted to say such things as 'this may be good enough for New Yorkers but in London it just won't do ... ' Reviews of that kind were inevitable. John's response was 'maybe', but he thought an impetus from New York would overcome that. I wasn't sure. He said think about it and we'd talk, together with Jocelyn, when I visited.

12 August, London

... Dexter is flying in tomorrow from NY for talks. He must have a tremendous deal up his sleeve to be rushing here in order to set up *Shylock* ...

---

42 Meaning 'countryman'.

13 August – on a train to Leeds

John D phoned from the Savoy last night.

'In with the fleshpots after all these years.' He raved on about how good life now was at fifty. 'Work, sex, relationships, everything!' Told him I feared I was not going to grow old gracefully. 'You will! You will! I promise you. You'll see. Have I ever lied to you about serious matters?' He has to shuffle dates around but will be ringing to fix a time to meet. He's come mainly to talk to me and Jocelyn. 'You'll love it when you actually see it on stage, but,' he warned, 'you'll hate it when I talk about it.' Left me filled with dread at the prospect of a 'director's concept'. The world hasn't seen what I have in mind and already a director is having 'concepts' about it. [Note: On 8 September *Shylock* opened at the Royal Dramatic Theatre in Stockholm to enthusiastic reviews. That same day, at 1.30 in the afternoon, my mother died. My sister rang the theatre instructing them not to tell me until the morning after the first night. We flew back at once to London. I have no record of the production in my diary, just a memory of mixed feelings. Dusty found it impressive and a leading critic wrote extensively that Wesker was now 'one of the world's great dramatists'. Not a word in the British press ...]

16 August

... lunch with John D and Eddie Kulukundis. It seems as though it's all going to happen; steaming ahead. John had been with me the evening before and showed me his plans for the staging. Appears to have found a good solution. Now in Jocelyn's[44] hands. Will see her next week.[45] He's so exhilarated – and exhilarating. Has he really mellowed or is he incredibly sweet because he knows this is the play he wants to do to keep him for the next years? Sir John Clements[46] has agreed to play Antonio in New York. I go there 24 September to met Mostel and one or two other actors. We've all agreed to open in New York first before London, *providing* the right bed partners can be found. They're

---

[43] Imprisoned Soviet biochemist.

going after producers Whithead and Stevens. The former puts on Miller's plays, the latter owns the huge theatre in Washington's Kennedy Centre. John has turned down an offer to direct Miller's new play. He doesn't think it's very good. He doesn't think highly of *The Four Seasons* or *The Golden City* either! He has also, much to my surprise, agreed to consider directing *Shylock* in Munich in the 77/8 season.[47]

[44] Jocelyn Herbert, brilliant set designer of *Shylock*, who designed my first five plays which Dexter directed. Dexter was by this time artistic director of the Metropolitan Opera House in New York many of whose productions he mounted with Jocelyn's designs.

[45] Oddly no record of that meeting which my appointments diary records as having taken place at 6.30 on 6 September at her house.

[46] Star of British stage and screen 1940s to 1970s.

[47] It didn't happen.

ENTER ZERO MOSTEL

[1976 *continued*]

25 September – Saturday, about 6.30 a.m. John's house, New Jersey

I shall soon be reading *Shylock* to John. This trip, so far, has been packed with events. It's an extraordinary experience to find I've written a play which has made everyone – John especially – look at me in a different way.

He tells me:'You are writing better now than you've ever done. Everything has lead towards this. It's a muscular language, your ideas are clear ... why are you complaining about growing old? Our development is parallel, I too now feel there's nothing I can't do ...'

Arrived in Chicago about 9 p.m. (2 p.m. local time). Found a bus to get me to the Astor Towers – near to it. Had to walk a block. Note from Kate Mostel[48] that Sam Cohn[49] – Zero's agent – would pick me up around 7 p.m. for the theatre (Zero in *Fiddler* – terribly sentimental show but it's had over two thousand separate productions around the world, and he is a tremendous presence on stage).

Tried to sleep an hour or so but couldn't. At 8 p.m. I was watching the show – i.e. 3 in the morning. He was playing in a barn holding 4500. Packed. Every groan he uttered drew applause from the audience. Made me wince. We ate in the pump room – where the 'greats' once ate. I couldn't really talk with Zero. He expected me, I'm sure, to be full of questions and conversation but I was too tired. Fortunately he didn't strain to be funny as I'd feared.

Next morning woke at 11.40. Joined him in his suite (where Zsa Zsa Gabor stayed!), along with his wife, Katie, Sam Cohn, Arlene – a writer's agent from ICM. It was still not possible for me to talk as I'd hoped. What could I say with everyone around except chat about this and that? Sensed they were all waiting for me to begin. I began humbly.

---

48 Zero's wife.

49 Now vice chairman of ICM (International Creative Management) Holdings.

'When a great actor like Zero agrees to do your play you don't just say "thank you" and wait for the first day of rehearsal, you pick up a plane and fly to him ... I just wanted to know how you saw Shylock ...'

He replied: 'I never know till I'm doing it.' Discussion over! No, not quite as abruptly as that, more was said, but not much. I'd seen enough on stage, besides. He'd make an incredible Shylock. John would control him, and the text awes him sufficiently to contain his irresistible urge to fool around all the time.

Though he did make one foolish suggestion. 'It's a pity that Portia makes the discovery about the pound of flesh and blood in the same way as she does in Shakespeare. Shouldn't Shylock and Antonio know this long beforehand?'[50]

I pointed out that if they did then Shylock would lose his big '*fool, you*' speech. There'd also be no play.

What did I expect to hear from him? Had we time alone I'd have probed; with three others present I could only observe him. He had the weight – certainly *that*; the stage presence; the talent to control his speeches; the intelligence to give them the quick of instant invention; the anger and contempt. But we didn't talk much about the play. It seemed wrong to press him. Insulting. Instead I showed him the John Allin folio of prints – which I'm constantly seeking ways to market – and asked his advice. He immediately rang Jack Tanza, vice president of a big gallery – Knodler, I think – and set up an appointment to meet with him on Monday morning.

They took me for lunch to a place called Arnie's. My first request was for their attractive Art Deco menu. Chose a hamburger. Not especially nice. They all seemed to think we'd had a pleasant day. I felt not quite with it. Pity I couldn't see Chicago – Saul Bellow's city. I had, though, the feeling that ICM – Zero's agency – were out to make a fuss of me. There was no mistaking that I was the creator of something a number of people wanted to have a part of.

---

[50] It is of course a criticism one could make of the original. Surely someone in Shakespeare's ghetto would warn Shylock that you couldn't cut flesh without drawing blood. But neither would anyone be fooled by Portia's disguise as a man, certainly not Bassanio. Both represent human gullibility and all too familiar lapses of intelligence.

John D had laid on a huge limo which took us from JFK airport to the Algonquin.[51] No! My baggage went to the Algonquin. Sam, Arelene and I went on to Sam's friend's flat, Esther Margolis – she handles publicity for Bantam Books – where a few people had gathered to watch the big debate between Carter and Ford on TV. She laid on Chinese food.

I was to have stayed at John's apartment but he had forgotten, had sublet it and booked me in to the Algonquin at his own expense. This worried me but Sam Cohn assured me the production would pay for it; and later John told me that I was to shut up about it because he had a long standing debt to pay me: during those months he'd spent in prison[52] I'd resisted other offers, waiting for him to come out to re-direct *Chicken Soup With Barley*. I was moved he'd remembered and felt so deeply about it.

A scriptwriter who lived between Dublin and Switzerland was there with Ellen Burstyn the splendid actress from the film *Alice Doesn't Live Here Anymore*. She was very actressy and cuckoo. Also an actor named Charles somebody who's in the new King Kong film, funny and sweet.

The Carter/Ford debate was unbelievable. They talked only about money, calling upon statistic after mind-boggling statistic, talking in hundreds of billions. Carter seemed as though he just wanted to laugh at Ford all the time, and was using great effort to hold himself back. Had they told him he smiled too much? Ford looked worried, like the man in power looking anxiously over his shoulder at who was coming up behind. Which was the case. And then the show broke down. For twenty-five minutes. No sound. The connection with Mars had disconnected, or something. In 1976! And yet – I enjoyed it breaking down. It was absurd and human, there was no fury, and no one was going to lose a job. The two world leaders didn't even look ridiculous, just sounded it when they spoke.

Next evening met John in Sardi's for a meal. What a reunion. We were last in Sardi's in 1962, I think, for *Chips With Everything*.

---

[51] Famous hotel in New York where Dorothy Parker met regularly with other wits and intellectuals at what became known as the Algonquin Round Table. Not to be confused with the group that Zero Mostel met with, usually in Chinese restaurants, called the Group of the Oblong Table!

[52] In 1958 John served six months in Wormwood Scrubs prison charged with 'molesting a minor' a young boy he'd been rehearsing (see page 43).

We reminisced, talked about Zero and scheduling. I pointed out that if Zero wanted an option to perform the role in London, and was going to be in it for eight months in New York then the play wouldn't be seen in London until about autumn '78. He'd have to think about that. I was aware all the time of how John was anxious to reassure me the extent to which I was to be involved with every detail of the production. Was he remembering that in 1972 I'd been indignant that he'd gone ahead with the design for *The Old Ones* at the Royal Court without consulting me? Perhaps I'm not being fair – there was no sign of effort. We were like two old friends, plotters, with a great deal of experience behind us. A warm relationship. Our backgrounds and tastes *were* similar.

4 October – on a train to Leeds catching up with New York diary

New York! New York! ... Met Roberta Maxwell at Sardi's with John. Lynn Redgrave was there with her manager husband. Everyone seems to be moving to the States. A man came up to me, solemnly took my hand and said: 'I'm a great admirer of yours Mr Shaffer.'

John continues to be outrageous, taunting Roberta about her passion for young boys. I took her off for dinner to Francesca's where we talked about the play ... She's going to be splendid ...

Saw three plays. 'The Oldest Graduate' – part of the *Texas Trilogy*. Not great but had a quality I liked. And *Streamers* by Rabe, well directed and acted. A good writer but suffers from what seems to me a strong American strain of debilitating sentimentality – posing the easy confrontations. And *For Coloured Girls* – fantastic black girls giving incredible performances, female put-down of the male. Accurate, often, but this, too, was flawed by that sentimental centre ...

Had breakfast with two directors of the Roundabout Theatre who want to direct *The Old Ones*. One of them, Gene Feist, said: 'One of the things I love about your plays are their titles, like *Hamlet of Stepney Green*.' When I corrected him – Bernard Kops wrote that play – he wanted to crawl under the table.[53]

---

[53] These days I'm mistaken for either Harold Pinter or the actor, Anthony Sher. Wonder if any of them are mistaken for me?

Later met up with Alan Schneider (who directed Albee's *Who's Afraid of Virginia Woolfe*, *The Texas Trilogy*, and much of Beckett; now head of the Julliard drama school). Told him he *must* direct *The Old Ones*. Said he would. So that's set up![54]

Met one of the directors from the Chelsea Theatre who wants to do *The Wedding Feast*. They had abandoned the idea because Jenny Sheridan – from my agent's office – had written a bad letter outlining my stipulations. It had upset them. Cleared that up. Let's hope ... May have three plays in New York next season.[55]

Had a call from Stockholm while in New York from agent, Eva Tisell, to say the director of *Shylock* at the Royal Dramaten had made cuts and put them in the post for my approval. The cuts didn't arrive. Decided to fly to Stockholm for a run-through, see what I could do. Discovered they'd cut several important passages. Shylock's 'invention of God' speech for example, robbing his personality of a mischievous sharp intellect. The actor was reduced to playing it too sweetly. Also the new Portia passages were cut from the court scene leaving her to seem a thinly-drawn character; and the outraged exchange between Bassanio and Shylock – gone! reducing tension. Plus other smaller sections had disappeared. I was very angry but didn't want to upset them before their opening. Simply advised how they might tighten up the production, bring back tension to the last scenes. Now wish I'd been there from the start. It's such a savage form of censorship, to cut. So cowardly to inform me at the last moment when there was little I could do. (Now wonder what the Stockholm production of *The Four Seasons* will be like.) The actors from *Shylock* had been nervous. Said the director, Staphan Roos: 'You're like an institution in Sweden.' Not much help!

Phoned Dusty from Stockholm to tell her time of arrival. She informed me we'd received an invitation to the first night of *The Four Seasons* in Paris. I'd forgotten about that production.

Remembered: Zero had a buttonhole in defence of sharks. 'I identify with them.'

---

[54] Didn't ever happen, though.

[55] Nor did *The Wedding Feast* ever make it. 'The best laid schemes ...'

1977

2 July, London

Am recovered from New York. How to describe events, where to start? Well, a thousand dollars and my new suede jacket were stolen from my hotel apartment. It was not broken into, someone with a key entered easily and took the cash I'd been given for the air fare – two air fares in fact because I'd bought Jocelyn's ticket as well. Depressing. Police and hotel management blamed the victim for his stupidity. There's a Kafka story in it.

I'd been enjoying the city up till then – it happened on the Sunday, four days after my arrival, a city about which one feels ambivalent – dirt, cracked sidewalks, pitted roads alongside a vulgar vitality, an energetic enterprise providing everything, its friendliness – even over-friendliness. Vulgar because everyone is on the make. The city possesses an energy at once repulsive and compelling. Will I survive there for a month?

The flat I'm renting – 117 West 11th – is attractive, spacious. Nice landlady, Sylvia Price, old time Party member; left her husband, who remained more to the left, and is hooked up with an elderly boyfriend, also ex-Marxist who can't quite lose his old arguments, and sounds like my Uncle Harry[56] with his 'Y'see?' The patterns of Jewish life over there are almost identically paralleled to Jewish life in England. The face, the type is mirrored uncannily, from Sylvia, a librarian, literate and working class to Bernie Jacobs the tough head of the Shubert organisation, through to Merle Dubuskey – press and publicity man. All recognisable, familiar Jewish types.

The buzzing atmosphere around the play is tangible. We've ended up with the most prestigious and talented assembly of actors seen on Broadway in the last decade. People gasp when we list them. Costs are soaring into the regions of $650,000. The lawyer, Mr Cotton, said he'd never heard of such costs 'for a dramatic play' (as opposed to a musical). And they're full of awe and respect for the writing as well. Merle Dubuskey kept quoting

---

[56] Also a party member. Dead now.

it at me; David Wyler who works for Marvin Krauss (the producer's management – all very departmentalised over there) told me he considered me the greatest living playwright. Absurd but nice.

Bernie Jacobs. Met him in his office where he obviously enjoys conducting interviews while signing letters, taking telephone calls, answering other people's questions – a room which Ken Tynan might describe as Jewish theatre-baronial. Bernie said at once he thought it a great play 'but needs a bit of editing, speeches too long for American audiences'. I winced at first to hear a New York producer say, predictably, what one expects a New York producer to say. 'You winced,' he said. I explained why. He was a little startled to be told he was a predictable New York producer but he recovered quickly and continued a flow of speech it was almost impossible to interrupt. I did manage to tell him the speeches aren't long and suggested perhaps it was that he read slowly. He said on the contrary he read very quickly, then went on to assure me he allowed artists complete freedom. He would say his piece but theirs was the final say, so if the show failed it would be their fault and only theirs. But on the production side, 'I'm a fascist! I don't believe in democracy in business affairs.' He seemed paternalistic, a kind of Marango.[57]

I told him: 'Mr Jacobs, you've been in theatre longer than I have, that's for sure, but I've been writing for twenty years, I've directed my own plays, I've seen them performed all over the world in thirteen different languages, and John and I have worked together on six of them. I'm experienced. Only the play matters, not the sacrosanctity of my lines. I don't believe my lines are sacrosanct. If something has to go it will go. John and I will know that.'

He put his arm around me, pressed me to him, and said how happy and successful it was all going to be. 'I expect this show to win all the creative awards going.'

It was pleasing to see the place John D has earned for himself on the Broadway scene. Everyone wanted to be in the play, and he conducted auditions beautifully. Fan letters arrived in his

---

[57] The paternalistic owner of the restaurant in *The Kitchen*.

office, and I heard one actor turn to him and say: 'Whatever happens I must tell you these have been the most pleasant and courteous interviews I've ever had in the theatre.' He'd meet them on stage, put them at ease, apologise that he kept calling them back (he'd seen about thirteen hundred actors over five weeks), was witty and kind, made them read in groups – Bassanio, Graziano and Lorenzo, for example – and gave them the chance to do it again.

The running of auditions was highly organised. I was impressed to find myself presented with a board with light attached, and the names laid out on sheets – very professional. Just one blemish. The only actress I wanted to audition, Susan Galbraith, was down for two appearances but failed to turn up from Minneapolis. I spoke to her later on the phone. She said she had received the confirming letter on the morning she was supposed to be there. John had, from the beginning, wanted Julie Garfield (John Garfield's[58] daughter). I saw her and thought her too sweet. A good actress but didn't match the tough Jessica I had in mind. I asked John if I could talk to her. I gave her, and the actor auditioning for Lorenzo, a note. The boy changed not a bit but she'd picked up something. I've agreed to her because she's a good actress and also John very desperately wanted her – but I've got my doubts.

The biggest shock was the boy John wanted to play Lorenzo. Three were in the running. One I thought was ideal – handsome, dangerous, Polish-looking with a Polish name. But once again John preferred a young boy, the one actor who seemed the most boring of all we auditioned. I was amazed, and told John so. He said never mind – in his opinion that boy would be a star in five years 'as sure as apples fall off trees' – but he'd take the gaunt one, an actor he'd worked with before – played one of the horses in Shaffer's *Equus* – and knew would work hard. Like Julie – not my choice, too frozen for my taste, but an acceptable compromise. A tall young man. Texan.

We looked at designs for posters. Out of five offered, my choice coincided with John's – an old print of a Jew, a merchant, with

---

[58] Hollywood movie star, born Julius Garfinkle (1913–52)

modern typography. I suggested the typography should echo the type face from my Cape book jackets, and that an abstraction of the image be made into a logo to be easily recognised.[59]

We discussed the publicity campaign with Merle. Said I wanted to keep a low profile, maximum three interviews: a duet with John, a personal profile, an in-depth discussion of the work. I'd do one extra interview for Philadelphia and another for Washington. Merle pointed out that if the play was a success then everyone would be after me in the following days. Told him I'd stay for forty-eight hours after the opening. He pulled a face.

'Seventy-six?' I offered.

The problem was how to project the play. *The Merchant of Venice* was hated by New York audiences, and though they might warm to my play, how were we going to get them there to begin with? I didn't want to talk about it before opening but a press release had to be formulated. About one thing I was adamant – it wasn't a rewrite of Shakespeare and mustn't be offered as one. Of course, Zero Mostel was the big draw, but that presented another problem – how to prevent an audience thinking they were coming to a comedy.

Merle had prepared a brief press sheet which got off to a bad start claiming I was the author of 'Chicken Soup With Everything'![60] On my return to London I posted some biographical sheets, press cuttings, and other material to help him fix me in Broadway's busy firmament for a brief moment. Here in Europe one doesn't take New York or American theatre seriously, except for their musicals. Their dramatic talent is swallowed up by Hollywood where it then rots. They, on the other hand, view European theatre as the sticks. The fact that *Shylock* opened in Stockholm, or that Yugoslav TV are presenting a month of my work would mean nothing to them ...

'Sardi's,' John told people, 'was Arnold's and my first taste of New York theatre high life.' Lunched there with him three times this trip. He, or the production, paid twice. The third time I insisted on paying. He told me how mean Peter Shaffer was.[61]

---

[59] My advice was not taken.

[60] A confusion of two plays: *Chicken Soup with Barley* and *Chips with Everything.*

[61] He certainly wasn't mean with his time, as I was to discover later.

'Never seen a man reach so slowly into his pocket as the check arrives.'

Took my landlady, Sylvia, to the theatre. Took Al Levinson and his wife, Eve, to dinner at Francesca's – preceded by one act of Stuttgart Ballet doing *The Sleeping Princess* which John had given me tickets for imagining it was for the new Balanchine ballets. Wrong theatre!

Burt and Korby Britton[62] took me to lunch at a gorgeous restaurant called Maxwell's Plum, joined by a publisher whose name I've forgotten. It was from this lunch that I returned to discover $1000 and the jacket gone. Met up with Burt and Korby again and insisted they help me get over the loss by letting me pay for theatre tickets for *Ashes*,[63] in which I hoped to see Roberta Maxwell perform but she had got herself released in order to prepare for the *Shylock* rehearsals. Fine play but we sat on the side and missed half the text.

Being with John in New York was like being with an old relative. He reminded me of incidents in the past I'd forgotten. He keeps a diary and one day he's going to write a book of autobiography in the form of a web: in the ring of the year 1948, where was Tony Richardson, Bill Gaskill? In the year when he was in prison, where was Jocelyn, Peter Hall? It's a vivid image. I told him I'd pinch it as a framework to help me write my novel.[64]

He reminded me of the party at Larry Olivier's flat. 'We'd all been telling him he had to begin entertaining those foreign visitors, and so he'd got all the young writers together, and that was the occasion when you decided to be honest and tell him you didn't like his performance of Othello. He had to disappear into his study to recover for five minutes and then he said ...' I've forgotten what John's precise and very funny formulation was, but something like: '... "not only do I have to suffer all those heavy foreigners but I also have to listen to pipsqueak authors tell me their opinions of my performance".'

---

[62] Burt Britton, bookseller *extraordinaire*. Korby, his wife, expert on women's fashion, antiques dealer in partnership with Julie Belafonte.

[63] By David Rudkin.

[64] Which I haven't done, so far.

Poor Larry. He was an awful Shylock, too. I'd not tell him any such thing now. John loves theatre stories and gossip. Expressed concern that most books on theatre got everything wrong. 'New one on Larry and just about every fact and date is wrong.'

Told me of Cole's[65] book on Coward in which he, Cole, prints a letter from Noël to me telling me not to wear my wife's sweater in future. In fact Noël *said* it to me as I was leaving his house in Switzerland. Where *are* my notes from Coward? Are they in these diaries, or tucked in Centre 42 files under 'C'? Or in my 'special' box? Must check.

Sunday, next day

Couldn't sleep last night. At 3 a.m. got out of bed and finished writing the New York section above, and read through a book of Jewish photographs called *Family Album*. So many people I'd not realised were Jewish. Offenbach, Pulitzer, founder of the Westminster Bank (my bank), Fischer Verlag (my German publisher and agents) ... Prince Albert. *That's* why Princess Margaret looks Jewish!

Crawled into bed at 5 a.m. Took half an hour to fall asleep. Woken at 9.30.

One of the actors we'd auditioned, Jeff Horowitz,[66] the boy I liked for Solomon Usque, read Paul's speech from *The Kitchen*. It had sounded good. Made John and me nostalgic. 'Not bad for a first play,' I said.

Donald Howarth was in New York on an Arts Council grant to write a play combining *Doll's House*, *Hedda*, *Cherry Orchard*, *Three Sisters* and *Seagull* all in one. 'To save sitting through all those boring old classics.' Jocelyn and I disagreed with him as we ate his superbly cooked chicken in mushroom sauce. Conversation got around to asking each other what we considered was our Achilles' heel. Jocelyn thought it was her guilt for having been brought up in a privileged environment.

'Too nice, that,' I suggested.

Donald felt it was his wish to please, or rather not to oppose those he really felt were stupid, which resulted in him being abused by those he'd despised.

[65] Noël Coward's valet, housekeeper, guardian ... everything.

[66] Now runs Theatre for a New Audience in New York

I thought I had too many weaknesses through which I could be got at. This drew from Donald a comment it seemed he'd been waiting years to make – nothing to do with an Achilles heel at all.[67]

'You're dauntless,' he said. And when I responded I quite liked that he went on to quote Olivia of Malvolia. '*Oh you are sick of self-love, Malvolia, and taste with a distempered appetite.*' He accused me of what he termed 'bilious self-love'. Under protest he retracted 'bilious'.

'No,' I said, 'it's not "self-love", it's my Jewish barrel-chest, makes me look arrogant.'

Dusty mistakenly came to the airport to meet us on Wednesday instead of Thursday, and rang John in an agitated state. He told me to ring her. 'She wasn't angry. Why should she be – I'd have thought she'd have been relieved to be without you pontificating around the place.'

Picked him up at the Met for lunch. As we walked down the steps I said: 'Can we get something straight? You have this journalistic view of me as a pontificator. I'm not. On the contrary, I care only that people should be equipped *against* pontificators. People are frail. I believe society should be organised to allow for human frailty. *That* may be what I pontificate about.' 'A bit like people feeling violent about violent people,' he argued, citing *The Golden City* which he thought contained 'the most awful flat dialogue you've ever written – full of pontification'. A complete misreading of the play, but he was enjoying himself. As we walked on, an administrator of the Met's ballet section passed by with her young son of about fourteen whom she introduced to John. 'And mothers should know better than to introduce their young sons to me.'

We went on to discuss our different personalities, or rather he did.

'I hate parties, socialising, small talk. At seven on Friday everyone at the Met knows I can't be had and I'm off away to the house to put my feet up, listen to my records, read, potter. People now know not to ask me out. They're frightened of me, they feel

---

[67] I wrote down at the time what he said, and read it to him for verification.

I can scratch their eyes out. But you,' he couldn't resist adding, 'they're frightened of you because they fear they'll get sucked up in all that sweetness.'

I enjoy John's good spirits and his delight in his outrageous, wicked comments. He told me how I always seem to be merely tolerating other people's stupidity. Well, sometimes. But often I'm merely trying to find a confident air with which to cloak feelings of intellectual inadequacy. Mostly, though, people play silly games or let their hang-ups hang out, and I can't hide that I can see them. 'Also,' I suggested, 'Lindsay Anderson was one of my early mentors and I think I imitate his special kind of patient haughtiness.'

'Ah! Perhaps so!'

Everyone impressed with the cast. Each event contributed to a sense of the excitement ahead, except for my meeting with the lawyers – that filled me with consternation. I'd not really grasped the potential earnings involved. I had guessed they'd be more than I've ever earned before, and on the advice of my accountant, Anton Felton, had called for a clause in the contract to delay the money coming – £17,000, and no more, for two years. The rest to be kept by the Shuberts till we decided whether to take a year abroad and save on tax, or let it in and pay most of it to Inland Revenue. I couldn't see myself staying out of England any length of time. Robin, my agent, had said it would have to stay with the Shuberts and couldn't be put into a bank to gain interest. I checked this and found it could be – though 30% would go in US Federal Tax. So what? I was with the Shuberts' lawyer to effect the change.

He, Mr Cotton, was looking at me with some bewilderment as the author of a play which, costing so much money, was going to require a high box office return and, consequently, a high royalty for me. I had taken the risk and accepted only 5% until recoupment after which I would jump to a constant 10%, plus 10% of the profits. The alternative was the sliding scale of 5%, 7% and 10% depending upon the take. So, If the play grosses $100,000 a week (and they hope for $130,000) with a $70,000 break-even figure (i.e. $30,000 profit) then it would take 22 weeks to recoup during which time I'd have earned $5,000 instead of

$10,000, meaning I'd have invested 5000 x 22 = $110,000! ! But at the end of a year I would earn $410,000 – an unbelievable sum. The prospect of it sent me reeling down Fifth Avenue and through Central Park to 72nd. I was in a daze the rest of the day and into the next morning after which I took John to lunch.

The daze didn't prevent me taking in John's suggestion for new rewrites to the warehouse scene. He'd been reading more on the decline of Venetian society and discovered that despite the decline young men were still being trained for trade and diplomacy. Bassanio, he said, ought to counter Lorenzo's complaints about idle youth in Venice ... 'I don't want to give the nit-pickers a chance.'

I had made a list of things to discuss with John over lunch. Which theatre to perform in – it had to be big enough to earn back money for the backers, but not too big or it would lose the play and tire Zero. I reported to him on my discussions with Merle concerning publicity. Merle had come up with the idea of showing text to selected critics before the first night since we didn't want important reviews rushed through in an hour and a half merely on one viewing. It was a demanding play, they needed to know something about it before the curtain went up. I had at once agreed. John didn't need much persuading.

The last item on my list was a confession – the huge royalties looming ahead. How was I going to handle them? What did *he* do? He confided he earned about quarter of a million dollars a year and had a tax haven in the Bahamas. It made no difference to him, he said, except it facilitated his work. He used the money. 'I'd forget about it,' he advised.

But I couldn't, and tried to explain. 'Look,' I began, 'how can I contemplate writing a play on the life of Jesus[68] with a quarter of a million bucks in the bank?'

'Why not?'

'Because Jesus was a man who said give your riches to the poor, and I'm going to have to have an attitude towards that. If I approve it will be asked "well why don't you do the same?" If I don't approve it will be said he's rationalising his own situation.'

---

[68] Something I'd been planning for years.

'Ah ha!' pounced John, 'you're only worried about what others are going to think.'

'No,' I replied, 'I'm worried about what *I* will think; that I won't be *able* to think, that I'll have a block.'

'Peter's got a block since he's earned all that money on *Equus*,' John told me.

It all seems silly now that I'm back in London where the air one breathes is thick with failure and neglect. Love this country though I do, it induces a sense that everything will fail. And sure enough I return to discover that neither Robin nor Doddie[69] have pursued the Royal Court to see if they'll take on *The Wedding Feast*! I feel *Shylock* will flop anyway.

---

69 The producer who mismanaged the transfer of *The Wedding Feast* to London.

NEW YORK! NEW YORK!

[1977 *continued*]

[Now begin five weeks of rehearsal prior to an 'out of town' opening in Philadelphia.]

WEEK ONE

30 July, 117 West 11th, New York

Driven to airport by Cape's car. Picked up Jocelyn on the way. New chauffeur. From Jamaica. Before reaching Jocelyn's I engaged him in conversation. He said, 'I used to work for the African embassies. No more. They had diplomatic immunity and they used to abuse it. One place I worked they didn't stamp my cards for a year. Couldn't do a thing. Another place, a new ambassador arrived and decided to drop my salary, take it or leave it. I decided to get out. You used to have to bow and scrape, man. I mean I know you got to show your employer some respect – but these new African states? They expect their subjects and employees to treat them like gods! You wouldn't believe it that these men have a civilised education. They go to Oxford and Cambridge and they quote Shakespeare at you but no sooner they're home they change back to old tribal mentalities. Only their families can get jobs and rise in positions. They all talk about freedom from slavery and colonialism and the need for democracy but there's not one democrat amongst them. They don't understand the meaning of the word. I mean I believe in majority rule but I still can understand the white Rhodesian's fear. Black Africa is so behind the times ... and they're all full of excuses – about colonialism and slavery, but that was a long time ago. I don't believe you can go on making excuses. It's twenty years, man! In twenty years things should have changed. You take a country like Israel, incredible country. They're building tanks and aeroplanes there. Black Africa can't even produce a pin, man! And they're so rich, they've got so much raw material ...' I asked him did other blacks share his view. He said most West Indians did because they came from a democratic tradition, but they'd be afraid to admit it. I asked how he knew so much. He replied it was because he'd worked a lot for the embassies and because he'd read. I've reported only a small part of his conversation which flowed as fluently as I've recorded it, though was more vivid.

Plane was twenty-five minutes late taking off. Smooth. No anxieties about flying these days. Had long talk with Jocelyn about the past and the condition of loneliness. Of course she feels lonely at times, but she's been living alone for nearly thirteen years now and is used to it. On the other hand she works, has good relationships with the children ...

'But we're all alone, even in a partnership, that's what makes it exciting – those two alonenesses coming together.'

I recalled for her the time George [Devine] came to eat with us in Clapton Common, the first flat that Dusty and I had in our marriage, and how he was one of the first to visit us from that alien but wonderfully thrilling new world of 'the real arts'. Mum thought so much of him, impressed with his courtesy and warmth.[70]

Jocelyn had recently spent time on a project with Lindsay Anderson[71] who was feeling, as I had been feeling, bitter and ignored.

We talked at length about the play. She told me: 'Riggs[72] reports that he's never seen John so excited about a play as he is about *Shylock*.' We were both thrilled to be on a journey embarking upon a new production together again.

Confusion on arrival. The Shubert organisation's company car was at the Pan Am building while we hung around the British Airways building. Sent out messages. Finally met up with the driver and got to the Village around 4 p.m. Sylvia came from Library to show me round her lovely apartment, so centrally situated. Went shopping immediately. Everything I needed was round the corner. Shopped in Jefferson's Market and the fabulous Balducci's. Bought cards, old photos of US. Ate in the Grand

---

[70] Jocelyn and George Devine became lovers until his sudden and untimely death in 1966.

[71] Lindsay Anderson, film and stage director, worked often with Jocelyn as his designer. He was the man responsible for reading my first play and promoting it at the Royal Court. I owe him the launching of my career and named my firstborn son after him.

[72] Riggs O'Hara, John Dexter's life-long companion, playing Graziano. John met Riggs when Riggs was a brilliant young dancer in the original production of *West Side Story*. They remained together till John's death. Riggs has edited a book of Dexter's memoirs, *Honorable Beast* published by Nick Hern Books.

Ticino, homely Italian restaurant on Thompson. I must have looked so much like a tourist but I can't help it, everything delights me. Fell into bed at about 11.30 p.m (4.30 a.m. London time) with a copy of a book called *Shylock*, the history of a character by Herman Sinsheimer, 'Shylock from the Jewish point of view'.

Shakespeare used the currency of his time – the usurer, the sly Judas, the cruel Christ-killer – to subvert medieval myths and create the greatest Jewish character since the Bible'.

Really, now?

Saturday, 30 July, New York (can't think why it's still the 30th?!)

Dreamt that two productions of *The Four Seasons* had taken place. One which the actors thought highly of; I didn't. The designer was selling his designs in a folio in a street market. I was asked did I like them. Said yes but thought they were more working drawings than finished designs. Designer agreed and seemed impressed that I could tell the difference.

Woke at 8 a.m. I love this apartment. Switched radio to the non-stop classical station which I soon located, and made breakfast – Turkish coffee, salami, tuna fish salad and tomatoes. Wrote up diary. Shaved and showered. Read more of the 'Shylock' book. Friend rang and I realized how much I wanted simply to be alone to read, listen to music, shlomp around in my dressing gown. Rang Korby to set up meeting for her to view the folio of Stepney Streets which I hope she'll sell. Rang Joan Kahn[73] who says Harper's paperback people can't set up edition of *Shylock* in time for first night – three months away! So I'll try to find another paperback publisher. Made date with her to go out with the family when they arrive. Rang John D. He's invited friends and cast to his birthday party. Sounds in good form. Talked about whether Jessica and Nerissa needed to be in the courtroom. Yes,

---

[73] My editor at Harper's. Dead now.

or the last scene wouldn't work. But he may be right that some small amount of dialogue needs to be written in order to tie up the loose ends of Shylock's pained relationship with his daughter. Must look at it. Or perhaps wait till rehearsal.

Arrangements to get to his birthday party had changed. No coach.

'I thought that would be vulgar for such distinguished people! Separate cars from 9J (his apartment in town) leaving at 12 a.m., returning at 6 p.m.' What kind of wild birthday party could that be ending at 6? Well, we'll all need to be ready for the next day I suppose. Only fifteen birthday guests coming, not all the cast as he'd originally planned.

He outlined the schedule for Monday, the first day of rehearsal.

10.30 a.m. – Equity arrangements
11 a.m. – meet the press
11.30 a.m. – reveal and explain model of the set to the cast
1 p.m. – champagne brunch
2 p.m. – slow and 'slightly pissed' read-through

We rehearse two weeks in Minskoff's rehearsal room on 44 and Broadway. Then two weeks in the Imperial Theatre. I learned from him that Zero's wife has had an accident – fell and needed twenty-nine stitches. Apparently always does that on the verge of a success.

Sylvia has arranged her spices in alphabetical order for me.

Sunday, 31 July

Spoke on the phone with Zero who announced he'd lost forty pounds. 'I've no clothes to wear,' he complained. Plans to lose another ten pounds, he says. I'll pop over to see him today before going off to John's party. He sounds fit. Says he feels on top form and that he now knows the play. 'But,' unable to resist the quip, 'I still think it's marvellous!' Told me he's warned the producers he won't perform it or even sign his contract until they give us a theatre other than the Imperial, which he thinks is a barn. 'I'll hold out to the last minute. Make them sweat. Who knows, maybe it'll work. Trouble is I can't be *really* angry. Can't produce real anger.' I hope he can on stage.

Looking out of the window I see that many other flats are shrouded with green plants, breaking up the brutal edges of concrete and glass. Sylvia says it's a recent phenomenon, the green-growing. Part of the counter-culture. She made a fish dinner last night here in her/my flat for Alex, her boyfriend, and me. After which we strolled the streets of Greenwich Village and listened to a young man reciting poetry by heart, on request, for a fee, badly but boldly; another young couple played sonatas for violin and viola against a background of car honks and a fruit grinder. They were not bad. Both sets of buskers had appreciative and generous audiences. Ended having coffee in a place called the Elephant and Castle. It was 1.30 a.m. I was bushed. But woke early. It's now only 8.30 a.m.

Can't begin the damn one-acter for the National Theatre. Have made two false starts. Nothing comes. Why? Because it's an imposed idea rather than a recreated experience?

Have brought with me a new book on Jesus called *Jesus the Jew* by the scholar, Geza Vermes. In his preface he quotes Martin Buber:

> We Jews know him in a way – in the impulses and emotions of his essential Jewishness – that remains inaccessible to the Gentiles subject to him.

Which I suppose is why I want to embark upon the play.[74] Must stop writing. Burt Britton due any moment.

Monday, 1 August – 6.15 a.m., the big day

Burt came round yesterday to collect the folio of 'Stepney Streets'. He said the accompanying text[75] on the front page had made him cry.

---

[74] I've had a lifelong ambition to write a play on the life of Jesus which would attempt to reveal him as the product of Jewish society that he must surely have been.

[75] Excerpt from a private and wild play I wrote in 1969 *The New Play* intended more for personal catharsis than production – writing it helped unblock a play I was having difficulty with called *The Old Ones*. Since revamped and entered for the Onassis Play Competition, 1997. No wins!

'I hope you don't mind me saying the things I say to you. It doesn't embarrass you? But I read this and I know you're going to be one of the few playwrights who'll last. You're a poet ...!' I'm not, of course, but I love hearing it.

Drove to Zero's apartment on Central Park for a coffee. A huge continental-type space, glass-cases filled with '*objets d'art*', walls covered by notes from people such as Ira Gershwin (it's like stepping into the pages of a book of theatrical history) and original prints and paintings, many his own work. I'd heard he painted and expected to hate them, but they're not without power. He's got no 'voice' of his own, though. Bits and pieces of other painters float through his canvases. He showed me a folio of small sketches he'd done while studying the play. Some were impressive, most were nonsensical. Together they produced an atmosphere but not one that I recognised as belonging to my play. Cervantes no doubt would have said the same of Picasso's illustrations of *Don Quixote*. He's lost so much weight. Still a big man but I'm glad I suggested he try to shed some. The coffee was weak.

I left him to go on to John's flat where I met Roberta Maxwell (Portia) and Marian Seldes (Rivka), and the car which was to take us to John's country house – Ocean Boulevard, Atlantic Heights, in New Jersey. Marian teaches acting at Juilliard. She talks a bit like Dorothy James, cooing and breathy – not as I imagined the strong Jewish sister of Shylock, but then she'd burst into mimicry, or a 'role', and I saw her strength. Roberta, sparrow-like, seemed in a state of wide-eyed, suppressed excitement. She's just made a film in Canada about rape. Said it was scary and violent, had nothing to do with sex, but with assertion ... Had to live through four separate takes.

In Ocean Boulevard, John's party was in session. Guests had already started eating. Peter Shaffer[76] was there, and Ned Sherrin[77] – both remarked how well I looked, startled, as though I'd been a cancer sufferer. I think they expected me to look fatter and greyer and – God knows what! More harassed probably. Julie Garfield

---

[76] John had directed many of his plays.

[77] Ned Sherrin, writer, director of musicals.

(Jessica), someone called Joe, and a woman called 'Chippy' who designed children's clothes and, I was told, went to nursery school with John in Derby. She knew Mike Henshaw,[78] had been in the same school class as he. Mike and his brother, she said, were 'sinister', whereas John was always in a high state. 'He used to bully us in class.'

John was in good spirits, which meant wicked spirits. When he introduced Peter and me he added, mischievously: 'You two know one another don't you – one from the commercial theatre and one from the legit theatre?'

'That's how they always divide us,' smiled Peter.

'An old trick,' I agreed. I asked Peter if he felt that John directing *Shylock* was like letting your wife sleep with another man? He misunderstood at first, thinking I meant: was letting *any*one direct your play like letting your wife (the play) sleep with another man. After I explained that I was referring to his long association with John he entered into a detailed exposition of the problems involved working with directors – '... always worthwhile in the end but ...' I found myself agreeing with most of what I heard him say but hadn't actually listened to everything he said. A recent and disturbing habit. I switch off from what people are telling me. My mind wanders. Often because something they say prompts another thought. The same happens when reading. But one can reread a paragraph, it's not so easy asking your companion to repeat most of what they've just spent a long time very carefully articulating. Peter told me John had 'forbidden' him to read *Shylock*. Why?

Thank goodness the girls were there. Nearly everyone else was queer. But the girls sat liberated and free with their legs decoratively splayed. Everyone was excited about the next day's reading. I drank too much champagne and stretched out beside Jocelyn on the couch. John loves the idea of us three being together again. Towards the end of the afternoon we smoked a little pot. My first in years.[79] At 6 p.m. promptly, Brent – John's

---

[78] Michael Henshaw, accountant. Born in same town as Dexter, whose accounts he did on the side. Dexter handed him onto me. In 1962, when a group of artists got together to create an arts organisation called Centre 42 and I was appointed its director, I asked Mike to leave his job working for the Inland Revenue and risk losing his pension by coming to work as 42's administrator. He took the risk, and subsequently met many artists to whom he became accountant. He has prospered.

[79] Not that I ever smoked on more than half a dozen occasions in my life.

assistant – got us all out of the house and on our way back to NY.

I drove back with Roberta and Chippy and the man she'd brought along called, I think, Tony Hall – a children's book writer and novelist who spoke all the time about how lonely writing novels was and how lucky I was to have an editor like John Dexter, and people (actors) to help me through. It was a putdown which I ignored. Roberta handled him stylishly, though. She's a no-nonsense lady who comes back with a punch. But she's also a little innocent. I teased her, warning that they all – she especially – had to perform the play in a strictly English accent. I think she believed me.

By 7.30 I was back in the flat, stoned and nowhere to go, with no energy to pick up a phone or attempt work. Tried watching TV. Dozed on the couch. Zero rang. Wanted clarification of a line in the play.

'What does it mean, "*all law is diseased in parts*"?' I began to explain but he interrupted to say: 'John told me you'd changed it.' Had I? Not that I could remember. He said never mind he understood what the line meant anyway. Strange! Why had he called? Must be alone in his flat and feeling in need of contact with someone from the production, as we all were alone in our flats – Roberta, Julie, Marian, John Clements ... waiting, eager and anxious for today's 'battle'.

John had said in one of his moments of high exuberance during his birthday party: 'I've been waiting and preparing for this moment for six months. Arnold's been waiting for over a year ...'

Over two years in fact. The first typed draft is dated May 1975.

Fell into bed about 10.30. Woke up at 5 a.m. Excited. Anxious. This is the day. Started writing this diary at 6.15. It's now 7.15. Will make coffee, write some cards – but that play, that one-act play, when will *that* come?

Later – after read-through

It is most odd to have had such a thrilling day and find myself alone in this flat, *again*, eating a fish salad, when I – we – should all be together. It has been no ordinary day and yet I'm here, by myself, being ordinary. ZERO HAS LEARNED ALL HIS LINES!

But the beginning.

I finally walked out this morning – it was difficult to leave the flat in any way that made sense, that fitted to the occasion. Something special should have happened. I should have flown to rehearsals, or walked all the way, or met someone first and walked with them. But I'm doing everything alone. Feels absurd.

First stop – the tiny post-office on 10th. Bought stamps, posted my cards, walked a couple of blocks, dithered in a stationary shop, bought more cards, a pen, a notebook, panicked about arriving late and took a cab to Minskoff's rehearsal studio on 1515 Broadway. Got into lift with Zero.

Actors and others milling around. Equity procedures to be attended to. Said hello to my cast. John had the inspired idea to make Nerissa black. His first choice of black actress for the role had declined protesting that, being black, she didn't want to play a 'hand-maiden'! Sam Levene (Tubal) complained (half jokingly) about his part being cut. Zero, loudly to the others, expostulated, jokingly of course: 'My God! The writer's here! Awful man! Can't write! No heart!'[80] He made, so Roberta later told me, funny faces towards my turned back.

The Shubert management came in looking like the Mafia, strolled among the players, benign and proprietorial. When they left, John D. said to them very pointedly: 'See you in five weeks time!' The only 'outsider' he permitted to remain for the read-through was the intelligent Roger Berlind, one of the co-producers. John has no fear of anyone. The money's been invested. He was in charge. An air of marvellous anticipation floated between all present, each one carrying their own excitement and pushing waves of it to one another, reassuring each other that – no! they weren't mad to be feeling what they were feeling.

Press line up. Photographs. TV. A brief chat with the *New York Times*. No one allowed to move from Studio 4, where we were assembled, to Studio 2, where the designs and model were to be viewed, until John and Jocelyn had laid them out. I'm impressed with the overall organisation. Lots of typed sheets full of useful information.

---

[80] I've since come to realise that people joke in the States as a way of camouflaging insecurity and a consequent latent violence.

Finally everyone is seated before the model. John, vibrating with an energy so enthralled that it embarrassed him, called Jocelyn and me to his side, and began: 'First you must forgive us aliens. We've worked together on six, seven productions before, but here in New York we feel a bit lost and dependent upon you ...' It was a before-the-battle address which delighted and stirred them. He gave them confidence pointing out that though he knew exactly what he was doing and had constructed a framework it could nevertheless be changed leaving room for them to grow and offer anything *they* might discover in the text. 'You don't have to do research for this play, it's all in the text. But if you want, Arnold will answer questions or refer you to books.' I told them there was a factual mistake in the play which they could make a game finding out.

'The only mistake of the play is that it's too long,' John also couldn't resist quipping, but it was half-hearted because the amazing reality was, uncharacteristically, he was 'reverential'. How mellow he has become.

He then explained how the set would function and described his method of working. 'I block in four days and, don't worry, I have a run-through so that we can all see the length and breadth of the play, so that I can see which of my moves aren't working, how the flow is going, and so on. Some people say it's a bad way to work but it's the only way I know how ...' Then he invited everyone to sit down to a champagne lunch which had been paid for by the Shubert organisation and laid out by Sardi's — theatreland's very own restaurant.

By 2.15 everyone was sitting around the table desperately anxious to begin. The buzz was tangible. I watched Roberta who was opposite me, her sharp eyes birdlike, sitting in a tight, wound-up state, waiting to be let fly. It seemed to me I could see her heart beating fast. There was a brief delay as John Clements and Zero had to be measured up for costumes — then, we were off. Not with my play but a five-second exchange between an excited director and his mega-star. Zero, on diet, had drunk nothing and eaten little.

John said: 'It's a pity that the first line of the play has to be said by the one member of the cast who is not drunk!'

'I *am* drunk,' Zero replied, 'with sobriety!'

John had told them to give the reading *some*thing, but no one was prepared for what followed. It was not simply that Zero had learned his lines but that everyone was in the grip of an inspiration which spread like sunlight upon exuberant seas making thrilling sense of the play. It *is* a dense play, full of ideas, but it flows, it has narrative, vivid characters, AND IT IS FUNNY.

After the excitement of reading through the first three pages, Zero came to the following passage addressed to his friend, Antonio:

Cardinal Caraffa! He's fortunate it *is* my God in charge or he'd be in hell by now. Oh forgive me. An arrogant joke. First I tire you, then I depress you, then I insult you.[81]

'And I tire myself also!' he added. The joker! Unable to resist the ad-lib, the wisecrack. Even at such a moment. But it didn't distract.

John had seated people in special relationships: Jessica next to her lover, Lorenzo; Shylock and his dear friend, Antonio, at either end of a long table; Portia next to Shylock, and so on. The positioning enabled them to speak to each other, play with and for each other. As a result everyone knew they were locked into a special experience, private, personal, intoxicating. Time and again actors hit the right note, the precise meaning. Zero of course was emotional, couldn't completely contain his feelings, but a combination of long experience and his inimitable humour gave his rendering a distance which offset it. Clements read with sober, straightforward intelligence which, contrasting with Zero's emotionalism, set up another pocket of electricity. It took all my sense of propriety to force myself still and not leap about with delight and gratitude. At one moment I turned to look at John. It was like the first night of *Roots* at the Belgrade Theatre in Coventry nineteen years ago when it was obvious that the cast had grasped his direction and were in control of my play, and that the audience was responding. I had turned then to look at him.

---

[81] These lines were subsequently cut from the play.

He was crying. Now, once again, his eyes were shining, damp with pleasure and pride at what he had put together and was hearing for the first time.

(Zero has just phoned while I'm writing this, lonely but also excited, to inform me of that same moment when John had tears in his eyes. And Riggs, with whom I had coffee afterwards, confirmed what he had told Jocelyn – that John had not been so excited by a play in years and that he'd been playing with the model endlessly and reading and rereading.)

In the rehearsal room was one wall of mirrors. It had been covered up with brown paper but, during the reading, the paper had begun to peel off, gradually revealing us to ourselves. It was an eerie happening which added to the sense of drama, and oddly, the joy. The joy was contagious. Lorenzo who'd not met his Jessica till that afternoon kissed her to round off their love-scene. Zero delivered his history-of-Italy – the Renaissance speech – with panache. The first act was over. It had taken 1 hour 57 minutes. (2 hours 56 minutes for the whole play. Surprised. Thought it would be about 3½ hours long.)

Lots of jokes.

'Anyone who wants to relieve themselves before we begin again, do so now,' said John.

'I've just relieved myself,' said Zero, 'and missed! Can we do it again?'

'You didn't put enough feeling into it,' joked John.

'Zero hasn't got any feeling,' said Sam Levene somewhat sourly and out of tune with the moment. Some of his camouflage had dropped revealing the tip-end of resentment.

The second act went at a slower pace, the air gone from the excited balloon of an afternoon. Sam Levene seemed to be deliberately mumbling his lines in defiance of Zero's full-bloodied rendering, unable to hide his envy of his old friend's role. His mumbling affected some of the others whose reading dropped in temperature, they too began mumbling. Levene even moved away from the table to sit alongside the wall when he'd no more lines. John is thinking of bringing back his (Levene's/Tubal's) speech to the courtroom which I'd cut for the Danish production. It's tempting but we must wait and see how long the courtroom scene lasts. It must not be made endless. Despite his surliness, I like Levene; he'll give a great performance. I just hope he's not too unhappy. No one else is. The reading ended leaving us all drained but elated. Pray we're not deluding ourselves.

Had coffee with Roberta and Riggs afterwards. Riggs, before she was cast, had asked Roberta which part she'd like to play. She said Jessica.

'You're playing Portia!' She'd been content. She seems in a perpetually stunned state. Riggs talked about the evenings, speculating how they'd be filled, spent as playtime.

'I want,' said Roberta, 'to save my playtime till Philadelphia. I want to get this part out as soon as possible, out there and tested and worked on straightaway. No messing and waiting around with *this* one.' I know what it is about her – she hovers. That's it! Poised as though for some mad moment.

Riggs expressed fears that John wouldn't talk much about this play and its roles.

'I hate it when he says "don't *tell* me, *do* it!" I hate that line more than anything. My most hateful line. Because sometimes you *can't* "do it" till you've talked, because it may involve moving this character here or that piece of furniture there. I'm just anxious he especially won't be able to talk to *me*.'

'Don't worry,' I assured him, 'if *he* can't talk to you then he'll ask me to talk to you.'

He seemed glad of that since earlier he'd expressed a fear that the Graziano of the first act was not the same as the Graziano of the second act.

'In the second act he's more vicious.'

I told him that sentimental, weak people often do become vicious, mean. He thought that helped.

Roberta casually announced that she was late for a date, but didn't seem concerned. It was obvious that no one wanted to leave anyone.

Wednesday, 3 August

Seem unable to sleep beyond 6 a.m. I go to bed late – 1 a.m. last night – yet some mechanism is getting me up at this odd hour.

Though this morning it was Dusty who woke me at 6.30 saying she was arriving on an earlier flight. In passing she also let me know the income-tax people had written to say they weren't accepting post-dated cheques. God knows why. They'll get them at the same speed anyway.

Arrived at yesterday's rehearsal, to find white mugs all laid out with our individual names on tape glued to them. Zero made a spectacular entrance laden with two huge cakes for the cast – from a famous shop whose name I've forgotten – one a cheesecake, the other a dried-fruit and apple-tart. Delicious.

First day of blocking.[82] John seems full of energy. First three scenes relatively easy with only two characters in each. Then comes Scene 4 with ten! But that's to be blocked after lunch. He asks me to join him at Sardi's to talk over his new thoughts. He'd greeted me in the morning with two observations: that the second act was better constructed than the first, tighter; and that he wanted me to look out in the first act for repetitions. The odd line here and there to be cut, the florid ones! It didn't need chunks cut out, just snippets. He pointed out some. I told him I'd work on it.[83]

We also talked about how thrilling the read-through had been and wasn't it extraordinary that Zero had learned his lines. I asked shouldn't we be worried? John said no, that's how it should always be. Noël Coward had insisted actors learn their lines before rehearsals began.

'And *I* say to actors – you can take your own time, use what methods you're used to for learning lines, but I won't be able to help you until you've put the book down.' A good tack, I'll remember it. I too believe you can't really work until the book's down.

Nice spread in the *NY Times* today.

Told John I was reluctant to put back the Tubal speech until we were absolutely sure we needed it. I didn't want to make that 'tight' second act longer. Let's wait; the speech was standing by. John had pointed out that by the time the last scene in Act 1 came

---

[82] The positioning of characters on the stage.

[83] Though I'd restructured the play from three to two acts at his suggestion.

(Antonio's dinner), a long time had passed since mention was made of Shylock's loan to Antonio. I gave him some new lines to open that scene, which referred to the loan.

'You work fast,' he said. I do!

I suggested that since the big Nerissa scene had been cut he ought to think about getting the actress, Gloria Gifford, to look for a special personality to compensate. Told him about the extraordinary actress in Sweden who offered an earthy Brechtian-type, a mocking peasant character who, despite having few lines, had made her presence felt whenever she crossed the stage — which the director had made her do frequently even though the script didn't call for it. Told John I wasn't too worried about any of the actors except the one playing Lorenzo, Everett McGill, who'd started off on the wrong track — neither intelligent nor controlled enough. He hadn't been my choice of actor. Hope he can do it.

'After about the second week I want you,' said John, 'to begin taking the actors out one by one for dinner to talk to them.' Suits me!

Before blocking Act Two John lay on his back with his legs in the air for six minutes. Zero constantly joking. I had the feeling that one day someone would become impatient with him. He breaks concentration, both his and others. And indeed later in the afternoon he asked me, as I was lying down on his couch in his special room, looked after by his personal dresser: 'Does my fucking around get on your nerves? Perhaps I'd better stop. I'm doing too much. I'll stop tomorrow.' It made me laugh, he looked so anxious. He continued: 'Well, a man's got a conscience about these things.' Which made me laugh more.

John makes a mess of the middle of Scene 4. He too is full of jokes, but anxious jokes, and erratic direction. He has Shylock sitting down ahead of his guest, Rebecca da Mendes. Zero points it out. I whisper to John 'he's right'. John changes the move. He seems nervous. His high spirits now come over as agitation. He openly confesses he's got the central part of the scene in a muddle but says it'll do for now, adding: 'It's ages since I've handled more than two or three characters on stage at once.' He's disarmingly charming, joking about his failure. I can see moves which are wrong, but have no fears that he won't see them later on. As he runs through the bustling family Scene 4 again he hold his hands out in front to regard them. I ask him why.

'To see if I'm still nervous.'

'Were you nervous this morning?'

'All day. And I will be until this week is out of the way.' Very reassuring.

Walked to 1 Lincoln Plaza, John's apartment. It's also where Judy Rossner[84] has a flat. I'd been invited by her for dinner. Bought a good Meursault and arrived hot and sweaty. She offered me a shower and kimono to cool off in. Her apartment is on the 40th floor with an incredible view of the Hudson, the Lincoln Centre, statue of Liberty, up and downtown. There was a sunset of a red I'd not seen before. 'Laid it on specially for you,' she said.

Judy was brown, tanned, and still caught in that faint but constant smile of incredulous delight with her 'delayed' success. She showed me a copy of her new book, *Attachments*.

'Still gives me goose pimples.' It does for us all to see ourselves in print. And she got them again when I told her Maggie Drabble[85] had both heard of her *and* read her book. She's a nice mixture of ripeness and innocence.

Asked about rehearsals. I reported how things were going. Felt her attention was only partly in New York. She had to be here for an interview but really wanted to be back in her country house. Work rhythms had been broken, to my advantage though – she could give me dinner. Good cook, too. We talked about coping with success. I'd been sort of 'famous' for a long time, I said, but I felt the success of *Shylock* – which everyone told me was assured with Zero Mostel in the lead – might throw me. She said not. At least the success of *Goodbar* hadn't thrown her. But perhaps that was because she's a different kind of person. I have this fear that too many riches diminish one's moral authority to discuss *anything*.[86] No such fears attached themselves to Judy and her work.

---

[84] American novelist. Came to fame with fourth novel *Looking for Mr Goodbar* which was made into a movie.

[85] Eminent novelist; editor of *Oxford Companion to English Literature*.

[86] Having lived on an overdraft the rest of my career this is not a view I hold with much conviction now!

Thursday, 4 August

I love the sight of the small urns with constant coffee and hot water. And Zero's cake lying around – warm and cosy.

John blocks the warehouse scene. It's a joy to watch his delight as he develops an idea to have Graziano pull and unroll, with an exuberant flourish, bales of cloth in which he swathes Bassanio, testing which colour will suit him for the clothes he's having made for his meeting with Portia. Graziano ends being tied up himself in length after length of many colours 'or as much fucking about as Miss Herbert (designer) will allow us', cries John, 'and that ain't fucking much!'

'Oh,' I coo at him, 'you know she'll indulge you.'

'Hasn't done so yet. That red will be bronze by the time she's finished, you'll see.' The scene shapes and grows under John's inspired direction. 'We'll litter the floor with damasks and silks, all the trade of Venice, even sprinkle them with spices.' Suddenly Lorenzo's words are brought to life:

... and our painters paint their Virgin Marys like whores. Sumptuousness! There's too much of it. Leads to effeminacy![87]

John mumbles with excited agitation: 'Forgotten how I'm going to get it all cleared up and away for the next scene now.' But he does.

'I trust,' I whisper to him, 'that you've noted the way I've played around with Pinteresque dialogue in this scene.' I was referring to Graziano's complaints about Venice being in the hands of old patricians:

A burning issue. I burn whenever it comes up. It comes up burning and I burn.

'Oh,' says John wickedly, 'I thought that was pure Wesker. You mustn't denigrate yourself, dear.'

Zero arrives. Embraces me with over-loud and over-sized kisses. Poor Kate, his wife, is in hospital and, he complains: 'Sick people

---

[87] The last three lines were cut from final text.

are terrible. "Bring me this bring me that, do this do that!" I'm tired before I begin.' I love the way he talks Yiddish. Makes me regret even more that I understand so little. He goes to his room performing a false trip on the way, then pretending he's blind and can't find the door handle, turns to get his mug instead.

'Wish they'd make each mug coloured, takes me hours to read which one's mine.'

The Lorenzo/Jessica love scene comes up next. John wants to put this back to where it originally had been, towards the end of the play. Their love possesses a strange quality and I feel it should come earlier so that we know about it sooner. I urge him to try it. He does so but completely fails to understand the scene's intention. He makes them embrace on first meeting. I want them to be chaste, poised on the *edge* of passion, to draw back and play this strange word game which they play so well together that it brings them closer until they can't contain their passion any longer, and *then* they embrace. Perhaps the scene needs a line or two to help it along; or perhaps it can't work at all. But I want it tried. I'll talk with John at the end of the week.[88]

We come to the long Renaissance speech set in Antonio's house after they've all eaten dinner. John's big moment. He's worked out some extraordinary blocking. Halfway through there's an announcement that a bomb has been put in the building. Bombs have been found throughout the day and one has gone off on 42nd Street killing one person. The rumour is that the perpetrators are a small Puerto Rican terrorist group. We talk about it. Sir John (Clements) wants to remain in the building and continue working. I certainly do. The stage management also want to stay on, and most of the actors. We agree to ignore the scare on the assumption that it's probably not true, and if it were then the ground floor was too far away from the third floor to affect us. The bomb would go off in the lobby. The building might lean a little, but no more ... Zero continues rehearsing the scene with great fun, milking the bomb scare, his hilarity growing as John gives him tables and other props to move around the set as a way of illustrating his idiosyncratic history of the Renaissance.

---

[88] The word game was cut from final text.

... The land in three pieces, then. But does everything stand still? Impossible! Watch in the north how the German Holy Roman Empire disintegrates; in the centre how the families of Rome brawl among themselves; in the south how the French house of Anjou fights the Spanish house of Aragon ...

Zero rushes around laying down something to represent the German Holy Roman Empire, something else for the families of Rome, another something for the French house of Anjou.

'Not only do I have to learn the fucking lines but I have to move the furniture as well! Look what I've become − a fucking furniture remover. Get the Contrini Brothers.[89] What's he doing to me? He started out liking me, admiring me, then he went to this fucking Voodoo man. Where was I? *Who* am I? Where am I? I don't know where I am any more, pushing these tables around here, there, there, here! I wasn't looking forward to this afternoon but the thought of a bomb under me as well ...'

John enjoys him but it makes the plotting of a difficult scene even more difficult. I'm not sure John's ever going to be able to hold back Zero's steam-rollering New York Jewish ebullience. But when the scene is finally blocked, with tables strewn around the place, Zero looks about himself in wonder and a certain excitement and asks 'will it work?' The rest of the company are sent off. He goes through it again. Alone.

The casket scene is blocked next. Simple. That'll work. The advertising men bring the poster. It looks good in red with the print of the old man running down the side, but the title is lost by being the same size and type as the star.

ZERO MOSTEL

in

THE MERCHANT

by

Arnold Wesker

with

JOHN CLEMENTS

SAM LEVENE

---

[89] A firm of removers.

I don't mind my name being half their size but it's madness both to lose the title and to have SAM LEVENE so large. He had insisted on the size in his contract and the Shuberts had given in. Why? Because he's claimed as a Broadway name – lots of movies and one of the leads in the original production of *Guys and Dolls*. But his part in *Shylock* is small while Roberta, for example, has an overwhelmingly larger part. Her name takes second place in small print lower down. Otherwise the poster works.

Another good day. John enjoys me being there to watch the unfolding of his direction. Or seems to, anyway. He walks upstage to an actor, demonstrates a move, an action, and returns giving me a look that searches for approval. Mostly I smile admiringly, often I don't return the look – I fear he'll become irritated to find himself searching for approval. Many performances not going in the right direction, mainly Zero's – little subtlety. But I've no qualms. I don't expect much at this stage of rehearsals, and what Zero is doing is making courageously bold offers. I'm confident that in the end the production will reveal what I've put into the writing. Meanwhile I derive pleasure making little cuts on the way, and John has promised me a long session of first-stage notes on his direction and actors' performances.

Walk down Broadway with Roberta who buys me a drink in the Theatre Pub on 50th. She's loving it all. Has great faith in John who, she says, is so strong that he gives you the tone as well 'and you trust him because experience tells you his ideas are better'. Did she mind me being there? Oh no, she enjoyed it. 'In fact when you were out for a long while this afternoon I missed you.' I asked how she liked New York (she's Canadian). She's settled in, has friends, but she prefers to work in total concentration – immersed in her part, her play, thinking about it, unceasingly feeling it within her. We made a date to sniff some cocaine together. It will be my first experience.[90]

Returned to the flat. Sylvia there with her daughter, Erika, and Erika's friend, Coco. Took Sylvia off to a new fish restaurant – felt she should be fussed over before going off on holiday. We'd planned a movie but the Gassman film we'd agreed to see was not

---

[90] I'm appalled to read that I seemed not to have been appalled.

on. She returned to her boyfriend, I returned to the flat. Fell asleep in front of the TV. Shame! Shame! Slept till seven this morning. Dozed till eight. Gets better.

Strolled over to the Imperial Theatre with John, Jocelyn and Zero. He'd played *Fiddler* there for a year. They're repainting it for us.

Friday, 5 August

Yesterday John finished blocking the whole play, ahead of schedule. In three days! Some lovely shaping but not everywhere. The Jessica/Lorenzo love scene is unhelpfully plotted. John gives Jessica a dud note about her meeting Lorenzo empty-handed. 'Not even money,' says John. 'It's as though Lorenzo wants her to bring money and she's daring him to admit it.' I intended no such nuance. On the other hand, why have mention of money at all if it's not significant? On yet another hand, perhaps John has given the reference too much significance. I don't think Everett McGill as Lorenzo is going to be very good. My choice, which was overridden, would have been better. And I hope Jessica will become less breathy. At the moment she's on one note up in the clouds. John's beginning to get at them for pronunciation.

'The "geddo"?' he snaps at Jessica, 'the "geddo"? What's a "geddo"? Sounds like an extinct Australian bird – the One-winged Geddo! Distinguish between your t's and d's. The word is ghetto. And "not", not "nod". Look after the consonants and the vowels will look after themselves, as GBS said.'

Z arrives to begin his big scene with Rivka (Marian Seldes). Needs his dietary drink before starting. Cries out: 'Oh Jesus! My potassium! I left my potassium in the bathroom.' His dresser has to race back to Z's apartment on Central Park West for the bottle. 'I'm not directing a play,' complains John, 'I'm directing an old people's home.'

Zero can't resist fooling around as he rehearses. The prompt helps him at one point. He shouts at her: 'Don't help me. Help me sexually but that's all. No, forget that line. I couldn't manage it.' He tried to pick up the text but is lured into an exchange of wisecracks with Sam Levene.

Rivka continues, regardless.

'Does their duologue disturb?' asks John, 'or can you work?'

'I thought it best to press on,' Marian replies good-naturedly. How long will everyone's good nature last, I wonder?

J goes on to stage the rest of the scene beautifully so that by the time Graziano reads out the list of ships lost at sea it becomes chilling, moving, even at so early a stage.

Zee's overacting worries me. Surprised he doesn't understand the simple rule of starting explosive speeches low in order to give himself somewhere to go. He's exploding all over the place. Example: castigating Roderigues for delighting in the conversion of a monk[91] he threw his glass on the floor. Another: he began the *Oh horror of horrors* speech explosively and stayed exploding up to the last withering line *And you, I suppose, have been chosen instead*, which should have been low, cold, contemptuous. He even spat afterwards! Crude acting. Perhaps it's good to use these early days to get it out of the way. John dined him out last night for a chat. Let's see what he does in the run-through today.

John hasn't got the Jessica/Lorenzo relationship right. Seems unable to understand Jessica's fierce contempt, like her father's; nor the way in which Lorenzo is frightened of her. John continues to get at Julie for her Brooklyn mispronunciation. In the afternoon break, she weeps. I console her, assuring her that he's not really getting at her and that she's only crying because of the pent-up excitement of the past weeks.

'I'm a cry-baby,' she says, sniffing.

John blocks the court scene magnificently. 'Choreographic stuff, huh?' he says, preening his self-delight.

Zero says: 'But you promised me a song.'

'Don't you think,' quips John, 'that we've all had enough of your singing?'

'*You* should earn such money!' You can't out-best the star.

Difficult not to get caught up in Zee's joking around. He sits out there making faces at the stage management, other actors, me. At one point I turn away with a pleading grimace which says 'Pack it up.' John catches it and misunderstands. Snaps at me:

---

[91] Deleted from final version.

'Don't *you* join in Mostel's games or we'll never get through rehearsals!' He feels less nervous if he can snap at me.

We get through the court scene. The problem is to forestall the audience thinking Shylock's courtroom speech ends the play. John asks me to remind him how I envisaged the transition to the final Belmont scene. It's the song, I tell him, the song must begin before the courtroom scene ends; it would also help if the final Belmont scene is silhouetted halfway through Shylock's courtroom speech so that he shuffles away through what an audience can see is the scene to come. John fails to make the transition work this time but stages the last scene so beautifully that I *kvell*[92] with pleasure. At around 4 p.m. Dusty phones from the flat. She, Tanya and Dan have arrived. I'd arranged for them to be picked up from the airport. All's safe.

Saturday, 6 August

Sylvie made a splendid dinner for us on the night of Dusty's arrival. I bought some cheese and wine, she bought the steaks. Fred and Linda[93] came. Fred's a fine poet but doesn't talk much. Tanya and Daniel flake out at 10.30. Dusty at 11 p.m.

Next morning I take the family to rehearsals to meet John and the others. Dusty says later that she almost couldn't bear to be in the room the air was so tight with 'professionalism', John so fierce and certain of himself. I suggest that what she saw was John trying to get right the moves he'd made a mess of in the big Scene 4.

Zero arrives.

John yells in that jokey anger which at any moment can spill over and become real: 'Right, you! Into your room at once.' And wheels him in a diagonal line across the rehearsal room before he has time to make his first joke.

'But he hasn't said hello to Dusty,' I say.

'He can do that later' retorts John pushing him into his room for a few words. When they emerge John orders: 'Now, go and embrace Dusty or I'll never be forgiven for it.'

It is to be a run-through. Dusty, experienced with rehearsal tensions, wants to get out quickly. Tanya wants to stay and watch. I

[92] Yiddish for 'swell with pride'.

[93] Fred and Linda Feirstein. Both therapists; Fred's also a poet and playwright.

deliberate whether to ask John if she can stay – she wants to work in theatre, dammit, how else can she learn? And it *is* my play. I risk it. John pulls a tortured face and says no, it's too early, too rough, too raw.

Dusty flees admonishing Tanya. 'You shouldn't have asked.'

Tanya understands. She's not hurt. I am. This tight exclusiveness in the theatre depresses me.[94] You don't run-through first time with a huge audience, but the spirit of openness towards a few trusted and serious ones ... Though I'd direct in front of everyone.

In a mood of irritation I watch the run-through. They've achieved a great deal in a short time but Zero's acting continues to worry me. He talks as though drunk, rushing through the text, pausing only now and then to score bull's eyes. And he conducts himself like the star Zero Mostel, with no attempt to search for a sixteenth-century Jew in hostile Venice. It's early of course. If only he'd act with less vanity. The scene where he smashes his glass is so silly, unsubtle; and because he gabbles his *Oh horror of horrors* speech it comes out in the wrong order. He opts for easy rage rather than a dangerous hissing of the lines. And he still screams that last line *And you, I suppose, have been chosen instead*, when it should be offered icily.

The run-through over he asks, preening himself ready for compliments: 'Well, you happy? You got anything to say?'

'My dear Zero,' I reply, 'we've got five weeks of work ahead of us. I'll have things to say then.' From which I hope he understands that I don't believe in his powers of instant achievement.

The plan was to have lunch followed by a talk from John, then me. He changed plans. He was so depressed for having badly blocked the family Scene 4 that he needed to reblock it to give himself a peaceful, more creative weekend. Poor John. He's determined to make a success of this play. I'd not realised how vulnerable he felt. Jocelyn had to console him over lunch.

Afternoon rehearsal.

John began: '... I'm going to pick on friends first.' Julie winced, but it wasn't to be her. Everett McGill was chosen for the first whipping, the tall, good-looking, gangling Texan. 'I don't want you to think I'm being British about this but – articulation. In five

---

[94] Less so now. I understand the need to rehearse protected from outsiders, though I'd still direct in the presence of others.

weeks it will be near to the way Arnold wants it but − once you get into the Imperial it will not be emotion that will get you through but articulation. Now, Everett, what's 'soggodo'?'

'Soggy dough?'

'Right. What's "nooze"?'

'News?'

'Right. What's "demended axe"?'

'You've got me there.' And so on, a list of utterly incomprehensible words of which everyone was guilty. Wish he'd directed some of his quips at Zee.

'Next, posture. You're all going to be given costumes which, unless you prepare for them, will throw you. Go to the galleries, there's some nice Titians there. Look at them. Study them. Find yourself a look, a posture, a personality. Be ready to receive your costumes, don't let them swamp you. Next. Don't pity yourselves. Don't get into sentimental tones of voice, high registers. And feel free to move − except where I've given you a glass to pick up ...'

He broke down the way he was going to work: next week an in-depth analysis of scenes, then a week in the theatre getting used to volume and sight lines, followed by a fourth week of a scene each morning and a run-through every afternoon. 'Most actors get worried about run-throughs but I've always found an actor gets more out of them than he's ever imagined. He gets greater control ...' He ended with reassurance. 'I don't have to tell you we've assembled the best cast possible for this play, and I know you're all capable of doing most things standing on your head.' A large part of leadership is bullshitting. John is a born leader.

Zero announces that a restaurant owner has invited the cast to an evening meal in the first week they start rehearsals in the Imperial Theatre, and I invite everyone to a party on Tuesday in my apartment. The actors go home happy to a weekend of work.

John Clements, however, sends me away with a shattering observation: 'Here I am, Antonio, with not a penny to my name, I'm cleaned out, wiped out, not a cent to get me from A to B, but no one cares a damn about me. Shylock goes into that long monologue without a thought about me, and I've been through one hell of a traumatic experience, I've risked death for him, but . he's offered not one word to me. What do I do? Where do I get my money from? Where do I go? Shylock's behaving incredibly selfishly.'

The observation shocks me. I've no reply. Feebly I thank Sir John for pointing it out. How I amend – God knows! What I've done, obviously, is forgotten my play doesn't end as Shakespeare's, where Antonio's ships have been found. In my play it's not so. Antonio's destruction is total. The answer must lie somewhere in his relationship with Portia. I'll think on it.

Meet Zero and Jocelyn in the lift. Zero's contract allows for a limousine to be at his disposal. They're on their way to the shoe-maker for his special feet. The car will drop them, take me to the flat, then come back for them. The limousine impresses the innocents, Herbert and Wesker.

'You must know how to handle producers,' Zee explains.

'You're a star,' I say, 'we're only talented.' Zero quips back – I forget what. I reproach him for ignoring my rare wit. 'You complain that I don't smile,' I say. 'It's because you take up all the space.'

Says Jocelyn later: 'I always feel so boring in Zero's company.'

In the evening Dusty, me and the kids go out with Joan Kahn to an expensive Chinese restaurant. She's a small, Yiddisher-mother type. Could be one of my unmarried aunts. Has been an editor for thirty years and is now torn between lingering enthusiasms for her authors, and urgent compulsions to write her own books. Feel guilty giving her my manuscript of stories. Nor am I mad for Harper to handle me. They're not quick on the ball, too large. I prompt her to remind their salesman to take advantage of the thousands of dollars' worth of publicity the Shuberts are spending. She makes a note. Because she's on holiday (albeit in her apartment writing) I don't ask why it hadn't been done as soon as the *New York Times* profile had appeared.

I fear we're an intrusion, and though she assures us she likes to have the family of Weskers around her, I sense she's only half with us. Conversation is tortuous, she seems unable to follow a thought through. Like her office her mind appears to be in a mess, she can't find what she wants in it. I try to establish coherent conversation: question her about her writing, about the state of the US under Carter. She begins a sentence but rarely takes it anywhere. It's as though four Weskers are too heavy for her to hold. In her flat, though, she confesses to great fears about Zero and warns wisely about the need to control him. I assure her John is tough.

We're all in bed by 10.30, although Evan rings Daniel and hauls him out to a friend's apartment. Which he enjoys.

Next morning

Visit Statue of Liberty. Took subway to 42nd Street hoping to find there a line to the boat. Wrong! Looking for help I approached train driver who, as I reached him, closed the doors and took the train off with me yelling, 'You're not very helpful!' Finally reach Statue. Stand at foot of this most universally acclaimed image of freedom. Only 'man' could be ingenious enough to build it and stupid enough to want to climb it. Dusty stayed on terra firma – tall buildings fall, she reasoned unreasonably. Daniel, Tanya and I walked up its narrow stairway. It was 110° inside.

Walked around the Village, coffee and beer at O'Henry's; bought wine for John Clements' lunch tomorrow, shopped food in Balducci's for Tuesday's party; dinner with Zero. Poor Kate was laid up in bed but Zee took us to an extraordinary Rumanian restaurant – Parkway on 46th Street – lots of little dishes served by Karl and Suzy. Over-ate again.

Shared with Zero John Clements' observation about being left alone. 'Actor's talk!' he snapped, rather unfairly it seemed to me. 'I like John Clements very much,' he added in a tone suggesting that perhaps he didn't. 'You take it poetically. Doesn't have to mean anything so precisely.' I disagreed, and we entered a short debate on whether art has to mean anything. He talks like a university undergraduate not very interestingly. Later he asked did I think people minded his constant malarking. I said, to begin with – no, but it would need to be controlled because people needed to concentrate. He pooh-poohed the idea, and expressed the generally accepted wisdom – which I despise – that one should hold back until on stage. 'Spontaneity!' he proclaimed. Nonsense. He'd been yelling and screaming through rehearsals and had smashed two glasses – what was he holding back? Told him I didn't like actors who held back – one didn't know what to expect or if it was going to be right; also, it selfishly threw other actors off-balance. Did the message reach him? He's probably the kind of actor who, with childlike perverseness and defiance, argues and gives the impression of not listening but really worries and takes notes[95] to heart.

In the restaurant someone asked him how he lost so much weight. 'One day I blew my nose and it all came out.' As he saw me into the taxi he said to the taxi driver: 'Drive carefully he's pregnant!'

Tanya made the observation: 'I like Zero but he makes me feel I've *got* to like him. He makes me feel obliged to fuss over him.' And she's right. His whole being demands special treatment, attracts sycophancy. It makes me – and obviously Tanya – feel uncomfortable.

Monday, 8 August – before going to rehearsals

Yesterday was a typical Sunday. Dusty prepared lunch. Time enough to walk into the Village to buy the ridiculously huge *Times*. Had coffee in O'John's. Shopped at Balducci's.

John Clements came for lunch, nothing too elaborate. Dusty made a halibut in white sauce, accompanied by a bottle of Meursault; avocado, cucumber, tomato and onion salad; cheese and coffee. He declined the *mille feuille*. Sir John is a very English, haughty theatre man, used to being in control. A manager in his youth – ran a theatre in Palmers Green. Generous about Zero.

'A great actor, we can all go home. It'll be his show. Most powerful. And very intelligent. He knows what he's doing.' I asked did he think the theatrical raging would go, and a little more ice creep in? He had no doubt of it. 'I know just the type he is. Rushes in all emotion from the start and gradually whittles it away. Used to do it myself.' I agreed it was courageous to take risks. Felt reassured but not entirely. Daniel feels awkward in his presence.

---

[95] 'Notes' are the comments given to actors about their performance. The individual 'note' can be given during a rehearsal, or a batch can be given after a run-through. Playwrights give 'notes' to directors both about direction and an actor's performance. All 'notes' go through the director unless he or she suggests the playwright give them directly.

Something worries me. One day during rehearsal Julie told me that her stepfather was the attorney who looked after Zero's trust and affairs. I match this with another moment during the dinner with Zero when, out of all the cast he *could* have spoken about, he observed: 'Julie's going to be good in this, she's a good little actress ...' And I recalled the extent to which John had argued for her, and hadn't offered me many other choices. In fact he confounded my one request for an actress, Susan Galbraith, to be auditioned. I put all these things together, and conclude – Zero wanted Julie in. Could it be? She may be a good actress but is, at the moment, the very wrong actress. She'd better become right!

After lunch John Clements suggested a cut. He thinks the reference to Venice's economic state is parenthetical and unnecessary. 'I was trained for the law, and all my family were in law. Stick to your single argument, don't wander off. You weaken your argument when you call upon other sorts of evidence. I know it. Absolutely certain of it!' He spoke emphatically, loudly, almost angrily – a trick he'd learned to help get his way in life, and one his argument shouldn't have needed.

Interestingly, months ago, while discussing the play, John D had said – contrary to everyone else's view – that he wanted *more* history in the play. What about Venice in a state of decline? The very cut Sir John was calling for. Promised I would think about it. We both smiled.

'Do that!' he said.

I showed him the handful of lines I'd written in response to his other observation about Antonio being ignored at the end of the courtroom scene. He seemed unimpressed. The problem with 'introduced lines' is they always feel like 'introduced lines' until they're worn in. His non-committal attitude made the lines seem even more 'introduced'. We'd wait to try them out, I said. At least he should know I was thinking about them.

Nevertheless he was generous about the play – as he was about Zero (in contrast to Zero's attitude to him). Indeed, I was flattered that this actor-knight had left England for a year, was transporting his paralysed wife – the once beautiful actress Kay Hammond – with paid help, in order to play merely the second lead in my oh so heavy play.

He returned to his hotel. 'Awful room, dark place ... must learn some of these lines.'

I shall never cease finding it moving that people struggle over lines I've written. Others design, some build sets, a director spends long evenings working out how best to shape on stage what I've imagined in my head. Extraordinary.

Hot and humid days. Walk around the Village. Eat at Maxwell's Plum. Cable ride to Roosevelt Island — Dusty terrified being suspended only by wires. To Serendipity for dessert. She is utterly happy — no responsibility, enjoys the heat. Only problem is she attracts mosquitoes. Woke up in the middle of the night, too hot to keep a sheet on her. Threw it off saying: 'All right mosquitoes, I'm all yours!'

WEEK TWO

Wednesday, 10th August — this records two days of rehearsal, 8th and 9th

On the 8th: Jocelyn was in the rehearsal room, cool, hard working, exuding reliability in every smile.

Entered a little conspiracy with her. 'See if you can persuade John that he doesn't need to *rush* from the court scene to the final scene in Belmont. It's fine for the other scenes but he can take his time on the last change. Portia can't address her last speech to a parting Doge.'

She nodded as though she had already considered the problem.

Spoke with John myself. He presented me with a huge problem — which I'll describe later.

So we began. It's the first day rehearsing in depth. John seems calmer, enjoying himself. He choreographs little moves, little hints of speed ... (must break off).

Sunday, 14 August

Had to stop. I love the family being here but couldn't concentrate on this diary with them in the flat. They've left for Maine. Can now spend all day catching up with the week's work.

Dusty rang from Camp Searsmont this morning. Her voice has

returned – she'd lost it in New York from a mixture of pollution and the changes of heat between cold air-conditioned interiors and hot streets

'It's idyllic up here,' she said. 'Cabins tucked between pines on the edge of the lake ...'

Zero has given her the address of his house on a nearby island, full of painters.

Return to rehearsals ... that day, Monday the 8th. So, we began. It's the first day rehearsing in depth. John seems calmer, enjoying himself. He choreographs little moves, little hints of speed. The actors pause to get right small points. Sir John asks what does '*and all past*' mean?

I explain: 'Everything passes, time passes, Shylock's books remind you you're old, that all things must pass ...' He seems surprised not to have understood all that himself.[96]

While John D talks to John C, Zero wanders over to check pronunciation of names, places.

'"David" or "Duvid"?' I remind him that John has asked for exotic pronunciations at all times. 'Duvid', therefore.

John D doesn't understand '... *their spites, you see, it revealed to them their thin minds ...*'[97]

'What "spites"? Who is "their"?' Pounced on like that it makes no sense to me, either. I have to think about it. Read it over.

'It means that books of genuine learning revealed to *those warriors of God* – the clergy who had called for the burning of Jewish books – what spiteful, thin minds they had.'

Sir John asks: 'Is it to be Julius third, as the Americans say, or Julius *the* third?' We agree on 'the third'. He asks again, this time picking on Zero's line: 'Is it to be Isaac of Corbell, or Corbeil as the French say?' He is not going to let anyone get away with anything and is, throughout, at John D's request, correcting everyone's pronunciation. He goes on to question Shylock giving Antonio a present of a Talmud which, Shylock has just informed him, still has to be hidden. It's inconsistent. I agree. Zero suggests

---

[96] In fact he was right to be confused. I used the word 'past' when it should have been 'passed'.

[97] From Act 1, Sc. 1: 'When fever strikes them, you can't trust those "warriors of God". With anything of learning? Never! That's what they really hated, not the books of the Jews but the books of men, I mean – MEN! Their spites, you see, the books revealed to them their thin minds...'

the present should be the work of Maimonides: *Guide to the Perplexed*. Better, and very apt.

I ask: 'But in order to get the full humour, which should come first – the author's name or the title?' They share neither my humour nor my concern. I put the author first.[98]

I sit listening to these first lines of the play remembering that awful night in my study in the Black Mountains when I nearly gave up. Here they are, now in reasonable shape, but that night – nearly two years ago – in my isolated hideaway I'd written a version of these first scenes which had seemed a catastrophe. The dislocation of time, setting, and atmosphere always amazes me. From that study in the Black Mountains to this rehearsal room on Broadway, a heatwave outside, and a cast who've committed a year of their lives to it.

These pages are worked from scribbled notes I make in rehearsals. Zero sees me scribbling and says: 'Oh, look at Arnold writing notes for me.'

'No', says John, 'it's his journal, his New York journal. If Kafka can do it so can he.'

A confrontation follows between Sir John and John D, over that part of the text which Sir John thinks is unnecessarily confusing, and which we had discussed over lunch. It raises an interesting question which brings me closer to John – we're both excited by history and its patterns. Here is the passage[99] Sir John wants cut, one added months ago at John D's request.

SHYLOCK I will not have soiled a friendship with my fellow man.

ANTONIO And if Venice represents anything any longer to anyone in the world it's through its laws, more important than a fusion of the best political systems, more important even than our constitution.

SHYLOCK The laws must leave me to conduct my loves as I please.

ANTONIO Especially now when the economy is so vulnerable.

---

[98] In the final version I make *Guide to the Perplexed* the first words of the play, with the name following.

[99] In the final version this rather clumsy passage is rewritten, though history is still left in.

SHYLOCK   My dealings with you are sacrosanct.

ANTONIO   The French markets are gone, the English are building faster and better ships, and there are fools talking about dangerous protectionist policies. We are a nervous Empire.

SHYLOCK   I *will* have trust.

Sir John wanted to cut everything except the first and last line, to read: '*I will not have soiled a friendship with my fellow man. I will have trust.*'

He reiterated all he'd put to me over lunch. 'The argument is about law. Stick to the argument. I come from a long line of lawyers who taught – always stick to one argument. If you bring in any other it's a sign of weakness.' I again point out that in real life one *does* reach out here and there for any argument that might persuade people. 'Ah, that's real life. And reality and theatre are different things.'

'I know *that* argument,' I tell him. 'But you don't see the contradiction of your own position. You're saying not everything in reality can be made to work on stage and yet you're asking for the reality of a legal mind to be exercised on stage. *My* point is: you can't be literal. Theatrical demands necessitate using this moment to add to the tapestry of Venetian life. It's also dramatic. It allows Shylock short bursts which demonstrate his stubbornness.'

John D argues for all of it to be kept in, but I can see that the exclusion of one line might help. There is one thought too many: '*... more important than a fusion of the best political systems ...* ' It's a mind-bender in the midst of all the other things their exchange needs to achieve. I'm grateful he prompted the cut – the kind of line that makes a passage seem ten times longer than it is.

Zero jokes: '*He's* cut something, *I* want to cut something.'

Later I talk about the last speech in that scene.

'It's a moment central to the play. It's here that Shylock is justifying his bond for a pound of flesh: "*Barbaric laws? Barbaric bonds!*" It needs to be pointed.'

As Shylock is thinking up the mischievous bond he has a line: .
'*We'll cheat them yet.*' I suggest to Z that he's exaggerating this

moment by banging his fist on the table. He seems at first to resent my saying so but later comes up with a marvellous reading of the line – he discovers it, slowly, wickedly, on the spot. '*We'll cheat them yet.*'

I talk to Sir John and Z about the '*I know, I know*' passage at the end of Act 2, Scene 3. It is carefully and musically constructed. Each of them has a bout of panic, and each an opportunity to reassure the other. They would enjoy it more if they found the music.

ANTONIO   I cannot raise the money now.
SHYLOCK   I know.
ANTONIO   Nor can you lend it me again.
SHYLOCK   The Ghetto's drained, I know.

And so on. They listen, but throughout the week have not made it work. I don't think they understood. Will try again next week.

John constantly interrupts rehearsals with stories 'Did you ever hear about …?' I can't remember them all. He's an incorrigible gossip and myth-maker.

'Who'd ever think that twenty years after calling me "comrade" on the Aldermaston March we'd still be working together?'

'I *never* called you "comrade".'

'You did just. You also said, "The fascists will be at Hyde Park, comrades," or some such thing.'

'You're a myth-maker,' I accuse him.

'No I'm not. It's all down in my little book.' Perhaps he's right.[100]

Later in rehearsal John gives a note to Bassanio: 'You have an extra antenna which warns you, lets you know when people are off you.' Gives me pleasure each time he understands so accurately. 'Just find those moments when your character shifts gear. Be quick to hear his [Antonio's] tone.'

He gives another accurate note some days later (he gives many but some require greater perception than others, and he rises to

---

[100] He wasn't. He was confusing it with a line from *Chicken Soup With Barley*, imagining I'd said something a character had said. On the contrary the character of Ronnie, based on myself, actually says in the last act, 'I even blush when I use that word. Comrade!'

it); it's in the court scene, when Shylock is consoling Portia for her sense of helplessness. *He* is consoling *her* when it's *his* tragedy. Such generosity of spirit shifts her anger in his defence to an even greater anger attacking of the court of Venice. John, with brilliant insight, perceives Portia's jump from one moment to the next. I delight in his cleverness and grin at him encouragingly as he points it out to her. In his jerky, embarrassed way he deliberately misunderstands the grin.

'All right, don't be so smug about your text.' But I know he knows.

There's a touching moment as Portia begins the casket scene with nerves. Her face flushes red, her voice shakes. She's in a flat spin but continues courageously, professionally.

When done John says: 'Now, Roberta, I like everything you're doing, you're doing it very well, but it's all too dry at the moment. The intellect is there but no humour ...' Second time round she's bolder but still lost. 'Be happier, richer, bigger. Use your voice, take up more space, Portia shouldn't be flustered – ever. The costumes will help. Flow. You're responding to the dryness of the text.' Roberta grows, flutters a bit but grows.

On the 9th I arrive at 9.45 to go through the casket scene with Bassanio (Nick Surovy). John arrives at 10, unexpectedly, and to my surprise I find it nerve-wracking to rehearse with him there. Is this why directors feel inhibited with the author around? I get used to it, as indeed John has become used to me. It's a question of habit, trust, familiarity – no more nerve-wracking than an actor performing in front of other actors.

I break down the casket scene. Give names to each paragraph: 1. Cool, cocky. 2. Less cocky, shaken. 3. Revival of spirits. 4. Knots, panic. 5. Then – when Bassanio's back is to the wall – adrenalin takes over and he realises which casket it must be. I suggest he starts with confidence, no movement in body or face as there is none in the words. Then face, body and language gradually crumble. It helps, but Nick is an actor of facial and vocal tricks. He'll need controlling.

Before John begins rehearsing he tells me, ominously, that he wants us to lunch together. There's a weakness in the court scene.

We are to discuss it in full over food.

But he casts a few shattering stones at me now. 'There seems to be something missing from the debate. Not enough cut and thrust. All the issues in the play must come together in the court which should be a "court enquiry" not a trial ...' He wants to bring back the long Tubal speech, partly because 'everyone's waiting for a big Sam Levene moment, and partly because Tubal reintroduces the issue of "the minority who has need of the law". *That's* the issue. We *need* the debate clear and hard in this scene.' My head is a whirl. I suspect someone's been getting at him because Sam Levene's part has been cut.

Rehearsals begin. John embarks upon a series of savage attacks which unnerve Jessica and are to embarrass me as the morning progresses. He tells her not to whine, to be firm, mix humour with exasperation and rage.

'It's a very important scene [Act 1, Scene 4], the first-time we see Shylock's family and hear about him from everyone else ...' He mutters fiercely to me: 'If I don't get this scene right I won't get the rest of the play right ... I've forgotten how to direct.' He adds movement, makes her go back again and again to the beginning, ideas sparking off him by the second, infusing her and the scene with energy, bustle. He snaps: 'Tell us about the household, I don't know anything except that Shylock collects books, tell me more, facts . . .' He throws another aside at me justifying his ferocity. 'I've got to get *this* scene going.'

'I *wrote* it for you,' I tell him not without some truth. I see John directing everything as I write it.

He's failing to get the whine out of Julie's voice.

'Don't gabble, make it clear. It's coming.' She attempts it again.

We shall be six to eat at midday. Yesterday it was eight, the day before seven, and tomorrow, no doubt, more again. And is he up? He's not even awake yet. Eleven o'clock and he sleeps ...

It's still not working.

'Now we've gone back to "Sara Solomon" ...' He decides to have Tubal in the scene from the beginning rather than have him make an entry. 'Don't like two people coming in together.' As rehearsals continue he attacks Julie again and again. 'Colour! Colour! Do two things at once. Move up and down the line otherwise we'll all be very bored and I'll have to give you a bar of music and say where each note is!' He sings words to himself in high and low notes. 'Don't do it exactly like this but get that kind of variety.' He's relentless. I fear she's going to burst into tears.

The actor playing the small part of Rodrigues is a curious mixture. He seems bright but laughs too much and too heartily at Zero's jokes. Even when nothing's funny he appears on the verge of laughter. Maybe he's just ecstatic to be part of the show. Inevitably he becomes the second of John's 'whipping boys'. The poor fellow has to make an entry at the same time as he calls for Shylock.

'Call your first *Shylock* outside [off stage], the second inside, the third one by the edge.'

'Is there a 'third' *Shylock*?' asks the boy anxiously, knowing there isn't and that John has made a mistake. His terror increases tangibly as he realises John will be angrier to discover Rodrigues only needs to call out Shylock twice. The boy attempts his entrance again calling, '*Shylock? Shylock?*' John's electrifying mixture of inspiration and malice is in full gallop. He throws down his pen in exasperation. Attacks again. 'Why the pause between each *Shylock*? Is something going on there? Like acting? Don't build your part up at the expense of other actors!' The boy takes it well. The scene grows in energy and bustle. John leans over to me. 'We need another line about Tubal also having an appointment with Shylock at the same time.' I invent a cheeky addition (in bold):

RODERIGUES	Asleep still? My appointment was for eleven.
TUBAL	**As was mine.**
RODERIGUES	'The plans,' he cries 'the plans! You want me to contribute to the building of a new synagogue? Let me see the plans first.'
TUBAL	**'The accounts,' he cries, 'the accounts are in disorder!'**

The Tubal line is invented to echo the existing Roderigues one, and the Roderigues passage is broken up to accommodate it. John likes the addition.

'The author has a rewrite,' he announces. 'Wiz, come over here. Give it to them.'

I go centre stage and dictate.

Rivka, ever appreciative, writes down the addition shaking her head, incredulous at everyone's genius, murmuring: 'Lovely. Just lovely.'

John has asked for trimmings. I suggest cutting the passage between Usque and Rebecca concerning the Spanish Inquisition's treatment of the Moslems. John says no, let's 'keep it all packed' until we reach the theatre at the end of two weeks. Sam Levene, nicely building his scene, stumbles on the word 'proclivity'. He can't pronounce it. Tries again and again. Finally, with beautiful timing, he looks heavenwards and asks in his Bronx accent: 'Why did I have to get myself such a fancy writer!'

Work on scene 4 continues till 2.15. Three and a half hours on one scene! But it's a long and difficult one. This and the court scene are *the* two nuts to be cracked before feeling the play has been controlled. John is flaked out but not too flaked out to see that one of Shylock's lines kills the joke of another.

That's not a sin. *Most* people have never met a Jew before. There are a hundred million people in China who've never met a Jew before.

'The second sentence kills the humour of the third,' John points out. He's right.

It's a pleasure listening to Sir John. He makes simple, unostentatious sense of every line, giving the exact inflection, the precise emphasis to a word.[101]

---

[101] Later, in 1979, I discover this quotation from a playwright, the late John Whiting: 'There are times when anyone writing for the theatre longs for the control over performance that a score and the presence of a conductor dictates in music. A line in a play holds just so much sense and no more. Just so much emotion and no more. It is when an actor begins to invest a line with meaning or emotion which it doesn't hold that this control is necessary. The really great actors exercise their own control. They give a line an essential rightness of sense which makes it seem impossible to read any other way. They also make the emotion a kind of atmosphere in which the sense can freely exist. Lesser talents often try to over-humanise.' [from: *My Diary. 20th Century*. February '61].

I offer Zero a line reading. We banter.

'All right,' he says, 'but not with your face. I'll find my own way to say it with your intention. You're a writer!'

'Every actor has that alibi – "you're a writer".'

'I'm not every actor. I'm every other actor.'

'Every *other* actor, then.'

'I'm every *third* actor.' He can't resist besting. Nor does he find an acceptable way to deliver the line. It follows Antonio's insistence that he must follow Venetian law which forbids dealings with a Jew without a contract. Shylock grins mischievously as the idea comes to him for a pound-of-flesh bond. Antonio mistakes the grin and asks is he not persuaded? Shylock replies: '*I'm persuaded, oh yes, I'm very, very persuaded. We'll have a bond.*'

It's the last four words to which he's not giving meaning. He's delivering them in the sense of: '*We will certainly have a bond.*' It should be delivered in the sense of: '*All right, if that's the way they want it – we'll have a bond all right, and what a bond it will be!*' The accumulation of many such tiny misreadings can tip a play over into being something other than intended. But he'll get there. He *is* a fine actor.

Then comes the explosive lunch. I'm not sure what John is trying to tell me. Perhaps he's talking through his own fears. As we walk to Charlie's Diner he repeats them.

'I feel I've forgotten how to direct ... No energy in me ... no shape. There's usually a shape by this time.'

I reassure him a shape is forming and that if he's lost anything it's a sense of time. 'We've only been going five days,' I remind him.

Having humbled himself confessing his shortcomings he feels he's earned the right to be fierce with me over the court scene. 'Something is wrong. You can't be realistic about the entire play and then do a romantic switch. You're not Shakespeare ...' I apologise for not being Shakespeare though it seems unnecessarily harsh to remind me of this fact. 'You've researched the play's background thoroughly but what about Portia? Can women be in the court at *all*? You don't know, do you?'

What is he *really* saying? Is he right? If so then the whole scene will have to be rewritten. How? I'm not going through the nonsense of making Portia disguise as a man. Besides, can't poetic licence be taken? He must be talking about something else. I try to discover what. 'If there's something else you're driving me towards, tell me.'

He protests he's not. I'm not convinced. Is he preparing his argument for taking the Lorenzo/Jessica scene out of the first act into the second one? Perhaps it's all to do with bringing back the Tubal speech so that Sam Levene can have his big moment. I like the speech but I don't want to disturb the tightness of the second act. Isn't the compactness of the second act what John applauds in contrast to the sprawling first one? So why does he want to make the second sprawl? I break down the court scene for him and point out the logic of its structure. He accepts it. But something else is going on. I can feel his mind fidgeting uneasily.

In the afternoon we rehearse the portrait scene. Again he picks on Jessica, trying to bludgeon the monotony from her voice. The actor playing Moses begins to irritate me. He's sweet, diminutive – a hunchbacked Jewish actor of the old school who's played in Israel and the Yiddish theatre. It's his thin voice bordering on the vaudeville which grates.

I underline words from Jessica's speech to help her achieve variety and melody into her voice. I tell her the speech gets better each time. Am worried she'll break down, but she takes it well – 'I feel it, but I'm not used to working so fast.'

Riggs as Graziano is anxious. John over-reacts, snaps at him. To me he says: 'Never engage the family. Thank God we live in separate establishments.' John calls out: 'Riggs! Turn round and say that Aretino quote *facing* us.' Riggs turns full on. John bangs down his pencil. 'Don't make a twit of me! Not right round, just half round.' He moves in to demonstrate.

Everett as Lorenzo begins to shape a character. Though the wrong one – as a vain fop – yet it *is* a shape. It signals control of his material.

Zero is *so* vain, gabbles until he reaches the high points, and then takes off. We're rehearsing Antonio's dinner in which Shylock gives them a history lesson about the Renaissance, rushing around the set using items of furniture and fruit to illustrate the story, *like men on his chessboard of history* as my stage directions say. I make a cut in the Renaissance speech about the creation of the Laskaris grammar books. A fascinating piece of information but it holds up the flow. Flow and rhythm is important. Point out to Zero that the list of classical Greek writers is written in rhythm. 'Yes, I know,' he says, 'I was resisting it.'

'But,' I press him, 'it fits in better with the action of plonking down the fruit which you're using to represent those classical writers.'

He replies, 'I'm still fumbling.'

'Every time I point out something, he says he's fumbling.'

'Well, I am. I'm thinking about words, the movements ...' He's right, of course, and I hastily acknowledge it.

'We know, we know! We sit here helpless with admiration that you *know* so much of the text.'

'That's what's known as arse-fanning,' he says.

'When you know *all* the words,' says John 'you'll have to come in with a white flag on your head and then we'll know we can have a go at you.'

I give Z a note on the last 'bubble bubble' section of Renaissance speech:

Amazing! Knowledge, like underground springs, fresh and constantly there, till one day – up! Bubbling! For dying men to drink, for survivors from dark and terrible times. I love it! When generals imagine their vain glory is all, and demagogues smile with sweet benevolence as they tighten their screws of power – up! Up bubbles the little spring. Bubble, bubble, bubble! A little, lost spring, full of blinding questions and succulent doubts. The word! Unsuspected! Written! Printed! Indestructible!...

If he begins on a high note then he gives himself nowhere to grow to. After all, I tell him, it's about the word as a tiny seed which grows to explode the tyranny of demagogues, so make the speech grow in the same way. He takes the note and makes it work.

John says to Roberta: 'Now, less of Joan Crawford and more of Marilyn Monroe. No, Marilyn is wrong. Vanessa![102] With radiance!

---

[102] Vanessa Redgrave.

Don't rush it. Long-bow it. Enjoy it.' She tries. It doesn't work first time.

'Stop deliberating, Maxwell,' John admonishes her. 'I didn't buy you for your acting ...'

I'm not understanding what she's doing but she looks so interesting that I'm happy to wait and see how she develops. At the moment her performance is actressy. I don't believe *this* woman has *read* Catullus and Ovid.

Wednesday, 10 August

John arrives determined to crack the court scene. He has problems he says, but – 'I know what I'm going to do.'

'So what are you worried about?'

'I'm worried about whether I can communicate what I want.'

'You're potty!' I keep needing to reassure him.

'Don't call me "potty", I'm older than you.'

'Yes! You *are*!'

But I, on the other hand, have real problems. Not only whether women were allowed in to the courtroom in Venice – which I've asked Burt Britton to investigate for me, but what do Lorenzo and Bassanio say to Portia and Jessica when they arrive unexpectedly? They're not in disguise. And then there's Sir John's point – what is to happen to Antonio at the end of the courtroom scene? He's the one who's just been on the point of death – I'd been so caught up with the relationship between Portia and Shylock that I'd neglected to wind up the affairs of poor Antonio.[103]

John breaks off, as he frequently does for light relief, to tell me that someone's chasing him for details of Doris Lessing's personal life. The same woman who rang me up. I apologised for putting her on to him. He's decided to say nothing. 'Doris would hate it.' He adds: 'Did you ever think when we were young together she'd become a grand old lady of literature?'

'Well, she was pretty established even then,' I said. My first image of her is vivid: in the pub alongside the Royal Court

---

[103] Proving my point that rehearsal is where the last draft is written and so the author needs to be present.

Theatre sitting on the first bend of the bar, beautiful and just gone forty. Flushed, both of us, to be having our plays done – mine by Dexter at the Belgrade Theatre in Coventry; her's – also by Dexter – for a Sunday night 'production-without-décor' at the Royal Court – the framework in which he was later to mount his sensational production of *The Kitchen*[104]. Doris's big rise to fame came after *The Golden Notebook*.

'But I still think the early African stories are better,' said John. 'That's what they'll say about me.'

While John continues rehearsing, I work on the women's entry into court. When done I show him the new text. He sits everyone down to explain.

'It's all been going wrong up till now. The problem is that we haven't introduced the women to the court properly, nor made links. We've got some new dialogue and we've got to find the cut and thrust of the debate.'

The court scene had opened with Bassanio at full throttle.

Shylock! Will you speak! [No response] He says nothing, offers no explanation, simply claims the bond. Look at that scowl. Have you ever seen such meanness in a face before? [To Shylock] He was your friend. You boasted a Gentile for a friend ...

But now, because the women are entering as soon as the court scene opens, something else is needed to open it.

BASSANIO	Portia!
LORENZO	Jessica!
BASSANIO	Did the women say they were coming?
LORENZO	On the contrary, Portia felt there was nothing to be done.
BASSANIO	Nor is there! Silence! For two hours this court of enquiry has had nothing but silence from him. Shylock! Will you speak? ...

In these additional six lines we:

---

104 My first play.

1. Signal arrival of the women.
2. Reveal the court has been in session for two hours.
3. Reveal that Shylock has been silent throughout.
4. Inform that it's not a trial but a court of enquiry.

Economy!

John sets up new blocking. It seems brilliant to me. The three women are centre stage in Belmont. '*Are women granted entry into the courts?*' asks Jessica. Portia declares: '*They'll grant these women entry to the courts.*' Bells boom out. One! They turn to face the wipe.[105] Two! The wipe is swiftly drawn revealing the court. Three! Doge and aides stand, the women bow low. Four! They sweep forward upstage seeking permission to enter, and then fan out to their different positions – Jessica to one side of the Doge, Portia to the other, while Nerissa, the maid, dissolves into the Christian crowd. Portia talks silently with the Doge. The cut and thrust begins. John calls for the first lines to be delivered as whispers across the stage. Bassanio's voice rises from whispering:

Silence! For two hours this court of inquiry has had nothing but silence from him. Shylock! Will you speak?

It's electrifying. But something is missing – Bassanio and Lorenzo seem not to share their surprise, they're not working together; a speech of Graziano drags. John mutters to me 'too long, too long'. Because I think it's Riggs who's dragging his lines, I do nothing. (Though later I discover John's right, and cut a sentence.)

Roberta doesn't help, delivering her speech on justice as if it's a passage about *her*. She fails to understand that her outrage is against a too rigid application of the law.

Shylock is consoling her with irony, '*Impartial justice, lovely lady, impartial justice.*'

She thunders back:

Impartial? How? *I* am not a thing of the wind, but an intelligence informed by other men by other men informed. *I* grow. Why can't they? What I thought yesterday might be

---

[105] A designed curtain as opposed to the stage curtain.

wrong today. What should I do? Stand by my yesterdays because *I* have made them? I made today as well! And tomorrow, that I'll make too, and all my days as my intelligence demands. I was born in a city built upon the wisdom of Solon, Numa Pompilius, Moses!

John says to leave her to get it off her chest.

Sam Levene has difficulty mouthing the unfamiliar structure of his new lines for Tubal. He's only just been given them. But he soldiers on adding, as if part of the text: '... and I'm reading this badly.' John, not without a touch of panic, turns to me: 'Take him aside later and take him through it.' It becomes unnecessary. Next time round he makes good sense of the speech.

John drives his actors, speaks fast, moves groups, urges them to deliver dialogue boldly. Nothing must get in the way of this animal he's whipping forward. He snaps at me — another passage is too long — the lines where Lorenzo tells Graziano to shut up. I'm not persuaded.

I'm caught up in John's energy and, in the wake of his adrenalin, sit in a corner struggling to shape lines to meet Sir John's objections. The problem embarrasses me a little. I'd neglected the awful plight of Antonio, the threat of death hanging over him. I've allowed him to focus only on his defence of Shylock with no sense of his own impending doom. Lorenzo is frenziedly reminding the court that usury is a sin against charity. *The people suffer from it.* Antonio replies:

	The people suffer from ignorance, Lorenzo, believe me. To deprive them of knowledge is the sin.
LORENZO	Knowledge! Knowledge! How Shylock's books have muddied your mind. A man can be strong and happy with no knowledge, no art. Turn to the shepherd and the tiller and the sailor who know of the evils of usury, without books, without art. Real knowledge, simple knowledge is in the wind and seasons and the labouring men do.
ANTONIO	You say a man is happy with no knowledge or art? There is wisdom in the wind, you say? The seasons

tell all there is to know of living and dying? I
wonder. Is it really understanding we see in the
shepherd's eye? Is the tiller told more than the
thinker? I used to think so, sitting with sailors
roughened by salt, listening to their intelligence.
They perceive much, I'd say to myself. But as I sat
a day here, a day there, through the years, their
intelligence wearied me. It repeated itself; spent
itself upon the same complaints, but with no real
curiosity. How alive is a man with muscles but no
curiosity? You wonder why I bind my fate to
Shylock, what I see in him? Curiosity! *There's* a
driven man. Exhilarating ... I'd have died before
now if no man had kindled my poor soul with his
music or wasn't there with his bright thoughts
keeping me turning and taught about myself. Even
now. With this old age ...

At such a dire moment he would not talk about 'old age'. I
exchange the last six words with a line I hope illustrates a sense of
his own plight.

...with his bright thoughts keeping me turning and taught
about myself: *Yes, even at such an hour I remember these things.*

To help further highlight Antonio's situation I give Graziano a
new line in a following speech:

As I thought. Bewitched. *A knife hangs over him and he defends
the man who holds it.*

I notice, too, that Zero has sobered up, he larks around less
between scenes except for one awful moment. When Portia
explains '*... this contract contains nothing but contradictions... It cannot
be executed because torn flesh draws blood. It cannot be executed because
precise weight cannot be achieved.*' Zero does a silly little dance as if
he was in a Mostel musical! What follows, though, he delivers
movingly. It's as though having been allowed his little bit of

nonsense he 'behaves' in return.

The morning ends jubilantly. The court scene is beaten into shape. John says I should have lunch with him in order to give him my notes.

'Then type them out so they're in front of me.' I've never known him to be so expansively open. My notes are not extensive. There's little of which he's not aware.

My main note is to do with Zero's total misunderstanding of the Jessica/Lorenzo scenes. 'He needs one big, harsh note along these lines: "When you're accurate you're stunning, when you're not you're like a Broadway star rushing through what you think are boring lines to the juicy ones. We don't want to see a Broadway star but a sixteenth-century Jew."' John agrees. I continue. 'He seems to lose concentration. Acts like "Under the Spreading Chestnut Tree", emphasising the words with actions. "Me" – points to himself. "Earth" – points to the earth. And he sounds drunk a lot of the time. Slurring his words. Other times he sounds like Jimmy Durante – monotonous and gruff, which is all right for a brief sketch, but not for a whole play ...' And so on.

We agree that I will direct the Jessica/Lorenzo love scene where I want it in the warehouse, after we've met the Venetians for the first time. John thinks it's not right there. If I can't make it work then it goes back into the penultimate Belmont scene.

Later, rehearsing the scene where Tubal and Roderigues are looking for the runaway Jessica, John whispers: 'Here! Here is where I'd like to see them for the first time together.'[106]

His insults continue pouring over poor Julie. 'What are you looking at you silly tart? And neither are you St Joan so just look straight ahead ...' So venomous I can barely look up. It dawns with horror that this is a repeat of the Wanda Rotha affair. John had engaged that venerable old star of German stage and screen for *The Old Ones* without consulting me. I had warned she would be wrong. She proved to be wrong though was not given a chance to give even what she had because John gave her hell. Similarly he'd engaged Julie against my advice, though this time with my agreement, and was giving her hell, too. Only occasionally does

---

[106] He's right. It's where I subsequently place it.

he find words of encouragement. He was also barking furiously – though not as viciously – at Everett whom I had just as energetically advised against. It's a pattern.

At the end of the scene he turns to me. 'Any notes? You can tell them as long as they don't contradict anything I've said.' They don't. They only confirm what he has said to them.

Lorenzo asks: 'Can I tell Arnold that if he finds anything missing he should tell me?'

'No! I don't think anything's missing except good acting.' John knows how to get away with such rudeness.

It's a tone which allows Everett to parry in his Kentucky drawl. 'You got the best.'

'I got the cheapest.' John needs to have the last word. 'Let's get on now. Take it from – oh, whatever the boring line is.'

The young Venetians have been rehearsing the warehouse scene on their own and are now showing what they've done. Cloth is all over the place. A mess. And Lorenzo doesn't really understand what he's saying. Why should he? It took me ages to understand what I *wanted* him to say. John again picks on him – prodding, nagging, complaining. He's restless. Resets the scene, and reads aloud passages making simple sense of the lines. He understands the text so clearly that it's incomprehensible to me how the actors can't achieve the same sense. Slowly he brings order, discovers the scene's shape.

He sends me off with Jessica and Lorenzo to talk through the love scene. I'm honest with them.

'John doesn't think the scene works where it is, or even *how* it is.'

I explain: I want a love scene in which the man wants to show he respects his lover's mind. No embrace to begin with. Lorenzo feels physical love has to be earned through a meeting of minds. Maybe what I want can't work, I confess, but I need them to help me try to make it work. They understand what I'm after. In the run-through at the end of the week they *show* they've understood. But I've not blocked or rehearsed the scene. John agrees I can do that next week. I promise that if I can't make it work he can replace it where he thinks it will.

Thursday, 11 August

First time with Shylock and his sister Rivka. An important scene. Rivka reveals clearly the nature of Shylock's dilemma.

To assert the dignity of your mocked people you have chained your friend's life to a mocking bond, that's what you've done.

The scene is all over the place. Marian is moving too much. She needs to find a stillness that drives. From now on everything must drive. John doesn't seem to push them. I ask for three minutes to show him how the passage is broken up. He says: 'Tell *them*.' I try. Marian seems to understand. Not Zero. It's difficult. I itch to re-block the scene.

On the other hand Zero beautifully delivers Jessica's elopement letter.

'Reflect on our quarrels. They have said all. Your daughter, Jessica.' 'Our quarrels.' What quarrels? How could she have called them 'quarrels'? Enemies quarrel. 'I am not what you would like me to be.' What did I want you to be, Jessica? My prop, my friend, my love, my pride? Not painful things, those. Are they? Oh, Jessica, what wretched, alien philosophy has taken up your mind, muddied it with strange fervours? Where are you now? Oh, vulnerable youth. You must be so lonely. So lost and lonely. So amazed and lost and lonely. Oh daughter, daughter, daughter.

Then came the big STOP – Antonio's scene with Shylock where they both face the inevitable outcome of the bond they should not have signed. Sir John questions something. It's a small point but it might be the central weakness of the play, and it challenges John D.

'Look, I say here, "*we shall both be put to death*", and then a few lines later on I say, "*but some explanation must be made*" [as to why they agreed to such a bond in the first place]. How can I ask for an explanation to be made about something I've already . conceded is beyond explanation?' Those weren't his words but that's what he meant. John needed to assert his authority. Categorically he told Sir John that he didn't understand what he was on about.

'You're being too logical!' It was true. 'You've quickly understood Shylock's dilemma but now you're asking him to explain it to the court.'

'But how can I? How can I ask for an explanation to be made? About what? I know we're going to be put to death!' Both men stand firm. They don't fight, simply argue their positions. I admire Sir John for holding up rehearsals and risking the irritation of other actors to get clear what he can't understand – an old pro who's been around for so long that neither director, author, nor other actors intimidate him.

They continue arguing for about twenty minutes while I try to work out what's really wrong, even try to rewrite lines. But John doesn't want the simple structure of that exchange broken. Nor do I, it was so artfully done. On the other hand, I'm worried that the weakness is showing through. I try to reason it out.

- The 'barbaric laws' push Shylock into the 'barbaric bond'. (Aided by his exuberant personality which led him to take risks.)
- The time for repayment is up.
- Antonio has lost his fortune.
- The city won't lend him money – he's a bad debt.
- Shylock can't find the money – the ghetto is drained by an unexpected tax.
- Shylock refuses to ask to be relieved of the bond; it would set a precedent threatening the Jewish community which relies on Venice honouring its bonds with them to be allowed to live and trade in the community.
- Antonio understands this, but (and *this* is Sir John's point) why doesn't Antonio ask Shylock to explain just that: that precedents mustn't be set which will threaten the Jewish community?

I think I see his point. John says it's implied. I attempt compromise suggesting alternative dialogue.

John is reluctant. 'Let's leave it for now. Arnold will think about it. He can't come up with the right solution on the spot.'

Now, as I'm writing this, I look at the passage and feel Sir John may be right. But it's no great problem, simply a question of transposing four speeches from Antonio. The final passage reads:

SHYLOCK   ... Just promise me silence in the trial.

ANTONIO   Will we make no explanations? The court must understand.

SHYLOCK   Understanding is beyond them. I protect my people and my people's contract. Besides, honour would be accorded me if I pleaded such explanations. 'He saved his people!' It would be grotesque. Just promise me silence at the trial.

ANTONIO   That's contempt, Shylock. Unworthy of you.

SHYLOCK   You must let my pride have its silence.

ANTONIO   They won't think it's pride, they will mistake your silence for contempt.

SHYLOCK   Perhaps they will be right. I am sometimes horrified by the passion of my contempt for men ...

'*Besides, honour would be accorded me if I pleaded such explanations. "He saved his people!" It would be grotesque.*' That's the answer to Sir John – Shylock doesn't want to appear noble when he's behaved with such foolish irresponsibility. I shall put it to John D next week.

My director *does* bully the smaller roles. Poor Roderigues.

'You're still not enthusiastic enough.'

'Still?' the unfortunate boy is foolish enough to question.

'Yes! Still! Don't ask me when I'm telling you. You've moved nowhere this morning.' (I suspect this actor was one of John's playthings for a night and that's why he's bullying him). In fact he's expecting more of the boy than his too few lines allow. I've worked out others to help him achieve what John wants of him, but John won't hear of them just yet.

Something is missing from John's method of directing. He doesn't set the mood of each scene before launching the actors into it. For example: rehearsing the last Belmont scene he doesn't remind Antonio and Portia that they've been together for two weeks since the court of enquiry, and therefore the mood hanging over them is still that of melancholy. Everyone has made a mistake. Shylock – he's bankrupt, lost his precious library; Portia – the caskets have led her to be partnered to an adventurer; Jessica – to escape an intellectually oppressive father she's fled into the arms of a religious fanatic; Antonio has lost a dear friend. Only the young Venetians are loutishly jubilant. Perhaps John is waiting for the bulk of the play to be oiled in before he can make this last scene work.

On the third run of the scene he calls a halt to tell Jessica to enter slowly. 'Slower, slower. It's a hot night.' The first clue he's given them. Then to Antonio and Portia he offers a totally wrong note to move and speak swiftly when telling each other what they will now do with their lives. But the lines call for a sad and slow delivery.

Sir John agrees. 'I heard your note,' he says to John D, 'that it was a hot night, so I went slower.'

I mouth to him 'you're right'.

My hope is that when the elements finally come together, when they've got the court scene right and can hear the sad, Sephardic song, then they will understand the melancholy in the writing. The last scene, though, did take a kind of shape. And the Lorenzo/Jessica relationship became clearer. Nerissa, thrilled to have the last lines of the play, is approaching the right sardonic mood for the ending.

And heroes you are, sirs, true. No denying it. True, true, heroes indeed. Heroes!

Her final '*heroes*' is done with her eyes – very beautiful they are, too.

John moved back to the first Portia/Nerissa scene. His energy seemed to have recovered. Great delight not only watching him hit moment after moment but interspersing them with gossip.

'That time in *The Cherry Orchard* when Svoboda[107] was designing, Sir Larry was so ill he was rehearsing in a wheelchair. There was a disagreement between them. Larry wanted a projection of green leaves, Svoboda didn't. They kept it up for the

---

[107] Joseph Svoboda, brilliant Czech designer who has worked around the world.

entire period of run-throughs, Svoboda not relenting, until one day, from his wheelchair, Larry said [John imitated him very well], "But Joseph you don't understand, I'm a dying man and I want green leaves." He didn't get them.'

It's been another larky day. Full of useful direction, just not as hard working as I'd have liked. John D seemed to be treading water, perhaps feeling relieved to have cracked the court scene the day before – no small achievement.

At the beginning of the day, during a scene in which Sir John is struggling, John D called out: 'Quiet! Sir John is trying to act.'

'That'll be the day,' quipped Zero, 'with all those decorations weighing him down.'

It's the stage manager's birthday. A cake has been bought. I buy him chocolates and a cup with SLAVE written on it. When I nibble at the cake and chocolates John admonishes: 'Stop eating the cake. You've got your butty in shape, keep it that way. You might even get to play Marchbanks again. With a good wig.'[108]

In the evening I meet Dusty and the children at Downey's. For old times sake. But the triple-decker Dusty wanted no longer existed. Not a very interesting meal. The proprietor recognised my name, though. Always a bonus.

Went to the new James Bond film. Magnificent first sequence of the ski-chase ending in the parachute jump over the precipice. The rest seems faintly immoral to me – the light-hearted killings, I mean. Not the sex, which was dull. Dusty is a delight to be with, she can still close her eyes in fear over such films.

Friday, 12 August

Begin with penultimate Belmont scene. Julie has picked up notes I gave her, and is better. Silly sounds and gestures remain but she's worked hard. I whisper this to John hoping he'll tone down his blasts. He does somewhat but can't resist one harsh note about a sigh – which I thought was rather good.

'It's in the line! Doesn't need your sniffs, grunts, sighs, farts, snorts ... I've told you!'

---

[108] Reference to my performance in an amateur production of Shaw's play, *Candida*, when I was seventeen.

He offers them a key note: not enough sense of crisis. He's right. After another run at the scene I mouth a silent 'better' to Julie who almost collapses with relief at such encouragement. She's beginning to look tragic, not unlike Jeanne Moreau.

Lorenzo requires constant pushing. Either he's bewildered or not very bright. Can't make up my mind which. John rearranges the Belmont scene so that some of my notes to both Jessica and Portia need reconsidering. With renewed insult he – perversely I think – has toned down the drive I gave to Jessica. Will need to handle this situation delicately or, between him wanting to show he didn't engage Julie under pressure from Zero (if that's the case), and my wanting to give her confidence, we'll tear her apart. His rearrangement of the scene is better. He's taken them out of a corner to command the entire centre stage.

Move on to court scene. John attacks it furiously, rushing from Jewish side to Christian side, orchestrating the rumbles and murmurs first of one then the other, like a conductor, except that he's orchestrating emotion as well.

In his enthusiasm for history John had reminded me of the Fourth Crusade in which Venice – that Christian state – urged the Crusaders to attack the Christian Byzantine Empire; they wanted their trade routes! Immediately wrote a piece for Antonio to be delivered during the court scene.

Sir John not happy. 'This new dialogue is absolutely unnecessary. Verbiage! All history is about Christian state fighting Christian state.'

I quite like the addition but leave the two Johns to fight it out.

John the knight has another point with which John the director disagrees. 'If I talk about Imperial Rome everyone will think of lions eating Christians and Nero fiddling while Rome burned. It needs some explanation to show what they're talking about when they talk about comparing Imperial Venice to Imperial Rome.' John D agrees and says it was Republican Rome they were thinking of. Not sure it is but I'll check.

Saturday, 13 August

Yesterday's run-through long and boring. Burns only here and there. The new 'economical' lines seem perfunctory rather than economical. Just because they're new perhaps? Rivka is better. And Lorenzo and Jessica. Antonio is down. Portia is just lovely to watch even when she doesn't know what she's doing. Zero has his moments. John gives them a few brief notes saying it's as good as could be expected after two weeks. Next week they *must* put down their books because he can't do anything with them otherwise. 'And we'll be in the theatre, which'll be a shock for you.'

Dusty and the two children left for Maine. Tanya's boil has burst. She feels better. Dusty has lost her voice. Sounds sexy. She'd rung Lindsay the day before and on hearing his voice so close had burst into tears.

'Everything's all right, mum,' he reassured her. 'Don't cry, it's expensive!' She misses him. Wishes he was with her.

I return from the airport hoping to see an off-Broadway show which Riggs said he was going to – closed! Walked home through the Village where the sidewalks are thronged with vendors, opera singers and poets. I love the atmosphere. Get home. Can't sleep. Write cards. Am in bed at 2.30 a.m.

Have spent all day – with breaks to rest my hand – writing these twenty pages, from 11.30 a.m. till now 8.30 p.m. Nine hours! Must get out for some air and a bite to eat. Had wanted to read through the play, collect my thoughts. Too tired. Perhaps I'll take in a movie – a Japanese film, *Realm of the Senses*.

WEEK THREE

Monday, 15 August

Our first day in the Imperial Theatre. Builders, painters, scaffolding. It's huge. John takes me aside.

'We are doing the first Portia scene and I want to get certain things straight. It's Beatie Bryant[109] who's got to university, got her degree, and is now saying, "Words and knowledge are not enough I have to put them to work." Right?' I agree, enjoying the parallel.

He informs me that Sir John, mistaking his call, came in this

---

[109] Central character in *Roots*.

morning with an idea. 'I told him to discuss it with you. It's to do with the logic of the situation. I don't know whether he's right to think of logic at such a moment but take him off and talk it through with him. He's concerned about a man who's had this knife hanging over him and there's no resolution.'

I show him the rewrite of the '*I know, I know,*' section. He accepts.

I ask: 'What about the new section at the end of the court scene?'

'Sir John hasn't seen that yet,' adding, 'perhaps *that* will appease him.' We'll see.

Rehearsal begins.

'Don't shout, ignore the echo, that'll disappear when there's scenery and an audience.' There *is* an echo. Very different from the rehearsal room. The actors look lost. Jessica and Lorenzo being around I grab the opportunity to go below stage and rehearse the 'love scene'. I feel awkward to be starting in the middle. Really need the momentum of having directed everything. My first ideas for blocking change. I shift, reshift; think, rethink. Lorenzo becomes a different character.

'Whisper the words into her ears like a kiss. You're making love to her with words. *Earning* the right to physical contact. Be precise in your movements, firm. We've only a short while to communicate a great deal. Every gesture must deliver a message ...'

They enjoy it. I feel it's insufficiently rehearsed but it will have to go before John.

Return in time to see the casket scene. Working better, but Portia is not making sense of those lines.

... Don't think from my response that I'm a calculating woman, though sometimes I wish I were. The truth is I'm impulsive. My responses shape at once. I know a man, a situation at a glance, but my mother said, 'Humility! Your impulse may be wrong.' You'd rather have my love relaxed and confident, Bassanio? Be patient ...

'Tell her,' John orders. I will, after I've spoken with Julie.

I take Julie to lunch and talk her through scenes, reminding her that Jessica is like her father, fiercely intelligent, capable of contempt and sardonic ridicule. She understands but, I fear, won't ever be able to carry it off. In rehearsal she shows me she's understood but hasn't yet found how to make it work.

Says John to her: 'Forget about the emotion. You can pop that in at the dress rehearsal. At least make sense of the text so that whenever your *emotion* dries up you'll have the *sense* to fall back on.'

I feel something is wrong with the text. Lorenzo is held up. The urgency we're looking for is blocked. As I rearrange lines to release energy John sings out a suggestion.

'It's one I've just this second written,' I cry out delightedly.

'If after twenty years we didn't come together ...' he says.

Sir John arrives. I take him below stage to the dressing rooms. He really wants to talk to both John and me together. I show him the changes. He's not impressed. Something far more radical is disturbing him. Roughly it's this: 'Here's this man, Antonio, wise, intelligent, a patrician of Venice, he's spent all this time and energy persuading Shylock why he has to sign a bond. Is he then going to allow Shylock to word such a monstrous contract? Surely he'd know the repercussions would rebound tenfold. And look at the reality of it. All right, so Antonio accepts the details of the bond, what happens next? They have to get it witnessed by three Venetians, two patricians and one citizen and then registered. Which patrician is going to allow such a bond to be signed? And more − knowing that he's put his entire fortune in one voyage, Antonio would be crazy to run such a risk. *He* knows about pirates. He'd *never* agree to such a bond.'

I've concertina-ed it, but that's the substance − a formidable criticism. At first I'm worried, then slowly I gather my reply which, also concertina-ed, was this:

'First, we must accept that a man's intelligence can lapse, especially in the case of Antonio who's spent himself persuading a steamrollering Shylock to agree to a bond at all. But let's imagine what they might have said. Antonio might have reminded Shylock of the risk − *all* his fortune in one voyage, to which Shylock would have said, true, you're a fool, still, do you imagine I can't lay my hands on money in the ghetto so that you can borrow again to repay me? To which Antonio might have said, but what if the city decides on a tax raid of the ghetto for ready cash, which they frequently did, and it all happens at the same time? To which Shylock would, rightly, say – you're absurd to imagine such coincidental calamity could befall. Antonio might be uneasy but he wouldn't be able to resist Shylock's persuasive accusation of unreasonable pessimism. Next – they wouldn't go to just anyone in Venice as witnesses, they'd find men they both knew and could trust, who'd indulge them in the outlandish bond. Lastly: we *are* dealing with a fable – that does allow some dramatic licence.'[110]

He was not persuaded – or rather he could accept my explanation but – there was more, 'much more'. He wanted to save it for a discussion to include John.

Then he said something extraordinary. 'I'm in a difficult position where I'm not in control of the situation either as director, manager or lead actor. I haven't *not* been the lead for years but, honestly, I've not read a decent new play in recent times and so my leads have been in classics, revivals, and when this came along I thought it was so good that I was prepared to travel three thousand miles and agree to the *second* lead. So it's difficult; perhaps I should have seen this earlier on – I did. I liked everything up to the court scene. And that's my point. This awful thing is hanging over the court and we aren't taking enough notice of it. A man is going to die, in a horrible way, his flesh is going to be cut from near his heart. It's barbaric, monstrous, a most cruel and gruesome thing, and Antonio is prattling on. About what? I'm going to die. Horribly! What's happening in the court to register this?'

He seems not to understand that, confronted with death, people often talk about what touches them deeply. Nor does he comprehend the degree of spiritual surrender both men, old and tired, have accepted. The fight is gone from them. Antonio was tired even from the start of the play. Mind you, communicating this sense of *weltschmerz* is not helped by Zero laughing on his line, '*And I love thee, old man,*' instead of delivering it sadly, utterly drained. I'll make these points when we're all together.

I'm in time to see the 'love scene'. Needs work to flow faster

---

110 I'm not sure that last argument persuades me now. The rest stands, however.

and be light, but the mood is there. John complains it has added to the running time. Refuses to believe it will play faster. Mutters, ominously: 'You've played right into my hands.' He simply doesn't like the scene. 'Let Jocelyn see it,' he says. He trusts her and probably believes she'll agree with him.

We hear the song sung for the first time, carrying us from the courtroom to the final scene. It doesn't work yet but it will. The actress singing it has a lovely voice but is nervous – Rebecca Malka, who also plays the maid. Graziano is strong and good – Riggs uses his voice well. Later JD asks me what Sir John has said. I report briefly. Promise more detail tomorrow, but warn him it may loom as a major problem. John instructs me to begin talking with Zero. I had planned to let the week pass, he says no! As soon as possible. I phone Zero. He's not free until Wednesday evening, or a lunch hour after that. He doesn't eat, still dieting.

Drinks in Charlie's with some of the cast after rehearsal. Roderigues wants to discuss his problems. 'I'm not a bad actor, and don't think I'm making it a big problem, but it is hard to achieve all that energetic bustling in and out of the house with so few lines.' I agree.

As we talk I realise what's missing – something idiosyncratic to help define his character. On the spot, in the restaurant, I write lines to help colour him in. A dangerous thing to do because now I have to persuade John they're necessary.

Tuesday, 16 August

Arrive early to discuss cuts and additions with John. Zero grabs me to talk about this and that. He's abandoned his artist's beret and is wearing a *yarmulke*. We sit in his room which he's got doormen scurrying around to furnish. Ask his advice about obtaining additional first night tickets.

He pulls a face as though I'm a fool not to know: 'I'll get them for you. I order a hundred tickets for my friends and relatives, not prestigious people, just old friends, I don't have any new friends. I'll say, "I feel ill, I can't perform, I need more tickets." Leave it to me.' He enjoys being helpful, needed, indispensable.

John comes in. Tell him I'd like to discuss the cuts.

'Next week. I believe we should do *all* the cuts together or else we won't know if they're a benefit.' What's he plotting to present me with? Cautiously suggest that Roderigues needs a few lines to colour him.

'He needs a kick up the arse.' Knew it!

Rehearse the first scenes all morning with Shylock and Antonio.

SHYLOCK   ... Imagine this tribe of Semites in the desert. Pagan, wild, but brilliant. A sceptical race, believing only in themselves. Loving but assertive. Full of quarrels and questions. Who could control them? Leader after leader was thrown up. But, in a tribe where every father of his family was a leader, who could hold them in check for long? Until one day a son called Abraham was born, and he grew up knowing his brethren very, very well indeed. 'I know how to control this arrogant, anarchic herd of heathens,' he said to himself. And he taught them about one God. Unseen! Of the spirit! That appealed to them, the Hebrews, they had a weakness for concepts of the abstract ...

John encourages Zero into a more mischievous delivery of this speech. But words are lost, muffled. '*For from that day on they were currrrd.*'[111] They were *what*? John advises: 'Let's get the broad lines fixed first, we'll go into detail when the sets are up.' He leans to me conspiratorially. 'I've told Sir John that in the court scene he becomes a changed man and feels "if I'm going down I shall go down fighting", and so he rages against the reactionary patricians whom he despises and tells them everything he's ever wanted to tell them.' I hadn't thought of it in that way, but it's effective. Will it work? I fear what Clements is planning to lay upon us.

Later I let John read the relevant parts of this diary concerning my conversation with Sir John. He reads my entry about the Lorenzo/Jessica scene, which prompts him to talk about the need for 'air' in the play. 'I should have seen it before but I didn't realise

---

[111] The word was 'cursed'.

how slowly I'd need to pace the play. It needs time, lots of scenes need more time. At the moment it's going to run four and a half hours.'

I know what he's talking about. An urge comes upon me to cut and cut. Treacherously I contemplate cutting the character of poor Roderigues entirely, and to halve the *'poor sages'* speech, and to let go the *'absurdum'* quotation, and Usque's *'I'm not in print yet...'*[112] In other words everything I had imagined contributed to the bustle of things. I put to John the idea of cutting out Roderigues. He became excited. 'It's tempting, tempting!'

On the way to lunch he asked: 'What time is Zero's party tonight because I'm getting laid.' 'John, that's the second time you've informed me you're getting laid. Forgive me, I'm bewildered. What do you mean? You have a boyfriend? An arrangement? Or what?' He explained. He had a little place, another *pied-à-terre*, to which an agency sends a young man. I was astounded.

'I don't know what you heterosexuals do but WE'RE very well organised. Happens three times a week. When I'm working I'm very horny, not so bad when I'm not but when I'm working I need to be distracted and this is the best way. Takes my mind off the play, the actors, you. Oh, the power of money.'

Over lunch I tell him he should consider the cuts *now* to save re-blocking later. His view is completely opposite – he wants to get right what exists. 'Then we can more easily accommodate changes.'

He animatedly talks about the film. 'I see three winter months in Venice with exactly the same cast who know all the text – none of this bolstering up with stars ...'

'What are you talking about?' I ask him, 'we're choked with stars. And why winter? Do you see snow?'

'I see this set in a wet Venice. My favourite time there. Wet Venice and sunny Belmont. And we'll hire a warehouse and build all the sets in it.'

I caution him: 'We'll all have to do it for nothing to do it our way.'

---

112 Most of which subsequently did go.

He disagrees. 'If we can make *this* work, we'll find the money. No problem.'

I'm not so certain about using *all* this cast. And what about the pressure that will be put on me to use an experienced film director?!

John informs me that the advance booking for Philadelphia and Washington is very good. Zero had said: 'You'll see, halfway through Washington the word will spread and New York will be sold out before we arrive.'

Afternoon spent inventing, animating, tightening up the family scene, Scene 4. My itch persists to get up there and direct, probably inspired by John's top form. It's looking better but Zero drags lines. I urge John to urge him. He does. The scene moves more swiftly.

During the Tubal/Abtalion exchange,[113] I whisper to John: 'Now here's a passage could go.' He asks to see how. I show him my script.

'But what would Levene say to cutting his part?' asks John.

'You've given him back his big Tubal speech in the court,' I remind him. 'Besides either we're going to risk giving New York a full three and a half hours or we *all* make sacrifices – me with the script, actors with their lines ...'

'... me with my favourite pieces of directing . . .'

'Right! Of course I'd prefer to present New York with a tough, three-and-a-half-hour bull of a play, but if you want cuts ... There are two phases to cutting: lines, words, phrases here and there, trimming to allow flow; and *then* the big cuts.'

'And you want to do the trimming now?'

'Yes. Why don't we spend an hour together before the big meeting with Zero, Jocelyn and Clements?' He agrees.

John runs Scene 4 again. We stand at the back of the theatre and chatter – letting the actors get on with it.

'When this scene has settled with the new blocking you've given it – which is much better – then you must make it brisk ... Abtalion, why is he going so slow?'

'Making the most of his moment.'

---

[113] Abtalion is later dispensed with.

'Shylock should be swifter when he comes in to introduce the Portuguese. Why can't he see he must bustle?'

'And what's going wrong with Bassanio in this scene?' John also complains.

'He's lost eagerness, forgotten that he's trying to persuade Antonio to lend him three thousand ducats.'

'But what can I do to change it?'

'Break up the scene for him,' I suggest. 'Show him how different passages have a different pace, change gear. Give him headlines.' Beat. 'Or I'll do it.'

'Yes, you do it. I'm not above taking advice from anybody. How do you think I got where I am?'

I write a breakdown for Nick of the Antonio/Bassanio scene where Bassanio, as a long-forgotten godson, comes to ask Antonio for a loan.

After rehearsal we're all Zero's guests at the fabulous Romanian restaurant – except John, who joins us later. I sit with the beautiful Gloria Gifford, and Roberta, and William Roerick, playing the Doge, who for the last years was the boyfriend of E.M. Forster.

Gloria is bright and talkative, afflicted with swiftly offered, firm opinions. Claims she can sum up people at once.

'You're very unnerving to be with, then,' I tell her. I enjoy the way she relates the play to her life: Bassanio is like her father, Lorenzo is like her fanatical brother who is Vanessa Redgrave's Workers' Revolutionary Party representative in the States. I spend most of the evening talking with her.

John D engages Sir John, and later whispers to me that he thinks he's persuaded Sir of the mood in which Antonio must face the court scene: '... Like a British galleon going down with all canons firing. But,' he adds ominously, 'I don't like the "revolutionary" change he's got up his sleeve to tell us tomorrow.'

Neither do I. What can it be?

One by one everyone leaves. I'm left with Pat and Brent – an excellent stage-management team, intelligent, willing, quietly efficient. I share a taxi with Brent. We collapse into a fit of giggles when I observe it's going to be all right except for a few.

He asks who?

'Not telling,' I say.

I ask him.

'Not telling,' he says, but suggests: 'You tell me who you think hasn't got a prayer and I'll tell you if you're right.'

Because I trust him and because he tells me he's been working on this play for a year and two months 'and I think it's a gorgeous play', I confess my fears about Julie and Everett. He agrees about Julie but says Everett is a slow worker and will make it. I say maybe Julie will in the end. He thinks Roderigues 'doesn't have a prayer and I'm not just talking about eight lines'. I don't tell him I'm toying with cutting the character.

He then lets slip a word which confirms one of my suspicions. He talks about the 'politics' of hiring Julie.

'That's an interesting word,' I say, 'it confirms something I felt all along. Julie was Zero's suggestions wasn't she?' My guess throws him off balance, and he can barely hold back a nod. So it's true – John hired Julie at Zero's insistence, and that's why he's whipping her. Pity.

We talked about the length of the play. Brent can't make up his mind whether it's the text, John's direction, or the acting. I'm not sure either. We'll only know when John has speeded up his choreography and when actors like Zero stop dragging their feet. Brent shares my fear that something must be done soon about Zero. When I tell him we're waiting till the end of the third week he reports a very worrying Zero remark. I had sent Brent to make a date for me to meet with Zero. Zero had said to him: 'What do they want from me, don't they know I'm going to play this play my own way?'

Christ! Was he serious? He can't be. He's listened to our notes and improved his performance. Nevertheless Brent is right – he rarely does the same thing twice. Seems unable to fix a moment. We never have a chance to evaluate what he's doing because next time round he's doing something else. No discipline. Or is he leaving himself space in which to be always fresh? This would be fine *if* he showed us he understood the essential drift of a passage. Brent reports that after they gave Zero sheets of the words he'd missed out he complained those words weren't in his script. Stage-management checked. They were.

We parted agreeing that somehow it would end as a brilliant

production. Brent thought John and I worked 'fantastically together'. 'You balance each other. And John loves you. You won't ever have a more loyal director. He wants to protect every part of the script and you.' We'll see what happens tomorrow when Zero, Jocelyn and Sir John put their criticisms to me.

Two fascinating pieces of information come from Gloria and Pat, which link. From Gloria: that this play is 'the talk among *every*body — actors, directors, producers, agents. They've all heard marvellous things about it and they're all talking!' From Pat: that Gloria and others are keeping a journal of the rehearsals and lots of publishers are interested in them. I know John D is keeping a diary. Possibly Marian is. Roberta had said: 'Oh, I'm writing on one or two pages.' Wouldn't it be intriguing, I say to Pat, to print a book with each day written up four or five different ways, the same moment seen by different eyes. Or different moments seen. A kind of theatre *Rashamon*. Of course, one wouldn't be able to print the whole truth. Some observations would be too personal, or too cruel.

I'm up till 1.45 a.m. writing this.

Glorious letter from Lindsay Joe. My son thrills me. Will send it on to Dusty.

Wednesday, 17 August

I've made my first mistake. Will explain later. First ...

Rang LJ at 2.30 a.m. to tell him how I loved his letter. He sounds in great form. Must try to get him and Dawna[114] on a cheap Laker flight to New York for the first night. Fall asleep around 3 a.m.

Because I had arranged to come in early to speak with Everett, my internal alarm woke me up at seven, eight and eight-thirty.

To play the role of a religiously fanatical Lorenzo, Everett had got into his mind the notion of a fundamentalist from the Southern States. 'You can't talk to them. They're mad.'

I tell him, yes, that *is* one kind of religious fanatic, but wrong for Lorenzo who is more intellectual. Everyone in the play is. The

---

[114] Lindsay's girlfriend at the time.

performance should crackle with alert, animated minds arguing, declaiming, full of energy ... I make him read his lines as one speech, skipping other people's lines in order to find the continuity. He feels the session was helpful.

The mistake. Last night I'd written a memo to John re Zero.[115] The problem of Zero needed to be faced. Foolishly I prefaced the memo quoting Zero's words as reported by Brent: '*Don't they know I'm going to play this role my way?*' John was shaken. I tried to dilute their impact by suggesting Zero was probably being his usual jokey self. I saw John take Brent aside to tell him off for 'upsetting the author'. I regretted my thoughtlessness and later apologised to Brent. *He* should have told John, not me, or told us together.

Sir John points to a rewrite in which Antonio says: '*And courtesies also. Remember I've borrowed three thousand ducats on my godson's behalf.*' He suggests it's inconsistent. 'Antonio wouldn't relate money to courtesy. The money would have nothing to do with it.' He was right. John had wanted the money referred to because it had not been referred to for the last dozen pages. Sir John said it would come better from Graziano. He was right again.

We rehearse Antonio's dinner. The scene begins dully. John takes Zero aside – my memo to him is fermenting. John runs the scene again. It's not working. Sits beside me in despair, asks what *is* the matter with them? I tell him what I told Lorenzo: everyone should sparkle, bristle with ideas, argument. Zero brings everything down by being lugubrious.

John mutters: 'We're going to have a row today, I can see it. Oh well, if we're going to have one let's get it over with.' He lams into them with harsh notes. The scene immediately changes gear, and works. Zero's good nature – and John's reluctance *really* to fight with him – avoids a confrontation.

I give Zero notes on single words.

'Zee, it's not *occupation* it's *profession*. They're not the same thing. A profession is grand, and Shylock uses the word sardonically in reference to his parents' trade: reconditioning mattresses.' He takes the point. Later I say: 'Zee, it's not '*so* what can we do?', it's '*but*

---

115 See Appendix 2.

what can we do.' With *but* you can then make better sense of the next lines.

...You have us for life, gentlemen, for life. Learn to live with us. The Jew is the Christian's parent. Difficult, I know. Parent-children relationships, always difficult, and even worse when murder is involved within the family. But what can we do? It *is* the family! Not only *would* I be your friend but I *have* to be your friend ...

After some resistance he takes the note, and says: 'Good, now I'll remember it.' But he can't resist the wisecrack – 'And don't do it again!'

'I will,' I retort. 'You take notes so well, and it's a delight to watch you catch fire.' I schmooze. But the scene *is* a difficult one.

'Why can't they just *do* it?' complains John. 'Why am I so tired, exhausted? Perhaps I need a fuck *every* day. Very good for one!'

The final run of the scene is incredibly dreary.

'It's not working,' hisses John, 'it's not fucking working.'

I lean over to help. 'The moves you've given are all he needs. He's *adding* to them. They're unnecessary. He's performing for *us* rather than telling *them* a story. He's not *excited* by what he's telling.'

John leaps up on to the stage and drives Zero through the scene, animates him. Better. But Zee hams so – rolling his big eyes, snaking his arm, wriggling his way across the stage.

John informs me he'll be setting up for two days in Philadelphia and that I'll be taking over rehearsals.

'You can have fun, then.'

Interview over lunch with David Kissel of *Women's Wear Daily Trade Magazine* which I'm told has a huge circulation and a good arts page.

Afternoon begins with the court scene. Sam Levene doesn't know his new Tubal speech.

'He could have learnt it by now!' mutters John, murderously. 'I'll get some energy into this scene if it kills me – and it probably will! I knew this was going to be an awful day.'

I say 'good afternoon' to Gloria. She replies with an abrupt 'hi', as though determined not to appear familiar having spent most of the previous evening talking to me. And it *was* talking *to* me. At one point last night I tried to say something to her but she didn't let me get in. I asked, very English: 'Can we have a *two*-way conversation, darling?' She snapped back, very New York: 'Don't get fresh with me, Arnold, because I can be fresher.' Pow! Dangerous New Yorkers.

The court scene gathers strength, then flounders. I want to cut lines and add a few. John says not yet. Pity. Cut a line you can unblock a section; cut another you can advance the pace. John can't get it right. He let's it run while he and I sit at the back making bets about what 'revolutionary suggestions concerning the ending' Sir John has up his sleeve. The run-through of the court scene is dreary. We exchange comments about it like giggly schoolboys.

'Horrible blocking!' says John.

'It's not working,' I point out, 'because Sir John is resisting this whole scene. He's dragging.' Why? To help his case for the evening? It's also not working because Zero is so bloody ponderous and hammy. Makes a meal of everything.

John gives no notes at the end, simply says: 'Thank you, that was fine.' I wish he'd incorporated my new cuts to see if they worked or not. And I wish he hadn't put back the long bloody Tubal speech.

I tell him: 'If we face a crisis, and cuts have to be made, and Roderigues has to go, then that Tubal speech has to go.'

'We'll lose Sam Levene!'

'You'll call a meeting and tell everyone that the play is too long, that we all have to make sacrifices, that the author is cutting, and therefore ...'

'Don't direct me in my role as director!'

In good spirits we go off. I'm in a car with Sir John. John D shares Zero's limousine. I chat with Sir John, jovially. 'We're all very curious about this "revolutionary" suggestion you have.'

He dismisses it apologetically as if his poor mind couldn't think up anything special. He's only sorry to be upsetting the apple cart at this late stage.

I tell him nothing disastrous can happen. Either his idea is good and acceptable, or it is misguided and we'll argue him out of it. 'John and I have been throwing this play backwards and forwards for a year and a half now,' I tell him, 'I've worked on it for three years; good friends have contributed their ideas to it; good minds have engaged with it. It can take a knocking.'

I am in no way prepared for what is to follow. Not merely the play but I personally am about to take a knocking.

In the apartment have been laid out cheeses, biscuits, chopped liver, wine, cake, nuts. We nibble the bits and pieces. John sits on the floor to my left, Jocelyn and Zero at right-angles on a couch to my right, Sir John at the other end of the low table in front of me. John D says, 'Let's begin.' And Sir John begins.

He goes over the ground he's already been over with me: Antonio wouldn't let such a bond be made, not enough recognition given to the horror hanging over them, too much extraneous gaff being talked while this man is under sentence. And then along comes Portia with a solution which anybody in their right mind would have seen straightaway — for example the Doge, who would have known at once that if you cut flesh you draw blood. Sir John delivers his case superbly,[116] pacing it slowly, precisely, (albeit a little pedantically), and comes intoxicated to his own solution which he delivers with such tingling excitement in his voice that he captures all of us — even me a little. John D squirms in his chair with excitement. This, more or less, is how the venerable knight delivers his 'revolutionary suggestion'.

'Portia comes with this declaration that if you cut flesh you draw blood and therefore the bond is not sensible, at which point everyone turns to Shylock, who says: "You see, Antonio, a nonsense bond, as we knew, but," and he turns to the Doge and continues, "but do you imagine I didn't know that if you cut flesh you draw blood? Did that have to be written in the contract? I draw breath when I raise my arm to cut the flesh, does that also have to be written in the contract? The bond stands and you must uphold it. Not even the Doge can tamper with the law. I will have my bond." And so the court of Venice must grant him his bond. He picks up the knife, approaches his friend, raises the knife and

---

116 Nicely avoiding any mention that someone in Shakespeare's play should also have known that if you cut flesh you draw blood.

then – throws it on the floor. He won't do it. He can't do it. He turns on Venice and says, "Look where your laws lead you, to the slaughter of one of your own. But I won't do it." And so the Jew has exercised mercy. Mercy – the supreme virtue before which every principle must fall. And there you have a real *coup de théâtre*.'

It was brilliantly executed. I hope he performs as well on stage. From then on a lot was said, impossible to recapitulate it all. Zero claimed it corresponded with worries he too had about the moment – he hadn't felt Portia's lines were enough. 'Not "sensible"? What's that? "Sensible"!' Jocelyn regurgitated the observation John Clements had made to me – and, presumably to her – that no one was taking any notice of Antonio in the court scene. John added fuel to the fire saying my play had no real equivalent to the 'quality of mercy' speech, no sufficiently high dramatic point, and that really I wasn't facing the implications of Shylock using the knife. Was he really going to cut his friend's flesh? When the moment came would he have done so?

The combined onslaught unnerved me. I tried to steady myself with questions. 'What would be said of a man who keeps his friend in a state of suspense,' I ask; 'who outrageously mocks the court to such an extent, and ends up doing the one thing he doesn't want to do – namely, breaking the bond and setting a precedent which puts his community at risk?'

Clements replied that Shylock and Antonio had such a friendship, 'beautifully created by you', that he would forgive and understand his friend using such a ploy; and that the act of mercy would rise above all else.

I didn't believe it. It was unsatisfactory. Something was wrong. I couldn't put my finger on it. The argument grew and expanded. I had the sense that Sir John was compensating for not being 'the manager, the director, or the leading actor'; more, that he was going to be the first of those who will be intensely irritated by the play – tampering with Shakespeare and his treatment of the Jew. How ungrateful of Wesker not to acknowledge that Shakespeare was being as generous as possible towards a Jew! Yes, I know Clements was calling for a Shylock who would stage a *coup* in which the Jew could emerge as the merciful one, but something else he said made my antennae suspect his motives. He admired the writing but, 'I don't agree with everything, you know!' There's something else is in his head. Something, something. It will emerge sooner or later, I feel it.

Perhaps I misjudge him. Certainly I felt angry that he'd brought up this gimmicky suggestion and disturbed us all. We argued back and forth, raising our voices, and as I came to understand my own feelings more and more, so I became more and more confident, though I didn't always say what I meant. When John asked me would Shylock cut the flesh, I said, without hesitation, 'Yes.' And when he next asked, dramatically thrusting a knife in my hand, would I do it to him, I replied as dramatically, as confidently, but more acting the role of the leader confronted with impossible decisions than as the person I think I am – incapable of treading on a fly. 'Yes,' I said. It was this reply that shocked him.[117]

But as I began to think more clearly I retracted. 'You're talking about another kind of play. My play is about "barbaric laws – barbaric bonds", simply that. That's all I want to explore. There's a beautiful friendship, everything seems cosy, along comes a godson to borrow money, no real problem there – but it's the beginning of all that goes wrong because then reality has to be faced: the laws of Venice. Barbaric laws which produced barbaric actions. You want a play about what happens when a man actually has to kill his friend. What does he do? I didn't think about it this way when writing, but now see that I instinctively avoided what I felt I couldn't honestly handle. I don't know what Shylock would do – nor what I would do – and so I didn't let the situation get that far. I use Shakespeare's device and bring in Portia. Fault me for that but that's the play I want to write".[118]

Clements persisted. So did I, asking again and again why would Shylock break the bond and do the very thing he knows he can't do: set precedents which will threaten his community? They considered this a callous view because one man was actually going to die. Here! In front of us! After all, confronted with imminent death who would pause to think about what *might* happen to the Jewish community in ten years' time? I insisted that they, the

---

[117] And from which perhaps he never recovered.

[118] This is not a coherent response, nor am I certain it's what I believed.

Jewish community, would. The threat was real for them in a way that it wasn't for us today.

John used harsh, blackmailing tactics to get me to relent. At one heated point I called him and Sir John sanctimonious. This struck him deeply, he became vicious. I reminded him that he had once described me as sanctimonious. He denied it. I apologised and wished that he took quips with the same grace he expected of me. I was wildly emotional, a bit out of control, but I was hurt by what I felt to be John's betrayal; I couldn't understand why he was falling for Sir John's corny and sentimental idea. Actually, I could very well understand why. He had not licked the court scene, and was probably regretting giving Tubal back the big speech. Nor was Zero performing well. And Sir John had attacked as 'nonsense' the new crusade lines which John had asked me, during our pre-rehearsal discussions, to add. The knight had also told John it was madness to bring the Doge on at the beginning of the court scene. 'He shouldn't be there to listen to all that political arguing back and forth.' Interestingly I'd left the Doge out of the court in my earlier draft, John had asked me to bring him in. Sir John even thought Portia shouldn't enter until later, which again was as I'd originally written it. But I didn't agree with that. I'd hate to lose John's marvellous moment when the women face the wipe, which moves aside revealing the court, and then sweep in to the sound of bells.

Zero left first. Then Sir John with great apologies to me. I lingered.

'I know you want me to go, John, but I have just a few things to say first, they're not upsetting ...'

He became acrimonious and asked me to leave at once. He said he'd not merely learned something new about the play but about me, too, and it had surprised and upset him. He insisted he had *always* believed the bond to be no more than a nonsense bond, and one that both Shylock and Antonio knew had no validity. How then, I thought to myself, could it ever have got to court, a scene he'd spent so much time trying to get right? But I didn't put that to him – he seemed in need of whipping himself into a fury.

I continued: 'I want to remind you – you wanted the Doge and

Portia there from the start – I agreed. You wanted the play cut here and there – I cut. You wanted the Tubal speech put back – I agreed. I'm standing by with big cuts if the play needs it. And I accept Sir John's point that Antonio is neglected – I've written a scene to meet that need. All the time I'm listening, working, co-operating – but I will not, and you must know it now, accept John Clements' suggestion. I think it's a cheap and gimmicky one.'

'Is that all you want to say? Good. Now go!' I couldn't understand what merited such rudeness.

'And, John,' I say, 'don't be stern with me.'

'I'm not stern. Just go or we'll quarrel.' Quarrel? He was rage incarnate. I kiss a sympathetic Jocelyn, and leave.

I want to take a plane back to England. Feel wretched. Fuck Clements to have brought up this ridiculous idea and get between John and me. But, strangely, I'm not *so* disturbed as my unhappiness suggests. Somewhere I feel strong and confident. I return to the flat to answer letters and write this up.

A sixth sense waits for John to ring and apologise. The phone rings. Someone for Sylvia. It rings again – Dorothy James. At 11.30 it rings again. It's John, his voice incredibly sweet and conciliatory. Jocelyn must have got through to him. He says something like: 'Sorry about all that – am I interrupting anything?'

'I wish you were!' He wants us to meet. We fix tomorrow after rehearsals. I feel better.

Next call is from Dusty. I relate what happened. She tells me how lovely everything is up in Maine.

At 12.30 Zero rings to ask how I feel. Has John been on to him urging him to ring and comfort me? Zero is lovely and reassuring, says how it's all better to be out in the open and how he kind of likes it that Sir John has the courage to do that. Claimed the discussion clarified things for him. He thinks Sir John will feel better even if his idea isn't accepted. 'Don't indulge yourself in anxiety, my friend.' Bless him. I just hope his performance becomes less ponderous and hammy.

2. 15 am. I'm whacked. And this will be utterly inadequate as a record.

Thursday, 18 August

Breakfast with Lenny Quartz[119] at OG's in Soho. Told him of the Clements idea, gave it all I could, made it sound good but in no way did I come to like it in the light of morning.

In rehearsal was grateful to find my voice could strike a calm and cheerful note. I called out: 'Good-morning, everyone. Good-morning, Johns.'

John D blew me a kiss, and called me over. 'Let [Sir] John tell you the Joan Littlewood[120] story,' which Sir John did.

'Joan Littlewood found herself in a lift with Zero Mostel and said to him, "I'm Joan Littlewood," to which he replied, "and so am I"!' I laughed, and the world was sunny again.

John called me to the back of the theatre. 'The reason I got so upset last night was because of something you said which either I didn't understand or found so disgusting it nearly made me cry. You said you *would* take up the knife and cut my flesh.'

'I retracted,' I said quickly. 'I was so overwhelmed by Sir John's performance of his idea, so confused by it, that I said yes, I would cut your flesh, and so would Shylock have cut Antonio's. But once I got myself together, I realised that's not what the play's about.' We had little time, and I suggested we couldn't discuss such an important issue in snatched moments. Then he told me he couldn't keep tonight's date because he had to talk to 'sound', and I wondered was he now going to begin avoiding me?

He went off to rehearse, I went down to the basement to phone lawyers about getting my visa extended.

Suddenly Brent appeared. 'John wants you, quick.' I came up. John gave me an imploring look. I was missing the first scene.

'It's up fifty per cent!' It was true. The play was alive for the first time. Zero had made the speeches his own and we were beginning to hear words clearly. Sir John acted as though relieved of a great load. The scene flew a fire. We had a play!

Not so the next scene with Portia. She was slow.

'No gaiety!' I whispered to John, and asked: 'Have you

---

119 Professor of Theatre, New York University.

120 Brilliant stage-director who brought to fame London's Stratford East Theatre Royal with such productions as *Oh What a Lovely War!* and Brendan Behan's *The Hostage*.

deliberately taken away the activity?'

'Yes, cramped the dialogue. We can bring back more activity once it's settled. What she's doing is not because she's off colour but because she's deliberately thought this out. And she's wrong!'

On to the next Shylock/Antonio scene, and they're still alive. Not *as* good as the first one but ... And then Scene 4, the long family scene. Julie will *never* be a Jessica. I'm resigned to it. With luck John will lose her in clever staging. He rearranges the Usque and da Mendes scene so that Shylock, as I had suggested, is politely standing to them, not sitting while they stand. Usque picks up an inflection I gave him. It works. I no longer feel the need to cut the Moslem/Inquisition section.[121]

John is vindicated, that's why he wanted to get it working before making cuts. 'That way I hope we'll only cut excess flesh.'

The problem of 'to cut or not to cut' occupies me constantly. As we watch Antonio struggle for lines I show John what I've written to fortify the bond-making scene. First, the original sequence of lines.

SHYLOCK A nonsense bond.

ANTONIO A nonsense bond?

SHYLOCK A lovely, loving nonsense bond. To mock the law.

ANTONIO To mock?

SHYLOCK Barbaric laws? Barbaric bonds! Three thousand ducats against a pound of your flesh.

ANTONIO My flesh?

SHYLOCK You're like an idiot child suddenly. (Mocking) 'A nonsense bond? My flesh?' Yes! If I'm not repaid by you, upon the day, the hour, I'll have a pound of your old flesh, Antonio, from near that part of your body which pleases me most – your heart. Your heart, Dearheart, and I'd take that, too, if I could, I'm so fond of it.

I've changed the middle lines:

---

[121] Though I do, finally.

SHYLOCK ...three thousand ducats against a pound of your flesh.
ANTONIO Is this a joke?
SHYLOCK Oh no! Not a joke.

John says it sounds as if Shylock really *wanted* the flesh. I changed it again.

ANTONIO Is this a joke?
SHYLOCK The flesh? Yes! The bond – no![122]

'Ah! Good!' says John, 'that answers everything I've been straining myself to tell you this morning. The flesh is a joke. He *never* intended to take the flesh.' Of course not.[123] Now it's clearer. He has to go on stage but grips my shoulder in passing – a favourite gesture of approval.

Portrait scene before lunch. That's better, too. Cleaner. But I suggest they should all be frozen in their pose – it would be funnier, less fussy, encourage more crispness. John says he began that way but it didn't give them a chance to spread, he'll bring it back later.

Lunch with a journalist from the *Philadelphia Post*. Bump into Sam Cohn in Sardi's dining with Bernie Jacobs and others from Shubert Organisation. They ask how it's going. I say: 'You see Dexter and I smiling still.' Sam asks is his client behaving? I say yes, he's a joy to watch, just that he doesn't enunciate; 'Tell him,' I suggest. Sam says he'll wait till Philadelphia, it would be unfair to tell him before. Quite right.

After lunch I listen to the Renaissance speech begin to work for the first time. Strange to me why Zero still glides dismissively over certain passages, as though not important. When he gives due weight to *all* the text he'll burn brightly throughout.

Even Lorenzo rose to deliver.

And Gloria's 'Hi!' was less cold.

Casket scene next. Bassanio dull. He knows what he's doing, and has come alive in other scenes, but this run he was just boring.

'Perhaps,' I whisper to John, 'he's got his period on.'

---

[122] I dropped these clumsy changes in the final version.

[123] These were thoughts under pressure. The reality of his dilemma does not permit him to 'intend' or not to 'intend'. He can see no alternative.

'Whatever period he's got on it's not the sixteenth century.'

Portia protests she feels cramped. It's not yet happening for her – but for her I have no fears. She's anxious though. I hear her resisting John's notes. He's tender but firm, encouraging.

Nerissa is not yet a presence.

Runaway scene. Jessica will never, never be right! Tubal and Abtalion still talk like New York Jews from the Bronx.

Letter scene. When Rivka follows my suggestion to move sparingly, the scene works. When she panics and moves too much, it goes to pieces. Shylock reads Jessica's farewell letter with feeling but because he doesn't enunciate clearly one doesn't know what it's about. Rest of the scene not bad – nice relationship growing between Usque, the playwright, and Rebecca da Mendes, his patron. But the '*I know, I know*' passage has no shape. All on one level.

Shylock's 'contempt' speech is moving, and will grow. Belmont scene nearly works – needs re-blocking. Julie apologies to me saying she's at crisis point. Promises to go home and work more. I remind her she needs simply to be still, allow her voice to move her.

Gloria is upset. Explains at length about not having money to pay in advance for the hotel in Philadelphia.

John re-blocks the court scene. I sit writing in between looking to the stage. It opens with the court in uproar and the Doge in recess. The bells chime, the uproar dies down, the women sweep in. John is a whirlwind pushing and reshuffling. He moves Antonio to the Jewish side – an inspired stroke. Every one of the crowd's 'shouts' now make an impact because they're well positioned. The actors are able to make sense of their lines because the right person is near to aim them at. Here is a great director at work. It's thrilling to watch. John turns to me for approval, holding up his thumb. I clap my hands in delight. Everyone's ideas are now brought together. One idea leads him to another. Even Tubal's speech slots into place though I would still like to lose it. John rushes backwards and forwards constantly needing to tuck in his shirt which his ever lifting and flailing arms pull out of his trousers which keep slipping and he must keep pulling up. Everyone knows it's going well. The air is full of gaiety and wisecracks.

I watch John place Bassanio in a kneeling position by Antonio to whisper quietly instead of shouting, '*And why are you so close to him* [Shylock]*?*' which enables Antonio's following aria to rise like sweet morning mist. '*You say a man is happy with no knowledge or art* ...'[124] It's breathtaking.

Then a curious thing happens. Shylock appears at Antonio's side. Where did he suddenly come from?

He says: 'I was to be there all the time but I was just resting.'

It looks awful now. Antonio's breathtaking moment is winded, stolen by Shylock who hangs immodestly by. I rush up to the stage and urgently whisper to John what he's lost. He's surprised. 'Tell me why?' I explain. He says, 'OK,' and moves Zero away. It's better, I say, but not good enough. Then Sir John, wisely knowing that this moment on stage is his, says he'd like to take up Arnold's suggestion. He moves across the stage. It works. The first half of the court scene is cracked. The way forward to the second half is clear. The dynamic of an actor finding his space is fascinating. As we watch it run-through I tell John that he's got it licked, and that I don't want to cut anything.

'But you will?'

'Yes.'

'Let's do it by trimming,' he says, 'not by hacking. I don't want it to bleed.'

'You've cemented in the Tubal speech so I can't prise it out.'

'I'll tell Sir John he can lose the Byzantine/Crusader passage if he tries to make the rest work.'

'I'll keep it in the printed text, though.'[125] Rehearsals can be a bartering market. Sir John is splendid, and I tell him so. He said he was happier now with John's new blocking, and especially with the Doge in the background.

Everyone is exhilarated. Except Gloria who's still unhappy about the advance rent she hasn't got. I give her a note to keep looking at Portia, full of pleasure, anxiety, and guardianship. Says she was just thinking of that. 'Like I beam at my son.'

Dusty was amusing last night on the phone from Maine. 'The

---

[124] Quoted earlier.

[125] I don't!

camp was full of those lovely Ashkenazi women. You'd love them. Not all beautiful, but striking and handsome and full of life.' I don't think I've ever heard the word 'Ashkenazi' on her lips before.

Friday, 19th August

John has instructed each actor to prepare a Shakespeare sonnet. A sonnet a day – to practise breathing. This day begins with Lorenzo. John D turns to Sir John – both agree that apart from the weak couplet at the end it is very good.

'Why doesn't Zero say something?' John asks.

'You didn't ask me,' Zero sulks. 'I'm not British!'

'You don't usually wait to be asked.'

I turn to Jocelyn. 'I couldn't understand it at all.' She agreed – his reading was incomprehensible.

Run-through of the play begins.

Antonio and Shylock: Good. Comfortable. Shylock enunciates with greater clarity.

Portia and Nerissa: Portia had complained to John she couldn't 'glow' as he'd called for. She was doing so now.

Antonio and Shylock: Nearly. The 'invention of God' speech needs to be more a shared joke between them.

Scene 4 (bustling family in Shylock's house): Much of it looks good. Controlled. But the poor Portuguese guests are still left standing while now Tubal and Abtalion sit. How can John let them be so discourteous?

Warehouse scene: It's going to be brilliant – colour, cloth, and wit. Jocelyn thinks the young men shout too much.

Love scene between Lorenzo and Jessica: Still not working, but intention is evident. John likes neither my rewrites nor how I've directed it. Perhaps he will direct it better.

Portrait scene: I'm still not happy with the way it's going. There's too much moving of heads instead of conversing while looking ahead. They should pose. And Zero doesn't know how to deliver that last line:

The Pope calls for vows of chastity, but God only ever ordained matrimony. To whom should I listen?

He's not simple enough, not wry enough.

Antonio's dinner scene: It's taking shape. Zero in control of his material. Still too much of a 'performance' out front instead of addressing the other actors on stage. He's pedantic rather than exhilarated – fatal.

The casket scene – Bassanio confesses he still hasn't got control of it. 'I feel I'm travelling alongside it and every so often I click into place, and then I'm out again. But it'll come. Just let's talk about it more.' I had told him to take his time and approach the speech absolutely confident that he was going to solve the problem of which casket contained the portrait.

What an eccentric test of love. Whose mind constructed this?
'By his choice shall you know him. '

As John watches he writhes. 'Too slow, too slow!'

It *is*. I feel it's my writing. Why can't actors be brisk and thoughtful at the same time?

John says: 'I know what I'll tell him, that he's the first comic on after the interval and he's got to get the audience back in the mood!'

'Perhaps he needs the addition of the word "now" with a clap and ringing of his hands?' *Now! What an eccentric test of love!* John grabs at that idea.

Portia remains compelling to watch but not yet there. She'll get it, though. She needs slowly to erupt.

Loggia (running away) scene: Not working. I ache to direct that one myself. Even Tubal and Abtalion aren't urgent.

Shylock letter scene: Rivka is becoming tremendous. She's found the drive, and wrings Shylock by the neck, not letting go. Her movements need greater precision. We talked about it, and she knows. I'll position her later.

Zero executed a terrible melodramatic action on his line, '*JESSICA, you've been grabbed by air!*' He clutched at his stomach as though afflicted with wind! Though the general mood of the long 'crisis' scene is good, sometimes moving. Just moments here and there not making sense.

Penultimate Belmont scene: Not quite right. Portia needs to be eyeing the young men with growing doubts.

Court scene: First half still works though it was down a bit. John has given Portia an extraordinary movement. She throws the scrolled-up bond to unroll on the floor – like a salesman demonstrating a carpet – curtseys down with it and, as she decrees the bond to be '*not sensible*', moving through her half-dozen lines, she slowly rises from her curtsey in triumph. John was anxious it needed more rehearsal and that I'd not like it. Reassured him it was *very* good. The second half of the court scene is in no shape. Could barely watch it.

The last Belmont scene: It will only work in the set, and when the song can be heard. Nerissa not delivering her lines with sufficient scorn. '*And heroes you are, sirs, true. No denying it. True, true, heroes indeed. Heroes!*' They're the last lines of the play – they carry contempt for bigotry the world, over. She hasn't the weight.

I rush with John and Jocelyn across the road to lunch at Sardi's. Bob Livingstone[126] is there. He'd wanted to transfer the London production of *Roots* in 1959. 'But,' says John, reminding me why it didn't happen, 'we couldn't bring it over because Larry Olivier was fucking Joan Plowright.' Good God! I hadn't known that. Our poor careers – what they're at the mercy of.

John asked Jocelyn for her comments on the run-through. Her main comment was that there was too much shouting.

John abruptly pointed out how hard he'd worked to get them up to any level of strength at all.

'Well you asked me and I'm telling you!'

I was perversely relieved to see he snapped at her too.

Most of my lunch was spent going through proposed trimmings, which I was to give to the cast in the afternoon. We agreed on most of them. No time to consider them all. The big ones – like cutting the character of Roderigues – we decided to leave till crisis time.

'In fact,' said John, 'we'll tell the cast that the big cuts are hanging around. Make them sit up, work harder, learn their lines ...'

The cast gathered in the space where the front seats had been

---

126 Producer.

removed. John encouraged them with his approval, and reported the play in a satisfactory state though lines were still unlearned and they hadn't found the rhythm either of the language or the play. He told them I would be announcing cuts but that if the play dragged, '... Arnold has bigger cuts standing by, very drastic, even to the extent of losing a character. None of us want that but the play is important and we may all have to make sacrifices – of favourite directing moments, favourite acting moments, favourite dialogue ...' It was a good speech, preparing for battle.

I echoed John, reiterating how thrilled I was with the state of the play, and assuring them that these snippets were not a reflection on their acting but on the excessiveness of my text. Added that as I was going to have them for two days while John was setting up in Philadelphia we could get closer to the text. I listed the cuts, and could feel the actors sighing with relief as I jumped pages in which they appeared. Jeff Horowitz, a good actor playing Usque, took the greatest brunt, and took it well. The play, he later told John, was more important. The shock for me was discovering *five* actors who feared their character could be lost: Nerissa, Abtalion, Usque, Rebecca, Roderigues. Gloria waited for me in a terrible state. Was Nerissa under threat of execution? I reassured her at once. How could she have imagined such a thing? Who would Portia have at her side? Who would have uttered the last lines?

'I had to know,' she said, 'I couldn't get through the weekend otherwise.' Poor bloody actors! What nightmares they go through.

John's next problem – a bizarre development to which Zero had alerted him. It was becoming known that Zero was not in a musical. Box office was being affected. Worse – everyone will be going to Philadelphia from New York, after which the word will spread like wildfire. Zero said, 'This sort of shit has to stop from the start.' The Shuberts had asked the press office to do something about it. They'd set up a radio interview for John in Philadelphia. What good could that do?

John left it to me to take Zero and Sir John through the new passage I'd written about the making of the bond.

Sir John's first reaction was negative. 'The bond is a ridiculous one and the only way we can get on with it is to skate over it as quickly as possible. If we raise any more doubts it'll only heighten its absurdity.'

We argued backwards and forwards getting high on Zero's chilled Muscadet. (Not Zero, he was still on his diet.) It was a good set-to. John had insisted that Sir John had never given his text a chance in the court scene; Sir John complained of his difficulty in learning the lines; Zero believed they ought to try my ideas. It was agreed. I'm grateful to Sir John, his doubts had pushed me to greater clarification, and in the process he had been compensated for 'not being the lead, the director, the manager ...'

Joined John in the basement to listen to a tape of bells.

Zero followed. He had a last thing to say. 'Look,' he said, 'I understand Sir John. Why don't you help him, cut away those lines about the fourth crusade, he doesn't want to say those things about the fucking Byzantine Empire. And also, you've got to understand, I've got all those emotional lines and he's got the dry text.'

I exploded, and read him Sir John's speech.

Justice? For the people of Venice? The people? When political power rests quite firmly in the hands of two hundred families? THAT, though he talks of principle, is what Lorenzo is impatient for, to share that power. You use the people's name for through their grievances you'll come to power. One of their grievances is what you call usury. The usurer's a Jew, and the Jew the people's favourite villain. Convenient! Easy! But usury MUST exist in our city ...

When I'd finished, Zero was amazed.

'Christ! I'd forgotten that's how they could have been said. You're right. Jesus! If only Sir John could have heard you.'

I glowed, and thought − Zero, my love, if only you could hear me render some of *your* lines!

Went off with John to Charlie's Diner to discuss the last of the trimmings and give him my notes. I'd lost a page. Wonder who'd picked it up and what it said?! John was high. Took the notes excitedly. He was off to New Jersey to do battle with the second half of the court scene. He'll come up with something brilliant, I know. Riggs and Jocelyn had been waiting half an hour for him in their car outside Sardi's. Riggs was furious.

'I'm sorry,' I apologised, 'but it's the first time I've had him – in a manner of speaking.'

'Oh I don't mind,' complained Riggs. 'It's just that I get my hands chewed off if I'm *five* minutes late, even for taking an old lady across the road.'

Lovely Italian dinner with Jocelyn at Livono's in the Village. Talked endlessly about John and the play. She has a few problems with the set wipe – it may be too narrow, the actors will be seen moving into it.

She gave me her notes from the run-through. As the actors didn't seem fully to understand what they were saying, she suggested my two days with them would be better spent sitting and reading through the text. I agreed. She observed how little time John gave to directing relationships, so concerned was he with the overall look. I think his policy is: bad actors need a good production to hide them, while actors who are good don't need him. She related something 'Georgie' [George Devine[127]] had said to John about him being marvellous on the plays which need a lot of choreography, but not to forget to do plays with two people occasionally, to keep his hand in. Shared with her my view that engaging Levene and Julie was a sacrifice John made to Zero, and that now, knowing Zero, wondered whether John had needed to. Had he felt so unsafe? Jocelyn was encouraging but as anxious as I was about Zero's performance. We both agreed he'd never get away with being so sentimental and loud in England where one would stop listening. And yet he was capable of finesse. Sooner or later John or I would need to confront him. It ought to be John – writers can always be dismissed as 'not understanding actors'. We're dining together next Monday, I'll put it to him then; also that he may have to face cutting Tubal's speech and losing Sam Levene.

Jocelyn enjoyed hearing my report of everything that had taken place. She's a rock to have on a production and I'm delighted she's doing *Love Letters*[128] for me – about which we talked briefly. She'll

---

[127] Co-founder and artistic director of the English Stage Company from which sprang, alongside Joan Littlewood's Theatre Workshop, Stratford East the now celebrated 60s revival of English theatre.

[128] Peter Hall had invited me to direct the stage adaptation of my story *Love Letters On Blue Paper* at the Cottesloe Theatre. Jocelyn first agreed to design it, then withdrew.

prepare some ideas soon.

In bed by 2.30. Awake by 7.30. Have been writing this all morning – Saturday morning. Am going off to the Met Art Gallery. Judy Rossner rang yesterday. Her new book has been well reviewed in the *New York Times*. She's delighted. Ecstatic actually. I'm halfway through the novel. Told her my initial criticisms were fading as I read on, but was having difficulty concentrating. She told me not to bother finishing it if I was under pressure.

Korby and Burt Britton took me to meet Harry and Julie Belafonte. The plan was to watch a movie Harry had produced and acted in together with Zero. Julie is a Jewish beauty, used to be a dancer with Katherine Dunham. Harry is of course Jamaican stock, very handsome, finely moulded head. Millionaires! From his records. A huge flat in West End Avenue on two floors, twenty-two rooms, full of art treasures. She collects snuff boxes in the form of shoes. He used to collect African art until they 'got through to me that I was hoarding', so he gave a lot away.

We weren't expected for food. Went for a Mexican meal and returned to watch the movie called *The Angel Levene*, based on a Malamud story. Zero is splendid. A modest, controlled perform-ance that's consistent from beginning to end. Convinces me that we can knock out his absurd excesses. I had been anxious about taking away his energy, fearing nothing would be left. Now I can tell John it's safe to tone him down – the differences between theatre and film notwithstanding.

Later in the evening

Rewrote the 'love scene' between Lorenzo and Jessica. He's written her a poem – a word game.[129]

Time flies. Realise I've been at it for nearly six hours. But at what? Have written eight cards and a letter. Talked with Dusty in Maine. Ironed shirts. Grilled some cheese and ham. Shaved and showered. Written up the diary. Paused now and then to read a poem. Six hours!

---

[129] Cut from the final text.

Later still

Took Gifford – Nerissa – out to dinner. She's bright and funny both about her role and those of the other actors. Talks about the need for a real relationship to exist between her and Portia. She's not getting on with Roberta. She, Nerissa, can't give unless Portia takes, nor take unless Portia gives.

It occurred to me – the play has many relationships between couples: Shylock and Antonio; Portia and Nerissa; Usque and da Mendes; Graziano and Lorenzo; Portia and Bassanio; Jessica and Lorenzo. The old gossips, Tubal and Abtalion. Even an embryonic one between Portia and Antonio as the play ends.

Gloria thinks Lorenzo is not warm enough with Jessica. 'See how he handles her like a Texas steer? And she has to speak through his arms? I mean her face is pulled back and her words go floating up in the air. Doesn't she know they have to see your face in order to give you a Tony award?' She has a sunny, open manner. Talked of her impecuniousness, how she 'scrounged' to survive. Used to buy for Bloomingdales, and last year collected cosmetic and perfume samples to give as Christmas presents. Her son, Adam, a child movie actor, has bronchial asthma. Informed me that Jeffrey Horowitz (Usque) and Mark Blum (Senator and ASM) are also keeping journals.

WEEK FOUR

Monday, 22 August

Greet John with news about Zero's film. He ignores my enthusiasm, and accuses me of not encouraging Zero enough. 'He comes up to me and says Arnold doesn't like what I'm doing.'

'That's actor's neurosis,' I reply. 'But now I've seen he can be exquisite and doesn't need to roll his eyes and go boom and have sinewy arms and that he knows the difference between incoherent rage and simple anger ...'

'Zero will be marvellous and great,' John reassures, 'and you mustn't worry.'

Tell John I've rewritten the love scene.

'Do it for me,' he says.

'Don't you want to read it?' I ask.

'I won't be able to react. And anyway I want to get these two moments in the court scene in order.' But he does read it, and makes no comment.

Sir John assails me with another suggestion. He wants Shylock to explain exactly why he doesn't want to break the law – the very explanation I want Shylock to withhold. I battle with him again. Tiresome.

John shapes the second part of the court scene with great simplicity, sending cold shivers down my spine. He has Portia deliver her interpretation of the 'nonsense bond' line by line; then one by one (line by line) a character stands up; the court's murmuring grows, grows, grows; by the last line people are crossing the stage excitedly until – and here is John's stroke of genius – coming as though through the smoke and rubble of an explosion Shylock moves slowly and with open arms towards Antonio, the crowd becoming silent, parting, to watch them embrace. It is a moving moment. After it my text seems redundant, an anti-climax. Needs rearranging at least.

John sends me off to Zero's room to talk through the new ending of the court scene with Sir John, Zero and Roberta. I reason it through, they read it out. Zero suggests putting it somewhere else. I say let's try it first. Give Portia the note of how to read, 'I *am not a thing of the wind*'. 'You're making it a speech about yourself whereas it's about them, the senators ...' She takes the note.

After John's beautiful staging of the second part of the court scene I rearrange the '*Fool, you!*' passage for Shylock. He now must emerge gently from that tender embrace. Zero suggests an alternative sequence of lines. He could be right. Return to watch John's inspiration continuing into the runaway scene – people in cloaks with lamps rushing about the stage.

After he gives notes from last week's run-throughs we lunch together at Sardi's. Sir John is there but we both decide we want to avoid his pedantry – though we later invite him to join us for coffee. My major note to John is a warning that the Tubal problem is looming.

I sit watching the run-through, and writing at the same time.

Zero still bumbling. Feel heavy with sleep. Think I'll go up to the balcony and doze.

Later

I did! Gave myself a neckache.

When I rejoin John he says: 'You know, there always is one run-through like this.' It was awful. As delicately as possible I tell him it's his task to give Zero a stern note about his incoherence. We sit like mischievous, mocking kids in the back row, growling and fuming and squirming and laughing, every so often throwing a line to one another the way it *should* have been done. 'Why can't they speak clearly?' John hisses. 'Why? Why? They aren't schooled in Shakespeare, that's their problem.'

We watch on, impressed now and then.

'This is the play Peter Hall turned down,' I remark.

'I'll tell them that,' he says. But doesn't.

When the run-through is over John says he'll give Zero notes in the dressing room, and advises I should stay away. He also suggests I stay away from rehearsals tomorrow morning while he goes through the Shylock/Antonio scenes. OK, though I have to come in to rehearse the new Lorenzo/Jessica scene.

The run-through hasn't left me happy.

'Your production is fine,' I tell John, 'it's just the play that's bloody awful.' He smiles. Later I say: 'I sometimes think there are many things an actor wants to do but doesn't because they're terrified of you.' *That* he didn't smile at. Made him think though.

His notes to the actors begin: 'Arnold and I knew the play was going to be a bugger, but not quite such a bugger. You *must* go home and learn the text and look for the rhythms and the *meaning*. You must ask yourself about the meaning of every line. And you must speak the lines clearly. It's no good saying you're Americans. English is your language. This text is not English or American it's Wesker, and there are special rhythms and you've got to find them. I can very easily give you the line but I'd sooner you found it yourselves. But if you *can't* I *will* ...

Spoke to Nerissa, told her she *had* to keep her eyes on Portia, like a bomber fixing the cross in the circle. She was Portia's guardian, adored her, cared for her, this was the woman who had picked her out of nowhere. 'You're too anxious about your future,' I said. 'Your eyes are roving, you're making feeble faces. Just play this play as if you're going to win the Tony Award after which you'll give up theatre.' She worried that if she came on strong it would throw Portia. Told her I'd talk to the two of them together.

Roderigues was hovering in the background but somehow never got to me.

Now realise that Sam Levene is one of those selfish actors who save it all for the first night giving nothing either to us or their fellow actors during rehearsal.

Antonio didn't push the last scene, and still had the book in his hand.

Shylock has no sense of the overall scene – he's slow when pace is called for. The first act runs one hour thirty-seven; at the right pace it could be one hour twenty-five, with a second act of one hour ten. They drag so.

Tuesday, 23 August

Zero rings about an arrangement for Dusty to visit his house in Montego Bay. He wants her to stay the night – a sculptor friend will put up the children. (Coincidence! She's just rung. She's going to the island with a party often. Still having a glorious time.)

Zero complained again about Sir John. 'If I hear another legal case-history I'll shit. But you know, he's alone, his wife's coming and that's a problem ... Tell him you'll try his ideas and then two days later say you don't think it sounds so good ... I believe you do what you're told. There's a million different ways to do something, I can do them all ways. If they tell you – you do it! What the fuck! He'll do it!'

I asked him about Belafonte.

'His problem is he freed the slaves. He fucked up the film with the love affair nonsense ...'

Rehearsals begin with tears. I notice that Susan, the woman handling publicity, looks unhappy. When I tell her so, she rushes to the back of the stalls. I go to comfort her. John had snapped at her that actors shouldn't be disturbed in the middle of rehearsal, they need the rest, breaks their concentration. 'And I hate women who cry,' she says, 'but I'm so tired of being treated like shit. I know my job, and I'm not being allowed to do it. The bookings aren't going well in Philadelphia and something has to be done about it. My mistake was to tell this to Howard [Zero's dresser and factotum] who told Zero who told John who rang the Shuberts who rang us, and I got the shit from that end also. But I was told that Howard was the best way to get through to Zero . . . And these bios [biographies of the actors] – they wrote them, they checked them, and now John insists they see the proofs, and I *know* what will happen – they'll want to change this and that, they'll see that other actors have got a line more than them, and it'll all be delayed and we won't have a programme for Philadelphia. I *know* it ...'

Why does John do it? Success should have given him security. Susan says Zero's also off-hand, rude.

Spent morning on the 'love scene' between Jessica and Lorenzo. I think it now has charm, just needs working in. Also rehearsed with them passages from their other scenes. Lorenzo asked me to read his lines in the warehouse while he read Graziano and Bassanio – something I'd like to do for all of them. He became more relaxed, made more sense – though in the run-through he tensed up again. Warned John it would be unpolished.

'But I shall be less generous and forgiving to you than you are to me,' he said.

John's work on Shylock and Antonio was productive. The run-through began with attack and went on to be very good. The stage was bristling as I wanted it. Scene 4 crackled with activity. The household was alive with vivid personalities. The '*I know, I know*' passage ending '*I love thee, old man*' was simple and poignant. And at last Antonio attacked the court scene.

Whispered to John: 'I knew that as soon as you'd directed your production you'd get around to directing my text.'

'Trouble is,' he responded, 'there's so much more of your text than of my production.'

The actor playing Moses is feeble, the play plummets when he comes on – he has such a tinny voice. Nor is Sam Levene the most sensitive performer. Jessica improves, will never fill the role, though. I identify text to cut from Tubal and Antonio's speeches. But – Zero is the central problem.

Told John that though Zero was now in control of the Renaissance speech he was performing it like Mostel not Shylock. He must calm down, find stillness, be poised like a hawk so that his anger is threatening rather than hysterical. The speech is a dangerous speech.

Jew! Jew, Jew, Jew! I hear the name around and everywhere. Your wars go wrong, the Jew must be the cause of it; your economic systems crumble, there the Jew must be; your wives get sick of you – a Jew will be an easy target for your sour frustrations. Failed university, professional blundering, self-loathing – the Jew, the Jew, the cause the Jew. And when will you cease? When, when, when will your hatreds dry up? There's nothing we can do is right. Admit it! You will have us always won't you...?

Actually I think Zero is crying out for help, to be told to stop his ridiculous actions. On a line from that speech '... *and were we to take up arms we'd be the world's marauders for sure ...*', he waves his knife, and shakes with fury like an absurd jelly. Surely John must hate such theatricality? Why doesn't he say something?

Around 11.30 in the evening Zero telephones, worried about Sir John who still doesn't know his lines. I take advantage of his call to give him notes on inflections for greater sense, and tell him how beautifully moving the '*I love thee*' sequence is. He protests a little, saying it can be done other ways. 'You can go *against* a feeling.' I tell him I know about actors who play lyrical moments lyrically when they should be playing against the text. (I should have added 'and angry moments angrily'.) But this, I told him, is one moment where he needed to float on the text. Warned him he had such a powerful presence that he could enter a stage, say nothing, and still bristle. He had to whittle away from himself not add. Bit by bit the message will sink in, I hope.

The second run-through in this week of run-throughs was good. First act ran the same time. Lost four minutes off the second act. John gave the actors excited notes, witty, speedily delivered not giving them a chance to talk back.

Main note: 'Don't talk fast, *think* fast. Think fast and talk clear. Repeat that to yourself again and again.'

Wittiest note: 'At the moment, Solomon Usque and Rebecca da Mendes are playing a Jewish version of *Brief Encounter*.'

Wednesday, 24 August

John to Portia: 'If you don't get this scene right you go straight back to the china factory.'

John to Rivka who hugs Nerissa with too loud an exclamation as Portia triumphantly finishes interpreting the bond: 'Marian! Stop acting!'

Worked one hour and a quarter with Rivka shaping her speech to Shylock, blocking it more precisely. John spent the morning cleaning up the court scene. Found time to rehearse Bassanio in his casket scene – invented new actions.

Jessica complained how mean it was that: '... The oldies are allowed to talk and answer back and waste the time for all of us – the young ones don't get a chance.' She confessed over lunch – a jovial affair with Usque, Nerissa, Bassanio and Luc Ponette, a visiting French actor – that she used '... to fuck all New York ... I was a very wild thing ...'

Third run-through. Running time: Act One – one hour thirty-four. Act Two – one hour twenty-five. Two hours fifty-nine. Under three hours. Not as good as yesterday but relieved to see Shylock's excesses in court scene have gone. Now he will be able to look dangerous instead of absurd. I want a Shylock of appetites, dignity and outrage.

Lorenzo was awful. Everything I'd done with him was lost – gabbling, flat, no drive, no vivacity. Rivka showed the results of our work together. So did Bassanio, some. And Jessica. John observed it was not as good as yesterday but was better than it has been.

'Two steps forward, one step back?'

'Exactly!' Nevertheless he seems confident. He got behind me, affectionately rubbed my shoulders, and said: 'We may not earn money to stop you writing your play on Jesus, but I promise you we'll get the play on stage as near as you've written it.'

John's notes were again general. 'You're getting better each time but you must try to find the language. It needs to be uttered clearly. The audience is not used to plays of language any more, or ideas, so we have to deliver it to them clearly and with rhythm. Not every writer writes this way. You have Tennessee Williams, we have Arnold. He writes in a special way and we must find out how.'

Went with Sara Sue Alexander[130] to see *Sly Fox* by Larry Gelbart, a 'modern' version of *Volpone*. Well directed, efficient performances, lots of funny lines. But it all depressed me. Something in the way the audience responded – with huge hilarity – that made me feel, irrationally, the audience would walk out of *my* play. Broadway was made for *Sly Fox* not for *Shylock*. There could not have been a speech longer than twelve lines.

Thursday, 25 August

John begins the day scathing poor Lorenzo.

'Where were your eyes? On the floor. Looking for the fucking truth. Being real. Well reality is not truth. You're on a stage, that's not reality. The audience can see you acting, they can see the set moving, they know they're in a theatre. They're not expecting reality. They're expecting a convention through which certain truths about reality *might* come ...' The sense if not those words exactly. And to Jessica: 'Lorenzo spent his time looking at the floor, and you fucked up the entire run-through with some Stella Adler crap ...' John glanced at my notes like Johnson making sure Boswell got it right, and underlined the words 'Stella Adler crap', adding 'CENSORED!'

Work with Bassanio on the casket scene again. It gets better but actors have difficulty doing more than one thing at a time – like being clear, emotional, swift and interesting ... in one! If they go swiftly they gabble or become monotonous or both. If they're clear they're slow. Work more on Jessica. She's showing signs of

---

[130] Friend, living in Paris, writing her thesis on the La Comédie Française.

becoming tougher, less breathy. Started off having problems with Sam Levene, imagining I would need to give him line-readings. I was firm, reassuring, and able to help both him and Abtalion. They were even grateful.

Third run-through had clarity, new things here and there, but was slow, slow! Put on four minutes in the first act (it's like weight-watching). Zero's excesses are gone but he's dull. Strolls through the play. Energy gone. He's not helped by Sir John who doesn't know his lines – John D says it's because he insists on being word perfect; if a word is lost he stumbles, unlike the American actor who will invent. I whisper to John that the warehouse scene was better. John whispers back (even though Zero was dull today): 'If we haven't got a Shylock in the scene we're in trouble.'

Sir John is tremendous in the 'Tiller' speech (and he now concedes the attack that can be got out of 'dry facts'): '*You say a man is happy with no knowledge or art ...?*

John leans over to mutter: 'He's going to steal this scene.'

A full stop in the middle of Graziano's 'Anafesto' speech holds him up. Says John to me: 'You scatter full stops like confetti. I think you should go back to Berlitz or wherever it is they teach East End Jews about English punctuation.'

The Renaissance speech is *so* draggy. No thrills. I put a revolutionary thought in John's mind. 'If Shylock uses the young Venetians in the scene as the City States instead of using the tables, then he'll be giving the works of Plato, Aristotle, and so on, to *them*.' He shudders at the thought of rethinking this scene, but as it stands it's worrying him.

During the run-through John pounces on me to consider four interesting line changes.

One in particular is worth recording.[131] John explains: 'I thought of this in bed last night. We agree Antonio is out of the picture for too long towards the end of the court scene. Therefore shouldn't he have this line?' He underlines the text he's referring to:

SHYLOCK   No books? Will you take my books? You take my life when you take my books. What nonsense now?

---

[131] The original diary explains all four, too tedious to list.

With John's suggestion it would now read:

SHYLOCK   No books? Will you take my books?
ANTONIO   You take his life when you take his books.
SHYLOCK   What nonsense now?

I agree.

A run-through in which Tubal, Jessica, Rivka, Nerissa, and Portia were up. Zero needs to pull his finger out.

John's main note was: 'The moment people see costume they think – oh, this is not for our time. You've *got* to get those words out clearly and with force and in a way that shows them this *is* a play for our time.'

Friday, 26 August

A morning of slowly going through the play, tightening, trimming. Everyone's lying around, relaxing, waiting their call. A time for close notes, line-clipping and wisecracking.

I suggest: 'How about a basket of food, a picnic to keep Nerissa occupied?'

'That will make *five* meals in this play,' John explodes. 'One day I'll write a book called *Food in Wesker*. CALORIFIC WESKER.'

Later – John turns to me, teacher-like, and asks: '*Why* have I called for a black quill pen and not a white one?'

'Because,' I answer, pupil-like, 'a white one reflects the light. Distracting.'

'Right!' He's pleased with himself. Why then is he making Antonio and Shylock move around in their set while Portia and Nerissa conduct their first Belmont scene? It steals the girls' first appearance – just as distracting.

Coffee and chat with Rivka. Tell her how good she was in yesterday's run-through, but she had dropped her level on two occasions.

She knew. 'I need Zero to *be* in that scene with me,' she explains. 'He thinks every time I stop I've dried. Or he thinks, "Oh, it's *her* moment, let her get on with it." But I need him to pick up cues quickly.'

Tell her I'll speak to John but that she ought to put it to Zero – he's a pro. He'll understand.

'There's a line I want to cut,' says Sir John to me. 'It's my most unfavourite line of yours in the play: '*It had a sense of doom which it seemed to enjoy rather more than it was anxious to warn of.*' I didn't oblige.[132]

The love scene *can* work. John barely touches it as though it were leprous, quietly tolerates it. Checked with Marian – whose taste I'm learning to trust – to see if she thought it was a valuable scene. Her reply at once was an encouraging 'yes!' She thought it gave Jessica a chance to be different.

'And,' I add, 'Lorenzo a chance to smile.' But I've made him less passionate in his kiss, which leaves Jessica the passionate one who must make the advances.

I buy lunch for Jessica, Usque and the singer (Rebecca Malka). Love being with actors during rehearsal, they're so generous and eager to make the play work.

John re-blocks the Renaissance speech, using Graziano and Bassanio as the City States.

> ... Nothing stands still! And as the dust of war and madness settles what, gentlemen, is revealed? City States! The magnificent City States of Milan, Genoa, Florence, Venice!...

Great laughter when Shylock names the City States (in the wrong order) as '*Milan, Genoa, Venice and –* ' taking Bassanio by the hand and sitting him down '*Florence!*' Later in the speech Zero can't resist saying:

> ... And where, where I ask you, could that worldly, new education come from to produce that new law, that new government? Tell me. Why, from books! Where else? And where *were* the books, Florence ... ?

Everyone convulsed, including me.

Zero points. 'Look! Even Sarcofocus-face is laughing.' He insists upon this image of me as humourless.[133]

---

[132] The line referred to a bad poem Lorenzo had become well known for. I later gave it to Shylock to display his critical powers. In the end both the poem and the line went.

[133] Because, I suppose, I can't laugh all the time at a man who works so hard at being funny.

Meanwhile the Renaissance speech seems funnier and lighter. In having Shylock use the young Venetians to represent the City States it also becomes a story to which people on stage are listening, and so the audience will listen, too. Shylock, thrillingly, uses Antonio to become Cassiodorus –

... A sweet and intellectual man. Dubious elasticity of conscience, perhaps – always able to make himself necessary to the different rulers of the country, but still. A statesman! A scholar! And for what is this man remembered most? His administrations on behalf of monarchs? Never! During his lifetime he'd succeeded in preserving through all the devastation of civil wars and foreign invasions a great collection of Greek and Roman manuscripts ...

A chair which Shylock tosses to Lorenzo becomes the printing press; a bowl of fruit, which he lobs one by one at Bassanio and Graziano, become the books –

Plato, Homer, Pindar and Aristophanes, Xenophon, Seneca, Plutarch and Sophocles, Aristotle, Lysias, Euripides, Demosthenes, Thucydides, Herodotus...

And the '*little lost spring*' becomes the last apple which, when the bells toll to call Shylock back to the Ghetto, he eats. All comes together.

John yells at me from the stage as I'm chatting with Rivka: 'Author! Put this into your journal: "He's the Rocky Mountain Goat of directors." 'I'll explain what it means later.' At which moment two other people rush – presumably to *their* journals. John adds: 'Fucking begins at forty-five with somewhat mechanical precision. Put that in your journal.'[134]

Other scenes are re-blocked: the runaway scene – Jessica is now too angry. She must find humour, replace her anger with bitterness. The second Belmont scene – Bassanio lost a lot of things he'd found, seems unable to sustain a high level of energy.

---

[134] I did, but now don't understand it!

Antonio continues to stumble over his words but in a straight run he shapes, articulates, balances his sentences completely unlike the others – cool and clear and very English. Am not certain I now know what Portia is doing. She articulates too clearly, too steadily. Needs to relax more. The ribald 'bone' joke isn't working. But the court scene is going to be explosive. When Zero leaves the stage with '*I'm so tired to men*,' it is delivered with two thousand years of Jewish history behind it.

Tubal moved centre stage for his speech. John took me to the back of the theatre where we conduct most of our private conversations, and confessed what I knew: 'This is my dilemma, and I know it's of my own making but I can't do anything about it. Here's this old man [Sam Levene] with a sense that it's all over for him. We *can't* cut his speech now, but we can snip it. In Philadelphia we …' I didn't let him finish, saying he shouldn't worry, I understood his problem and would do what he wanted, but I eagerly accepted the chance to snip away at least *some* of Tubal's lines.

John observes brilliantly: shouldn't the letter from Jessica be read by Shylock *before* Rivka comes in? Idiot! Why didn't I think of that?

Had dinner with William Roerick who invited Jocelyn, Gloria, and Donald Howarth. Donald couldn't make it, he's setting up one of his plays. Bill showed us round his small collection of Pipers, Sutherlands and a Henry Moore. Pretty apartment. A fine meal of spinach and sorrel soup with sour cream. Sea fish and shellfish kedgeree with sour onions. Apple mousse, cream, and bitter chocolate.

Joss was late because she was involved with costume fittings. Her designs will look beautiful. Gloria had originally complained about her costume. 'A huge caftan. Made me look like a cow. Urg!' Teased her, said I don't want her to look as though she's walked out of *Vogue*.

When Jocelyn and Bill moved into another room to look at some *objets d'art*, Gloria burst out that Portia was not coming through. 'She knows the text but doesn't fit the right passion to it.' Not exactly true but I know what she means – Roberta is trembling on the edge of her role but hasn't yet tumbled into it.

She's bright is Gloria. Not a great actress – perhaps this is not the role she was made for – but she is *so* full of the play and convinced she, and it, will be a success. And she communicates it. Might make a better director.

Saturday, 27 August

The first run-through with a small audience: Kate Mostel – Zero's wife; Sam Cohn – his agent; Gerry Schoenfeld – chairman of the Shubert Organisation; Marvin Krauss – production manager; Howard Rodney – Zero's dresser; Jocelyn, and Andy Phillips (lighting designer).

Both Joss and Andy thought it was up. Kate cried. Gerry was happy. Sam was ecstatic. Marvin said, crassly: 'Where did you learn so many words?' The cast thought it went well. Graziano thought it was good but now they needed more public. For my money the run-through was – adequate. Now it needs fire breathed into it. Zero is not merely ponderous from beginning to end, he has no sense of – as John puts it – 'the rack' in the court scene.

John told them: 'People are fluffing lines. You've had four weeks. In five days you face a public. I don't want *anyone* fluffing lines from now on. Your control of the play is fine. It's good. You have a confidence, but I want to say one thing. There is enormous snobbery in this country about style and the classics. If you make this play work you will be telling the managers that Americans can handle style and language. Managers think it's only the English who can do it. If you pull this off you will open up all sorts of possibilities for your colleagues. Don't bugger it up. You have an enormous responsibility.'

John went off to Philadelphia – not without a little panic. I'd planned to have everyone in on the first day, Monday, give notes explaining the play's 'scheme of things', make links for them, and – as a distraction – read from my story *The visit*. John, perhaps regretting his decision to let me take over, gave Zero and Sir John and Roberta two days off to learn lines. Roberta rebelled, feeling that two days, was too long to be away from the play. He asked me to take 'the Jews' on one day, and 'the Christians' on the next. I managed to arrange for everyone to be together from five till seven on the second day for the court scene. John need not have feared, I would never undermine his authority.

Before he left he gave me a present of an ounce of grass. When will I ever smoke it, and with whom?

WEEK FIVE

Monday, 29 August

John was still in the theatre as I arrived to conduct rehearsals. He had a cold.

'Don't you remember I always have a cold before opening night? It's a tradition.' I didn't.

First session with Portia and Nerissa. Tension as we sit round the table. They irritate each other. Nerissa makes great sense but talks too much, can't make her point succinctly. She relates the play to her own experience which is good, but her experience is not Portia's. At one point Nerissa, talking about Portia's '*gimcrack men*' speech, said something like: 'Don't you know those sort of men ...?' Portia, impatient to get on, burst with exasperation. 'I don't *have* those sorts of relationship, Gloria!' Gloria was hurt – the price of self-exposure.

Think John may be right not to become too involved in discussions with actors – they talk too much, too foolishly, to be helpful, and then discover they actually don't like each other. But - valuable changes were achieved, and much of the talking *was* helpful.

It's not easy to seal up the cracks in another man's production, which is what John wanted me to do while, presumably, wisely conserving his energy for the cracks which will appear once actors are in costume on the set.

Jessica improves, Lorenzo seems awkward in his role. Graziano is over-acting now that he has more confidence. Bassanio will be good if he can hang on to what's been agreed.

John is right – I don't always punctuate wisely. Changed full stops for commas, which allows more flow.

Nerissa bought two of my volumes in the Drama Bookshop for me to sign. She had to pay in full. I put $3.50 in one edition saying she should buy the first as a dutiful actor but I'd buy the second in appreciation of her 'services to the play'.

Julie took me to meet her mother – John Garfield's wife. He was a hero on the screen when I was a youth. Startling to be in her apartment, a penthouse on Central Park West. She is now married to Sidney Cohen, a powerful labour lawyer who also handles Zero's (and Anthony Quinn's[135]) affairs. He had defended showbiz people through the McCarthy trials. Felt I'd touched history here. They took me to eat in the Restaurant des Artistes.

We leave the day after tomorrow. No – tomorrow! It's 00.45 hours. Off to Philadelphia in the morning!

Later

03.30 hours. Can't sleep. Weather humid. Sidney Cohen's house is full of original paintings – Picasso, Matisse, Kandinsky. His grandfather was a famous Talmudist who wrote commentaries and published them. Came from Vilna. He and Julie's mother adore New York. I picked out a leather-bound book from their shelves called *The Force of Evil*. Opening it I received a jolt – it was a typed manuscript of a film, punctuated by photos of John Garfield – who was known as Big Julie. His widow now looked like a very tired woman. Must try to find out their true story from little Julie. Did he commit suicide?

Later

05.00 hours. Have been writing an article for *Playbill*. When will I sleep?

Tuesday, 30 August

Approached today's rehearsal with some apprehension – how would Zero behave? The morning went well. Amused them by reading from *The Lexicon of Musical Invective* – a book of reviews of music by great composers. '*The length* [of Beethoven's 9th Symphony] *alone will be a failing cause of complaint to those who reject*

---

135 I'd earlier written a filmscript commissioned by Quinn based on a Dostoevsky short story called 'An Unpleasant Incident' which I later made into a play – *The Wedding Feast*.

monopoly in sounds...' A good start – upstaging Zero who'd never heard of the book.

We make textural changes, I find lines to cut. It all contributes to smoothness and clarity.

Gave a note to Rebecca da Mendes about the irony in: '*I shall never understand this habit of using our misery to feed our wit.*' She's been at sea, getting little help from John D. My note was the last straw. She wept. Not an outburst, but quietly to herself. Decided at once to take her and Rivka to lunch at Sardi's. There we chatted. Marian told us how, after Saturday's run-through, '... Zero stopped me and gave me a thousand notes. I was very angry. He told me I should love him a little more. I hate actors giving each other notes. I never would and I resented it. I know what I'm doing. But when I left him I began to wonder ...' 'Did any of his notes touch you?' I asked. She said she wondered about her ferocity – on the other hand she knew it would settle. I told them how Zero had taken the youngsters aside to tell them about pronouncing their consonants. Him! Who drops words and mumbles what remains into his beard.

Asked Angela (Rebecca da Mendes) about her background. She had a very scholarly, strict father, a professor of whom she was terrified, and called 'sir' up until the day he died, aged ninety, last year. The intense days of rehearsal, the approaching opening in Philadelphia made her weepy. Tears rolled down her face. I reassured her. When we left she held my arm. She was feeling more secure. Good.

The first part of the afternoon went well, but when I came to the court scene, with the entire cast before me, I encountered my first difficult moment. I had carefully planned my notes but they were no match for Zero and Sir John who got into a gallop of piss-taking like kids playing up because teacher was away. The 'temp' was in charge – no need to take anything seriously. They were unstoppable, the fool pushed them both.

Finally I went up to Zero, put my hand on his cheek like a father to a son, and said: 'Be a good boy, let *me* have this moment. It's the only time I'll have with you...' They became quiet. I was able to continue.

'You are in your room – you know its contours. Now you have

to live in it. Fire has to be breathed on the play ... Remember, the stage is alive with vivid characters, intellectually bright, full of wit ... ' I quoted lines. 'Shylock says the ghetto rocks with argument, so should the play rock with argument. There's bustle, bustle, and more bustle: Shylock with his Portuguese guests, with his partner, with his daughter, his architect. Bassanio hustles and bustles for a loan ... Portia and Nerissa bustle to put their Belmont house in order ... Jessica and Rivka bustle around the house ... Graziano bustles in the warehouse ... There's the intellectual bustle of Shylock inventing God, telling his story of the Renaissance. Ideas crackle on the stage, and relationships. Not the obvious ones of Shylock and Antonio, but Portia and Nerissa, Shylock and Portia, Graziano and Lorenzo, Tubal and Abtalion, Portia and Antonio. Look for the echoes — Shylock's love of learning echoed by Portia's, they even mention the same books! Pay attention to the echo of lines: Antonio's '*I'm so weary of trade*' echoing Tubal's '*I am so loath to lend and deal in this trade.*' Shylock's '*I am so tired of men*' echoing Portia's '*Something in me has died struggling to grow up.*' Shylock says he loves '*the scheme of things*'. Look for 'the scheme of things' in the play. The plot, the scheme of things in the world outside the ghetto, the world of Jewish trade, the Venetian Empire, the Renaissance, the world of *autos da fé* ...'

God knows if my attempt to pull the strands together worked. We read through the court scene. I was going to run it but sensed they'd resist — Zero or Sir John would — so I packed them off home holding back the youngsters for the Belmont scenes. They were delightful. Things began to happen which hadn't happened before. Portia and Nerissa had a relationship going. Bassanio was almost perfect. Jessica lost her emotionalism in '*I sometimes think the sadness in my eyes ...*', found bitterness instead. Truer, subtler. Told her to keep still and screw up her eyes instead of opening them wide. She wasn't sure of that — but it worked. Even Lorenzo relaxed.

Nerissa bought me chocolates as a 'thank you' for signing her books, and took me for a drink after rehearsals. She's special. Everything about this venture excites her — beginning with auditions through to getting the part, the dramatic champagne reading, the buzz that followed — to be in a Dexter production means something. '*This* is Broadway. Nothing will be the same afterwards. I can only do movies from here on ...' Everything makes her eyes shine, this black girl – stout and beautiful. Not *my* choice for Nerissa. Perhaps, finally, not right for Nerissa at all. But she's determined to make it work. I urged her simply to be friends with Portia. It was important. She added: 'It's *going* to be a success. I know it!' Her childlike delight and enthusiasm are infectious, reassuring. We will all be on the bus tomorrow. 'Rebecca will sit next to you,' she said as she boarded her taxi home. She meant Rebecca Malka, beautiful and affectionate if a little intense. 'I don't compete,' she added, not realising that she'd let slip a state of affairs of which I was unaware. 'Compete for *what*?' I asked, opening her taxi door. She sped away.

At this moment, as I write, I'm a little high on lack of sleep and Jack Daniels. Must pack. Collect my wits. Go out to eat. It's 22.30 hrs.

We're off to Philadelphia in the morning: It's exciting. What are our futures?

OFF TO
PHILADELPHIA
IN THE MORNING

[1977 *continued*]

Wednesday, 31 August

Considering how little I slept the night before last, you'd think I'd have slept well last night. No. Kept waking what seemed like every hour and going to the fridge for a drink. The heat! Was I *so* anxious? Am I?

Awake at 8.30. Began slow packing. Parcelled up two bottles of Liebfraumilch and red Italian plonk, all magnum size, plus the bottle of champagne Burt gave to Dusty and me. Ironed a couple of shirts, collected and collated my papers.

Limousine arrived 11.15 to drive me to the Imperial Theatre. Waiting for the bus to leave, the air is full of excitement and chatter as though we're about to embark on a camping holiday. Boxes of props loaded on. Rebecca takes photographs. Sir John and Zero go off in limousines – separately! Absurd extravagance. They offered me one but I wanted to go in the bus. What – miss the fun? I savour every moment.

Angela (Rebecca da Mendes) was driving to Phili in a car, Roberta was going by train.

'You really *are* keeping away from the crowd, aren't you,' I had said.

She'd nodded. 'There's going to be time enough for it.'

Gloria's room-mate, Mary Ellen, brought Gloria's son, Adam, to wave us off. Marian's friend waved *her* off. As the bus eased away I reached for a bottle of Liebfraumilch. Gloria had a bottle opener. Everyone took swigs.

Chatted with Mark Blum and Jeff Horowitz – nice boy. Sam Levene tells us he started out in medicine but wanted to be a salesman; thought he ought to take classes in speech to become a better salesman, and was urged by the head of the school to become an actor. His brother didn't speak to him for five years.

Dozed a little. Julie sat by me. I like her a lot. She has a great singing voice, sings folk songs, Hebrew ones too. We sang together, Rebecca and Leib (Moses da Castelazzo) joining in. I loved it. It *was* like my old camping days in Habonim.[136]

---

136 Zionist youth organisation.

On arrival made date with Marian to visit the theatre immediately. Telephoned her room within minutes: 'I'm unpacked and there's absolutely nothing keeping me in this hotel.'

'Let's go,' she whispered swiftly, 'I'll see you in the lobby.'

We walk through the doors of the Barclay Hotel and I say to Marian, looking at my watch: 'At 2.37 p.m. Seldes and Wesker walked through the doors of the Barclay Hotel and strode out into Philadelphia's streets.' We bought some fruit on the way.

The first words John uttered as we walked into the theatre teaming with stage hands and technicians were: 'Stay away. Stay right away!' But there was a grin, somewhat drunken, on his face. He told me everything had gone wrong. They'd built the set shoddily in order to save on the budget – no ironwork frame, the cheapest wood, badly put together. Jocelyn was nearly in tears. John had got on the phone and told Bernie Jacobs that seventy-five per cent had to be rebuilt for Washington and he'd agreed. Perhaps that's the way they work – cheap set for out-of-town try-outs until the production looks as though it has a chance of success. It looked adequate to me, though when the wipe was drawn it did seem without elegance. Perhaps lighting will change that, or as I think about it perhaps it's the proportions of the theatre – the stage opening is not wide therefore the set seems bunched up. I reassured them it looked fine and they reassured me it would *be* fine. Andy (lighting designer) in generous mood. Let slip that though he didn't, as he usually does, have a stake in the show yet he was rooting for it.

Told John I'd like to report to him on my rehearsals. He said: 'Oh let me just see it!' But I insisted on five minutes. We sat down there and then.

Descended into the cellars to see the costumes which are magnificent. Blossom is the show's wardrobe mistress. He's a huge queer, efficient, maternal, very English, and of long experience. Within ten minutes he'd told me the tragedy of Mary Ure.[137] She was mad. Gentle one minute, raging the next. He gave me a hot tea with honey and whisky. Must give him my velvet shirt to clean up with his cleaning contraptions. Every stage of the process

---

[137] Actress, came to fame as Alison in *Look Back In Anger* by John Osborne, whose second wife she became. Committed suicide 1975.

excites me, and everyone is high with anticipation. Sir John and Zero arrive. The stage hands know him and begin, without being aware of it, to sing and whistle from *Fiddler*. Gloria asks me to join her for a dinner-theatre production of *Carousel*, in which an actor friend is appearing. She has to change her hotel first – she's at the Morris where, she'd been warned, 'the cockroaches stand up and defy you'. I find her there with her actor friend, Austin. She's transferring to the Drake where we help her cart her belongings; from there to the Riverside Theatre. Our seats are comps, but not for the dinner. We eat in the very good Riverside Restaurant. She's a delight to take out – everything is an experience. She feels it's the beginning of stardom – I haven't the heart to caution her.

The dinner theatre section is full of an overweight audience badly dressed in those opulent-brightly-coloured-ill-shaped-ill-matching styles with which so many Americans adorn themselves. I thought we were sitting in a transitory area before having to move off into the theatre. But no – the theatre was there, in a tiny space in front of us. Suddenly there were lights, it began, the tiny space was flooded with 'a show'. And we loved it. No great performances – except perhaps Austin who is impressive, possibly even with star potential. He sparks together with Gloria, real friends. She claims she goes everywhere to see his shows. Ate later – together with the male lead (Austin played the villain) – in a restaurant called Fiddler. Surprise!

Back at the hotel lots of messages from obscure cousins related to my Uncle Perly's wife, Betty. Obscure I think even to her.

Asked Marian Seldes to check the local bookshops for the recent Harper (two) volumes of my plays. She called on three stores. No sign of the books. Why are publishers never on the ball? She told the shops she'd call back so they'd better get hold of supplies!

Thursday, 1 September

Typed out short article for *Playbill* in the morning. Collected Dusty and children at 1.15. They looked tired but had had a marvellous time in Maine. Full of stories. Lots of tears when they left. Children ate hamburger and frites in their room, and fell asleep. Dusty and I walked the town. I wasn't enamoured of an acidy-green dress she was wearing. Bought her two others and two pairs of shoes to match. Popped into the theatre for a few seconds but she couldn't bear the strain. Had to flee after some minutes.

We returned to collect Tanya for a meal – Daniel slept on – but I insisted on calling in at the theatre on the way back. The court scene was up and in progress. It looks marvellous. The costumes are sumptuous, and Andy's lighting has done miracles. Dusty didn't want to stay but I did, the atmosphere irresistible. Scenes being talked through, staff, actors and technicians dotted around watching, listening, admiring. Dusty said Zero spoke as if he was stoned. Tanya asked if he was drunk. He will be magnificent if only he's clear.

John made no sign of hello to us. I wasn't going to wander over – he can so clearly signal 'unwelcome' at times, makes Dusty's skin creep, she says, though she declares she loves him. When he was on stage I moved in to tell Andy and Jocelyn how splendid it all looks. It will look better she said. The floor will be constructed in time for this Philadelphia opening but the super-structure won't be ready until Washington. Drove back to the hotel in the limousine hanging around for Zero and Sir John.

One o'clock call for tomorrow. A run-through. Then the first preview. What kind of an audience will it be?

At this stage – seeing the cast struggling to wear their costumes as though born to them, watching them move in their set, realising they were near to facing a public, noting concern on their faces – I felt now they and the play were pulling away from me. As the days pass it will shift more and more into John's hands. He'll need to refer to me about text, I'll have things to say, but now he will become the hub. Till this part of the process it was the two of us together shaping the meaning and action played out in front of us. Now John is to become a kind of whirling-Dervish spinning many elements into a weave. I was to become a strand – the most important perhaps but nevertheless a strand among strands – actor, set, lighting, sound, stage management. Even the producers – John had to weave them in, too.

False start to dress rehearsal. Go to John on stage to reassure him it was looking strong. He muttered: 'This is going to be the first of your plays I've fucked up.'

'It looked great last night,' I told him.

'Good of you to say so.'

'How's your cold?'

'That's the least of my problems.'

He had planned this opening: bells boom out, house lights down, two Christian valets enter from one side of stage, and bow to two Jewish valets who've entered from the other side. They position chairs and tables, the wipe slides across to reveal two silhouettes of Jessica and Lorenzo in the centre, Portia and Nerissa to the left. He didn't like it and took it away. I asked why, it had looked good. Needed more rehearsal he said.

The play proceeded. In American! Will I *always* hear my plays for the first time in a foreign language? Of course everything goes wrong. Lines are fluffed, the wipe gets stuck, Andy is still playing with the lights, John is still directing scene changes, the older actors with the exception of Marian are at low ebb. I'm used to rehearsals going to pieces at this stage but as Zero continues to stroll through the play I can't help suppress a welling and treacherous honesty seeping like hot flushes through me. My wish to be supportive loses its nerve. Before me is unfolding little as I had conceived it. Perhaps the worse moment is when Dusty and I finally face our mutual recognition that the set disappoints.[138]

'It's not elegant,' I admit.

'Exactly,' she says, sadly. We had both not dared admit it at first. The set is *so* sparse, there's nothing for Portia and Nerissa to clear away. Belmont has no clutter and so there's no atmosphere of a woman coming to make order out of chaos. In fact she's wearing a coat and a hat, looking very rich and cared for. No intimation of the tough young woman I'd created, plain, determined, no nonsense. This Portia looks elegant, even spoiled. Where's the peasant mother in her? The dotty father?

My love scene is *certainly* not working.

And yet I have faith that John will attack and shape the text,

---

[138] Jocelyn left it out of her splendid book of designs: *A Theatre Workbook* (Art Book international 1993). Photographs of this production can be found in the Methuen Student Edition (1983) of the play under the title *The Merchant*.

the emotion, the atmosphere of the play once he's mastered the technicals, and the cast have faced their first audience. At least I hope so.

I asked Jocelyn would she mind if I made two observations about the set.

'Say anything you like.'

Sweet lady. Did she not think that the top of the screed looked truncated, squared off? Below, all was elegant, but it didn't reach up – I should have said it didn't soar. She agreed, and said changes were planned. Next – I had very deliberately called for two visual elements: the dark and gloom of the Ghetto contrasting with the colour and vivacity of Venice. Between them John and Jocelyn had either abandoned the idea, or the set didn't allow for such contrasts, or it wasn't yet working.[139]

And the new air-conditioning is going to drown half the text!

We didn't get past the wipe which should have taken us into the court scene because the wipe didn't wipe! It got stuck again and again. After the sixth failed attempt John turned to Jocelyn: 'I think it's actors-out-of-costume-time, don't you?'

'I do.'

The actors were instructed to de-robe and attention was given to fixing the wipe.

It's 5.30. The actors must rest. There is time only for topping and tailing.[140] The public is due in two hours.

Sunday, 4 September

FIRST PREVIEW – FRIDAY 2 SEPTEMBER, FORREST THEATRE – WITH AN AUDIENCE

That John and the cast pulled anything off was a miracle. The actors were just thrown together for that first public performance but somehow they rose, as actors do, nerves and adrenalin shooting off in all directions, lines fluffing one after the other, technical failures like mines exploding around them. An achievement!

---

[139] My diary records no response to this.

[140] Beginnings and endings of scene to rehearse set and light changes.

In the audience were people from New York. One, a producer's wife, wept and seemed to gaze at me as though she didn't believe I existed; the other, Gloria's boyfriend, Tom the lawyer, who Gloria says couldn't stop talking about the play and my 'genius'. 'Genius' or not it's significant that even with the play in a technically under-rehearsed condition, two New Yorkers were bowled over.

But people did walk out. Susan of publicity reminded us in the interval that half the house was papered with people who'd been surprised to discover *Shylock* was not a musical. Their walking out meant nothing. On the other hand many others walked out after the court scene. Once Shylock is dismissed the play seems over, and the last Belmont scene – extraneous. Shakespeare's problem!

But much *was* depressing. I scribbled the following notes in the dark: Zero mumbling, Lorenzo gabbling, words glossed over, swallowed, Sir John fluffing, fluffing. Two androids enter in front of wipe while house lights are still on, the audience doesn't know the play is starting. They 'sssh' each other. There's applause when the lights go up on Clements and Mostel. The manuscript of the Papal Bull doesn't look old. There's no sun in Belmont. Portia strong but lost words in a panic. 'Creation-of-God' speech gets laugh and applause. Antonio fluffs a line – says to his godson, Bassanio: 'I may be your godson, Bassanio ...' There's applause after Scene 3. Clements gabbles. Antonio/Bassanio – dull. Applause after Scene 4. Lorenzo gabbles. Box of cloth left in portrait scene by mistake. CUT ARETINO QUOTE? CAN'T BLOODY HEAR

After Shylock's Renaissance speech I leaned over to a young couple who were enjoying themselves, and asked had they been able to follow it. They said no, they'd lost the thread, but they'd been held because it was Mostel. 'He's so great.' So, audiences will watch him even though they don't know what he saying. That's not good enough. Makes me angry. Such vanity to imagine just being there on stage is sufficient. Whole sections aren't made sense of. I want to cut the Deuteronomy passage in Scene 4, and the interpretation of Jessica' s letter, simply because you can't hear the words, clarity is gone, and what you *can* hear he makes no sense of.

I came away with ideas for more cuts. Bassanio's casket speech . can be trimmed. As Jocelyn says: 'Choosing the caskets is what that scene is about. To talk about plagues, and Portia's cleverness, and opening banks, is superfluous.' But she's wrong to think all character information about Usque and da Mendes is a bore. I want minor characters fleshed out, and some of their exchanges placed elsewhere. Bassanio's outburst in court can be reduced to one sentence; Shylock's parting speech can be honed. The major conflict will explode trying to get the Tubal speech cut from the court. John's view that Sam Levene, being an old pro, should be allowed to bow out gracefully from the profession is an unfair burden to place on the play, the production, and the other actors.

Ended the evening in a deli near the Barclay with Usque, Rebecca, Jessica and family.

Next morning, Saturday, up early to be taken somewhere by Fred Goldman – an old acquaintance – that turned out to be one of the memorable experiences of my life – the Barnes Collection. Stepping into that first room was a physical shock. I gasped. The Renoirs, the Cézannes, the Seurats. Cluttered, Dusty felt, but it was the very cluttering of all those riches that moved me. It began with a mere thirty-second glance, a sweep of the eyes that began as a gentle curiosity and ended in a force that sent me reeling back into the hallway where the others were chatting, having not yet entered.

On closer inspection I saw that the paintings were in fact symmetrically hung – the fleshy Renoirs, Cézanne's *Card Players*, Seurat's *The Models*, canvasses I'd only ever seen in books or as postcards. Confronting them was like confronting stars in the flesh. On closer inspection still, Fred pointed to their juxtapositioning – a calm Modigliani between two wild Soutines, for example. After the first recoil, on re-entering, I had to sit. And, sitting, I experienced what I had experienced only once before – tears. I wanted to weep as I had done in Kyoto standing before the rock garden of Ryoanji.

I crept, almost flinching, from room to room. Little Corots and Daumiers and Boschs as well. Some anonymous Flemish and German painters. At least two Van Goghs I'd *never* seen. Here was Courbet's *Woman With Doves*, Cézanne's *Fruit and Tapestry*. *What* is it that makes one want to weep? What precisely is the quality of the experience one's going through? Familiarity? Being in the presence of spirits who defied mockery? Contact with an artist's unique ability to cherish? The past always carries a quality of melancholy, but when charged with the singular passion of creativity exercised in innocence it is overwhelming. I felt I didn't mind if the play flopped, I'd seen the Barnes Collection.

5 September, Monday (continuing Saturday's events)

After the Barnes went for brunch with Jules, a distant relative who is a tax lawyer. He's the son of a cousin of Aunty Betty who is my aunt by marriage. Pleasant family atmosphere orchestrated by his wife, Bernice, one of those 'Ashkenazi' women – in a home with the personality of a modern shop window.

Fred and Linda Feirstein were in town to see the Saturday matinée. Rang and left a message with the box office that I'd see them in the interval. Jules drove us into town after brunch. We found Fred waiting in the foyer. Why? It wasn't yet the interval what had happened? No show – it had been cancelled. Zero had been taken ill.

A ZERO'S DEATH

Here's what happened. The audience had been seated. A quarter of an hour before curtain up Zero had gone pale, heart palpitations, sweating. He'd looked frightened. Marian had clutched Julie, and said: 'My God, the first time! Never in thirty-five years of performing have I been in a show that's had to be cancelled.' Zero was in hospital. The report is that it's a virus. Saturday's evening performance was cancelled, so is tonight's.

My first thought was – this has been arranged between John and Zero to give John a chance to get the show in better shape. When I put this to John later he said no, on the contrary, *he* had thought Zero had imagined that he, John, had wanted him, Zero, to fall ill. It was no prank, John assured me. It looks as though the opening night is going to become a preview and therefore we must press for the opening to be on Wednesday. Not that it will stop the New Yorkers from coming down. Dusty, though, will miss the first night.

Dusty and the Feirsteins returned to the hotel, I went to the office. Roger Stevens, one of the producers, had been looking for me. He'd driven down from Washington with his quiet wife, Christine, to see the play. Now he was at a loose end. John was in the theatre rearranging the blocking and lighting. We commiserated with one another. With a mixture of comfort and encouragement I told him what a miracle he and the cast had achieved. He brushed that aside and said, excitedly, how he had all sorts of new ideas for the blocking and ending of the play.

'Now that I know where I'm going, I don't feel so ashamed of what I've been doing to your play. And we must talk. I'm sorry we've been so distant these last days.' I understood. These were days in which the author takes a back seat. I could see his problems and thought he was tackling them in the right order of priority. With equal enthusiasm I told him I knew where cuts should come. We made a date to meet at his hotel on Sunday at 2.30. I rejoined Dusty, Fred and Linda at the Barclay.

My first instruction was for Tanya to phone the hospital and send this message to Zero:

YOUR AUTHOR NOT WISHING TO BE OUTDONE IS SICKER AND HAS BEEN FLOWN BACK TO LONDON IN THE QUEEN'S PLANE. YOUR CONTRIBUTION TO HOSPITAL FEES SHOULD BE SENT THERE.

We heard later it was never received. The American hospital, unfamiliar with English humour, imagined it was a prank.

Roger Stevens rang. I invited them over for coffee. Roger said he'd like white wine. Ordered two bottles of Pouilly Fuisse. The tall, grey-haired, distinguished looking New England gentleman, arrived with his tall, pretty, inscrutable wife. She rarely talks, and *he* mumbles so modestly into his chin that it's a strain to converse with them. He's pleasant and wily, and has been responsible for many fine productions over the years. Told him I was surprised that, given such an expensive production, the sets had been shoddily constructed, and now had to be remade. And why had there been so little time for a proper get-in? He explained how costly technicians were. But look, I replied, it's becoming even more costly – because of the pressure Zero has fallen ill. He took the point.

I asked had our new ambassador to Washington, Peter Jay,[141] been invited to the Kennedy Centre opening. If not, he ought to be. The Stephens couple launched into criticism of the clumsy way the change of ambassador had been effected. The previous one, Ramsbottom,[142] had been admired, respected, warmly liked. Washington was shocked by the way Peter Jay had been imposed upon them.

'Not,' said Roger, 'that I haven't heard anything but the highest reports of his ability, but Ramsbotham had to return three weeks later for an operation in hospital, and they could have made the change then with no problem.' I said I knew nothing of the ways of politicians but suspected there were other reasons which couldn't be announced. I'd only met Callaghan a couple of times but felt sure both Jay and his wife would be interested to attend the first night of a British play. Roger divulged that he was trying to get President Carter along, and would be obliged if I kept that to myself. It seems not only does he come to first nights, he also reads texts of plays.

They drove back to Washington. Dusty and the children were picked up by Austin for *Carousel* and dinner. Fred, Linda, and I ate

---

[141] Recently appointed by his father-in-law, James Callaghan, the British prime minister.

[142] Sir Peter Edward Ramsbottom, Ambassador to Washington 1974 to 1977.

at the deli on the corner. They had come specially this early because Fred felt it to be a time he could be most useful. Wasted. We talked of this and that but I was anxious to get to the theatre by 8.30 to see what was happening.

A curious sight: I sat listing the cuts I wanted to make, Jocelyn was re-drawing the set, John was re-blocking the change-overs, Andy was re-lighting. And Marvin Krauss, the production manager, was presumably re-planning. A hive of activity in the stalls.

Rosie runs the bar and Jewish restaurant across the alley from the stage door. She looks like Mama Dinken who runs the Kosher restaurant in Tokyo. And Mama Dinken looks like all our Jewish aunts who in turn look like Sophie Tucker.[143] Andy loves sitting in the corner of Rosie's bar, drinking whisky. Jocelyn says she'd have gone mad without Rosie to come to. During the first preview Dusty and John had a drink there together. He introduced her to Rosie as 'the woman I've known for twenty-five years'. John confided in her his problems with Sam Levene, and how he couldn't get rid of the old man of the theatre, and how he knew that Arnold would come up with his own cuts in the play.

In the evening a group of us found ourselves together eating in the deli across from the Berkeley: Gloria, her mother, her son and her boyfriend, together with Jeff, Marian, Angela and Rebecca. Austin turned up later with my family. A sense of crisis was drawing us all together in a huddle for comfort. Crisis, adventure, kids on holiday. The mood was warm, tense, verging on crazed. Gloria has a food problem – when she's hungry she can't wait to eat. Jeff, too, was eating huge quantities. I sat squeezed up against Marian with Gloria's voice teacher squeezed up against me. Facing us were Rebecca, Jeff and Angela. In that state we sat, ate, and began to laugh with growing hysterics as we went over the evening's rehearsal.

There had been two glorious moments of utter confusion. Can they be recreated? First the portrait scene. John had re-staged it. It now takes place on the other, prompt, side of the stage. The new position threw Marian (Rivka) who now posed with her body

---

143 Real name Sophia Abuza. Russian-born American vaudeville artiste, famed for singing 'My Yiddishe Mamma'.

facing inwards, towards stage right, and her head over her left shoulder facing towards the audience. The portrait showed her facing in the other direction. John told her to go over to the portrait in order to see which way she *should* be facing. Julie carried on with her text, Leib carried on painting, the androids rehearsed their moves, the lighting went up and down and Marian moved to look at the portrait. She took it in, returned to her pose, and fell at once into the same incorrect stance. John again invited her to look at the portrait. This time he took her there and demonstrated the direction her head should face. Jessica talked on, Moses painted on, the lights went up and down and Rivka returned to take up the same incorrect pose. She simply couldn't make her head do what her eyes saw. A third time John told her to walk over to the portrait but this time, to our amazement, we saw that she hobbled there. She had been under the impression that John had given her a *stage* direction to walk over in character! This had made Julie angry. 'Is he making you walk around during my scene?'

Squeezed together in the deli we were reduced to fits of laughter reliving the moment over corned-beef sandwiches, bagel and lox.

The other moment – which had Sir John in tearful fits under his seat – was in the big Scene 4 where Leib was playing Abtalion while Abtalion, Joe Leon, was getting ready to stand in for Shylock. Jessica entered and delivered her lines while Leib slowly turned the pages to look for his place. Impatient, she couldn't wait, and said his lines too, and then Tubal's lines at which point John cried out, 'Bring on the Portuguese' – who entered and delivered their lines, followed by Jessica delivering her lines and *again* Abtalion's lines while Leib continued slowly to turn, turn, turn the pages, and John kept moving on and on to the end of the scene, with Leib only ever having turned the pages slowly, slowly, and uttering not one of Abtalion's lines.

Next day, Sunday, we were brunched by another part of the family, all obese, in a house of furniture that was not only the height of 'Jewish baronial' but was also covered in plastic – a habit I despise. Jules, the first cousin we'd brunched with, picked us up, drove Dusty and Daniel to a baseball game while I took Tanya to join Gloria's family – they were going on to the *Good Ship Lollipop* and then to other sights. I went to my meeting with John in the Benjamin Franklin Hotel.

Two unmade single beds, some champagne, and an excited John. I could see I had to establish a determined voice at once. 'I think we've got a marvellous production on our hands but we've got a lot of hard talking to do.' That way he knew I hadn't only come to announce ideas for cuts.

'Yes we have, dear. And let me say straightaway it's all my fault. Your play arrived on my lap full of all the things which for one reason or another – my operas and things – I'd been reading about, and as a result I led you into the worse excesses: indulgence in historic detail under the impression that "they" should know what "we" know. I not only encouraged you, I fed you more of the same.'

Not quite like that. They were there because the play was about a man who loved the historic scheme of things, and because the details were fascinating in their own right; also because the play was about characters who were themselves affected by, and articulate about, the past and the socio-economic world in which they lived. If you say such details are boring you're saying you don't like people who converse at that level. Which of course is true for many theatregoers.

Anyway, that was only a shot across the bows. We got down to the cuts. I put question marks beside a number of John's suggestions for single-line cuts. He proposed we looked for what we could immediately agree upon and put others aside to discuss at the end. Most were agreed upon at once, John delighting at each of my suggestions, especially cutting Bassanio's onslaught in court. 'Oh, what a clever North London Jew I have for a writer.'

When we came to the Shylock cuts it gave me a chance to say how boring and vain I found much of Zero's delivery, and that I was cutting simply because he didn't articulate with clarity. John said he planned to tackle him. 'I've understood what you've been saying about "he's waiting to be directed" and I think you're right. Let's get over this crisis first.'

Tubal's speech was the problem. John conceded it had been 'an awful mistake' to bring it back but that now it couldn't be changed. Told him I didn't want him to feel pressured but I didn't think an audience would come to hear Sam. If they came it would be for Zero. Sam may have his fans but they were hardly likely to be *Shylock*-type fans! Losing him would not damage the show whereas his presence with an unnecessary speech was unfair to players and play. John agreed only that the play was important not the players. He asked that we wait to see how effective the cuts were. The Levene/Tubal affair could be thought about later.

I went into detail about Zero's performance – inaudibility, lack of comprehension, the cursory way he delivered important text ... John took the points. I talked also about the first Belmont scene – where was the activity, the bustle? 'I can't see the peasant mother in Portia nor the dotty philosopher-father.'

He hit back by attacking the warehouse love scene, not without justification. It was by now embarrassing me.

'It doesn't belong there,' he argued. 'It's not a love scene, and it anticipates their break-up. How about beginning the Logetta (runaway) scene with Tubal and Abtalion, then bring on the Jessica they've told us has run away, and have your love scene there?'

I could see the point of rearranging the order but couldn't see how it was possible to put a love scene in the middle of an angst-ridden runaway scene. John attempted to explain but nothing made sense. Nevertheless, I told him, I'd apply myself to it. 'You've got me in the position you want – what's there I don't like, what could be there I'd *like* to write!'[144]

It was an exhilarating exchange lasting three hours. Left for the theatre to have my hair cut by Carol – hairdresser to the company. Met Dusty and Daniel at the hotel. They'd had a marvellous time at the ball game. Joined up with Tanya, Gloria, and her family at the Drake. Outside which were two horse-and-carriages which took us to Old Bookbinders, the fish restaurant, where we had a not very good meal that cost a lot of money. Dessert – unnecessarily large – and coffee at Fiddlers.

Today, Monday, begins with me giving the cast their cuts. They'd all been anxious about them. John announces very firmly: 'As it's

---

[144] It was only later that I understood what John was wanting and could see a way of doing it.

Arnold's play he'll give the cuts. I'd like no comments on them, neither complaints nor "thank goodness that's gone". When they're done you'll go downstairs and run them in, and then I'll want to start on scene ...' I forget which one. John spent the day making scene changes throughout. Cuts and changes – a lot for an anxious cast to absorb.

The children have been occupied with bowling, cinema, eating. We spent the evening with friends. There's an eeriness about the days. Zero's absence is felt. We're all worried he'll have a lot of catching up to do.

Tuesday, 6 September

The day we should have opened. Dusty leaves with the children to spend the day in Safari. I linger to write up the journal, then walk to the theatre buying Fanny May chocolates on the way for – I don't always know who I buy what for, but an occasion arises sooner or later for which a present is needed. I knew only that I bought a bottle of Sancerre for Carol who'd given me the haircut.

Julie is at the stage door reading a letter. She has a special 'in' with Zero, and tells me no one could see him but she's sent vast amounts of flowers. Four telegrams await me – from family and friends.

I seek information about Zero's condition from John in the stalls. It's only a virus, he tells me. Doctors think Zero will be able to work next Monday. John plans to spend the week cleaning up the Belmont and court scenes. He'll work with Zee on Sunday in his hotel, give him cuts and notes, run him into the play on Monday afternoon, preview Monday night, clean up Tuesday afternoon, open to press Tuesday night – a week late.

He asks: 'How's your love scene?' I tell him I'm working myself up to think about it. He puts pressure on me. 'Think about beginning Act II, Scene 2 with Tubal and Abtalion in the Logetta. In that way you get all your information about the ghetto being taxed, Jessica's elopement, and Antonio's sunken ships out of the way, leaving the love scene possible for a runaway daughter. But make it a love scene without intellect, without games about words ... You've got some strange tune playing in your head which means God knows what.'

John said he was going to take a sleeping pill tonight.

'Aren't you sleeping?'

'Good Lor, no! A couple of hours here and there, but then I wake up with ideas for the production. My hotel room is littered with yellow pads on which I've written my midnight ideas, and which, when I wake up next morning, seem utter gibberish ....'

The cast assemble. He tells them the plans, and sends Usque and Rebecca over to me because I've worked out a breakdown of their lines. Actually, it's not my idea. Usque came to me yesterday with the suggestion that if they divided their text it would correspond to what Rebecca says about '*I know his rhythms* ...' Makes their relationship sweeter, the passage lighter.

In the wings lurk Nerissa, Jessica, Portia, Bassanio and Lorenzo waiting to rehearse their scene.

John had told Bassanio not to open his shirt. 'This play is not about your tits!'

'I got the idea from you,' Bassanio now tells me. Nerissa cheekily asks if the box of chocolates in my hands are for her – she's not well. I say, of course. Jessica presses me about the warehouse love scene, is it gone? She's relieved to hear I'm about to rewrite and reset it.

I'm writing this in Rosie's bar where I've eaten chopped liver, gefulte fish, matzos, and drunk two glasses of wine. Charlie, the chief prop man comes in, buys me another glass of white wine, tells me my words grip him when Zero and Clements handle them; spoken by others they seem 'over-long ... and I've handled twenty-five shows!' He's probably right. Makes me think one should *never* work with stars alongside lesser performers, better to find a solid cast evenly matched.

Rosie has watched me writing this, and offers me another glass on the house. 'You're working so hard.'

I think I may have cracked the problem of the Jessica/Lorenzo love scene: a brief, passionate pause in the heat of flight from home. It lowers Jessica's temperature from anger to anxiousness leaving room for real anger in the penultimate Belmont scene.

Later

Yes, yes! I think I've made it work. Typed it in the office, and go in search of John who's solving the problem of Shylock's move from the court to Belmont. Before the court scene ends, at the moment of Shylock's last words: '*My appetites are dying, dear friend, for anything in this world. I am so tired of men...*', we hear the sad Sephardic song which carries us over into the last scene where, suddenly, four servants appear hurling a huge picnic cloth, billowing, over the stage. Other servants appear with platters of food. Now there can't be any mistaking that Shylock's last words are ending the play.

John has ordered a huge boar's head and lots of game. 'My biggest and, I trust, the last Wesker meal ever! Have you got a love-scene for me?'

'I have.'

'You want me to read it now?'

'Yes.'

'Oh, he's clever. Coughs up a love-scene at a twist.' He goes off to read it.

LORENZO	You're trembling
JESSICA	I'm frightened and I'm ashamed so I'm trembling.
LORENZO	Oh, those eyes. Those sad, sad, eyes.
JESSICA	Forget my eyes, Lorenzo, and tell me what is to happen next.
LORENZO	First be calm, if for no other reason than not to command the staring of others.
JESSICA	I've spent so much, you see. It's cost so much.
LORENZO	I know, I know.
JESSICA	The decision to break away – you can't imagine. To be cut off.
LORENZO	I know.
JESSICA	So I'm drained. I'll be all right soon but for the next hours my reason is numb and you must do it all.
LORENZO	Trust me.
JESSICA	Kiss me.
	(He hesitates.)
	All these months of meetings and you've not kissed me.

(He hesitates again.)

Haven't you kissed a woman before?

LORENZO A hand, a cheek.

JESSICA Not lips?

LORENZO Not lips.

JESSICA Then mine will be for first for you.

LORENZO And mine?

JESSICA Will be the first for me.

(They kiss.)

Oh, I have known that kiss all my life.

LORENZO (*Lifting and whirling her round*) Now, I would like to become small, nail your name, proclaim you!

JESSICA And say this is mine, and this, and here I've been before, and that skin, that smell, that touch so belongs, belongs, belongs that surely I was born the twin to it.

LORENZO Nail your name and claim your strength.

John thinks it almost works. 'The first part is great, pure Hemingway ...' He enjoys its monosyllabic brevity '... *a hand, a cheek* ...' 'But this section, '*Now I would like to become small*', may raise laughs and is – er – gluttonous.' Having the line pointed out, it worries me too. Nor is he enamoured of '*Oh, I have known that kiss all my life.*' That, however, is not one I'll relinquish – it's a virgin's line and I love it. Those aside, the new lines and the eradication of Jessica's temper makes the scene thrilling. John's instincts were again sound, productive.

Went back to Rosie's. John and Brent eating at one table, others of the cast scattered around. Ponder which new line can replace '*Now I would like to become small.*' Decide simply to cut it and add '*claim you*'. '*Now I would like to nail your name, proclaim you, claim you* ...' I take it back to John who's worried by '*nail your name*'. I point out its echo of Luther nailing his ninety-five propositions to the door of All Saints Church in Wittenberg.

Wednesday, 7 September

Couldn't sleep last night. Both Dusty and I woke around the same time. I had a pain in my chest. Partly nerves, partly heat. Continued reading Judith Rossner's new book.

Gave Jessica and Lorenzo their new love scene. They didn't respond too warmly. I talked them through meaning and intention, and we ran it a few times till they became familiar with it. Julie asked could she say only one *belong* instead of the three. Explained it was part of her ecstasy. Everett asked could he drop saying he's kissed *cheeks, hands but not lips*, could he act it instead? Explained the words contributed to the music of the scene.

Dusty and children joined me at Rosie's who laid out a light lunch of smoked salmon, mixed fish, bagels and cheese ON THE HOUSE. So generous. The children went shopping. Dusty and I visited the Philadelphia art gallery.

John had said he would be ready to rehearse the love scene at about 3.30. 'Am I going to have to do it with you around?' he asked.

'I'll go if you want, but I thought I ought to be around in case the lines don't work and need changing.'

'You're right of course. I'm just jittery. I'll just have to suffer it.'

At 3.30 we were back. Dusty asked Sir John if he wanted any messages taken to London. He gave her one. I watched the new version of the warehouse scene. The bales of cloth had gone!

John said: 'If you can cut the decoration out of your play I can cut it out of my production.'

'They were colourful," I said, 'I miss them.'

'Well you oughtn't to! No one could concentrate on the text while all that was going on. I expected you to tell me that five days ago.'

'*I* could concentrate on it, and I thought the joy of throwing the cloth around fitted in very well with what was being said on stage.'

'Well that tells me a lot about your text!'

'Did you *ask* anybody if they couldn't concentrate?'

'*I* couldn't concentrate. I don't have to ask other people.'

Was he right? I'm not certain. With absolutely nothing going on in the warehouse you don't really know it *is* a warehouse. The young Venetians simply stand around and deliver their lines. Is there any atmosphere? Certainly none as there was in Stockholm with barrels of wine and a Graziano measuring them. I loved our Graziano playing around with cloth, throwing lengths through the air, a display from which Bassanio could choose his wedding clothes – a real production number. And the text was not so difficult that it required intense concentration.

On the other hand John's made the first Belmont scene exactly as I imagined it – more ruins, and energetic activity from the girls. John has even picked up my suggestion (which he doesn't know, and I won't tell him, is from the Stockholm production) of them having a picnic. Unfortunately there's no time to do the love scene; postponed till the evening. Inform lucky John he'll now have his chance to direct it without my presence because I'm taking the family to the airport.

Dusty has her hair cut and washed in a new style which we all think makes her look younger. They eat in the deli on the corner – a last Philadelphia meal. For me just coffee. I've lost my slim line and am determined to stop eating. They speak to Zero on the phone, say their goodbyes, wish him better. He calls me a cheapskate for not paying the extra fare to keep them here. I can't. Now that the first night has been postponed a week till next Tuesday – the doctors won't allow Zee to start work until Friday – it would cost too much. Besides, Tanya and Daniel must get back to school.

Return to find John rehearsing the last Belmont scene. That too is radically changed. He's not only laid on a huge sumptuous meal of sixteen dishes, he's got this extraordinary parade of servants gliding slowly backwards and forwards carrying laden platters to the picnic, their slow motion walk contrasting with the fast moving, fast speaking trio of Bassanio, Lorenzo and Graziano. In the background the servant sings her sad Sephardic song. Antonio, Jessica, Portia stand, isolated figures in the archways, their backs to us. The effect is both curious and compelling.

'In your Jesus play,' exclaims John, 'there will be no food at all!' He paused. 'Oh my God! The last supper. I'd forgotten. And the wedding at Gethsemene. Of course – another Jewish story, food all over the place! I just can't think of a title for that book on food in your plays.'

'I'm more interested in a book on "Wesker's Women",' I tell him.

He's in good spirits.

Zero's illness is a mixed blessing. It's given John time to pull his production together but it has slightly demoralised the company who were raring to go and who now, left with long periods of inactivity, are prey to advising one another on their performances, – what John calls 'dressing-room direction'.

Two incidents disturb me.

During the session announcing cuts, Sam Levene said, sulkily: 'I had a dozen lines. Now you've cut three I only need phone in the rest.' Bitter and funny, but in front of the cast – unforgivable, especially after John had asked for no comments. Since then he's not responded to my day's greetings, though Julie tells me he's surly like that with everyone.

The other was Roberta's request for a talk. We walked around last Monday – Labour Day – for a long while before we found a quiet Chinese restaurant where we talked for two hours. She began by asking me to explain the nature of the bond. It seemed to me a strange request after so many weeks of rehearsal. My explanations developed into a short history of the plight of medieval Jewry and how the Venetians Jews came to live in the ghetto. Only slowly as she questioned more did it dawn on me what was going on inside her. I began to hear the voice of Sir John. She couldn't understand why Shylock insisted upon his pound of flesh, why wasn't he more merciful. 'Is his race more important than a man's life?' At one point she was on the verge of tears saying: 'Antonio is becoming the hero of this play, and it ought to be Shylock.' I was touched by her distress.

Later I phone Zee to find out if he's now rested.

'I'm so rested I'm like a plum pudding,' he says. The virus has been isolated and identified as one originating from a district in New York which sounded like Cocksucking. The Shubert Mafia came from the big city to visit him and, presumably, to gauge if he was dying or not and if a replacement was imminent. John had already phoned Sir Larry'[145] to see if he was free. He wasn't. John was building a list of others like Peter O'Toole and George C. Scott. Julie tells me that if it had been any other play the Shuberts

---

[145] Sir Laurence Olivier

would have cut their losses and abandoned it by now. 'It's only because they know they've got something special on their hands.'

Thursday, 8 September – 8.30p.m.
room 1725, Barclay Hotel

An hour and a half ago, at 7 o'clock, I had been in the wings watching the actors go on and off, wisecracking with them, enjoying the backstage atmosphere.

John had seen me, and called me down. 'Zero's been unconscious since six,' he whispered with his arm around me; 'it's his heart. Marvin's over there with him now.' I sat in the stalls behind Andy, and in a numbed state watched John continue beautifully shaping the court scene. Every so often he'd pause, and the three of us would toss replacement names in the air. Peter O'Toole still had drinking problems, Andy said. Topol can't act, said John. Edward G. Robinson and Peter Finch are dead, I lamented. The show had to go on.

Half an hour later, at 7.30, as John was taking the court scene to greater and greater heights, Marvin Krauss, the general manager, walked down the aisle to tell us that Zero's heart had stopped at 6 o'clock. He's surrounded by doctors but they couldn't get the pacemaker to resuscitate. I knelt in the aisle by John, we held each other's arm. Before us, on the stage, a group of unsuspecting actors were rehearsing my play.

'This can't continue,' John said, referring to the actors acting on stage. 'What do I tell them?'

'That Zero's had a heart attack,' said Marvin, 'and that we'll call them together tomorrow at one, and let them know what's happening.' John braced himself, took a cigarette, went on stage, told everyone to sit, and very swiftly announced what had happened. Marian and Julie at once dropped their faces in their hands. The others just sat, stunned. John sent Marian to Rosie's to look after Sam Levene who had been with Zero at 6 o'clock when it happened, and was now at the bar, drinking. One by one the actors left the stage, except Sir John who lingered, lost, sad and shattered. John D was numb, close to tears.

We floated around looking at each other, not knowing what to say or do. He was concerned for me and the play, I was concerned for him. Truth was – the air of helplessness was made up of many things. I felt helpless about poor Zero – we couldn't go to him, be by him, or even stand in the corridor outside his room; I felt helpless about John who'd put eighteen months' work and a whole lot of genius into this production; and about the company who had gone to pieces and were in need of what I was helpless to give them. I felt helpless about my play, in fact about all my plays which I now felt were jinxed. I remembered my mother dying on the first night of *Shylock* while we were in Stockholm; my father dying the night before the first night of *The Kitchen*; Kennedy assassinated while *Chips With Everything* was on Broadway. I recalled the fate of *The Journalists* which the actors of the Royal Shakespeare Company – 1971/2 season – had refused to perform, and a heatwave driving London audiences away from *Roots* which had made it to Shaftesbury Avenue ...

And they couldn't find Kate Mostel.

Sir John invited John D to sit with him in his hotel for a drink. He declined. I was about to leave the theatre, John called me back. He wanted to assure me we'd get the play on somehow.

Had to stop writing. Two phone calls just came through – from 'cousin' Bernice, and Ben Alexander. They've heard. It has just been flashed through on TV. Zero is dead.

My play has killed him. He had dieted for it, was under pressure for it, and – silly bugger – he'd overdone it. Oh Zero, Zero, Zero, now I'm crying for you. You were so rested you were like a plum pudding.

What ironies there are. Last night I found in a bookshop a copy of Bill Fishman's book *East-End Jewish Radicals* and bought it for him. It was to be his coming-out-of hospital–today present. My inscription was *Where this story ends my family's story begins. Thank you for coming out alive.* And the telegrams wishing me luck had begun to trickle in.

As I left the theatre I'd seen Brent in tears. I bought two bottles of white wine which I thought I'd need to see me through the night. Messages awaited me. One from Gloria *'who is at the Drake Hotel if you need her'.* The phone began ringing, Rebecca – to see if I was all right or needed company. Told her I didn't want to impose myself on the cast who would feel they had to console me. Fred Feirnstein had rung before from New York to find out how things were, and knew immediately from my voice that something was wrong. Now he rang again – he'd heard the news. Which made me think – has Kate? Were they able to find her? Jesus! they couldn't have announced it without letting Kate know first. I must send a telegram.

What about the rest of the cast? Should I leave them to lick their wounds with each other, or gather them together here in my room? To do what? To say what? Yet what are they saying to one another now? What are they doing now?

Paused.

Gloria came in to tell me people have gathered in Sir John's room. Minutes later Marian rang down to say I *must* come up to them. Gloria's gone ahead with the two bottles of wine.

Mel Albaum has just phoned, it's Fran's birthday. Family and friends are all gathered for it, and they've heard. Mel tells me his son, Evan, had a dream last night – that Zero had died.

Friday, 9 September

The papers carry the headlines. The story pieces together.

I went up last night to Sir John's suite, 11c. Marian had come to bring me up imagining that unless she came I'd not move. Gloria was there, Rebecca, Jocelyn, Blossom and his assistant. Jeff and Julie joined us later. Sam had been with Zero, had brought him some books to read. Zero had said he couldn't cope with those so Sam asked would he like him to go out and buy a *Hustler*? Zero then asked him to call a nurse because he was feeling dizzy. He fell. Sam tried to steer the fall away from a table but Zero was unconscious. Doctors rushed in, attempted to massage the heart, then opened him up to insert a pacemaker. Nothing worked. Within an hour he was considered dead.

In Sir John's room we talked, slowly at first, then relaxing into humour.

Roger Stevens rang. I told him we had to go on. 'I know it's your money but there's already been a lot invested, including a great deal of talent and time. It's a great company and John's production is beautiful ...' He was very much in agreement.

Jocelyn fell asleep on the couch. Sir John told stories about performing in the war. He'd laid on smoked-salmon sandwiches and red wine. Later we went to the deli on the corner. Riggs, Roberta and Bill Roerick had gone to church.

When it was suggested, Riggs had asked – but which church?

'Where the real God is!' said Roberta. So they walked for hours.

'But the only place open was a synagogue,' reported Riggs, adding, 'You see, we know the Messiah came so we lock the doors and keep people out, while the Jews, who are still waiting, keep their door open, in case.' Not true of course, except this synagogue's door does seem to have been left open. Julie and Jeff had also found a synagogue.

Now back in the deli were a bewildered trio of Bassanio, Lorenzo and Roderigues. I told them we were not planning to abandon the play. Related my conversation with Roger Stevens. They were cheered. At Julie's suggestion I ate a rice pudding – comfort food. She told Zero-jokes. The radio flashed through tunes from *Fiddler*, followed by the news item of his death.

Blossom whispered angrily to me (and with British determination): 'They shouldn't be allowed to indulge themselves in the drama of it.' He was talking about the actors. 'They should get up there and give a fucking performance ...'

I told him they had to mourn, it *was* a shock. But I knew what he meant.

At 3.30 in the morning I phoned Dusty who already knew. Mike Kustow had heard it on the 7 a.m. news (2 a.m. here) and had phoned Bishops Road. LJ had brought up the news to her. What could be said? I'd phone again when the situation became clear. Back in the hotel more condolence calls from friends. It was like a death in the family. Got trapped on the phone by a local reporter.

But I woke up in fighting spirit, and felt anxious to be with John D who, I was certain, was also in a determined frame of mind. The show – despite the corniness of repeating it – had to go on. Lists were being drawn up, names discussed. I arrived in the office to hear Marvin Krauss saying the boys in New York were all for keeping the show on. Roger Stevens was prepared to open in Washington with Joe Leon who, in yesterday's run-through with the book in his hand, was giving a good, clear reading of the text. God (and Zero) forgive me but at last I could hear my lines! Spoke to John on the phone. He *was* in determined mood. 'The play is a good play, and can take it.' I told him his production could also take it. We discussed names. Howard da Silva, he thought, had no humour. I pressed the idea of Barnard Hughes because Gloria, Marvin and Roberta all thought so highly of him – we need a great actor, not a star. John's production and the play will bring in the audience, and a good actor would be *made* a star. John was inclined to Jack Gifford – a good actor but, it seemed to me, with too thin a voice. I'd seen him in *Sly Fox*. A character. 'I'd go for the comedian rather than the tragedian,' John said.

His plan was to give the cast twenty-four hours rest – 'I couldn't rehearse them today, I just couldn't' – then slowly to get Joe Leon geared into the role. 'I think I can give him a few tricks to pull him up.' Then, if we could find the right actor within forty-eight hours he could be ready for the second week in Washington.

Sam Levene, 'suffering from permanent constipation' as Marvin describes him, held court at Rosie's bar last night where, I was told, Julie had hysterics. Jeff controlled her, and took charge, while Sam told funny stories about Zee and the war, criticised the play, and bad-mouthed the cast.

A television crew is on stage filming the set. Reporters are around. I'm in the theatre's office writing this. Phones ring. A photographer shoots the telephone operator answering calls. Rosie is being interviewed on TV. I'm avoiding them all. There's to be no ceremony. The telegram I sent Katie is to be my only token of grief.

To add to problems John has an opera to direct at the Met.

Later

It's been a day of phone calls with New York, and of waiting around. John talks to the first gathering of cast and technicians in the theatre. His lack of social graces stands him in good stead; he has no arsenal of emotional tricks, and can only be brief and direct, and thus, paradoxically, packed with emotion.

'We're all stunned. I'm not going to talk about him. I know how you feel and you know how I feel – I'd been talking about productions of *Falstaff* and *Galileo* with him, so you can tell from that. Well, we've not got Shakespeare or Brecht but we've got Wesker and, as the Shuberts have said, the greatest monument to Zero would be to get this play on. And that's what the plans are about. So I only want to put practical things to you. I have certain problems surrounding the Met, and our own logistics have to be worked out – such as where we rehearse and who we open with. I'd like us to go straight on and take Joe into Washington, and then see where we are. But I'm going to ask you to hang around till a call comes through. Might be an hour or so ...'

Everyone was dispersed and requested to be back by 5.30. John told Joe he'd better get to work at once. Joe sat in the stalls stunned and with tears in his eyes. John cancelled his production of *Eugene Onegin* at the Met – '... something I've never done before'. He was also waiting for news about a strike at the Met which might mean he didn't have *any* productions, not even *Rigoletto*. And, if the strike was called off, he'd have to rehearse that for six days in the evenings while doing *Shylock*!

John and I got on to the phones for a four-way conversation with Sam Cohn and Bernie Jacobs from New York. It was most odd. No one spoke till I said: 'John, you start talking.' He did, and said he wanted to finish the production with Joe Leon so that we could look at the play and see what we had, then replace him with Jack Gifford. Sam said Gifford had difficulty learning lines. John said Gifford or someone else, it didn't matter, we'd go into that later. The question was were they going to support the production? They said there was no question of that, but Roger Stevens – who was on his way to California – had to be spoken to, and they needed more time to think.

John had informed me that Sir John had talked about being released – apparently it's in his contract that he was to play alongside Zero. He was also unhappy about certain lines which he wanted cut. I'd already agreed with John to cut Roderigues which meant that an outburst of Shylock's would go, too. With Sam

Levene leaving the cast (he simply announced it) we could lose the Tubal speech in the courtroom. Together with Roderigues cuts we were now down to size.

I thought Clements' threat to withdraw depending on who was the new Shylock was shitty. And so – no more cuts. That was it. John was agreed. 'Good! That gives me a firm base. But I think he'll get good reviews in Washington, and he'll want to stay on.'

Despite John's upbeat determination I felt oppressed with a sense that the show was going to pieces. Little sleep didn't help. I returned to the hotel to find my pigeonhole full of telegrams and messages. Rang Dusty to tell her the show was going ahead. My voice cracked, delayed reaction setting in. I wanted to weep.

Dusty said she was sorry not to be there with me, and reported lots of phone calls. The Kustows had been round, lists – corresponding to ours – had been drawn up: George C. Scott, Topol, Alan Arkin, Guinness, Herschel Bernardi, Adler, Carnovsky ... But we didn't want to have actors who'd followed Zee into *Fiddler*. I reported the state of play, and said I'd ring back on Monday. Walked back to the theatre with Marian, both of us low.

Emotional times. John was on the phone to NY. A fierce conversation was ensuing. They wanted to postpone a decision, John wanted them to commit themselves to what they had. 'If you don't then you're showing little faith in the play, and I'll buy it from you, and you'll miss the chance of one of the biggest money-spinners of all time in addition to the lost prestige ...'

He insisted he wanted to know now because he had to instruct someone at the Met on the moves for *Onegin*. They were hesitating – dubious about Joe Leon going in to Washington. John was becoming angry. He becomes magnificent when he fights for something, emanating strength and confidence, his adrenalin high, feeding his love of power. The Shuberts were insisting they had to wait for Roger Stevens who was in transit and couldn't be contacted. John pushed and battered them, asking what they'd sell the production for, and where did they stand on the rights of the play, and he'd put the fucking show on with his own money! He hung up.

Before going back to the cast, who were waiting in the stalls, he turned to me in the aisle and told me not to worry about those ultimatums, he had some more things up his sleeve, and the time-schedule was not as bad as he'd painted. He just wanted to bring pressure to bear. But what now was he going to say to the cast?

He told them we were going ahead but that we didn't yet know where we were going to rehearse – New York or Phili. We'd know by 3 p.m. next day, Saturday, and everyone was to phone Warren at the theatre office to find out what was going to happen. 'This ... ' he told them stumblingly, '... I don't know how to say these words they're so corny, but they're true – this is what Zero would have wanted. He knew this was a great play, something special, and he invested a lot to do it.'

On those words I had to turn away. John's utterly correct, matter-of-fact voice – not without its strain and gentleness – made the moment unbearably poignant. He told them they were a fine company, still a lot of work to do but they had made huge advances. It was a brief but rallying speech.

Then came the harsh acts. John Davey had to be told we were scrapping his role as Roderigues. I went after him to say how sorry I was and that I'd tried – we'd all tried – to hang on to the character for as long as possible. He was on the verge of tears but very good about it. He understood. 'And it's been a privilege,' he said, then made a quick retreat through the iron doors of the backstage wall.[146]

John went into conference with Sir John. Later at Rosie's I asked him what had happened. It was all right for the moment, he said, but it mustn't get to the Shuberts that he was thinking about backing out. I told John it would leak out through Clements' agent, surely?

'No. We share the same agent. I'll see to it.'

The problems piled up. Jocelyn had phoned home to London and heard that her mother had fallen down and broken a hip. She was returning to London on Monday. The entire experience had been a nightmare for her – her set badly built, workshops, technicians, people in general not being helpful. But John was in good spirits – he had a challenge on his hands, he was off to New York that evening, Brent had lined up Abtalions and Tubals to be

---

[146] I subsequently reinstated the character of Roderigues and dropped Abtalion.

seen for Saturday morning. We were all in Rosie's – poor Julie looking haggard – having a last drink.

John kissed me and said: 'What a fucking awful mess I've made of your play, but it'll be allright. Don't worry.' I said it was not his fault but – pointing up there – *His*! He quoted John Fowles at me – something about we're all acting in a play that hasn't been written, with no set, no stage, no one knew when it began or when it will end, and there' s no audience watching. Something like that.

I tried to arrange that a bunch of us eat out together. In the end it was just Rebecca, Jeff, Gloria and me who went to the ship restaurant, the Mushulu, for a good meal. I bought a bottle of champagne. Austin and a girlfriend, Kate, met us and we went dancing. Great evening, full of jokes about Zero and the mess he'd left us with, and how Philadelphia had got one of us, who would Washington get? Austin drives like a madman. Jeff was non-stop funny about him: 'You drive like an existentialist, Austin, living from block to block.'

Saturday, 10 September

Another good day – the four of us stayed together and, with the help of Fred Goldman, visited the Barnes. The girls made sandwiches, we visited a friend of Fred's who opened her house to the embattled stragglers. We ate in her garden, drank wine, and fell asleep on the grass. Fred drove us back with Vivaldi playing in the car. Idyllic. While at the Barnes I rang the office and heard we were to begin rehearsals in New York on Monday at 1 p.m. – ACT 48 Studio. The show was on! Only then could I tell them it had been in the balance. Mind you, at this moment I don't know who's putting it on. John or the Shuberts or Stevens.

Now the four of us are going to eat our last supper in Phili.

Sunday, 11 September

But we first called on Rosie's for a farewell drink. She added another piece to the mosaic telling us that Zero had phoned an hour before his death saying how fine he was, ordering his chicken, asking if 'the kids' were there and were they all right, were they eating. Jewish father to the last. We all said sweet things about each other – how Rosie's was the one place Phili was worth coming back for. She said: 'You'll be back. I know it.'

Dreamt last night about Llantrisant,[147] walking in the street where I'd been billeted. Woke up heavy with thoughts about Zero. Three days ago he was alive like a 'rich plum pudding'.

I want to get out of this town. It's a beautiful city in which the inhabitants have felt for us – waiters, lift boys, people who've recognised us on the street – but we must get out, back to New York. I'm a doer, it's been frustrating sitting around unable to function.

Gloria wants me to go to the top of the Pen Tower with her. Fred will take us to brunch. At 1 p.m. we'll pick up the Avis car four of us have hired, and drive back to New York. And I must see Kate.

Pause.

Brent just phoned. John wants me at auditions on Monday morning. Asked him how things were. He reported that, 'John fought magnificently.' Brent didn't hear the conversation but when John came out of the Shuberts' office 'he was grinning like a Cheshire cat. He'd got his way'. I asked had names been mentioned. He said there were three acceptable to the Shuberts and John, but didn't know who they were.

Howard told Brent that Kate's not taking it well. She hasn't accepted it yet. Talks about getting the place straightened out for Zee's coming back.

---

[147] A village in South Wales where I was evacuated during the war, aged about 13, now the home of the Royal Mint.

NEW YORK – WE START AGAIN

[1977 *continued*]

Monday, 12 September, New York

Fred took us to *the* Kosher restaurant/deli in Phili — huge plates of smoked fish decorated with fruit, and the best roast beef in the world. Collected car, and drove through Buck's county, stopping on the way at a huge flea market just as it was closing. Gloria bought me a book on DANCING, Rebecca a turquoise stone. I loved driving through New York. Am staying in William and Claire's[148] rented apartment. Will see Kate sometime today.

A phone message was left for me in Phili to 'please call Louis Sager in New Jersey about the role of Shylock' — a poor fellow who thought this was his big chance now Zero was dead. People had probably told him how much he'd resembled Zero, and how he had been great in all those local shows ...

Later

A memorable day. Moving. Because these are emotional times it's easy for those of us involved to *feel* too intensely. But the fact is that everyone has risen to the challenge brought on by Zero's death. John especially has surpassed himself.

I arrived at the Winter Garden Theatre for thirty minutes of auditions to find a new Abtalion and Tubal. John was wearing a tie. Odd, I thought, till he told me it was a present from Zero for the reading on the first day. He looked drawn and tired. I squeezed his shoulder. He took my hand.

'Was it a great and difficult fight?' I asked.

He tilted his hand back and forth — so-so. 'The story is to be this. We're taking Joe Leon to Washington where the producers will see the play and we'll decide from there. Meanwhile names will come up, we'll give them scripts to read, and say it's not on offer but if it came up would they be interested?' John sent Brent out to buy a half bottle of champagne. Someone came up to tell

---

148 William and Claire Frankel, friends. He's ex-editor of the *Jewish Chronicle*, a writer on political affairs. Claire writes on art.

him that the flowers he'd ordered for Rosie had been sent. 'I couldn't face *that* one,' he said.

We auditioned five new people – the residue of a group John had seen on Saturday. We chose a younger, strong actor for Tubal, John Seitz. Julie was thrilled, she'd just worked with him. And for Abtalion – Boris Tumarin who turned out to be the director of the John Houseman touring production of *The Kitchen*.

'You realise, John,' I told him, 'there's the possibility you'll pull off the biggest coup Broadway's seen in years?' He understood exactly what I was thinking, and, I believe, secretly had known it and always wanted it – the opportunity to make a play work on Broadway without a star. He then told me something which he asked me not to 'memorialise', and which I won't, but we all, I'm sure, contemplated. (As I type this out I can't for the life of me think to what this refers. I obviously *haven't* 'memorialised' it!) Then he added he wanted me to tear up the memo I'd sent him on Zero. 'It's very strong, and that mustn't ever get around. His reputation is all that an actor has to live after him.' (Not true of Zero, there's his films.) I assured John that Zero's reputation was safe in my hands since, although the memo is critical, I knew that John would have eradicated Zee's excesses, and that Zee himself would have grown with audience response feeding him. And, as John said in his speech today: '... there was no doubt in any of our minds that he would have given his greatest performance ever'.

Slowly, with the champagne, John's spirits rose.

'You're right, we may have something very special on our hands. After all we've never needed stars before.'[149] When auditions were over he discussed with a member of management the question of Joe's salary. He wanted to make sure that if someone else, a name, *did* take over then Joe would not return to his old salary. 'I mean he could turn out to be a Judy Holliday, and become the greatest thing on Broadway, but in case ... a contract must be worked out.'

The morning was to be more auspicious than I realised – a press conference which *all* the producers were to attend, and where John was to make a speech to the actors which would also

---

[149] He was referring to *Roots* which had made a star of Joan Plowright, and *Chips With Everything* which had rocketed Frank Finlay to the top.

be a statement for the press.

'But,' John told Brent, 'you must grab me as soon as I've finished so as I'm not grabbed by the press. And someone must grab Arnold.'

I put it to John that perhaps we shouldn't avoid the press. 'I might have a helpful statement to make.' I'd planned a statement about *John* being the real star now. I wasn't asked.

Before walking to the rehearsal room on 48th, John embraced me. Photographers were there and a few actors. An atmosphere was accumulating. It was the 'first day' all over again. I sent out for three bottles of champagne for the cast. More faces appeared – Marian, Bill, Gloria, Jeff, Rebecca; then the producers – Bernie Jacobs, Gerry Schoenfeld, Roger Berlind, Sam Cohn; the publicity people – Merle and Susan; Andy and Jocelyn. It was like a wake. No – a gathering to look at the ruins, assess the damage. No – not that either, the ruins had been assessed. This was a gathering of those who were about to begin work on the reconstruction. It was the first time we, the Philadelphia stragglers from the battle-front, had met with the money-men from New York. The last time we'd been together Zero had been alive. Merle, Susan, Gerry and his wife had seen the one preview for which he'd managed to *stay* alive. A buzz rose in the room where we would soon be rehearsing, a humming made up of consolations, hail-fellows, anticipation – all a touch thrilling.

As Julie made her entrance with dark glasses John sang out: 'No dark glasses, Julie. Let's see your eyes. We'll have no tragic heroines this morning.'

'You anticipated me, John,' she came back at him, 'I was just about to take them off.'

John asked me to sit with Jocelyn and Andy, behind him. 'So that I don't see your face!' I understood why as he developed a great speech in which he hammered home that we may not have Zero but we *were* left with a tremendous play which had to be seen. He spoke strongly, hitting the right note every time. '... It's bad enough to lose an old friend, it's worse to lose a new one ...' No one could follow Zero, and no one was going to try. Zero interpreted the role in an inimitable way but all great roles had more than one way of being delivered ...

I haven't made notes, and now I'm very tired. Remember only that he was choked by the end and everyone felt compelled to applaud him.

When it was over I opened the champagne. Bernie, Sam and Gerry came over to shake my hand very warmly. I told them: 'I'm not unaware of the faith you're all showing in the play.' Their response was generous, they repeated that they thought it was a great play. 'And you've got a great man in charge,' I added. 'A genius', they said. And indeed John had been – I don't use the word lightly – magnificent.

Before rehearsals began Jocelyn told me she was going to stay on until the opening in Washington. She'd spoken to her mother who was recovering well. I was pleased and relieved. How could the set get into Washington without her?

Rehearsals began. It was like starting all over again. We had two weeks at the Minskoff with bits and pieces for props; the next two weeks we graduated to the Imperial stage; on to Phili, with sets, lights, costumes – and one solitary audience. Now, having tumbled downhill, we were starting the long haul up to performance pitch with a new Shylock in a poor rehearsal space where heavy gymnastic dancing thudded over us. It was fascinating to watch.

John is directing Joe in a way he never attempted with Zee. He's going at him word after word, line after line, making him sing high, low, making him colour the language, pointing out the music, the meaning, the rhythm, giving him new moves with an authority he seemed never able to achieve with Zee. And he's enjoying it, plying his directoral fingers in among the words, now able to touch and pluck at them, make them reverberate. Zero couldn't be stopped midway for direction as often and as energetically as John was now doing with Joe. Or perhaps he could have. Zero wouldn't have objected – John had said he was beginning to understand my advice about Zero's need to be directed. Now it was thrilling to watch him in his element moulding a performance rather than sitting back and directing it. His delight to be doing what he couldn't do before is palpable, though Joe is giving to the process a lot of his own invention and personality. There is clarity where before was none, or little; every sentence is given its full meaning, every feeling its full weight. It's only later that Gloria hands me some disturbing medical information: a symptom of Zero's ailment – his aneurysm – is a slurring of the speech. Does that mean his inaudibility was not Zero's failings as an actor but the result of what was afflicting him? If true, how terrible to know that only now.

As I watched rehearsals progress I became aware of an extraordinary metamorphosis in the relationship forming between Joe as Shylock and the aristocratic Clements as Antonio – to do with weight. Not bulk but presence. Joe is not a small man but he's more of a terrier than a Saint Bernard. He has attack but not the dominating, dangerous power Zero possessed. He can be heard clearly but he doesn't loom. I realised the cause – Clements' greater eminence off-stage is manifesting itself on stage. It's fascinating to observe. Perhaps Joe will grow to tragic heights – God knows we are willing him up there; and John will get more out of Joe than Joe ever knew he possessed, and, like a boxer in training, he asks for more and more. 'Keep talking,' he said to me. 'I'm resilient. John's showing me things in the text I couldn't see.' But his and Clements relationship is visibly different from Clements' and Mostel's.

It was a fine, energetic day's work on three scenes. An exhilarated John had been on top form. Before leaving I asked him what more John Clements had said about his contracting out.

'I'll tell you what *I* said. I told him I didn't want to hear any more of that kind of talk from him, and that I was surprised he'd brought it up at all at such a moment ... He'll be all right.'

There is, of course, a buzz around the play much greater than before. The big question reverberates: will it make it now without Zero? John loves that kind of challenge.

Saw Kate last night. Her two sons were there and a friend. Someone had bought her a new terrier puppy. She was in good spirits.

'It hasn't hit me yet. I'm encased in an ice box just now. When it hits me I'll give a *geshrie* ...'[150]

---

[150] Yiddish for 'howl'.

'Poor Kate,' I said, 'you not only have Zero's death to cope with but also all of us who come to see you.'

'And they all talk about the same thing,' she complained, 'that's what gets on my nerves.' Had I been talking about 'the same thing'? Told her how grateful I was Zee had ensured the play got into production – not entirely true, but near enough to be worth saying for comfort's sake – and how it's now Zee's inspiration cementing the cast's morale and ensuring the play's continued life. I wasn't sure she believed me.

The truth is I didn't know *what* to talk about, and decided I'd face the topic of dying head on. Told her that my father died on the night before *The Kitchen* opened in London; and that while I was attending the first night of *Shylock* in Stockholm my mother died. And now – Zero.

She nudged me with her elbow. 'You're afraid to put pen to paper, huh?' A Jewish toughie. Invited her to England when it was all over.

Off to Washington on Friday for interviews.

Tuesday, 13 September

Rehearsals continue, easing in the two new actors. Boris Tumarin, playing Abtalion, is slow; the younger, John Seitz, playing Tubal, is more vigorous. I'm told he's a gourmet chef specialising in Szechwan Chinese cooking. He talks like a cowboy which makes it difficult to believe one is in sixteenth-century Venice among Jews. Neither has yet read the play, having received the full text only today.

John began his attack on Julie again. It's true that she was gabbling but I felt he got at her too soon in this new process.

I heard her on the phone to a back specialist cancelling her appointment. 'Sidney? I can't come tonight I've got to see my psychiatrist. Sorry, it's very important.' She seemed agitated, and told me that if John screams at her once more she'll quit. 'I mean I didn't come with my mourning yesterday, I came in a good humour but he started on me straightaway. It's still soon, and I haven't looked at the text since it happened. If he doesn't think I'm any fucking good then let him fire me and let Rebecca take over.'

'John is going at you,' I consoled her, 'because he wants to get a good performance out of you. He yells so often at so many that it cancels itself out. He's also had a burden ...' I explained at length. She seemed reassured.

Joe said: 'As I rehearse the role more and more I find Shylock a *gruber jung*. A peasant.' It's a perceptive observation of character, but he must lose his stand-up comedy habits.

After lunch John and I exchanged notes. John to me: 'Victor Henry[151] ... Zero Mostel ... Who will you curse next? Me?' Me to John: 'I'm afraid that after this experience you have me for life, dear friend – learn to live with it.'[152]

I left early, around six – unusual for me. Chatted with John before leaving. He explained that he was exploiting Joe's comic strength to begin with, then he'd go for depth. Shared my thoughts about Joe being a terrier we could hopefully shape into a looming presence. John asked me to put aside time over the weekend to take Joe through the text.

Wednesday, 14 September

Woke this morning feeling gloomy. Can't escape the fact that it *is* depressing to be starting again. Fear it will never get off the ground. I bet some of the actors must feel this, too, especially people like Roberta and Everett who are not getting any rehearsal these days because attention must be focused on Shylock, Tubal and Abtalion. John's task is enormous. The sooner we get to Washington and into costume the better.

Liz Fowles rang last night. They're in town promoting John's new novel, *Daniel Martin*. She rang to greet and console. Tom and Malou[153] are also in town. Will see them tomorrow night. William and Claire have invited them for dinner.

Phone Gloria to ask her to check a place where I think I've lost my credit cards. Her humour is a great tonic. She had me giggling at 8.45 in the morning.

---

[151] An actor I directed in *The Friends* who set out to wreck the play and virtually succeeded. A car accident left him brain damaged. He died.

[152] A parody of a line from *Shylock*.

[153] Tom Wiseman, novelist, and his wife.

Found John had woken up in a similar mood – heavy, lethargic. Reaction had set in for him too.

'I'm so doped,' he announced to Nerissa, 'between last night's sleeping pills and this morning's dentist's whatever-it-is he put in I'm absolutely without energy. This will be a recap rather more than anything else.' But it turns out to be more, and his lethargy turns into a rich, loamy seam of inspiration. I recognise the mood – creative tiredness. Nice. Intimate. Relaxed. The actors take chances and soar. They turn on John, who in turn, turns them on. His wit opens up. Everyone loves him, and he loves them.

Brilliant moment with Bassanio follows. John seats us in a semi-circle in front of him, and delivers a lecture on the soliloquy being an introverted event but one which works only when taken out into the audience. He instructs Bassanio to use us as an audience, to ask questions of us.

What an eccentric test of love. Whose mind constructed this? 'By his choice shall you know him.' What shall you know of him? That if he choose gold he will be a man without a soul, with a purse where his heart should be? But a man without a soul may have cunning, surely? Greed does not preclude perception, and a greedy man may well detect misfortune where his instinct leads ...

The long soliloquy comes alive in a way it hasn't before – when his eyes actually engage us, that is. Nick has difficulty keeping his eyes – and argument – from roving.

After lunch John attacks Scene 4, creating a new dynamic, new rhythms. He helps the cast adjust to the new actors. 'You hate them and wish they weren't here and wonder why they were brought into the company, but you've got them – so learn to live with them. It's easier to listen to new people than to remember what the previous ones were like. Rhythms! Rhythms! You may wish you were playing in a Harold Pinter play but you're not so you'd better put up with the author you've got. Find *his* rhythms...' John is forging them into a company, but not without difficulty – something is happening behind the scenes.

Brent returned from being away all morning, and reported that

Marvin Krauss was angry. Didn't know what for.

'Over the Clements affair?' asked John.

I leapt to ask what *was* the Clements affair. 'Is he still playing up, wanting out?'

John waved it off muttering something about no one being irreplaceable. 'I'm going to blow him up one day soon,' he said.

Clements has been fluffing lines and looking as though he wishes to God he were not with us but three thousand miles away in England. Is he doing it deliberately to be sacked? After six weeks he still gets small speeches wrong. John is furious with him.

Later

But Clements was better in the opening scenes. I love John making connections, like telling Shylock that he must have more bustle and pride when he talks about the ghetto.

'He knows they're "*thin achievements in stone*" but loves the ghetto being a place where debate goes on. Remember – Lorenzo tells him "disputation is a sacred right".'

Connections!

Joe very different from Zero in the '*daughter daughter daughter*' scene. Brings tears to my eyes. Watch John end the day taking Joe through Renaissance speech. No one else in the rehearsal room but we three and three stage-managers. Images of Zero flood back. I remember with guilt complaining that he blurred lines which I imagined to be vain acting but now know to have been a symptom of his ailment. Joe will be good and clear in this speech but will he ever achieve the equivalent of Zero's little laugh on: *I am so tired of men?*

Thursday, 15 September

Morning. Stage management take Tubal and Abtalion through their moves. John is at Met. I'm recovering from a hangover.

Afternoon. Devoted to court scene. More evidence of John getting closer to the text. Gave Joe almost a line by line reading. On rerun of transition from Belmont to the court, where Portia says, '*Holy Mary Mother of Christ! I have it! ...* ' John made everyone stand, poised to enter, while he worked on Roberta for ten minutes making her deliver those lines again and again and again and again till they are each one different.

> What can I do? I pity men their mad moments but a bond is a bond. The law demands its forfeitures. A pound of flesh is a satanic price to conceive, even as a joke, but ... I have it! Holy Mary Mother of Christ, I have it! But no! No! No, no, no, no, it's too simple. That's not law. The law is complex, devious. This is common sense. Justice. The law is not to do with justice. No. It *can't* be applicable. And yet – who could possibly deny ... the law may not be just when it demands strict adherence to an agreement which may cause misery, but it does demand strict adherence. Then surely ... dare I? I'm no advocate. My temper's not for public places ... and yet ... a wrong is a wrong ...

John becomes more and more animated as the afternoon wears on, and rehearsals increase in temperature. Court scene is much happier and lighter without the Tubal speech but it doesn't stop John turning to me and making scissors signs with his fingers to snip the odd, unnecessary line. Even cutting four beats from a sentence makes it smoother.

John finally tackles Sir John.

'If you want to go, go now and let's be done with it!'

'What do you mean?'

'Well, I haven't had a decent day's work out of you for two weeks. Now, I don't want to discuss it but if you *don't* want to leave let's get on.'

Rehearsals improve tenfold, Clements along with them. In fact he delivers his big court speech in a completely different way – instead of raging he offers it with a whispered danger. I'm riveted. So is the rest of the company who've never heard such a rendering. The court scene, with Tubal's speech gone, is swift, tight, electrifying. John re-stages it so that there is no wipe – he's taken all the wipes out of the play – and we watch the courtroom slowly shaping and filling to the sound of ominous bells as the last moments of the preceding Belmont scene come to an end. The cast are thrilled by it.

At the end of the day John announces that Friday will be

devoted to the Jews, but that on Saturday they will have to run the play for themselves. He needs the full weekend break. He tells me that reaction has set in, stretches his hands to me. They're shaking.

Saturday, 17 September

Joe says the story of Jessica echoed a story of his sister who died young. He'd never cried over her until this play. '*Now* I could weep for her.'

Friday's rehearsal was without John. He was ill – something about too many sleeping pills. But actors find it a productive rehearsal. This morning's run-through is workmanlike. Not inspired, but a sound reading of the lines, except for Lorenzo who is very, very much better – relaxed and in control of all he's doing. Marian continues to be remarkable. No mean holding back from her, she offers something every second, and has done from day one.

I give them notes. 'Not serious notes, just a handful of little things which might help. But first,' I reassure them, 'I want you to know how tremendous you all are to have recovered and pulled the show together. You've had to start right from the bottom again. John's helped, and now he's paying the price ...'

In the afternoon spend three hours in my apartment – from five to eight – going through his role in the play with Joe. It's gratifying at last being able to touch the part, to lock with an actor. I give him the tunes which are in my head. He finds his own way to sing them, but at least it's the same melody. He's grateful. He could be powerful in the role. John has no doubt of it.

Sunday, 18 September

Helped shop for cast party which Gloria gave in her apartment. I love her little boy, Adam. Made me homesick. William and Claire came to the party but fled from the noise and heat to take Sir John to *Star Wars*! A group of us shifted to the bedroom – Julie, Rebecca, Leib, Jeff, Nick and his beautiful Jewish girlfriend, where we sang songs, English and Hebrew, to Julie's guitar.

Everyone seems able to play the guitar. I'm envious. Gloria remained in the other room dancing to Tony Bennett. 'Not my scene,' she said.

Once again I experience this warm sensation of companionship with my cast, would live in a commune with them if I could! Victor Henry and Diane Cilento[154] did a lot to destroy my feelings for actors, but mostly I love being with them, at least with those connected with my plays. It's moving to experience a group of strangers who are giving themselves to something I wrote many moons ago, worrying and working to shape and offer what I worked and worried to write, locked away in the Black Mountains of Wales. I don't want to leave them.

Monday, 19 September

We progress from the cosy, if claustrophobic, Studio 48 to the huge open stage of the Minskoff Theatre. Shylock and Antonio are ahead of us rehearsing. John D is with his secretary from the Met clearing up some last minute details in his other life. It's amusing to watch Sir John direct Joe. In the gap left by John's absence, the knight slips naturally into the role of director, albeit self-appointed. He's in his element. Some of his tips sound good but his role as surrogate director can't continue, even though Joe has expansively declared he'll take help from every and anyone.

John strolls up to ask how 'the other director' is doing. I tell him, not bad – but I'm worried about Joe having two directors. 'Not any more!' Then, changing the subject: 'I'm now an expert on marathon sleeping. Ten hours on Friday, eleven on Saturday. I made up for all that sleep on Sunday afternoon, though. They brought two adolescents to perform for me. I've decided I'm an old-fashioned voyeur who directs plays. That's my pleasure, to watch how the young do it.' I think John wants to shock me, I think he thinks I'm an innocent. [155]

He takes over from Clements to work with Shylock on the

---

[154] Cilento played opposite Alan Bates in my play *The Four Seasons*. She didn't get on with the director, and, like Victor Henry, wrecked the play.

[155] Reading this now I *am* shocked. Could he have meant 'young men'? He couldn't have meant teenagers.

'creation-of-God' speech, and gives Joe a way of doing it which is almost exactly how I'd directed him when we worked together on Saturday. 'Go up to Antonio, begin softly, almost like sharing a secret, mischievously, and then build.' Joe's not picking it up. He will, though.

The bustling Scene 4 falls into place with the three new actors, but the love scene persists in not working. John turns to me before going up on stage to 'do' something. 'I believe the Israelites once had to make bricks with only straw.'

'Off you go,' I encouraged him, 'like a good little Israelite.'

He mounts the stage and attacks the beleaguered Jessica. 'Has Julie got another note in her voice other than denotes a whine or wetting of her knickers ... We've heard it for five weeks ... Julie-one-note!' After a few attempts he becomes even more vicious. 'Will you be original and get something *new* out of your gut other than that note, for Christ's sake ...'

Julie has a nervous habit of pulling at the end of her long, black hair. Now she pulls violently. But, with God knows what reserves of resilience, she comes back and tries again and again.

At one point John brings himself to encourage her. 'That would be fine if only we could *hear* it ...'

I wince, but who knows? I could never work that way but perhaps his cruelty may yet evince from her a performance of great variety.

'I don't mind,' she later assures me. 'I was determined to come back fighting.'

John to Joe on his 'letter from Jessica' scene: 'The purpose of being a clown with Rivka is so that you can let it all out in the '*daughter daughter daughter*' scene. But pain, not tears.' Joe attempts 'pain'. John yells intermittently from the stalls 'QUIETER! SIMPLER! LONELIER!' It's not easy for Joe which is why I'm worried about encouraging his gruff, coarse, comic style. Will John be able to refine him? I hope so.

Tuesday, 20 September

Second day in this huge barn of a theatre. Cleo Laine will be singing here on October 5th.

We can work on the Antonio dinner scene because Riggs (Graziano) is back from Paris where he's been re-casting John's production of *Equus* for the French tour. John is on stage re-blocking and, in the process, reminding the actors what's supposed to be happening. He *so* understands what should be happening on a line, you'd think an actor would. It constantly surprises me how, for example, a line like the last in this following exchange is not perceived by Joe to be a hissing, bitter line:

SHYLOCK   But my parents – they tried a new profession. Very brave. Second-hand clothing! My mother went blind patching up smelly old clothes, and my father became famous for beating out, cleaning and reconditioning old mattresses. Bringers of sleep – not a dishonourable trade don't you think, gentlemen? Mattresses – bringers of sweet sleep.

LORENZO   And sweet plagues.

SHYLOCK   Yes! I know! Better than you, I know!

Joe/Shylock offers it angrily. Zero/Shylock offered it in boredom. Neither is dangerous. Neither came from someone you'd think twice about becoming entangled with.

John breaks up the 'autobiography' monologue and has Shylock run from one to the other of the young men, humbling himself as they turn from him.

If I'd been a damned physician, I'd not have to wear this damned yellow hat every time I took a walk. Physician! Now *there* was a profession to belong to instead of my own seedy lineage. Failures! I descended from German Jews, you know. My grandparents – grubby little things from Cologne. Came to Venice as smalltime money-lenders for the poor. But my parents – they tried a new profession ...

It's an inspired reading but will only work if Shylock builds from being humble to being arrogant on that last line of contempt – '*Better than you, I know!*'

Again, it's exciting watching John get in among the lines in a way he couldn't with poor Zee, painting the story of the Renaissance so that it's clear and thrilling, but over lunch I warned him Joe would break down soon.

'About when?' he asked. It's Tuesday today, we both thought about it, and in one voice said, 'Friday!'

'*Then* he'll be all right,' I finished off.

We discussed plans for producing the play in London. He was available from the beginning of April to mid-September but, he said, he didn't want anything to do with Eddie [Kulukundis] or Eddie's office. He would prefer to set it up with the Royal Court, certainly not with the National. 'Wouldn't work with a fascist organisation at my time of life. You and David Hare and all those other socialist writers can work with them if you like but it's too late for me.[156]

His main worry was that the commercial boys would not be interested in a production without a star. 'You're very mistaken to keep talking about me as the star,' he said. 'It doesn't work. Do you want to do something about it now or wait for after Washington?'

I told him *we* were a formidable team, and they'd give the money to us with *good* actors and no stars. He thought this naïve.[157] 'In which case,' I said, 'we'd better wait for Washington in order to see if we've made it work with Joe. If we do then we're in a strong position.' So it stands. Jocelyn has put the idea by letter to Sturt Burge who's now running the Royal Court. Frank Finlay is being pursued to play Shylock but hasn't yet been found.

A well-known English actress comes up to us.

She's working with Max Von Sydow and Bibi Andersson.[158] They'd been lunching together. 'They're so serious,' she tells us. 'No jokes. He says [Von Sydow] "We have a word for a little boy's cock in Swedish – *snoop*. Is there a similar word in English?" So I suggest "little John Thomas", and he repeats it, "little John Thomas". But with no smiles.'

---

[156] John was bitter at the way he'd been treated at the National after all the work he'd put into building up a company and repertoire under Olivier.

[157] He was right.

[158] Two fine Swedish actors.

'She's got a lovely face,' I say to John as she leaves. 'Is she a good actress?'

'One of the best, only she makes a mess of her career because she goes where the fuck is.'

We stroll over to Clive Barnes, John introduces me, makes an arrangement to phone him for advice 'now you're no longer involved'. Barnes was dismissed as critic of the *New York Times* six months ago.

Wednesday, 21 September

Begin day with Antonio's dinner scene. John asks me to think about adding a line to: '*Let me remind you of three distinct developments affecting the history of this extraordinary land of yours ...*' Something about '. . . and all the world'. The request worries me. To have Shylock observe that the history (of the Renaissance) he's about to tell them affected the world's history as well would be to give him post historical insight. Would Shylock in 1563 know about the impact of the Renaissance upon the world? Perhaps it would be better to have him predict it: '... and *will* affect the world'. No! That's worse. That's *really* being clever about what's known. John's reason for adding such a line is to lift Shylock's speech out of the limited context of Italy. But as I think about it, it becomes too much of a 'universalising' exercise. The strength of Shylock's Renaissance speech surely lies in a man talking about what he knows of his place and time?

When I explain to John why I'm worried about universalising that line he tries another way to explain his reasoning. He wants the end of the speech to connect back to the beginning, to make a full circle. I understand. But what to do? Will think about it.

Next the casket scene. He can't make Nerissa's bawdy 'bone' line work. He finds it obscure.

'Leave me *that* one, John,' I plead.

'You may have as many stunned silences in your play as you want, my darling.'

It's Nerissa who isn't making it work. Must talk to her. Or perhaps it's Portia who must help, with a certain tone of voice?

Love scene still isn't working. John can't draw a performance out of either Jessica or Lorenzo. Julie is incapable of getting variety into her voice. Everett is sweet and a good actor but, as I guessed from day one of auditions, he's no Lorenzo. Julie is a fine girl, a good actress for the right part, but she's no Jessica – as I guessed from day one of auditions. I adore Gloria but, as auditions showed, she's no Nerissa.

Lunch with John to discuss possibility of doing both *The Wedding Feast* and *Shylock* in repertory beginning at the Royal Court and moving to the West End, with Colin Blakely[159] playing both parts.

We speak to the famous English actress again. John asks her if she's free in April to do Portia. She is.

'You've turned me down more than any actress I know. I promise you I'll bring the fuck.' His outrageousness takes my breath away. I think my face showed shock on her behalf, but she seems not to mind, and tells her own story about a production containing ten young men 'and not a fuck among them.' She's obviously party to her own reputation.

After lunch John directs the Rivka/Shylock scene – almost for the first time. Tubal looks on from the wings, I'm at his side.

'He directs it like a piece of music.'

'That's the way I scored it,' I tell him. 'I always wanted to be a composer and John always wanted to be a conductor. That's why we work so well together.'

Then comes one of those memorable moments in a rehearsal. When Shylock and Rivka next run their scene Shylock brings himself to tears on reading the '*daughter daughter daughter*' letter, real tears out of which he laughs when Antonio appears. An extraordinary moment.

John turns to me ecstatically: 'Oh, I can still direct.'

John *is* high. He's working his way through the Shylock/ Antonio exchange, covering the entire 'disintegration' scene, taking Shylock physically in his hands and wheeling him around the stage, conducting his sound and pace as though Joe was his own image and he was making sure it acted well. It *looks* as though Joe is his puppet but it's not so. He's simply ensuring Joe

---

159 A splendid Irish actor. Dead

responds to the text. John's great virtue is that he has no ego other than to make work a text he respects. And to watch him these days is really to watch a great director in action. I didn't see the clown in the Shylock I wrote, I mean not as much as John sees, but he's contrasting the clowning with the tragedy which now looms large and true. Joe is loving it. He's never been directed like this nor had these qualities drawn out of him. He's over-acting just now but once his exuberance settles he will give a great performance. John strides back to me in the stalls as we settle to watch the 'disintegration' scene.

'Written a new play yet?'

'When you've provided me with adequate financial security I'll provide you with a new play.'

'I'm doing my best, but your demands are increasing so.'

Fresh attack on the last part of the court scene. The patience of actors who have to hang around for so long always amazes me.

John sleeps through the run-through of Antonio's dinner scene. I wake him on the last line and suggest he tells Joe he can't help much more until Joe has the lines under his belt. Also suggest that one day he should let Joe tell the Renaissance story without any moving of tables and people and fruit and jugs of wine. John agrees. One day no doubt he'll strip away the invented business as he did in the warehouse scene. Not everything I hope. Or would Shylock's Renaissance speech be better if simply told, with no business at all, a story with no illustrations?

In the break Portia and Bassanio, who were given only one run-through, grab the stage and work their scene on their own. Poor Christians, they're getting no attention.

Jessica *is* one note. Will she ever change? Not that the love scene is well staged.

'You're not happy with my writing of the love scene are you?' I ask John with a mixture of caution and enquiry. He isn't.'

'Can't you arrange for them to fuck one another?' I suggest.

'From what I hear he'd split her in half, and I'm not sure it'd help. In Texas the corn is not the only thing that grows as high as an elephant's thigh.'

The rest of the afternoon is given to the casket scene.

Thursday, 22 September

We're moving slowly through the play. Rehearsals begin with a strange quietness. Shylock is developing – oh God – a sore throat. John has asked him to keep his voice down.

Noise of laughter erupts from the wings. John shouts: 'If you must play kid's games do it in the street, for God's sake!'

Roberta tells me she and Bill Roerick had consulted the i-ching last night. Everything is going to be all right. We simply have to make it to Washington. John gives her and Nerissa in Belmont only cursory attention. Not sure I understand what's happening to her these days.

Run through Scene 4 twice. Second time round the two of us fall asleep. Wake up in time for a short exchange.

He says: 'The problem with Joe is going to come when the Shuberts say: yes, he's very good, but no one's going to pay to see him, and they're going to ask for Danny Kaye. I can be one step ahead only when Joe's good enough for me to ask can they guarantee Danny Kaye will give as good a performance.'

'But don't they understand that the kind of audience who will come to see Danny Kaye won't really like the play. They'll go away saying, "Danny's all right but the play ..."'

I ask John why he gets so angry with publicity, and suggest it'll boomerang if he treats them badly. He says he gets angry that they come to him and say we've got to do this and that because they're not getting bookings. Hearing which depresses me. Zero's death is beginning to affect our future. We need Washington, an audience, the sets, to raise our spirits.

After lunch

We hang around for Joe Leon to return from the doctor who's spraying his throat. Spirits rise briefly, due mainly to finding cuts. I go to the wings where the actors are waiting around, and call for Jessica and Lorenzo.

'Oh my God!' cries Brent, with rather more cheek than I care for. 'Not another love scene?'

'No, a cut.'

'Oh, good! A cut. You know how thrilled I get with cuts.'[160]

While the dinner scene is run through John tells me about the sexual services involving closed circuit TV on offer in New York. 'Much more interesting than this boring old play!' Later on, watching the actors perform, he quotes an incredibly beautiful line of Shakespeare.[161]

I tackle John again about publicity. He informs me he booked a lunch with them to iron out problems but they didn't turn up. It worries me.

I ask Brent what he thinks of Joe's performance. He wants to avoid an answer. I press, and he finally confesses that though John is drawing marvellous things out of Joe yet he's seen the performance before.

Snipped two questions out of Jessica's 'to whom does a house belong' speech, but it doesn't prevent the play from seeming very boring. Joe performs like a little clown trying not only to impress the other characters and failing, but failing to impress us, as well, with too much trying.

Friday, 23 September

Arthur Storch phoned from Syracuse about his production of *Love Letters On Blue Paper*[162] saying he felt something needed to be cut as the play neared its end – the Esher discussion. He sounded right. All goes well there, so far.

John dressed in brown three-piece suit and tie. He was gloomy. He'd had a Met board meeting, he explained. Told him I had a second director to deal with who wanted cuts. 'He's not the only one,' he said. 'There's the Shuberts. I'm asking Peter [Shaffer] down for the third day in Washington. The Shuberts will listen to him. They think he has a clear intelligence and we need to build

---

[160] The death of a star invites a breakdown of courtesies and sense of place. It's a lesson I never really learned: with a star in your play you are regarded with greater respect.

[161] The Shakespeare line is not recorded, can't think why. Was I interested in juxtaposing John's seediness with his sensitivity?

[162] World première by Syracuse Stage, 14 October 1977

up a battery of defence. I'm going to fight a star to my last breath. The only thing is — the play's not ready yet.'

'Are you talking about my text or your production?'

'Both.'

'What do you want to cut? Tell me. The love scene?'

'Not yet. I'm going to try and make it work.'

He ran it. I realised he can't direct that kind of passion and exuberance. I suggested that Lorenzo picks up Jessica and whirls her round in a rush of joy and exaltation. He hesitated, as though torn between feeling such an action might work and really wanting to cut it. Later he said: 'I think we're going to have a big fight.'

'You and me?'

'Yes. Can't think where it should be though, or when.'

'What about?'

'I want to get rid of digressions. There's a part in the court scene that's a digression ...'

He told me but I didn't register it, I was too chilled at the prospect that our relationship was under threat. Asked him to repeat it. He wouldn't. 'I'll save them all up and let you have them together.'

I begin to worry that the rich detail to which everyone had once responded is slowly being whittled away. Many of the cuts are good ones, others I'm leaving in the text. Is John now going to present me with cuts tailored to Broadway bums? He insists that no, he's only concerned with meeting the play's needs, no one else's. Now I can't be certain and must distinguish between what really needs cutting and what John doesn't know how to handle.

Spent lunch answering mail. John took Joe for a meal and gave him half a bottle of port. After it Joe *drove* through the play, sang his way through it. Incredible! Bernie (Mr Shubert) Jacobs came to watch, and kept dozing.

Am worried about warehouse scene. *Where* is it taking place now? Whisper to John that Graziano has great energy but no humour.

'Where *is* the humour?' he asks.

'In that he gets things wrong.'

'Is he supposed to know he's funny?'

'Yes. He's a clown. He enjoys clowning. Admits he's an academic failure.' John writes it down.

'It takes a long time but sooner or later one gets a good note out of you.'

Unjust. He's preparing for a fight.

After the first act Bernie Jacobs and Gerry Schoenfeld talk to us. They seem pleased. Gerry can see that there's greater clarity. Bernie hugs me and says we'll have a great success on our hands, adding: 'We only ever deal in success!'

John embraces him and says: 'That's the nicest thing anyone's said to me in a month.'

Great relief

'It's called "taking risks", says John when they've gone. 'And I'd told Joe I want triple somersaults on a tightrope. The subtlety will come later.'

'Joe's got energy,' I say, 'clarity, humour, colour – now he needs – majesty!' He agrees. 'And tenderness and lyricism,' I add. He agrees.

'But we mustn't give him those words, we must let him find them for himself.' John tells me what he said to Joe over lunch. 'I told him it's about time you were a leading actor. You've got Howard as your dresser, you're travelling first class, now behave like a first class actor. Be a bit of a killer on stage, don't be so reverential to Sir John.' He'd done as John directed. The knight looked quite taken aback at Joe's attack, full of surprises, from which he didn't really recover.

I'm writing this as I sit watching the second act. Joe has just delivered the contempt speech so movingly, as though he'd made it up there and then, for himself. And the change from his broad smile to a most tender '*I love thee Antonio*' made me gasp. Will he ever be so good again?

The thought strikes me that the court scene is too discursive – the centre doesn't hold. Does it need restructuring or just a word here and there to make the links to the centre? John thinks the latter. It's a confrontation between Dogma and Enlightenment, he says. Then follows a solid Dexter insight. 'I think that what the Venetians in this play have done to Shylock is turn him into the Shylock of the other play.'

Giving notes John tells them: 'Well, it must be clear to you all that Joe's taken off and I think has earned your congratulations.' The cast burst into applause.

WASHINGTON –
THE HIGHS AND THE LOWS

[1977 *continued*]

[The play now runs for 5 weeks as an 'out of town' try-out at The Kennedy Centre in Washington during which time more cuts are made, scenes merged and reshuffled, and a decision is held over to see if Joseph Leon comes up to standard and the play is able to make it on Broadway without a star.]

Monday, 26 September – Washington, Kennedy Centre, 6 p.m.

They have arrived. Again. Again gathered to perform. But for the moment gathered only for a line-reading. There they sit, before me in a semi-circle, oak-stripped flooring, white walls and ceiling, atmosphere hushed.

Actors line-read with differing degrees of intensity. Sir John races, as does Roberta, not pausing to act – though Roberta makes faces and uses her hands. Sir John sits casually with his legs crossed. Gloria continues to articulate too precisely, taking her time. Joe puts a little more colour into his lines than Sir John. Marian sits and shakes her head from side to side forever incredulous at the wonder of the word, the world.

During the exchange between Usque and da Mendes the idea occurs to rearrange their 'list of the dead' in Portugal. The rhythm has always worried me, the moment held up, poised too long.

I mouth to Riggs across the semi-circle of actors: 'Has John spoken to you about the warehouse scene?'

'Yes, but nothing has been decided.'

'I would like to see something come back.'

'I know, I have an idea how to use the fabric so that the text is not lost in the material.'

The line reading continues. Suddenly, Riggs bursts into loud acting, as if he'd felt 'we need to liven things up!' The room comes a little more to life.

Tuesday, 27 September

Phone call at about 9.15. Stern voice, determined, low in the belly. 'John here. Good morning. We must meet for lunch today to discuss cuts.' The first thrust. Stored till the pressure of an opening was upon us. Chill! 'We'll need an hour together, then lunch. They're cuts I'd hoped you'd see because I'd been indicating them ...'

Told him I'd been waiting for him to steel himself for such a call. I wanted to sign off but his tone changed. He lingered, became friendly. 'Now, what museums have you seen? You've been here a day more than me.'

'The Matisse.'

'See the permanent exhibition,' he commands, like a loving father. 'I'll see you at eleven.'

It was now my turn to steel myself. At 11.15 together with Jocelyn we went into an office. On the way I apologised to John for being late: 'I've been looking for some little scissors to buy you for a present.'

'You won't need little ones.'

'There's no room for big ones,' I replied, defiantly letting him know I was not taking more cuts easily. Between us we established a tense setting.

John began. 'These cuts are not made for time but because it's writing that's repetitious, boring or badly written.'

I reach for a notepad and write, mumbling his words, '... not made for time, but – repetitious, boring and, what was the third one?' I was attempting to deflate his intimidating tactic of brutal terror.

He snaps back. 'If you're going to do that for everything we'll never get through.'

He asks Jocelyn to start. What she says irritates me. I've heard it before – it's as though John has schooled her: repetitions, the story's held up, one loses interest ... I cut her short and suggest we deal with specifics. John begins. Some are sections, some are details: the end of the love scene, the word game, '*my father's an intellectual snob*', the beginning of the Belmont/casket scene ...

When he's done I thank him, say I've understood the intention behind the cuts, but I'd like to consider them. He says, of course, and we'll have lunch. I tell him, no. He asks have I a date? No, but I want to consider the cuts in peace, at my leisure. He concedes. Of course!

I agree to look at them for their repetitiousness but point out that there does exist a difference in personality and taste.

This, more or less, is what I say. 'Jocelyn is a bare bones person, I'm not. I don't like excess fat but I'd like to write a play that is succulent, that did for theatre what novelists can do for literature. Serious people don't come to the theatre because they feel it's all over in a fart, they've experienced nothing. I enjoy people in life who are precise, but I also enjoy those who can vividly digress. I want to be practical but I also don't want to lose pleasure in my play. That's the balance I aim for.'[163]

John is anxious to bring up another subject. It's startling. He asks: of the two plays – *The Wedding Feast* and *Shylock* – which would I prefer to see first?

'*The Wedding Feast*,' I answer.

'Good! Then if I do *The Wedding Feast* before April I'd like to do *Shylock* together with *The Jew of Malta* and the Shakespeare as a season at the Court, using the same company and gearing *Shylock* for transfer.'

I'm speechless. It was John at his most breathtaking[164] – he has the most incredible look on his face, a kind of anxious mischievousness, looking at me out of the side of his excited, sweaty eyes. I feel panicky.

'Look,' I tell him, 'it's bad enough taking the risk I've taken in writing the play – you've no idea the wrath that's going to descend. But to tempt them more by playing me alongside Shakespeare and Marlowe ... I think I'll leave that decision till after the first night when I see what kind of play has been left to me.'

Jocelyn thoughtfully suggests I be left to do one thing at a time – first consider the cuts. John says he has to organise his future but of course he'll wait.

I return to the hotel and discuss the cuts with Gloria whom I've come to respect. She's perceptive about other people's performances, and sensitive to the text – even though she is utterly wrong for Nerissa, not a classical actress at all, made more

---

163 The final printed version represents all I wish for the play.

164 Also his most manipulative – he was painting me a glorious future as a reward for being a good boy, and cutting!

for comic roles in movies. Some things I refuse to lose – Jessica on dogma and men writing books; the bone joke, the no Jews in England joke. Other sections I want to give only half away; some parts I'll trade; a few give up whole.

John is a little smashed from lunch. We go through my new cuts in a corner of the red plush foyer at the back of the theatre. He's not entirely happy with what I've accepted and not accepted but knows he can't push for more. When it's done, I ask, can we talk about his project because we must agree an approach to *Shylock* for London. I remind him it hasn't worked entirely as I'd conceived – partly due to some of the performances, partly due to the production which didn't have the bustle and detail envisaged. I leave that one to sink in, and ask him: 'Tell me about your plans for the Shakespeare. Will you cut it or do the lot?' He says he plans no cuts, seems to think *Shylock* can hold its own. What's left of it!

I pass the rest of the day arranging my flight – to Syracuse for the opening of *Love Letters On Blue Paper*, and the return flights to London – I don't need to hang around Washington for the five week run at the Kennedy Centre. It seems only Bernie Jacobs can authorise another advance if I want six air fares paid from the US end.[165] It's incredible but the one performance in Phili and the five and half weeks here in Washington earn the first $5000 advance. Half a week's royalty on Broadway will pay for the six air fares!

A call came through from New York. A production company in Montreal want to do *Chips With Everything*. Fine – a standby in case we flop.

7.30 p.m., technical run-through. At halftime tell John I plan to discuss major points of the production after the first night, but can we now find time for small things? It's a tense moment. He has that air of wanting to avoid me, wishing I were not there. As he's about to move off without answering I call to him again. He turns with a hostile look and waits, poised on the turn, daring me to hold him up or request *anything*. I dare. He says yes, we will find time. But it comes out viciously begrudging.

The run-through has not been bad, considering the cast have

165 For the family.

run nothing for two weeks and it's the first time on stage for Shylock, Abtalion and Tubal. Line fluffs – inevitably, a too slow beginning, and for some strange reason Sir John has turned into a surly Antonio – his way of being sad I suppose. God knows what Shylock sees in this Antonio or what this Antonio sees in Shylock for that matter. Still despite the general blandness, Shylock picks up in the dinner scene. Not, however, in the second act where he becomes absurd and ridiculous, doing a Hasidic dance (in sixteenth-century Venice) on *'yes, I! I! I! I!'*, and falling over backwards on *'No books?'* And how angrily he now performs the letter scene – no tenderness; and how irritatingly he receives the news of Jessica's leaving; and the bloody bells are *so* loud in the love scene! There's only one marvellous and quite original moment in the court scene: Shylock takes out the knife, says. *'Well damn you then, I'll have my pound of flesh'*, and having whipped the knife out violently he then holds it at arm's length with disdain and disgust. It's stunningly inventive.

On balance, though, I have a profound and mortifying sense of having failed to write the play I wanted to write. The stage is bare, and so seems my play also. Roderigues is gone, the Papal Bull is gone, half *'the Martyrs of Blois'* speech is gone. I'm depressed. When it's over I'll not hang around but return to the hotel where John can leave a message about a meeting to exchange notes. Even catching his attention to tell him that is difficult. He has problems, so I hover, wait for him to set his timetable for the next day's rehearsal, and then say. 'John, I'm going back to the hotel; leave me a message there when you've got yourself together.'

'What kind of a message?' He's moving one way towards the stage, I'm moving the other towards the exit.

'About a meeting?'

I'm about to disappear through the door as he says: 'Friday!'

I look back, angry. 'What did you say?'

'Say Friday morning?' That's *after* the first night. Should I tell him that's too late? It's not a moment to quarrel. I say OK, and leave.

Depression deepens. That frustrating period is approaching when I have notes to give and John has no time to receive them – the demands of the production take precedence over the author's concern for his text. It always happens, and after all these years I've still not learned how to handle it. The play is slipping out of my control – or rather my one contact with it, the director, is slipping away. I'm furious, really. Feel I'm here merely to sanction cutting what the director can't direct and the actor's can't act. I don't want to sit through further rehearsals or run-throughs until someone listens to my notes.

Perhaps it's not as dire as I feel. There's time enough after the first night. After all that's what out-of-town-time is for – putting things right. The irony is that despite all the cuts I've made, we've put five minutes *on* this run-through. It ran two hours forty-six instead of two hours forty-one. Had no stomach to hang around for his notes, walked back alone in the rain.

Wednesday, 28 September – next morning

Here, more or less, is Gloria's report:

> Well, John gave no notes except to say if you're wondering where Arnold is he's gone back to the hotel with a razor blade because despite the cuts we've managed to run five minutes over. He gave us our schedule and then said there'd be a photographer to which Sir John said he hoped not and John just ignored that one and took Joe for a drink. Then Julie, Nick, Everett, Rebecca, Jeff and me we came back for a drink and began talking. Julie whined and I got angry with her. I mean I really got angry with her. She was so negative. I said this is no time to be negative, we've got the stage there, the sets, the props, the lighting, the moves, the text – it'll all come together, what is this?... I got on that stage and you know what I thought? I thought, Jesus Christ! This is the first fucking time I've done this scene with all those props there and costume. I jumped down off the stool into the centre of the stage – my Errol Flynn entrance on Broadway – and I thought well thank God I didn't trip over my costume, that's what I thought. *I* wasn't on that stage. You know who was on that stage? My fucking costume! My costume was there telling me your body hasn't picked up that blanket, hasn't moved that object. Who

could act? Who could get anything right? *I* was sweating, Roberta was sweating, Julie was sweating. And when I looked at Sir John under the weight of all that costume I thought – I don't blame him for blowing up. Everyone has a different way of releasing their tension so he yelled at them to be quiet during his speech. Nick gets angry with him: 'That Sir John,' he says, 'why doesn't he learn his fucking lines?' Well he'll know his lines on the first night – what's everybody getting at everybody for? Jesus, I wouldn't like to have John D's problems. He's got the balls of the union pushing him on one side, the balls of the actors pushing him on another, and Julie whines on about why is he cutting me when all the others have so much that can be cut and blah! blah! blah! So I tell her that's ugly and disgusting and she gets upset with me but I don't care, it *is* ugly and disgusting ... And Jeff – I love Jeff, he's cute, him and Rebecca, I like them because they've got quick minds – Jeff says, 'Now, don't let's desecrate the lavatories!' My, he was sick with worry, I tell you. Jeff was so miserable with anxiety for this play, for this play and his part. And he *still* should be, we got five more weeks to go! But he also got at Julie and said how the magic could still happen . . . I knew John was going to go for me, I just didn't know when. But I was cool. I knew exactly how to handle it, though I didn't know what I'd do if he became personal, I didn't think I could handle *that* – except to say, 'It's you I'm *really* attracted to.' And when he screamed at me and said, 'You're supposed to have rhythm,' I replied, 'Well, you see, John, my mother doesn't have rhythm and *that's* my problem! ' I knew you had to keep calm with him because he can always best you and I hate being bested so I said yes John of course John anything you say John tell me what you want John. All in a very low voice so that he gave me a double look. He stomped away and then turned back as if to say, 'Are you handling me?' Of course after it was over I had to rush to buy the biggest bar of chocolate I could find, like one other time a director yelled at me I was very calm but when I got outside the rehearsal room I fainted. I mean you've got to understand about John that he's got a very short fuse, he's got such a short fuse it's hardly there at all and he's got all these people to deal with – actors, producers, publicity, unions, stage hands. No! I sure wouldn't like John's problems at this time.'

Her accounting of events is richer and fuller than I've been able to recapture, her perceptions sharper and funnier – a tonic as a companion, though not one who can stop me feeling I've failed to write the play I'd wanted. That Shylock Kolner household was written about *my* household, full of children and their friends and my friends coming in and out and the lunches and Sunday teas and meals for foreign visitors. There's always an event in Bishops Road and that's the atmosphere I wanted to recreate on stage – a ghetto full of life, '*a house never still*', a Venice bursting with trade. It's not there. All that remains are spare and bare bones. With Zero dead and gone it's become a play about a Shylock directed with boring Englishness by a pinched and dried Antonio – which is how Sir John is beginning to play him. Ironic! It could be said, as Lorenzo in the play says of Shylock and his ghetto,

> I've stood by him in the ghetto when he's showing visitors it's sights: thin achievements in stone which he's magnified more from relief they've any stones at all, than from their real worth. There's hysteria in his description of things, an earnestness, a hammering home. His tone is urgent, excited, ornate and – proudly erudite ...

I feel my play is *a thin achievement* which I've *magnified* and that Jocelyn and John have cut out the urgency, the excitement, the ornateness because they imagine it's hysteria, earnestness and a hammering home. I feel like Shylock being got at by Antonio to be sensible and tow the line of law. I ache to see Roderigues back on stage with an abundance of lines; I ache to see *more* people bustling around. Where are those *objets d'art* of Venetian interiors, the signs of Jewish ghetto life, the delight in detail? Jocelyn apologised later for getting at me in the office. I couldn't deny that there *did* exist a difference in our temperaments, and asked didn't she see that an absence of things could feel as 'full' as the material presence; that a spare silence could scream as loudly as excessive verbosity? She understood. It didn't help. John promises to return some of the fabric he'd originally put into the warehouse scene, but with reluctance I feel. I think back on the atmosphere of bustling Venice which obtained in the Swedish production – slow and lugubrious though the acting was. Dusty loved that and, I'm sure, will be disappointed with this production.

Or again – am I too much on top of it? I'm inclined not to attend rehearsals this afternoon, just turn up for tonight's preview. But my absence is felt, and felt to be critical, which is why John needed to explain my absence last night. I'd better go.

Later, just before first preview

There are strange moments in a play's progress towards its first night. Moments of anxious hostility. John and me eye each other from a distance, not speaking. It was the same just before opening of *The Old Ones*.[166]

I arrive at the theatre. An exclusive and excluding relationship has developed between John, Andy Phillips and Jocelyn. It feels to me like a ganging up of the English, the Gentiles, the interpreters. John's bought two bottles of wine, Jocelyn has bought some Camembert and rusks. I hear John say, 'We're going to have a party for the next three days.' There's no greeting to me, no, 'Come on, Arnold, wine to see us through the slow hours of the tech.' I retreat upstairs and watch from the balcony. Publicity Susan and a photographer are also there, watching and plotting the photo-call. But I've had no lunch, and can't resist the cheese. Call down to Jocelyn who asks do I want her to throw it up. No, I'm coming down. I cut myself a portion, and ask John does he mind if I pour myself some wine. Of course not. Thus provided for I go back upstairs to watch the tech of the second act, John exercising instant direction, tightening up scenes.

In the court scene Sir John has an inspired idea to bare his breast as Shylock whips out his knife and cries:

---

166 I wrote about it for the *Guardian*: 'Butterflies With Everything', 9 August 1972. Their title, not mine, which was 'First Nightmares'.

Well damn you then! I'll have my pound of flesh and not feel obliged to explain my whys and wherefores...

It creates a strong, tense moment. But I still can't bear Joe staggering backwards on '*Will you take my books?*' It's so undignified. Nor can I bear the harsh way he rushes through and delivers the lines which follow:

> Will you take my books? ... What nonsense now ... I? Plot? Against a citizen of Venice? Who? Antonio?... Was 'that' which I pursued 'plot'? Plot? Malice aforethought? ... There's no perception, no wisdom ... no pity there.[167]

Delivered with no pain, no weariness, no broken man. At one point I miss one of the rewrites. Bloody hell, I think, has John made a cut without telling me? I rage inwardly, but when the scene is rerun I see it's still there.

He rehearses the curtain call. Invents the choreography of it on the spot. Antonio and Shylock from either side in front of the curtain. Bow, go off as curtain opens revealing the Androids. Abtalion, Tubal, Usque and Doge move in one swoop from behind, withdraw to the sides, then come the three Venetian boys followed by Rivka and Jessica, Portia on her own, Sir John again, followed by Shylock who brings them all together. He's left out poor Nerissa. Her Broadway début! He rehearses the curtain call again and again leaves her out.

'You're so dark I can't see you, that's why.'

'I'm no darker than Julie.' Jokes and merriment.

They're racing against time to finish.

The unions are standing by to darken the house.

Nerissa and I have a drink in a hotel, pass the hour and a half until curtain up. She's so excited. It's overwhelming to be with her. Does it come from me or does she communicate the feeling it will go well? Whoever – it's what I tell everyone when I visit them in their dressing rooms to wish them luck and broken legs. They respond, excited. John is in Marian's dressing room.

---

[167] Slightly changed in the final version.

'May I kiss her good luck?' I ask, not to disturb an important last minute note. I kiss her, then turn to the sitting John and kiss him warmly on the head.

Only pleasure is around, no sourness. Oh, may their happiness last.

It's a good audience. Not full but well spread out. Lots of late-comers. A slow, controlled start. We know Shylock is a collector of books, that he's witty, effervescent, has a patient, adoring friend. The audience laughs at the gondola line. They laugh through the 'creation of God' speech. They laugh at Nerissa's '*why, her brain can hardly catch its breath!*' They're breathless through Portia's '*I am the new woman and they know me not*' speech. It's when they applaud the end of the long, bustling, Scene 4 that I know the play has taken off! But the biggest surprise is the applause on:

The Jew is the Christian's parent. Family relationships – always difficult, especially when there's murder involved.

It's an audience that seems to understand every nuance, and is attentive even through the Renaissance story. And Joe was magnificent. He so thrilled me as I stood watching from the back of the stalls that I had to bring my hand to my mouth to stifle a gasp of delight.

In the interval I rushed downstairs to tell them how well it was going. I didn't need to. They had all been watching it on the screen and were in a daze of excitement. Roberta had applauded Joe at the end of Act I. Even Bassanio, Lorenzo and Graziano had been held by him on stage. He made such sense of it, was so ecstatic telling his Renaissance tale. And the stage looked beautiful. I found myself not missing the cuts. The second act went well, except the changeover from the court scene to Belmont. Not rehearsed. Lights all wrong.

When it was over I rushed again to tell them. But still John and I could barely bring ourselves to do more than acknowledge each other in passing. What *is* it that goes on? He sends out vibrations, murderous and simple, which say 'don't talk to me, don't embrace me', warnings, perhaps, that there's more fighting over more cuts so he doesn't want to hear my notes on production or performance. I swear to myself there will be no more cuts. The curtain went up at 7.35 and came down at 10.35. That's not too long for an evening, and it will get faster. I expect a phone call in the morning from a stern voice saying, 'We must meet for cuts.' I've steeled myself to say, 'Not another word! Not another word!'

I attempt for the sake of company bonding to gather people together for food and drink. Most go their own way. I end up with Nick, Mark (an android), Gloria and Leib. Publicity and management are at another table. We're in the restaurant of the Intrigue Hotel!

Thursday, 29 September – day of first night

Yesterday there were two performances. In the matinée only a small house but attentive and, in the end, appreciative. John sat taking notes which he gave to people in dressing rooms. I moved here and there offering a few words but mostly saving it for a session with John.

The evening performance was nearly full – a benefit for computer people. They laughed in all the right places but, although on the verge, never found courage enough to burst into applause as that first preview audience did. Nevertheless good. Attentive. John has asked Peter Shaffer to fly down from NY to see it. In between shows I bumped into him and we had a coffee together talking about John whom he thinks may well be schizoid. I should love to talk more with Peter about our common director of whom we both have criticisms but who we obviously feel is an order of genius. John told me that we would all – the *Equus* crowd – gather after the show in his hotel, and talk over the play. The *Equus* crowd being Rivka, Portia, Graziano, Lorenzo and one of the androids all of whom had been in the Shaffer play at one time or other. It took for ever to get to his hotel. I had an appointment at midnight. There was little time left for me to be there. John had given me the wrong impression, there was no talk, it was to be a party – champagne, sandwiches, cheese and grass. He was dressed in a long black caftan and was fast becoming smashed – not my scene, really, though Peter is a great raconteur and had us in fits of laughter with Lew Grade[168] stories.

At eleven this morning I met John outside the theatre. We walked back and forth hugging the walls of the Kennedy Centre, avoiding the sunny sides, while he talked and put the position to me.

'We must tell the company where we stand tonight, and here is how I see it. You're standing on your author's rights not to cut any more. The management want – will want – fifteen minutes out. I'm on the side of management. I agree with them. Now, I can reduce the running by about two minutes or so by altering scene changes and the like, but what I believe is that some sort of tightening can take place which I'll talk about in a minute. First, as Peter told you last night, there's a focus missing from the Renaissance speech. Why is it there? You want it pointed by referring to the yellow hat. I don't believe only a visual thing will help. I can do it but it's not enough. It needs some line like that great line about "Thank you, and if you tell me where you're playing next week I'll come and see you."[169] I'd like the Christians to applaud Shylock's Renaissance speech and for him to say something about "but all this knowledge is wasted" or "it could be applied to the whole world if you knew how", or something to state what it had all been for. Now, I know you're not happy with what I've done to the play, that it's not what you wanted, but we've got a show here which still could work. If you want to stand by what we've got – fine. I'll tighten and improve. But I'm convinced that a week's work with you in New York could produce a new rearrangement along these lines: attention is lost by going backwards and forwards from the ghetto to Belmont to the warehouse back to the ghetto. If in some way we could bring the portrait scene into the big ghetto scene and get all the bustle over and done with, leaving a clear line to the warehouse and Antonio's dinner then we would have a compact unit, tight and focused. Remember, I'm not talking about cutting for time. Nor am I talking about whether you or I earn money. It's a question

---

[168] Lord Grade. ex-chairman of ATV.

[169] The last line of John Osborne's excellent play *The Entertainer*.

of how many people do you want to see this play? Do you want an appreciable audience for a few months or something that will go on for a year at least ...?'

He talked for a good three-quarters of an hour along those lines. The situation was put with warmth and professional clarity, coupled with the urgency of a statesman laying before the king the pros and cons of his dilemma.

These are the inferences I'm left to draw. If I stand firm the play will probably not go to New York. It will also mean John wouldn't direct it in London (which means no one would!), nor would he direct *The Wedding Feast*. Then there's the cast. If I stand firm they may not go to Broadway – a moral dilemma echoing Shylock's: his friend's life or the life of his community, my play or my cast? To say nothing of lost earnings. Perhaps that would be a good thing – not earning all that money. I could write the Jesus play with an easy conscience. On the other hand John was suggesting a possible solution which could be got ready for New York.

I replied that central to my hesitation is the feeling that I've always had: length is not the problem of the play, ideas are its problem. Ideas and argument are the nature of this beast. No matter what one took away it would still seem a long play because it's a 'think' play, it's demanding of the audience ...

As for the restructuring – I don't know. My instincts say – be firm, the structure is right. But I'm going to stop writing this journal and attempt to restructure. I have to do it now because I can't agree to something until I know it works.

Later – 4 p.m.

Drama! Drama! Drama!

I began to work. Gloria phoned – my contact, my spy.

'What's happened?' she asked animatedly. 'Where are you? How are you?' I told her I'm here, working, sweating it out, that I had been confronted with an ultimatum. She reported: John had told the cast that Arnold was feeling a bit battered and was walking and talking with Peter Shaffer, that a question of half an hour of cuts was involved (half an hour?), that Arnold was saying 'no more cuts', and that he, John, was in agreement with the management.

He'd asked the cast to look closely at their own text and see if any lines could come out. He gave them forty-eight hours to do that, pointing out that there were sixteen characters and that if each lost a minute that would be sixteen minutes. Not possible, of course, but as a guide ...

Gloria, sensing in my voice the drama and urgency of the situation, wanted to reassure me and at the same time argue for cuts. There was, she began, an over-abundance of riches in the play. 'If you'd invited people to a meal and spent three hundred dollars on food but a hundred and fifty dollars' worth had been stolen, and they'd come and eaten and said they couldn't eat any more, and if you were to say to them, "Ah, but you should have seen all those cakes I'd bought which you now can't eat because they were stolen," they'd say, "But Arnold, we've had enough, we couldn't eat any more, we just couldn't." It'd be the same thing.'

I'd been drinking bourbon on an empty stomach.

'I don't care about Broadway,' I yelled down the phone. 'I don't care about it. Someone has to say that.'

'And bring down everyone with them? That's *hara-kiri*.'

'And to say *that* is corruption.'

'I take it back. Not another word. I'm sorry. Forgive me!' She was marvellous, whispering almost, sensing the nature and intensity of an internal conflict.

'I feel as though a storm has been whipped up,' I continued, the bourbon really in control now, 'and huge waves are gathering and I'm the tiny thing in their path – management, John, the cast who want to go to New York, my future. All those things are poised over me.' Did she guess I'd half a bottle of bourbon on an empty stomach? Told her I must get on, try to restructure the play, asked would she please buy me some first-night presents on her way back, listed what I wanted.

I returned to work. When done I rang the theatre and spoke to John. He guessed I was in a high state because he was in one, too. Told him: 'I've been working.'

'So have I. I've re-staged the ending of Act I to make the hat seem significant.'

'I've got a better idea.' And explained. He became excited. .

'Also,' I said, 'I've restructured the fourth scene to incorporate the portrait scene and it loses the discussion about lateness and broken appointments *but* it does not lose us fifteen minutes. What I want from you is assurance that this is all, or I want to know *now* what else you have up your sleeve that you think is unnecessary.' He was in the middle of a ten minute break from rehearsal and I had *him* under pressure.

He answered: 'The fox fables passage and the Usque da Mendes exchange about skin bared to the wind, and other lines here and there.'

'John, I don't want to lose that exchange or the foxes' fable, and, besides, none of that will lose us fifteen minutes. I want us to agree here and now that this change I've made will be all.'

'You must speak to the management tonight and tell them. You and I will talk in the second act perhaps ...'

'No! I don't think I'll be able to tear myself away from *any* part of tonight, and I *don't* want to talk to management tonight. I want to be with the actors. My place is with them. I'll talk to management in the morning. I'll see *you* first and then them. *We'll* talk about my changes and your suggestions and then I'll be in a position to talk to management.'

He agreed. He had to rush off for the last hour of rehearsal.

I'm very high as I write this and I've got to a position where I've made a major structural change which I quite like.[170] I had originally followed the Shakespearean tradition of swift change from setting to setting. The new structure concentrates on longer and more solid blocks of text and action. Now it's going to be hand-to-hand battles for individual lines.

Think I must lie down and sleep for twenty minutes. It's 4.35 p.m. Curtain up in two and a half hours. John had said they'd done a good afternoon's work.

Later

I dozed. Korby rang to say she and Burt had arrived and were going off to the Matisse. She said she had a friend who owned a restaurant and had arranged for the cast to gather. Rang the

---

[170] But I returned to my original structure for the UK production in Birmingham, and for the definitive published text.

theatre and gave the task of co-ordination to one of the stage managers.

My meeting with Shaffer. He very kindly came for a quick half-hour chat following my talk with John. We walked round and round the Kennedy Centre. He said, briefly, that he thought it was a brilliant idea, marvellously written and conceived, a great *coup*, but two things worried him – he didn't understand the reason for the big dinner scene in which Shylock tells his Renaissance story. He loved, was riveted by it, but was waiting all the time for its relevance to be made clear. Second, he felt the play sagged in the middle, especially around the long, bustling family Scene 4. One debate too much ... or something.

'There always reaches a point,' he said, 'when you have to make decisions about what's more important out of two things going on.'

It was this which led me finally to abandon the exchange between Shylock and Jessica about the importance of keeping appointments, and to incorporate that portrait scene into the main family Scene 4. I was touched by his friendly concern and intelligent observations. His manner and tone were just right – aware of the presumption but accepting the responsibility of a colleague.

Having made these changes[171] I felt in a better position to face the producers. In a mad rush I collected the roses and half bottles of champagne I'd bought for the cast, fell into Angela and Gloria's dressing room to write out first-night cards, delivered them, and the bottles of whisky I'd bought for lighting technicians, androids and wardrobe staff; rushed upstairs to say hello to Burt and Korby, and settled down for the first night. It was not a bad performance, but I discovered later from Riggs and Gloria that John had, in addition to other things he'd said, told the cast how everything was in a state of flux, and the play may not go to New York because management want a half hour of cuts, and Arnold was standing on his rights ... etc. This had drained energy from them. Not his wisest tactic. Bloody stupid, actually, especially as he knew I was at work on cuts. Still, at the end there was great excitement.

Julie's stepfather, Sidney Kohn, who'd handled Zero's affairs, took me aside trembling, and declared me to be the greatest philosophical

---

171 I seem to have left out the other important structural change I'd made on that drunken bourbon afternoon in my hotel; I'd drastically restructured and shortened the warehouse scene.

playwright alive – a deliciously acceptable exaggeration. Then followed a most extraordinary encounter. My last call of thanks was to Sir John. Bernie Jacobs was in the dressing room with him. He could be my uncle, sallow-skinned with dark rings round his eyes, like Aunt Sara. He too must have come from Russian parents. He said his few words of praise, which I was grateful to accept for he was, after all, party both to the initial purchase and the subsequent decision to continue after Zero's death. After the New York flatterer the New York businessman. The play was too long, he said. I told him that work has been done, that John and I were meeting to discuss what more could be cut, but pointed out that though the play will be shorter it would not gain more than ten minutes plus another ten minutes gained as the play was run in. He ignored what I said.

'Because I don't want you to be under any misapprehension about where we stand. If it's necessary John and us will go over your back and make the cuts and get it on.'

He said more, as I did, but roughly my reply was: 'Bernie, you're talking to the wrong person. I've gone to law before now to protect my plays and I won't hesitate again. You shouldn't have said that to me, I'd already said we were contemplating cuts.' He tried to soften it by saying he had to be frank, that he had more experience than me, and so on. I was furious but glad I'd hit back. Silly old Sir John then took up my time with a boring story about how he'd directed a cut version of Ben Levy's *Rape of the Belt*, which Levy himself then directed a fuller version of in New York. The London production ran for two years, the New York one folded after three days. [172]

I wrote out a page of notes, and left them for John. [173]

Monday, 3 October – on train from Washington to New York. Story of first night at Kennedy Centre.

No party had been arranged. Marvin Krauss, the general manager, came to tell me the producers would like me to join them at dinner after the performance. Told him I had arranged for the cast

---

[172] Reading the Ben Levy story twenty years later I concede it is interesting. But I was in no mood then for Clements' moral tales.

[173] Appendix 3.

to eat together in Nathan's II and that I wanted to be with them, where I belonged. They were welcome to join us. They did, and with great generosity picked up the bill. Not everyone but most came. John, of course, stayed away. I proposed a toast to the producers who 'had they been anybody else would have abandoned the play'. It's true but my tone may have showed I still smarted from the encounter with Bernie Jacobs. Bernie accepted the toast seriously, and thanked me, his voice tight with deep appreciation, perhaps moved that I appeared to have forgiven him.

Talked at length with Gerry Schoenfeld (whose wife reminded me I'd promised her a long private talk about the play). I assured him, too, that work had been done on the play and more would be done. Nevertheless a date was made to meet with everyone the next morning at 8 a.m. in Suite 106 at the Watergate Hotel. I was in bed by about 3.30 a.m. and up at 7.30. Not only did I fall asleep thinking what I would say to them but I went on to dream about them, and woke up thinking about them!

Breakfast of scrambled eggs and coffee laid on. I ate, ravenously, eggs, which I shouldn't have done, but then I've been eating a lot of foods lately which I shouldn't have done. Present were Bernie, Gerry Schoenfeld, Roger Berlind, Sam Cohn, another member of the Shubert organisation – Phillips? – and Bernie's wife who said nothing.

I felt in an odd, almost false position. I'd already assured two of them that cuts had been made and more would result from talks with John. So why were we here? I felt thrown to the lions. John had honestly told me he'd chucked in his hand with management, now I was left to battle with them alone. But, as I later discovered, the timing had gone wrong.

I kicked off, asking could we get a few things clear. 'None of us can be entirely objective. My text makes me subjective. John's production makes *him* subjective. And your financial involvement makes *you* subjective. No one commands a special lofty height giving them clear vision. Next, I'd like it understood that we're all experienced and professional, we've all been around a long time, each of our opinions has weight.' I asked them to believe that I didn't feel my text was sacrosanct because *I'd* written it. But there was a grand design to the play which I wanted to protect, a quality to which they had responded, and perhaps I had to protect *them* against themselves. The play had already been cut and trimmed – evidence surely of a responsible attitude. I informed them John had asked the cast to look at their own text for cutting. I quoted John saying there are sixteen people in this play and that if each one cuts a minute we'll lose another sixteen minutes. I was aware of their investment of time and energy, and of John's and the cast's hopes, to say nothing of what it all meant to me, but I reserved the right to protect the integrity of my play.

They conceded this right which was, after all, written into the contract, but their concern was where *they* placed final responsibility. They'd given everything over to John – it had never happened that such total responsibility had been given to a director: casting, design, lighting, publicity and budgeting, even though contractually the last word on the text was mine. They were in a quandary and could only hope that John and I will be able to resolve our differences – but it was in John they placed total authority.

I said I understood and accepted such a chain of command, but repeated that I had to place trust in my own instincts, though of course I would, as always, be open to John's suggestions. And then I said something about which I now feel guilty, as though it were a betrayal. I pointed out how John and I began our careers together and that I'd like to think he had learned from my plays as much about the limits to which drama could be pushed as I had learned from him; that his courage and daring had been revealed to him through directing such plays as *The Kitchen* and *Chips With Everything*. Further, that great though he was as a director he was human, prone to error, and could as easily be wrong. My instincts were as valid as his.

They reiterated their support of the play and their belief that we were on the verge of an extraordinary event, but their faith and trust in the omnipotence and authority of John the director was total. In that case I said they would have to wait until John and I had gauged the extent of our differences before they made their final decision about what to do next. They also expressed reservations about some of the cast, but agreed with me it would be fatal for morale to make changes. John, I knew, would work on performances. Sam Cohn – the most sober and intelligent, perhaps the most sensitive, since they're all intelligent – said he realised John's energy had to be given to Joe Leon in these last two and a half weeks, and so other performances and aspects of the production had to be abandoned; and though they felt Joe had done marvellously he was not that huge personality they hoped would match a 'huge' play. Still, if Dexter and Wesker wanted to go ahead with him then Wesker and Dexter must know what they're doing. We were due to meet that day, they would wait to hear.

I rang John there and then, woke him up, made a date. Gerry was supposed to have met him at 9 a.m. He'd forgotten. It was now 10 a.m. We arranged to meet at the theatre at 12.30 where he was to give notes, rearrange the curtain call, tidy it up. After that we'd go off to eat and talk.

Returned to the hotel, and spent the morning writing my 'notes for John', three pages culled from the sheets I'd scrawled over during the last two performances. Didn't get a chance to finish them all, had to rush to the theatre.

Everyone looked strange. Roberta especially – her face creamed, wearing a hairnet – seemed weird, birdlike, stunned. Four actors weren't there because they'd been called for 1.30 instead of 12.30. We sat around the Green Room. John told them how good they'd all been, how now they must settle and: 'I beg you, beg you, beg you not to listen to other people or engage in dressing-room direction. Arnold and I are going away to New York to work on changes and sort out our differences. Fifteen minutes must be lost from the play, we have ideas ...' A short talk before going off to the Pelican Restaurant in Les Champs, the shopping area of the Watergate Hotel.

We spent a good three hours together. Reported on my meeting with the producers, told him honestly I had defended my own instincts alongside his, gave him the restructured text and my three pages of notes, then insisted he tell me in *full* what his other thoughts were and not surprise me day by day. I listed his suggested cuts.[174] We discussed future work plans.

---

[174] Appendix 4.

Something John said staggered me, and pointed to a difference in our personalities. He said how upset and anxious he'd been that afternoon before the first preview when I'd fled to the balcony. 'I thought – my God, Arnold's gone off to write another *Guardian* article, and then we saw you being photographed, and Jocelyn said that's the way Arnold is and has always been and you'd better get used to it.' I rounded on him. They'd completely misread the moment. They'd imagined I'd abandoned the team in order to be photographed whereas I'd fled from what I thought was *their* unfriendliness, from what seemed to me a triumvirate of technicians, English and Gentiles keeping out the writer who was neither Gentile nor very English. Told him I'd even written about it in my journal.

How could Jocelyn have said such a thing? I was glad *that* one was cleared up.

By the end he was a mixture of drunk, irritated and in need of air. I returned to the hotel to collect some sheets, he went back to the theatre where we later met again to go over my soldering of the portrait scene on to Scene 4, and talk about next stages. He was flying to New York to start rehearsals of *Rigoletto*; I was to join him and we'd work for the week in the evenings. He'd try to get Lorenzo and Jessica down to work on them during the day. Told him I'd join him in New York after Wednesday because I had to be in Washington for a symposium He needed a couple of days to get into *Rigoletto* and I needed time to recuperate and collect my thoughts.

He had to get an hour's sleep before the Saturday evening performance. I too returned to the hotel for a break. In the interim something happened. John's mood changed. His irritation, which began with the abundance of notes I'd given him, had taken root. He snapped at me about my not coming to New York at once. I was tired, vulnerable and off-balance. His anger, so different from the afternoon's spirit of warm friendship and work, sent me reeling. When he rages there is such malevolence in his eyes. He's trying to gain the upper hand, I thought, to assert his authority. If he says I must go to New York on Monday then it must be Monday. We snapped back and forth over other things – such as me repeating that something must be done about Portia, him saying that was his business and he'd already said he'd do it. It was my business also, I insisted, just as my text was *his* business. But my energy was at too low an ebb to fight effectively. I became silent.

The performance began. A full house and an audience which from the start got everything. I stood at the back. After a while John crept up behind me, and in a renewed friendly voice whispered about the need to re-do the poster. I was not ready for friendliness.

'I'm not taking it in, John, I'm too upset.' He moved briskly away, and I continued watching.

He came up to me again. 'Did you notice how much warmer Clements was in the first scene?' I had done. He wanted to make sure I could see that he'd already started putting my notes into effect.

Later he came back again, and whispered in my ear: 'If you're good I'll show you the *Washington Post* review.' I turned to him, my eyes alight. He said: 'Give me a kiss and come outside.' He offered me his lips. I kissed them, and we went outside to read Richard Coe's review.

Shylock is provocative and stimulating and should be one of New York's most arresting offerings of the season. In Shylock, Arnold Wesker has created a character of timeless appeal ... humour and logic ... the play's the thing and *Shylock* has the quality of a rich considered statement by an original inquiring mind ...

'But,' said John, 'the *Washington Star* is a bitch.' He hadn't read it, he'd heard. As the evening progressed he became more drunk, mellower, and more affectionate.

The cast received a good ovation. Performances had been up on the first night. Clements had delivered his 'tiller' speech the best ever. But the cloth from the last Belmont scene had been left on the floor, and Marian had slipped on it during curtain call. When I went down to see her she was in tears. The accident brought everything out. She hugged me and said: 'And I want you . to know that I think it's obscene asking actors to cut authors' lines. I do it because I'm disciplined and I do what I'm told but I hate it that they think they can mess around like that with a writer's work.'

I was touched, grateful for her tears and words. Not that I entirely agreed since an actor *can* have sensible thoughts on what's repetitive or redundant (though *some* of their suggested cuts are hair-raising, of which more later). I commiserated with her about her scene with Shylock in which he, because he doesn't know his lines, is crippling her performance, making her frantic. I also thought while watching that something was wrong in the centre of that scene – the logic and rhythm not as clear as it could be. I had thought this before but only now, as I've just paused in writing the journal, have I looked to see what had been worrying me, and corrected it.[175]

Everyone went their separate ways. I took Gloria, her mother, and son Adam out to dinner – my surrogate family. Next day, Sunday, we and Nick Surovy had lunch at Clydes, and visited the Smithsonian Space Museum. I loved it. A film about flying was projected on to a huge screen. It began with the balloon which took us through glorious parts of the States. We sat three rows from the screen engulfed by it. Everything about the day and that film made me float. I felt exhilarated. I also felt homesick, and found myself hugging, clinging to little Adam, and cooing at a woman's tiny baby. It's foolish but looking at babies makes me, like a woman, broody, and I thought: that's what I've got to look forward to – grandchildren!

That evening I heard some distressing, even shocking news. Dined with Nick, Gloria, Susan and Merle. I like and respect Susan and Merle but they were bitter about John's criticisms of them and the way they were handling press and publicity. For their part they were not happy with the production. They hated some of the performances and felt certain questions, answered in the text, were not being answered in the production. I told them of my battles with the producers. Merle said something about the producers having been misled. On our return to the hotel I took him aside to ask for clarification. Here came the shock. He

---

[175] Not recorded, but I suppose I cut and rearranged some lines.

informed me that John had told Marvin – these are his words – 'to get the producers down, the fucker isn't changing a line.' Suddenly a lot fell into place. John must have acted immediately after our confrontation early in the week when we'd just arrived in Washington and had met together with Jocelyn, and I'd accepted some but not all his suggested cuts. Enraged, he'd lied to the producers telling them I'd adamantly refused to cut, thereby enlisting their support. But since then we'd had our long walk round and round the Kennedy Centre, and I'd talked with Shaffer, and as a result had rewritten. That's why Bernie Jacobs' fierceness was ill-timed – the moment causing it had passed. So had the need for that early morning meeting with scrambled eggs. More distressing was John's betrayal. He'd thrown me to the lions after I had been co-operative and had made so many cuts and changes.

Gloria begged me not to quarrel with John. I should understand that his arms had been twisted by the producers and so he was twisting mine. The only hope lay in us not letting anything or anyone come between us. If John betrayed me I should not do the same but give people to believe we were in harmony and would resolve our differences. I disagreed. It was not the producers who were twisting John's arms but, crazy though it seemed, John was twisting theirs. He was in control of everybody.

It was an intense, emotional exchange, as everything has been. I was touched by Gloria's passionate defence both of John and our friendship in which she saw the ultimate saving of the production. It seems everyone, from management to cast, have this image of our relationship as something uniquely and immensely creative. The cast in particular keep a wary eye on us, watching our moods, the way we talk to one another. Or don't.

Went to the theatre yesterday – Monday – morning to pick up mail and tell Merle and Susan not to worry about the review in the *Washington Star* which I'd just read. It was a familiar attack, no one escaped – Jocelyn, John, the acting, the play. The critic was the journalist who'd profiled me, not unsympathetically, but obviously a softener for this the real blow he'd been planning. It was so vehement that we laughed. Not Riggs or Nick, though, they'd been cruelly singled out, and it affected their performances that night. I was anxious to let everyone know the review hadn't upset me, rather it had turned on my adrenalin – must be a great play to attract such vitriol.

Took the train to New York, arrived around 6 p.m., taxi to 117 West 11 to pick up a key from Sylvia and meet her house guests – she slept with her boyfriend for two nights so's I could sleep in her bed – then taxi to 1 Lincoln Plaza for dinner with John. The evening was totally unexpected. Moving, strange, perplexing.

He'd laid out deli food – roast beef, smoked salmon, feta cheese, and began to talk about the history of the theatre beginning with caveman drawing on the wall. I can't remember what he said but I wasn't very interested – or rather I was interested but he wasn't very interesting. I was more curious to see where he was leading. Paradoxically, though he wasn't interesting he was intoxicated, alive with purpose. His intention was to try and place my work in its historical perspective, though I don't think I understood why he needed to go back as far as caveman. 'Along came Zola and Ibsen and Strindberg and Chekhov with their naturalism, followed by Shaw with his theatre of ideas, and you I suppose fall between the two.' He went on to talk about finding a style for *Shylock*, 'which is a play synthesising naturalism, ideas, and a kind of classical shape ...'

After a while I told him I'd prefer to talk about my 'place in the scheme of things' from a different angle. I'd once seen a TV programme, I told him, devoted to theatre, which included a panel of theatre people – critics, actors, directors of various styles and isms – talking about their ideas and theories, and at the end Robert Bolt[176] appeared and made a statement which began (something like): 'I don't feel that anything of what has been said here this evening has anything to do with what I think I'm doing when I sit down to write a play.' I told John, 'And I feel very much the same a lot of the time. I'm driven to write only by experience. Not *all* my experience of course, but that which I think is significant, resonant. I'm not motivated by a wish to explore or prove theories about theatre or styles of acting or design. I only wish to organise the chaos of my experience, and it's the material which dictates the form. *The Kitchen* is the shape it is because the

---

[176] Playwright and screen writer – *Man For All Seasons, Dr Zhivago* etc. Dead now.

material dictated it. *Chicken Soup With Barley* fell into the traditional form of three acts because that's the way the material came to me. *Chips With Everything* was broken into small scenes because the events demanded those small scenes. I'm not a theorist. I believe everything is permissible if it works. *Shylock* for me is a sixteenth-century *Chicken Soup With Barley* if you like. I was prepared to accept the spare style of Jocelyn's sets providing the busy naturalism of the life described in the text was shown. Sometimes you've achieved this, sometimes not ...'

John wanted to talk about Antonio and Shylock in the light of his and my relationship. He said how much he identified with Antonio as the Christian being received into the Wesker house. He had this sharp memory of Dusty and me taking him into our flat in Clapton Common after he'd come out of prison in 1958, and that's why he responded to the Antonio/Shylock relationship. It had not occurred to me.

I'm trying to remember the sequence of our conversation. It's impossible. I must just lay it out as it comes to me.

He took a joint to smoke. I asked him to forgive me not joining in. As the evening moved on he became less and less inhibited, and wanted to continue talking about 'us'. Where did *our* relationship stand? He talked about the past and what pleasure it gave him that we were all still working together, that we had survived. He wanted to know how I viewed him.

'As someone with whom I don't share a *social* life,' I began, 'but a very intense *working* one. As someone with whom I share a history, one of the most important in my life since we began our careers locking into one another's talents. As someone upon whom I feel I could call for anything, and who could call upon me, providing there wasn't a mother dying ...'

'That photo of Leah[177] you sent,' he interjected, 'was a marvellous and strange one.'

I told him how Dusty and Leah had loved him. He'd known about Dusty but not about Leah. It brought tears to his eyes. 'Oh I'm pleased about that, I didn't think...well ...' And Tanya, with whom he'd had an initial clash, she too had come round to

---

[177] Leah, my mother.

forgiving his 'male chauvinism' and had responded to the cuddly bear in him. It all gave him pleasure. We talked a little more about the children, and what they wanted to do. When I told him Tanya wanted to act, and Lindsay to direct, he at once asked what they were going to change their names to 'because the children of famous people suffer'. I said I knew that, and had already advised them.

He wanted to talk more about my feelings for him and about the parallels in our lives. He said that when he thought about our relationship he always felt himself to be the feminine one of the two. With little boys he felt masculine but not with me. That's why he often lost his temper and raged, kicking against my masculine stubbornness. I was astounded by this confession. He went on to ask about Dusty and me. He said how he and Riggs had not lived together for ten years and had a complete understanding about living separate lives. He wanted to know what it was like 'on your side of the sexual fence'. I took some time before plunging into confessions.

'If you're asking me have I had affairs, well you know that because one hit the headlines. But, despite that, Dusty and I are closer than ever and find much in common. We share the same values about family and home and friendships, though we don't always like each other's friends. She doesn't have any affairs.' I resisted telling him about Elsa.[178] He said how magnificent Dusty looked these years, both he and Jocelyn felt the same – she was simply radiant, the best she'd ever looked.

Told him how astounded I was that he saw himself as the feminine one in our relationship since my perception was of him trying to assert a masculine authority over me and the text. It was his turn to be astounded. I told him that one of my anxieties in our relationship – I hesitated, he pressed – was that he'd make an advance which would cause us both pain and embarrassment. I was certain he'd always imagined me a latent homosexual and seemed constantly on the verge of putting it to the test. That's why I'd not smoked the joint, and was going easy on the drink, and had made it very clear that I was going to another flat that

---

[178] My daughter in Stockholm from a Swedish liaison.

night. I wanted to be in control of all situations. He said I'd nothing to fear. 'Not that somewhere in the back of my mind I don't lust after your body. But I just wouldn't.'

He put on a record of Ravel's *Concerto for Left Hand*, followed by the Mozart's *Mass in C*, followed by Noël Coward's *Bitter Sweet*, the while talking about genius and asking would we give up people, family, friends and wine to produce music like that. Said I feared greatness eluded me because I'd always put family first. On the other hand, art and family had never presented themselves as alternatives. John warned that moment may come soon where I might have to chose between staying longer in the States and returning home on schedule. I hoped not. Besides, that was not an extreme dilemma. He confessed he would sooner be conducting or composing music. I shared that with him.

We talked at length about *The Old Ones* and why his *Fiddler* ending had so distressed me. He seemed at last to understand what I had been trying to achieve. He apologised. He'd been ill, stretched on his back.

'In fact Robin Fox[179] said to me, "Why do you take it from Arnold? You don't take it from Shaffer or any of the others." And I told him it was in return for a guest-house room.'

This story left me speechless. Why did he take *what* from Arnold? My right to insist my play be done as I'd written it? The underlying assumption of Fox's remark is that the director's wish should be final, and how thoughtless of the writer to upset him.

It was another intense time. John dressed in his long, black caftan, becoming wild and red-eyed from smoking grass, physically on the move most of the time, talking so personally, relating to the play so personally, the emotionally charged music ... 'I've been looking forward for weeks to this evening,' he said. 'It's the first time we've ever really done it, sat down and talked like this.'

I was torn between feeling moved by his passionate concern about our relationship, and an uneasy suspicion that it was all a softening-up process to persuade me to accept his suggestions for cuts and restructure, though I feel treacherous thinking such

---

[179] John's assistant at the time, now a theatre and film producer.

thoughts because the evening was one of warmth, affection and trusting confession. One of the most pleasing of his revelations was the genesis of his taste for opera. Directing opera began for him when he directed the opening of the third play in *The Trilogy*, *I'm Talking About Jerusalem*. 'Making all those moves fit with the Beethoven *Choral Symphony* – that's when the taste began.'

We touched on nothing or little of the problems of *Shylock*. He let fall the information that Paul Newman was interested in the film of the play; that he was trying to persuade the Shuberts to open in a smaller theatre – the Plymouth where *Chips With Everything* had lived, and *Equus* had begun its New York life. Without Zero it *would* be more difficult to fill the Imperial, and running costs are less at the Plymouth – the difference between 1000 and 1400 seats. I thought it a good idea, though it's a pity not to be able to open in a theatre that's been redecorated for the purpose. Another problem looming on the horizon is that Joe Leon and Sir John are now asking for huge increases in salary. John told me he was refusing to be blackmailed by either, and had threatened to recast both parts and open two weeks later if necessary.

He kept mumbling about 'desperately wanting to present your work to a wider public – English speaking that is'. My suspicions are unworthy, I know, but I can't help them. He has such a Machiavellian approach to life – or do I misjudge? It's a dilemma. He's a browbeater. He doesn't direct that which he thinks should be cut, and he talks on and on about the text he thinks ought to go, or be trimmed. Between not being able to see directed what he thinks is undirectable, and not hearing text which actors mumble or want cut or don't understand or simply can't deliver, it's hell deciding what of my play works or doesn't. Sir John hates the description of Graziano – one of my favourite passages[180] – and therefore doesn't deliver it properly, or remember it, and so

---

[180] 'In my warehouse is a young man, Graziano Sanudo, in charge of the import of spices. Now *he's* a happy man, no melancholy in him, and I don't know that I can stand him around. He has no real opinions, simply bends with the wind, quickly rushing to agree with the next speaker. He's a survivor, not defiantly, which is honourable, but creepily, like a chameleon, blending with everyone to avoid anyone's sting. He laughs when every idiot farts out thin wit, fawns on the tyrannical, is reverential before the papal, and manifests the most depressingly boisterous happiness I know. Give me Shylock's melancholy, gentleman, and take away my man's smiles.'

John wants to cut it. Angela delivers her lines like Lady Bountiful which is why her exchange with Usque fails – John wants that cut, too. Julie whines, and so large sections of Jessica have gone. But I've wandered from that evening. Little more I can remember, anyway. Just that I left with the sense of a terrible loneliness in John, a man who thrived on intense work – *Rigoletto* during the day, discussions about *Shylock* in the evening, and phone calls in between about actors' salaries and opera administration. A driven soul pitted and plagued with anxieties, doubts and stomach pains. And as if all that wasn't enough he's planning with the Czech Cultural Ministry, through Svoboda (the designer), to create a production of *The Tempest* in a Czech set, involving film and slides of actors in masks which could be taken around the world using the actors of each country. An amazing concept.

This evening was a working evening with John from 5.30 till 10.30 with a break for dinner at the Ginger Man. I'd worked during the day on his idea of soldering the warehouse scene on to the dinner scene. I could see its advantages but, I told him, it made me feel I'd failed to write a good warehouse scene in which the images of what was being warehoused were linked to the debate between the three men. I reminded him of Antonio's words: '*The most important aspects of our Empire are its warehouses, packhorses …*' Shouldn't he be pushing me to improve the scene rather than incorporating it into – and making longer – the dinner scene? And what about variety? 'Aren't five scenes enough to satisfy your need for epic splendour?' he threw at me. I know less and less what's right or what works.

But the most important discussion of text revolved around Antonio and his attitude to the bond. No one, insisted John, picking up the old Clements' argument, was convinced that this man would allow Shylock to go ahead with such a mocking bond, unless he also shared in it in some way. The idea interested me at once for Antonio to say, 'Yes, great idea, let's mock the laws of Venice together, they need mocking.' Such a line would be echoed later by Portia: '*… There's not enough of mockery in Venice. We're a city boasting very little of intelligent self-scrutiny or ridicule …*'

I fly to Washington tomorrow to participate in a symposium,

then return Thursday in order, I fear, for John to continue brow-beating me into more cuts. We've agreed on much, and now only hand to hand fighting over words and lines is left. For example, Jessica's speech about to whom a house belongs. In the sentence 'look how my father smiles, swells with pride ...' I cut out 'smiles'. 'He's given me teachers to nourish and exercise my mind ...', I cut out 'and exercise.' And I delete the entire last sentence: 'He neither comprehends the conflict nor thinks my anger serious.' Repetitions and inessentials!

Perhaps when it's all over it will seem best for the play. At the moment I just fear that we're taming the magnificent lion.

Stayed up till 2.30 a.m. writing all this which began on the train from Washington, and continued in the hotel.

Wednesday, 5 October – on flight back to Washington

Couldn't sleep last night. Writing the journal hyped my mind. Must have dozed off at about 5 a.m., woke at 7. Thinking all the time about the cuts I'm making and resisting, especially the new idea that Antonio should be part of Shylock's mocking bond. One cut I'm thinking could be made is the exchange between Nerissa and Portia about her 'strange tutors ... the boring Lamberti from Genoa ...', etc.

'Very exotic names,' said John, 'but you're just showing off.'

Read through the actors' suggestions for cuts. Marian, who had wept on my shoulder and declared it was obscene to make actors cut a writer's word is the one who has suggested the *most cuts*, and those mainly of other peoples' lines! Joe Leon has suggested a very strange cut.

SHYLOCK   Then you must look out for a rare manuscript for me ... called the *Fox Fables* ... The English edition is beautifully handwritten and – this is what interests me – contains references, since omitted, to the writer's life in England and the indifference of its wealthy Jews to intellectual and literary activities.

USQUE   Perhaps that's why they were expelled.

Joe Leon suggested cutting the last line saying he doesn't under-stand it. English irony – difficult for the Americans.

Thursday, 6 October – on train back to New York

Was *so* tired last evening I couldn't watch the performance. Nor could I bear to. Everyone was shouting, and Joe Leon was on the verge of vaudeville, tearing at the bread and throwing it behind him on '... *the northern half breaks up* ...', and stuttering the line '*My b–b–b–b–books, would you take my b–b–b–b–books?*'

I'd gone from the airport straight to the theatre to join Marian in a public symposium which went out live on radio. Audience full of enthusiastic *Shylock* public. One young man handed me a thesis he'd written in 1973 – a Mr Winter. Glanced at the beginning, intelligent. A young poet introduced himself who'd seen *The Friends* three times at the Roundhouse in London. He gave me his book of poems and drawings; walt-christopher stickney his name – lower casing an' all.

Returned Susan Schulman's call in NY – she wants to finalise interview with *NY Sunday Times* and arrange for photographs to be taken of John and me with three principals. Told her I'd ring John in NY to arrange it. Everyone's terrified of speaking to him about these things.

On the phone he reminded me that Joe Leon and Sir John were asking for larger salaries – we may not *have* them as principals! Sounds as though their agents are handling it with clumsy greed. If the play is a success the actors should share in it but not hold us to ransom now. John firmly reiterated he would not be blackmailed by actors, there were others who could take the place of them both. He was serious about delaying the opening by two weeks. We agreed that just he and I be photographed at the Met.

Picked up a letter from Peter Shaffer which he'd taken the trouble to write at length on the plane back to New York. I was most moved by it. Arrived at just the right time – I'm in the mood to slash left, right and centre.

On the plane, 30 September '77

MY DEAR ARNOLD: this thought occurred to me on the way to the airport. You probably know it already, but it may be worth stating again.

When one starts writing a big piece one is invaded by so many thoughts and emotions they seem hard to contain or cope with. The energy one puts out in shaping them, making a vessel to contain them, making that vessel grand and accessible both − the business, in a word, of being a play*wright* in the sense of a wheel*wright* − is enormous: virtually all consuming. When the play is completed one can sometimes actually *want* it to be long on stage (you would really like *Shylock* to be 3½ hours, you said) simply in order to make a shape that *parallels* that energy. An enormous output of creative hammering, one thinks, must *show* as that. But one forgets that a play, properly cut (I don't mean made slick), *expands* in the mind of its audience: it can become as gigantic to them in receiving it, as it seemed to you when you first took it on, and started shaping it. One can look at a powerful, beautifully shaped work after the labour of making it so, all dizzy and sweaty from the grappling, and say to oneself disappointedly. 'Is *that* all it is?' But that is to fail, imaginatively, to ignore the way furious, inchoate energy funnelled through shape (and only so) reconstitutes itself as furious energy in the brains and psyches of its *recipients*. Reconstitutes itself because of you. The fire which started in the playwright's head must get dimmer and dimmer as it grows in the communal imagination of an audience. Your job is to convey sacred flame in a vessel. You can say, looking at that vessel smoking on the stage: 'How miserable. I have seen the *Volcano*, and all I caught is one wretched tongue of fire.' But that tongue properly placed and focused upon, *is* the Volcano. Your power to concentrate fire for an audience will make them feel it, and be burned by it, even though they don't know the volcano, and never can.

The more one concentrates work, the more one recreates for other people the vastness of the original impulse. If one doesn't, all one gets is the labour − the contemplation of which is fatiguing.

I apologise if all this seems obvious and banal to you. But it is sometimes difficult to believe that what one writes can detonate in a viewer's head with the same resonance that it had when one first put it down on paper − and always, of course,

when time has defused it for oneself. To make a vile pun:
diffusion can only defuse things for an audience. You're a good
man. Thank you for your good play. Love Peter.[181]

Spoke to Joe about the line he didn't understand '*Perhaps that's
why they were expelled*,' and discovered that he was right. It's
confusing. *Who* were expelled? The *rich* Jews? The *intellectual* Jews?
Perhaps I'll cut it – one of my favourite black jokes.[182]
Fled performance in the interval, returned to hotel, pasted up
the portrait scene into Scene 4, wrote three cards. Back to the
theatre to give Brent the rewrites to retype. Sir John confessed
he'd just given an awful performance, resorting to tricks. Told him
we had cuts that would please him. Went with Nick, Julie, Everett,
Gloria and Rebecca to dinner in Georgetown. Julie is wild and
funny. A friend had taken her to the Washington Zoo where were
housed 'all those fucked-up birds' which she then imitated,
making them birdlike but human, pecked and anxious. She *is* a
good actress, why is she not giving a good performance? She
talked to me about it. No one could understand why Jessica ran
from her father nor why she ran *to* Lorenzo. She wanted a quarrel
with her father in which his cruelty would be revealed. I pointed
out that Shylock wasn't cruel – that would be too easy. He was
just overpoweringly enthusiastic. But Lorenzo, I told her, was
going to be worked on by John, into something quite different –
to make him charming, dangerously charismatic so that one
understood *why* she was drawn to him
Next morning (this morning) at theatre by 11 a.m. to pick up
photostatted new scenes. Train to New York to meet John at Met.
Caught Boris dying in last moments of Mussorgsky's opera.[183] Sit
in John's office working on more changes. John warns that
someone might ask who I was – they were checking up on all
offices because Vice President Mondale was coming tomorrow

---

[181] Re-reading it now I'm reminded what a generous act it was, to have spent time on such a
helpful letter; and I would like to think that sight of my travails with *Shylock* helped him avoid similar
ones in the writing of his best play – 'Amadeus'.

[182] In the final version I made the black comedy line even blacker: 'Perhaps *that* accounts for the
massacre of London!'

[183] Boris Godunov.

night to the fund-raising gala performance. 'We expect him to give us four million dollars so's to pay my salary, so don't tell them you've been to Cuba.' No one called.

Went on to his apartment across the road in 1 Lincoln Plaza for a whisky and talk. He has a shower, changes into the black caftan, then unpacks his new toy, a complicated drawing board. What for? To do his basic designs on. He never lets a designer work without offering some of his own ideas.

I show him cuts – a mixture of actors' suggestions, my own, and most of his. John spells out his plan of campaign: he wants me to ask Sir John on Friday to consider putting in the two Antonio cuts for the Saturday matinée and evening performances; Sunday, go through the play with the cast scene by scene and, where there are changes, give them to be rehearsed Monday on stage; Tuesday night, management is coming to see if it's short enough and less confusing; I fly to Syracuse on Wednesday, and depending upon management's response, I either come back to Washington for a couple more days or go on to London; he is to instruct Brent to give the new scenes to the actors concerned for them to look at in preparation for Sunday.

The cuts agreed, we next talked about Antonio's collusion with Shylock. I'd not brought Antonio into the decision, he said; his role wasn't fulfilled. I could see that but argued it was Shylock's play not Antonio's, and that our problem was with Sir John the actor who was unhappy playing a second lead to an unknown. John disagreed. It was something else, something *was* wrong with the character of Antonio. The play was called *The Merchant*,[184] surely it had to be as much about him as about Shylock? I replied no, Shylock had to be the battling, steamrollering force.

'Well *you* give me a sentence to explain it to Sir John because I don't know how to do it and he's adamant that he, Antonio, wouldn't agree to the bond next day on thinking about it freshly.'

I considered a moment, and said: 'Ten years of friendship! In ten years of friendship Antonio has become used to Shylock's rhythms, allowed himself to be persuaded into indulging Shylock's excesses.'

---

[184] This is the one time I've left in the original title because it was part of John's argument. Not surprisingly it became one of the reasons for changing the play's title.

I drove the point, it seemed a good one. But John hung on. I thought, if he was so anxious then maybe something *was* wrong with the relationship between Shylock and Antonio. What?

We continued arguing over a meal at the Ginger Man and again on our return to the apartment. I read out to John some of the lines which would need to be uttered if Antonio is to be shown more as a participant in the mockery as opposed to someone who simply goes along with it. He became excited. We pumped each other's adrenalin.

The work was productive. We were both happy.

The evening had been interspersed with other conversation. I told him of a letter Dusty had written describing how she'd been ignored at a National Theatre first night, and it was all unexciting, and that John should come back to England to enliven the theatre. 'They don't want me back!' he spat out. I asked him why he thought it was so. 'Working class and non-university!' He was utterly convinced of it. 'All dons. The National is don-ridden.' He listed his experiences, including Tony Harrison's experience translating the *Oresteia* for Sir Peter [Hall].[185] He harped back on George Devine's non-acceptance of him in the early days of the Royal Court, and how he was used as a kind of dog's body at the National in Olivier's time – 'Oh, John can get *that* together.' Then he informed me he'd just been offered the running of the Lincoln Theatre – New York's National Theatre. He'd turned it down and had recommended it be run by two young directors under the guiding influence of an uncle, the chairman. He'd offered to be that chairman. 'Still, it was nice to be asked, and it helped me up my salary at the Met.'

I discovered from John why Jocelyn was making noises about not being able to design *Love Letters* for me at the Cottesloe. She felt I didn't like her set for *Shylock*, and I'd snapped at her over notes one day. It's true I'd cut her short that time John had asked her to justify more cuts, but I loved the sets.[186] They'd worried me in Philadelphia but they'd been rebuilt for Washington. Wrote her a card begging her not to let me down, saying I needed her for

---

[185] I faxed Tony Harrison for further explanation but received no reply.

[186] Beautifully lit by Andy Phillips they looked like paintings by Rembrandt, though they never achieved the contrasts I'd called for.

my début at the National Theatre. I hope she stays with me.

John and I talked about our conduct of rehearsals. What was really needed between us, I suggested, was an agreement on definite times to confer. Once a week, or every ten days.

'Oh, I thought that as long as you don't protest, that everything I was doing met with your approval.'

'No. Why should I jump up at once to object to something when I know that you'll change it many times again and that seven out of ten times you'll arrive at what I want? I hate jumping in. *You've* got to create the mood to talk as we go along, *you've* got to say when you're ready to receive me. I know my place and can keep it as long as I know I'll be consulted sooner or later at reasonable intervals.'

The evening approached its end – he was expecting 'somebody' at 10 p.m. I'm joining him tomorrow at the Met to hear the quartet from *Rigoletto*.

'You'll be witnessing one of the greatest quartet of singers of all time.' He listed them. I was to meet a Romanian singer whom he knew wanted to get him to bed, and he was contemplating doing it 'in the line of duty'. He rather liked her, she was striking. 'Everyone told me she'd be a monster, but she's as gentle as a pussy.' I expressed surprise and asked had he ever had a heterosexual experience before. 'Oh yes, but it doesn't work for me after the orgasm. With men or young boys I can say "Come on, let's have a drink, a smoke." I can't be social with a woman. I go cold, stiff.' I was to meet and approve of her.

I read him Peter's letter and he was amazed.

'You don't know as well as I do how extraordinary that letter is. He's never written to anyone like that.' He wanted a photostat of it, and asked me to read it again. I was moved even on reading it a third time.

Sir John's and Joe's salaries have been agreed. John D finally rang Joe and spoke to him personally saying 'come off it'. Bernie Jacobs spoke to Sir John. *And* we have the more intimate Plymouth Theatre. Won't need to shout. John reiterated the sad truth that had Zero been playing the role the play would never have sprung to such life. One of the problems of giving him notes John said: 'Was that I could never get him to stay still for long enough.'

Friday, 7 October.

Spent morning writing letters in Sylvia's flat. Had lunch with her and a Turkish guest with the lovely, unbelievable name of Dilmaron. Sounds like a spice or herb.

Was at the Met by 2 p.m. to watch John rehearsing the quartet from *Rigoletto*. Glorious. He can't yell at opera singers – they're all stars, only the chorus to scream at. It's a revelation being so close to opera singers in rehearsal. They appear to sing with no effort, as though not they but someone else inside them was pushing the sound out. John introduced me to Jimmy Levine, the music director, who arrived towards the end to revive their flagging voices. A young man, about thirty-six, he shook my hand warmly and congratulated me on *Shylock*. Rehearsal over we went into the auditorium to meet Placido Domingo, the great tenor. He'd just done *La Bohème*. He should have been rehearsing *Rigoletto* but a rather fine understudy was standing in for him. John, in his usual high spirited, outrageous way, said to both Placido and me: 'Now the one thing that the two of you have in common is that the same woman is trying to get hold of both of you. She was once Ravi Shankar's mistress, and has twice asked to be introduced to Arnold and once to you, Placido. I've only met her one time and I don't want to pimp for you both but if you're interested ...?' Placido seemed to be!

Rushed across town to see Claire and William, pick up mail – a beautiful letter from Dusty – then taxi to La Guardia for the 7 p.m. flight back to Washington where I now am. Found awaiting me the air ticket for Syracuse, and three phone messages. One to ring Simon Relph[187] at the National in London. What can *that* be about? Gloomily I imagined the worst – a delay in rehearsing *Love Letters*. Or cancellation. Or to inform me that Jocelyn's final decision is 'no' to designing it. Perhaps he's only checking to see if I've written the one-acter.

Saturday, 8 October

Rang Della.[188] Wanted to share the memory of today, the first year

---

187 Administrator of the National Theatre, now a film producer.

188 My sister.

of Mum's death. A year! So quickly gone.

Simon Relph passed on the disappointing news that Jocelyn was unable to design *Love Letters*. I rang her, filled her in with news of cuts and improvements. She's not accepting *any* work for two months. It's her mother, Gwen. She's improving but Jocelyn can see she needs care and attention. She can't handle Gwen *and* work which may call her away to meetings. I understood. She suggested Bill Dudley, the young man who had started to design *The Old Ones* for John, and then abandoned it – a trauma had struck his life.[189]

Returned to small tensions. Portia is telling Nerissa and Lorenzo what to do in her scenes. Julie is upset with her role and performance – she got very drunk in the Intrigue last night and became melodramatic about her father 'who was dead in bed with a woman who wasn't his wife; that's my tragedy!'

Gloria had invited a friend to see her act, an elderly man who had told her she wasn't in the scene at the end of the play. It's a note I'd planned to give her. She delivers her lines like an afterthought stuck on at the end. She hasn't found a way of weaving herself into the melancholy of the scene.

John and I are probably the closest we've ever been. I loved being with him at the opera rehearsal, and I think he enjoyed me being there, watching him. He shows off when he's got an audience.

Sunday morning, 9 October – rehearsal room at Kennedy Centre

Arrived in pouring rain to discover four actors standing outside stage door. It was locked. On arrival Gloria, resourceful as ever, went through the front to get to the back and let us in. John turned up tired and wet. Not so much tired as bleary with the first hours still in him. He'd been trying to block the portrait scene – I had soldered it on to the end of Scene 4. Hand him the restructured court scene plus a sheet laying out what I thought the restructure was achieving. He reads it, thinks it'll work. It'll be

---

[189] Recovered, but it was Bernard Culshaw who designed the play.

put in next Sunday when I won't be here – unless I bring Dusty to Washington.

Actors gather. John announces plans for going through the entire play giving cuts as we go along 'rather than all at once because you'll forget them'. He informs them there's a hard day's work ahead and that: 'Thank God we're moving into the Plymouth Theatre and *not* the Imperial: A smaller space, no need to screech. Just the old problem of nine dressing rooms and twenty-one actors!'

Begin with Scene 1. John tells Joe to stop taking so many pauses, rather to deliver his lines in one sweep. 'To be vulgar about it I'd rather you got one big laugh on "gondola" than four little ones on the way. And you've lost the excitement of your books. I'd sooner you lost your voice than that. But keep it conversational.' He sits with my notes before him but fails to give Sir John the first one about being surly. He gave it to him last week and Sir John took it but lost it again. He's still playing an English knight, bored and weary with the little Jew at his side.

The first Belmont scene – the cuts are given. It moves swiftly now because Portia is beginning to throb more, be a little more excited and less regal.

John sends out for four bottles of chilled champagne which we drink before settling down to the long task of rehearsing the re-blocked Scene 4. Champagne and the excitement of doing new work increases the levity level. I invent a new and – to my mind – very funny line for Moses which I plan to put in the text but not actually *give* to him because the old man, Leib, quadruples the time needed for delivering a line. John says: 'Oh, let's give it to him!' I do so.

SHYLOCK Ah, Moses, you're here.
MOSES No! I'm not here!

I pass a note to John:

Since Marian is not ninety years old would she not be better upright rather than bent? Does anyone believe that energy can be contained by such a doubled-up frame? A thought! Also: in real life Angela is very practical, efficient and with a lovely dry sense of humour. Why can she not play herself?'

He reads it and whispers: 'Agreed, agreed! With both of them!' Riggs sits on a sofa looking despondent. Told me yesterday he was desperately unhappy because the role of Graziano is now not the role he accepted to play. 'I'm too old to play roles with only four or five lines. I know why it's cut, and I agree, but I now don't know who I am.' He went on at length. I understood. Alerted John when he flew in from New York that Riggs was a problem looming. John thought he might view it differently once it was rehearsed.

Great energy after lunch. The big (and now bigger) Scene 4 looks as though it's working, has much more of the bustle I wanted. Can't imagine bringing back Roderigues into the play. John has brought the Portuguese more into the picture.

Gloria confides to me in a quiet moment: 'The only other man I know who's like my father is you-know-who? John Dexter. My father used to yell at me, and whoosh! I'd wet my pants. The same with John. He yells and I have to rush to the loo!'

John sets up the dinner scene, and talks to the three young men. 'Now listen you three, you are not the languid sloppy young men you've been playing up till now, you are three men of equal rank debating vigorously as the young men of Venice used to debate. Don't drop the temperature of what you're saying. You Bassanio are peeling an apple in one, you Graziano are dipping grapes into your wine before eating, no elbows on the table, but the debate going on is strong. You are setting the intellectual climate into which Antonio and Shylock return from their walk outside. The argument is going like the wind. Don't let Lorenzo get away with everything. Answer back. Debate! YOU ARE ALL OF EQUAL RANK!'

But when, I wonder, will he redirect Lorenzo to get charm in and stiffness out? I like his intention to project elegance and ease in contrast to the ostentatious bustle we've just seen in the ghetto.

'Everyone knows,' he says to me, 'the Jews have no grace.'

'Just brains,' I reply.

He pauses, thinks, then rejoins: 'Only they sometimes confuse information for brains.'

'You took too long to come back with that one.'

'Yes, I did, didn't I?' But he *is* a bester.

After one run through he explains more to the Venetians. 'Following this great wodge of Jewry come the young men of Venice. Arnold wanted the bustle of Venice in the warehouse scene, I couldn't get it properly. We'll get it here instead, another aspect of Venice. So you *must* get the energy of debate, as we imagine the young did in Venice. Contrast, that's what I'm after.'

He gets angry with Everett who seems to be resisting his direction. Whispers to me: 'We must change him. I can't direct this stubbornness. It's either that or stupidity.' 'Let him be charming,' I whisper back, 'and sweet, and let his fanaticism slowly surface.' He seems unconvinced.

John is full of stories. Where *does* he get them from? One, to illustrate the civilised cut and thrust of parliamentary exchange: 'I can't remember who it was in the Commons who said to an opposition member that he thought the honourable member would die either of the gallows or the pox, to which – was it Brindsley and Fox? – the honourable member replied: "That depends, Sir, whether I embrace your politics or your mistress."'

Monday, 10 October

Left last night's rehearsal at 8.30 for an interview with *New York Sunday Times*. John was slowly going through a bottle of Italian red Soave. He fears becoming an alcoholic. Brent thinks his drinking is irresponsible.

Last night, along with two others, I was to have been his guest at the Cellar Door to hear Barbara Cook. Marian and Gloria were my guests. Gloria said she wouldn't have come had Marian not accompanied us. Joe, Brent and Brian – a new stage manager – were there. Riggs and Roberta were to have come, they didn't. Neither did John.

Cook was great. The first nightclub show I've seen, I think. One song made Marian cry. When it was over we went backstage to see her. She's a friend of Joe's and Brent's. All six of us went, as my guests, for an omelette at Clyde's.

That night Gloria wept because she was feeling mediocre in the role. 'Jesus Christ! John's given me the right direction but I haven't picked it up. I disappear into the woodwork. I don't know what I'm doing, I'm a lump on the stage, and that fucking Portia gives me nothing, she's such a selfish actor, and I have to take those fucking notes she gives me every night. Every night. Well one night I won't take it. I just won't. I've got to stand up to her. I've got my own role, my own job to do, and she's got to let me do it ...' It went on longer and more poignantly.

Today John had his bottle of Mouton-Cadet from the start. We ran through both acts in the morning. The first - with the changes - is now six minutes shorter. I don't know how long the second act ran. Poor actors, on top of rehearsing they have to heave the play on to the stage tonight. John rushed off to New York at 2.30 for the gala performance of *Rigoletto* before Vice-President Mondale. He'll return tomorrow. I'm going to leave him to pull the courtroom scene together on his own next weekend – must get back to London, though I feel I should stay with it.

Riggs wants to get out of the show. 'My part's been slashed and I'm too old to play chorus boys.' He's desperate about it.

Tried to give a note to Angela to play her role with more of herself in it. She wept, said every time she played herself she was slapped down. She didn't know where she was.

John is hissing that he wants to get rid of Lorenzo. It depresses me that the minor characters have been whittled away and neglected. It's bad writing.

Tuesday, 11 October – mostly written on plane to Syracuse

Last night's first act *did* look better. We lost ten minutes. Now all the ghetto scenes are together and suddenly one moves into bright Venice and pomp, and *those* scenes are together. I'm getting used to it. It irritates me to think my original instinct was wrong. Irrational since each new draft is saying about the previous draft that my 'instinct' was wrong. Suppose it has to do with wanting to have made the discovery oneself.

Had a nasty confrontation with Riggs whose tongue is loose.

It flared up suddenly. He's distressed that Graziano has been whittled away and that he's received the worse notice of all. I'd been taking a great deal of his casual mockery, that kind of kidding which hides deep resentments. 'Why don't you just walk away from it?' whispered Marian to me one day after witnessing a lashing from him.

It happened this way. Last night, in the newly constructed dinner scene, Bassanio has the new line, 'Good God, Lorenzo, you're in love, like me.' Nick invented a light touch adding, 'or is it I?' Which is a send-up of one of Graziano's lines.[190] I thought Nick's improvisation was witty, and told him so in the afternoon's line-reading. He was sitting with Riggs. 'We were just talking about it,' Nick said. I could see he was in some distress. Riggs had been at him. I repeated that I liked the line. Riggs said he didn't, and threatened that if Bassanio said the line he'd say it with him. I can't remember the exact sequence of the exchange from then on, it just caught fire.

Riggs said: 'Oh, don't I count? I'm not in this scene?' I couldn't understand why he was saying it. Why should the line upset him, and why was he presuming to interfere, in such a hostile tone, too? It was that special sound of green-room sourness that brought back all the other shit I'd taken from him. 'Anyway,' he said, 'I think the time has come for the playwright to go away and leave the play to the actors.' Theatre cant like that drives me mad at the best of times, said with viciousness I couldn't hold back.

'Fuck off, Riggs!' I hissed at him angrily, something I rarely utter to anyone.

But he was in full flight and went on to say something about '... if you'd been doing your work over the last thirteen weeks ...'

'Don't abuse my good nature,' I warned. 'Don't lose respect just because I've been close.'

'I've lost all that, for you and your play.'

Nasty, spiteful little tongue. I told Nick we'd talk about it later, and walked away. Though brief in all, there was more to the exchange. Mortifyingly, it was delivered in public. I was shaken. No wonder John terrifies – in order to stifle the one or two mean

---

[190] 'Don't be surprised, my friends, not all Venetian aristocracy is bright, you see. Least of all I. Me. Least of all me. Or is it "I"? I'm what they call an academic failure ...'

voices a cast can throw up. The majority have to suffer alongside.

I cooled down and decided the best thing was to talk with Riggs and clear the air. The irony was that I had found some lines to take from Lorenzo and Bassanio to give to Graziano in order to bring him more into the scene. He was not needed till well into the reading so I asked Brent to call him out. Brent returned to say he refused to come till after the rehearsal. I was furious but don't have the temperament to make a scene – a scene being the last thing the company needed. That was John's role. I was supposed to be the calming influence. What to do?

I'd been having second thoughts about returning to London. It seemed ridiculous to have been with the play all this time and then return to London simply because I'd scheduled it that way. There was still a big rewrite to see safely home – the court scene. My predicament was manifold. I desperately wanted to return to the family *but* didn't want to abandon the play. Then again I didn't want to insult John by appearing to say I didn't trust him. On the other hand I wanted to be around in case of his excesses or omissions. The confrontation with Riggs made me want to flee. Perhaps he was the sign from hell that I'd been around for too long. Would it get worse? Gloria said that was nonsense and pointed to all the others who were constantly calling on me to ask this and that. (Her point was later confirmed when, on hearing that I was going to stay, Julie flung her arms round me, and Marian whispered: 'I'm so glad. If you'd gone they'd have betrayed you!')

Very few in the cast now liked Riggs. He'd spread poison, and had generally demoralised the company, especially since his bad notice. I had sympathy for his unhappiness and would have had more if I hadn't suspected he wanted to change his character from the fence-sitting buffoon I'd written to someone more sympathetic. He hated playing the charming idiot, as written. He felt uncomfortable. Somewhere along the way he'd screwed it up.

The trustees of the Kennedy Centre had a buffet that evening before the performance to which I was invited along with 'the stars' of the cast. Rostropovich was there.

For the performance I took my place at the back of the stalls standing behind John who was sitting next to Brent writing furious notes. He seemed in a foul, evil mood. I looked over to see what notes he was making. At least four were for Gloria. I had the distinct feeling that John had been stirred up by Riggs, and was now preparing to get at me through the member of the cast I'd befriended. I was preparing myself for battles and began a fantasy row in my head, a kind of rehearsal. But quarrels never turn out as one feverishly fantasises. I went backstage to warn Gloria that flak might be coming.

If they gang up on Gifford because we've become close I'll hit the roof. Julie shouldn't get at her. Perhaps she's not doing. How insidiously backstage tensions creep into one, and distort the vision. That's why John stays away and Roberta keeps to herself.

Julie said to me as I passed her by the noticeboard during the performance: 'One day when it's all over we'll talk about what's happened. I'm not a bad actress, I know I've got talent and one day I'll prove it. But it doesn't help to be so rude. It's bad enough having to act in front of one's colleagues without being further humiliated. It only makes one stubborn and resentful. I don't give of my best.' She sounded very sad.

Thursday, 13 October – on flight from Syracuse to New York

Before the performance began that Tuesday night, Brent took his place with me at the back of the stalls. He seemed upset. I asked him about John. 'Is he in a bad mood? Did he yell at you?'

'Oh, I'm so tired of the insults. I'm too old for it. John came up to me and announced that he was doing the Burton *King Lear*[191] and that he wouldn't be using me on the show. Well, that's all right, I could take that, but then he added that he thought I ought to do a lot more smaller shows. Well, hell. I was going to ask him was Riggs to be in the Burton *Lear* – but I didn't get a chance. It's worse not even being able to get a point in first.' He laughed sardonically.

It occurred to me: if John was going to do *Lear* in April when did he plan his production of *Shylock* in London? I had asked him some days previously – now that Jocelyn was looking after her mother – what about all those plans for *Shylock* and *The Wedding*

---

191 Richard Burton as King Lear. It never happened.

Feast and the season of the three Jew plays? He'd said let's wait and see how New York went, after all I may not like what he'd finally do. Certainly I should wait till the New York opening but I felt he was manoeuvring to be in a position where I would be asking him to do the play. Why do I always get the feeling that John plays power politics? I responded by stepping aside and saying: 'If the play is a success in New York and earns me enough money to carry on working I won't care if the play is done in London or not!' Let *them* chase! (Damn bumpy flight, this. I hate it.)

But I've drifted away from the main sequence of events. Steeling myself for a confrontation with John was unnecessary. After the interval I saw him with Brent at the bar. He waved a friendly hand, and I moved in to join them. He seemed neither on the attack nor on the defensive, nor did I sense Riggs had been complaining to him. He waited for me to start.

'Those lines you suggested I find for Graziano,' I began, 'to put him more in the scene. I have them.' I went through them one by one – two speeches from Bassanio, one from Lorenzo. And then, as casually as I could, I told him about Bassanio's improvised line which I thought was witty, and wanted put in – the one about *'Good Lord, Lorenzo, you're in love, like me. Or is it I?'*

'To which,' said John at once, 'Graziano ought to answer without doubt or hesitation "me".'

I was wrong. Riggs *had* been complaining to John, for John was so ready with Graziano's reply.

I'd been watching that scene in the first act and noticed that Nick had not put in his improvised line. Had he been frightened? I asked him about it in the interval. He was full of quiet anger.

'I just didn't want to face it. Riggs had threatened he'd foul me up in the scene and I don't want to be involved in the middle of a fag war. I want to work with Dexter again one day ...'

I told him he was right, and not to worry. I'd clear it with John first. Which is what I was doing, and John had capped it. When I later told Nick the decision he was angry.

'So it means that Riggs has won his battle.'[192]

---

[192] In fact I though Riggs' suggestion a good one, and had he said to Nick that he thought his improvisation was witty and wouldn't his suggestion add to the wit, I'm sure Nick would have agreed. Neither line exists in the definitive version!

Still in the bar John and I talked on. 'If you want me to stay, I will,' I told him. 'It seems silly to go at the last moment.' 'I leave it entirely up to you,' he said, and went on to explain his idea of having Shylock draw the knife and go straight at Antonio. It sounded to me a little melodramatic, cheap theatrics. The action also implied that Shylock *had* made the decision to cut, which I think is wrong. I told him how much I liked Joe's idea of drawing the knife on the wave of his anger during the '*Jew! Jew!*' speech and then recoiling from the weapon in horror, appalled at his momentary lapse into violence. We agreed to wait and see it. He added that perhaps after all he would like me to stay. Is this moment of drawing the knife going to be a big confrontation moment like his *Fiddler On The Roof* ending for *The Old Ones* — which I'd also hated and which he'd put in without referring to me?

We changed subject. He told me that Jimmy Levine and Placido Domingo wanted to get together with me for a meal. And was I going to hear him sing? John talked about me doing an opera, saying my terse lines lend themselves to opera. His idea was for an opera about an opera being performed in a concentration camp. He talked about other things but I found myself not listening, so much else was scurrying around in my mind. The variations on a theme of Dexter/Wesker quarrels playing in my head were momentarily suspended because John was warmly talking with me about the future, but I couldn't rid myself of the feeling that he was biding his time for the *coup de grâce*. After all how loyal was he being if he was contemplating the Burton *Lear* in April? (I later heard that Marian and Roberta had been asked to play in it.) Did that mean he didn't expect *Shylock* to last?

Still, he found time generously to buy records for the children and me, and got them signed by Levine and Domingo. A complex man. His personality rests on three pillars: a reputation firmly rooted in impressive artistic and administrative achievement; a bullying nature capable of malevolent terror; and back to back with the terroriser, the great charmer and enthusiast, full of stories and an infectious and dynamic energy.

After the play Sam Cohn, Bernie Jacobs, Gerry Schoenfeld and Roger Stevens gathered in the green room. It was Malvin Krauss's birthday, and stage management had put together nibbles, drinks, and a cake for him. I had put up a notice on the board inviting the cast to join me in a farewell glass of Chateau Margeaux '71 – I'd bought five bottles – but having decided not to leave, the wine became part of Marvin's birthday celebrations.

Bernie grabbed me with affection – and too much heartiness for my taste – dragging me around saying how much better the show was. Sam clasped his hands together in prayer before me and said it was a beautiful play but 'just a little, little more trimming'. They were excited and gave off the air of being privy to an event of great moment, begging me to stay on. Insisting! John, with his constant air of having to rush off somewhere (this time to talk with the actors), evaded them with only a few words, and fled, leaving me to handle them. Bernie managed to toss at him a wish that the opening wasn't so slow. John, in flight, firmly assured him it had to be in order to familiarise the audience with an unfamiliar setting. It had been a good audience that night, full and responsive. I assured the producers that John and I were friends and talking to each other. Bernie, relieved and in high spirits, asked wouldn't John and I eat with him in New York? Sam, knowing it was neither a good nor acceptable idea to us, held up his hand to put Bernie quietly down. I marvel and wonder at Sam's influential position in this set up knowing him only as Zero's agent. He impressed me, and I told him so – I respected his taste, intelligence and, in particular, his style.

The bosses flew back to New York. I joined a half dozen of the cast in a bar called the Greenery from where we went to Le Bistro Français for a meal, picking up a depressed Nick on the way. John Seitz, understudying Shylock, spoke so interestingly about the role and also his role of Tubal that I was prompted to add lines making Tubal into the kind of Jew who mistrusts all Christians, even Antonio a little.

Wake late next morning and have to rush to catch flight to Syracuse where I'm met by Susan Kindlund, the publicity lady, who whips me off to a TV and press interview, and then to meet Arthur Storch for a meal before seeing the show. (Damn it! *I'm* calling it a 'show' now!) On the way I hear her life story, about her aspirations to write, her laziness, her divorce, her ten years of writing to Albee, her struggle with overweight ...

Storch is an intellectual looking man. Jewish, Bronx, directs for Broadway but prefers to build up a regional theatre in Syracuse. Coincidentally he's about to direct a new play by a successful Canadian playwright who's just had an all time smash hit with a play called *Same Time Next Year*. The new play, starring Jack Lemon, is also about a man who's dying of myeloid leukaemia.

Storch's production of *Love Letters* is not bad but the set is poor. The two main actors[193] are excellent. The professor, absurdly, is played with a hint of being homosexual – simply because he has a long monologue about the death of his mother! The young trade unionist is badly cast. I wasn't happy about the way the letters were delivered. Storch, against my stage instructions, decided some should be delivered live as opposed to recorded voice-over. It was, he felt, too taxing to listen to them *all* as voice-over. He may be right, I'm not certain. I'll see during rehearsals in London. My instinct is that they should *all* be recorded because they're written by 'the other woman', the personality we don't see but who, through her surprisingly exquisite letters, should contrast sharply with the woman we see on stage.[194]

The preview audience was interesting, mainly teenagers from the university, and they were riveted. The play needs running in to get the music and rhythm right, but when the young professor picked up the hand of his dead friend to kiss it a lump came to my throat. Will try and get Sam Cohn down – up – to see it. Deserves to transfer – but with a different set. I ought to add that the set had to serve an O'Casey curtain raiser – which didn't help.

I'm in New York – Sylvia's apartment again. Opening date is definitely 16 November. A quarter page advert goes in to the *New York Sunday Times* this Sunday. We're getting ready for launching.

---

[193] John Carpenter and Myra Carter.

[194] *Love Letters on Blue Paper* is about a trade union leader who is also dying of myeloid leukaemia'. His wife, Sonia, writes him letters which she posts and delivers to him with the morning post. Neither of them talk about these letters. He gives them to a young friend, Professor Maurice Stapelton, to read as they arrive. As she moves silently about her housework we hear the letters as voice-over. They seem to be at first merely recollections of their past, but they grow in intensity. By the eighth and last we realise that they are letters preparing him for his death, telling him theirs has been a beautiful life together.

Later

A great meeting with John. Unpredictable as ever. I come away relieved and exhilarated. In the hall of John's apartment was a package to take up. He was in his black caftan looking as though he'd just woken up.

I asked him: 'Have you been asleep?'

'All day! I decided that today I was going to give myself a day off, and I've been sleeping all day.' The package contained those signed records. Brahms for Tanya, Scott Joplin for Daniel, *Force of Destiny* for me, Placido Domingo for Dusty, can't remember who for LJ.

Friday, 14 October

About yesterday's meeting with John. In the corner was set up his new toy, the drawing board, with a small model of the *Shylock* set lit up. He'd been playing around with re-blocking. I kidded him about abandoning me to management on Tuesday. 'You certainly fled leaving me holding the baby.'

'I want to keep everything clean,' he said. 'Let them talk to you separately and me separately until we're a hundred per cent together and then I'll come over on to your side.'

I reported they seemed excited by the first act but had begged for it to be even shorter, and that I'd told them more work was yet to be done, and they seemed reassured. John and I agreed on what we were to talk about – Everett as Lorenzo, and the new court scene.

I again talked through the character of Lorenzo. He was not a soft, loving brother but charming and energetic, full of compelling smiles, youthfully confident the world will be his, not imagining that he would go into politics until, in court, in a public place, he surprises himself and finds his political voice. This would allow for development. And in the dinner scene he should be patronising rather than contemptuous of Shylock, seeming to be friendly, his gracious smile hiding hostility until Shylock patronises *him*, and then his smile falters: '*And don't* play *with me, Signor!*'

John found that reading a revelation, original, but could Everett do it? His dilemma was to replace him or not. Said I hated the idea of replacing actors but that was *his* decision.

'What would you do if I wasn't here?' he asked.

'I think I'd work with him.'

'Then work with him!'

John would mull over it further. He asked me to read the court scene to him. As I did so he sat before his model moving the characters around, trying to re-stage, scribbling notes in his yellow pad. I think I read it well and showed him how Antonio's speeches were *not* lectures but explosions of impatience which added to the tension of the scene. He seemed excited, and talked about having the court go into silence after Portia's dramatic and logical interpretation of the bond, completely different from my stage direction calling for *a crescendo of noise in court*. I liked his idea, and encouraged him to it. He also wanted to make more of Antonio bearing his breast, perhaps get to his knees, and for Shylock to move forward with flashing knife and real intent. I couldn't go along with *this*. Rather than show Shylock willing to cut his friend's flesh I thought Joe's idea of recoiling from his drawn knife was truer and more moving.

We next discussed the problematic shift from the court into the final Belmont scene. He confessed: 'I'm at fault somewhere. We should be getting a standing ovation and we're not. Why?' We needed, I said, a foot in each setting moving as it does from Belmont to the court to Belmont again. I reminded him of two ideas contained in my stage directions: that the song should begin during the last line of Shylock's final speech in court, and that Antonio, Portia and Jessica should not go off stage but should remain after the court has been cleared. In this way it will be obvious that something more is still to happen, that the play is not coming to an end with the ending of the court scene. John knew such an arch was needed but didn't think my suggestions were the answer.

A good afternoon's work. Not simply because I'd finally got across to John how the melodies of characters could be sung, and what the musical structure of scenes might be, but also because he'd shared his uncertainties and their possible solutions with me. Here was not a man adamantly trying to force his ideas. We seemed to have reaffirmed a working relationship.

He showed me a half-arsed letter from the Arts Council asking what he was doing and was there no possibility of him working in England in the near future. He was scornful. 'They don't really want me. Covent Garden would never have offered me what the Met's offered. Here things are possible. There they're not.'

In the morning rang Gloria to find out what news of the previous night's performance. She was full of talk about a new atmosphere of hostility in the company.

'It's terrible, and I mean really terrible. Everyone's read the new court scene and they say it's not shorter, and why isn't Arnold cutting the play, why does he have this death wish about the play, because he's going to take us all down with him. Even the stage hands are talking about the show failing because Arnold won't cut it, and they can see their jobs going out of the window. It's awful and it's all being spread by Riggs who's talking everywhere to everyone. He said to me John's never had to work like this before, it's making him ill and, "I'll just tell John never to work with Arnold again, and he won't, John won't work with Arnold again, that's what'll happen".'

I told her he was crazy since I'd existed for twelve years without John.

She then went on to say that she too thought it ought to be cut. 'Antonio has three speeches which don't move the plot on, and every time he stands up we lose the audience because they think it's another lecture.'

That was because he wasn't delivering the lines as he should be, I said. And anyway the restructured court scene *was* shorter, it could be seen from the crossings out. Reported how excited John had become when I actually read the court scene to him so I was not going to be panicked into more cuts because an actor was delivering lines incorrectly. She argued hard – she's fearless – but finally conceded my points.

'And don't allow yourself to be stampeded by others,' I warned.

'Yes, I know,' she said. 'We're all little Grazianos really!'

She dined with Roberta last night, and had received a long lecture. 'I was saying how I hated theft, and she said you have a very strange set of morals, to which I told her, "You don't know anything about my morals." But I "handled" her. She didn't know I was handling her but I did, just riding her insults. She was getting at my friendship with you until I pointed out that I had nothing to gain from it since you were in England. It was John who could further my career, not Arnold. But all that was irrelevant. She came full circle, and by the end we were planning to go to dance and keep fit classes together ... It seems as if everyone gets angry with you until they talk to you. Like John Seitz the other night. He was screaming about you to me but then you came over and you talked to him in the restaurant and listened to what he had to say and he completely changed his mind about you. There's no one like you, I tell them, *no* one. I mean you mix and eat and drink with the actors and even pick up the bill, and no writer ever does that, while Roberta keeps herself aloof and that's not good for the company ...'

We agreed that actors could often be treacherous and easily panicked so that they demoralised each other. I could understand Roberta staying out of it all. I could even understand John bullying them because if he didn't spread a little terror (though I think it's excessive) they'd be erupting all over the place.

By noon I was at the Met to meet with John. Caught a snatch of the chorus rehearsing *Rigoletto*. He'd been working on the court scene and was almost in control of it. He was certain that the celebratory roar after Portia' s interpretation of the bond was wrong – too much like an ending. He was going to make it so silent that they'd be on the edge of their seats. We agreed more cuts.

I phoned the changes through to Washington because they were due to read through the new court scene at 4 p.m. Spoke with Brent who was eager to know what we'd decided. He confirmed we had a very unhappy company at this moment due to Riggs who was pouring poison into everybody's ear. 'I've never seen such unprofessional behaviour, talking loudly in the passageway and backstage – still, that's our problem, we have a cross to bear.'

I'm actually quite shocked but it's so serious I can't tell John. Not yet anyway. Everyone's nerves are on edge because they're getting nearer and nearer to New York, and we're still shaping text and production – a time of back-biting to replace shortcomings. All must be kept from John – let's wait to see how the cast is cemented . by Sunday's rehearsals. Once they can see solutions they'll drop recriminations. And if, in the end, it's a success then everything will be forgotten, and they'll come to believe it had all been happy – which I thought it had been, and indeed it was until Zero died and then Riggs received his bad notice and we pruned his character.

John's secretary adores him. '*He's* creative, I'm administrative, and my job is to keep him free from worry in order to create.' So she does his shopping, buys the presents he wants for people, makes sure food is in his apartment, takes his laundry to a cleaner's, arranges for his cash expenses to be on hand. She liaises with his contacts all over the world as well as with Riggs and the two women who run the New Jersey house. She also does things for his friends, like me. She says everyone is terrified of him but he's only ever been kind and gentle and generous to her. She finds him 'a scream', makes her giggle all the time. 'I have enormous respect for what he's done with his life and his whole lifestyle.'

In his office fridge are small bottles of champagne which he drinks with orange juice during his break. A wardrobe holds spare clothes. Cards from colleagues abroad and photographs of him with famous personalities, are pinned on walls. (In his apartment, too.) It's a cosy den. He occupies every space and every minute, answering letters and telephone calls even in his half-hour break, sipping his favourite drink meanwhile.

I return to Washington in a couple of hours. These last pages have been written in John's office at the Met. He's gone off to New Jersey to pursue further solutions.

Later

Delayed flight. Rain. Bumpy. Why do I fly? Rain in Washington. Arrive to Howard Johnson and a message to phone Simon Relph at the National Theatre. Within minutes I hear from Gloria: explosion during read-through of new court scene in afternoon – Sir John saying he will take cuts but not rewrites of speeches; Riggs overheard saying gleefully: 'Mutiny on the gondola, I hear!'[195]

G. tried once more to persuade me to cut the two Antonio speeches. 'That would really shock and surprise the cast, and

---

[195] Quite witty actually.

they'd all then feel you weren't trying to hold back, and you'd leave a good feeling ...'

'Gloria, don't lets you and I talk about it.'

'I know we shouldn't. It's just that I'm worried for you.'

'I'm a big boy, I've been around a long time, I can look after myself.'

'Oh [tweety-pie voice] you can?'

'With a little help from my friends.'

Later

Just had dinner with 'the crowd' at the Intrigue. Brent reported the following. Not only was Sir John refusing to learn the reconstructed lines but the reconstructed scene. (Brent was horrified to discover that none of them had looked at the new pages he'd given them until yesterday's read through.) In fact, he said, *most* people were unhappy with the reworked court scene, and Sir John was unhappy with me and John D. It appears he's trying to incite rebellion. One of the actors, he's declaring, should take responsibility and stand up to shout louder than John. Brent thought John D would massacre him. I agreed. Joe told Brent that Sir John was trying to involve him, Joe, into a common cause against John D. Brent had advised him to stay well out of that one. I hope Joe takes his advice.

Saturday, 15 October

Pulled comb through text and found more cuts. Snippets here and there, some from Marian's list which I've scrutinised again – most of her suggestions were intelligent ones.

Later

A number of friends at this evening's performance. Good, except that what's left over from the warehouse scene has no life at all. Riggs is playing a haughty Graziano who spits grape pips over his employer's floor. Madness! John will work on it tomorrow. Brent was asked by Sir John to call John D into his dressing room before the show. John told Brent to tell Sir John that he was not coming in to see the show, and that the new scene Arnold had reworked would be rehearsed tomorrow.

Gloria tries a new idea. Since she can't be, as written, the stern warning voice to the vibrant, youthful Portia because Portia has decided she's regal and that Nerissa is *only* her maid and not, as the script says, her *'friend and help'*, she decided to go to the other extreme and be very much the eager-eyed pupil. 'And she loves it! It feeds her ego. She was absolutely thrilled. I played innocent to her teacher. Yeach! But it's the only way to find an individual character.' It's true, Roberta can't bear her *any* way but submissive on stage. She upstages her every time. This way she'll be reassured that Nerissa can't command any moment. It's awful. Roberta gives a slow and ponderous reading of Portia – regal and dull, as Sir John is regal and, in the court scene, dull. Both simply perform as 'stars' rather than their characters.

Sunday, 16 October

John has asked Jeff Horowitz to come a quarter of an hour earlier – Jeff is the Equity representative. John tells him he intends to go ahead and rehearse the new scene, and asks for his support of an Equity ruling which says all actors must accept the discipline of rehearsing new scenes. Politician that he is, John has left nothing to chance. If Sir John wants to fight he is ready to throw the book at him.

His warm, enthusiastic mood is once again unpredictable. I'd imagined he'd be furious, icily steeling himself for a confrontation with Sir John. He whispered to me as I sat by him in the rehearsal room: 'We go straight on and do it, right? No point in talking to him in a dressing room. If he doesn't do it he's in breach of contract.'

'Absolutely. If you don't steamroller through you'll have chaos on your hands.'

In the event it went well. John gave a stirring, firm introduction before going into battle.

'Now, the producers as you know were very pleased and impressed with what we did to the first act, and I would point out it has nothing to do with cutting but with shaping and re-structuring. That's what we've done with the court scene, and we're going to do the court scene now the way the author has written it because that's what he wants and it's the way I want to direct it. The producers in their wisdom have been very courteous to Arnold and me, they've given us complete authority and trust, quite properly. Restructure and re-staging is what we're after, though if you imagine we don't have more cuts ready in case – you're mistaken. Next, we've done our cuts but we must pay attention to the acting. So far all of you, without exception, have been playing solo performances without listening to anyone else on the stage. Selfish acting. You *must* begin to listen to one another. It's no good Arnold cutting the play if you're all going to fill in the spaces with long pauses and solo performances. The court scene, as we now have it, is more concise and leaves a direct line for: one, Lorenzo to be chasing the issue of usury; two, for Antonio to be urging the court to get on with it; and three, for Shylock to be insisting upon his silence. We've got a hard day's work ahead of us because we have to learn it and block it *now* and put it in for tomorrow night's performance. I expect your full cooperation in this.'

That was it more or less, only longer. His tone was firm, workmanlike, but warm. No one could stand against it. Not even Sir John who must have come determined to say something. He did make little protests as the scene was blocked, asking for this word to be dropped, that changed. John checked with me swiftly each time. I could see he wanted to relent a little, not humiliate Sir John, so I acquiesced. Except for one whole passage – '*You will inflame the people's grievances for through their grievances you'll come to power ...*' to the end of that speech. Sir John's reason: that's already been said. It hadn't, and I instantly said no, which John upheld. Sir John backed down.

Of course, it *is* difficult to relearn a scene. It's even worse when speeches have been rearranged but are still similar to the original ones – especially for an older actor.

Before beginning to rehearse John calls for his slippers. 'You know very well the magic won't come unless I'm wearing my slippers.'

Mark brings them: 'Ah! Now you'll see genius rising. ' And he throws a kiss at one of the young androids, John Tyrell.

He's on great form, punching into every line of the dinner scene, squeezing significance and meaning for them out of each word. His good humour gets him into a gallop but I'm not convinced he's always galloping in the right direction. The three young Venetians, for example – he's shaping a very *haughty* threesome. I'd make them more sympathetic, less one dimensional. It's as though he can't get energy out of them unless he makes them bite with viciousness. I can't stop him. Lorenzo ruffling Graziano's hair – a brotherly act – is the solitary gesture of warmth. The rest seems harsh, shrill. No intelligence there. Why? Their words are not inconsiderable.

Tuesday, 18 October – on flight from New York to London

Continuing Sunday's rehearsal. John made four major changes to his blocking of the courtroom scene. It surprised some of the actors. When we break for coffee he approaches me. His idea for silence instead of uproar after Portia pronounces on the bond is interesting but I'm not sure it solves the problem of the coda. Again I press him to consider beginning the last Belmont scene before the court scene ends. He said he knew exactly what I meant but was worried about introducing the song because music denoted ending.

'Right!' I said, 'It *is* the ending, but one *we're* controlling and it's therefore not a false one.'

'I know! I know! I'm just not sure how to do it!'

'Finish this new blocking through to the end and then see where you are.' He'd directed a lovely sweetness out of Lorenzo on '*No one doubts the Jew is human ...*' so that suddenly Shylock seemed like an arrogant bastard which is much more interesting because his plea '*My humanity is my right*' now means 'you don't have to like me in order to concede my humanity'.

John says: 'I just knew I couldn't start introducing warmth into Lorenzo in the beginning of the dinner scene, that I'd have to do it later. The courtroom was the best place to begin ...'

I reassured him he was right and that the warmth of this scene would now work backwards through the play.

After the break a run-through again. One by one new moves take shape. Jessica's moment is attended to. Shylock sweeps his bond under his arm. The Belmont song begins halfway through his speech in court. Portia remains and takes off her cloak on the spot instead of going offstage to do so. The androids enter and throw the picnic sheet over it (not too certain about that). The scene becomes clearer, more dynamic. The cast is excited. Suddenly everything is happening downstage.

'Much better,' I say to John.

'Always! I learnt it from opera.' Now the next important thing to do is change the lighting. The lighting must not fade down or it'll spell – *The End*.

I make a long attempt to explain the 'sword and scales' speech to Roberta. She has always imagined the speech was about Portia instead of about Portia raging at the inflexibility of the law. When she finally gets the point she becomes very excited.

I lunch with John in Les Champs and give him the new cuts. Small but effective. He's pleased with the way things have gone. I tell him that as usual he was unpredictable.

'You thought I'd be all fury?'

'White heat and steeled for a fight.' We talk over certain aspects of the play and I agree to write a sheet of notes before leaving. He mentions again the idea of an opera – *The Magic Flute* – rehearsed in Dachau. Told him that I felt the theatre was the writer's medium, the film the director's, the opera the composer's, but if he sketched out a rough shape I'd be happy to play second, third fiddle. His enthusiasm determined me to listen to *The Magic Flute*.

After lunch Roberta came up to me and said: 'I love doing that speech now, thank you, thank you.'

My relationship with her began before rehearsals started. She was the first member of the cast I met in June last year. That should have given us a head start on friendship. It never happened. We had one meal together, then a New York drink over which she promised to introduce me to cocaine. She bought some but lost it.[196] When rehearsals began she seemed reluctant to get close.

---

[196] Thank God!

I wasn't going to pursue. The actors playing the smaller roles were friendlier – Bassanio, Usque, Nerissa and The Maid became my circle. My relationship with Nerissa especially has irritated a lot of people. Riggs in these last days has fanned that irritation, especially in Roberta. 'Arnold better not go near Roberta,' he was heard to say, 'she's furious with him.' So I didn't. I wasn't enjoying her performance anyway. But if Gloria could 'handle' her I decided I would, too.

A Canadian director had phoned wanting to direct *The Four Seasons*. I'd told him it depended upon the actors. I didn't know any, and asked Roberta, being Canadian, for advice. On Saturday the Frankels had gone back stage to tell her how marvellous she'd been. I dropped in. 'I want your advice,' I told her. The relationship was back again, and at the end of the performance I could give her a note about a tender moment between her and Shylock which she's missing. She understood it at once and was at once eager to play it.

Later, Gloria said how her own tactics – much against her instincts – had paid off. Roberta was loving the submissive Nerissa and – paradoxically – was treating her much more informally. Gloria was now getting feedback on stage. In the last scene for instance, when Nerissa has to utter the last ironic and difficult lines of the play: '*And heroes you are, sirs, true ...*' Portia was sharing a look with her which gave her confidence, a sense of belonging to the moment. I had also noticed how, in the casket scene, Portia was lying back in Nerissa's arms. Nerissa was being wooden about it, uncertain. I reassured her – it was an inspired moment, she should use it, take her mistress in her arms.

The process is a fascinating one. Who's to say who was right? Roberta forced Gloria to be submissive so that she could then be generous and achieve what I wanted – that is to treat Nerissa informally. Could she have achieved as much without humiliating Gloria, without making her feel so wooden that she couldn't relax unless Roberta approved? Gloria had to humble herself – was there an alternative?

Our competition on Broadway is *Golda*, the documentary based on the life of Golda Meir.[197] starring Anne Bancroft. It's 'the

[197] Israel's fourth prime minister

other' Jewish play. Rumours are that its story is non-existent but that Bancroft is brilliant. Last week, though, their costumes, scenery and photo-slides were destroyed by fire. PLO sabotage? On Monday (yesterday) John had to return to *Rigoletto* in New York. I take over a morning rehearsal for the dinner scene with the three young Venetians. Tension between Riggs and myself is subdued but there. He knows from Nick that he can have a few more of Bassanio's lines to bring him even more into the scene. They run them through. In his high-pitched, cavalier voice he asks a question of the other two. 'I don't understand why I'm saying, "*No more arguments, gentlemen, please.*" Have you been arguing?' I attempt to explain. He cuts me short. 'No, no Arnold. This is a thing for actors.'

For actors! More theatre cant! They discuss it and conclude the line is to be delivered not in the sense of 'no more arguments' but 'no more banter'. When they're done I come in very curtly. 'No, Riggs, you're wrong. It *is* argument. As John pointed out to you already these are young Venetians animated by ideas of the time – the vote, the aged in power ...' He quietly succumbs. They rehearse while I attend to another problem.

Sir John feels that with the new rewrite they don't know where they are. In the previous scene he and Shylock go off to eat in Shylock's house, when they next appear it is in Antonio's house. He's right. It's the result of rejigging the scenes.[198] I write in three new lines which clarify the move. He'd also thought that having Lorenzo misquote Ezekiel with Shylock correcting him was a cheap joke. It should be Graziano who misquotes. I don't agree.

The rehearsal continues with Riggs still subtly digging at me. They've lost a lot of what John got from them the previous day but they've found some other things like a gentle way of mocking Lorenzo. I attempt to show Lorenzo how he can bring into this scene elements of John's new line of direction – warmth and dynamism. He begins to play with it but it's going to take a long time for him to lose the old stiffness.

The actors assemble for the courtroom scene. There's a sad little moment when Bill Roerick, playing the Doge, snaps at 'the Jews'

---

[198] Which I've since rejigged back. The sequence now makes sense.

to stop chatting. 'I'm nervous, you see, and if you make faces ... Oh forgive me, Marian and I are best friends, I didn't mean to snap, I want to apologise to everyone ...' His apologies and everyone else's embarrassment grow out of proportion. Marian says: 'I'm mystified.' I take charge and ask has John called for interruptions at that point? No, they were to stop as soon as the Doge began. It was settled. It had been his imagination, or someone had mistakenly moved or spoken out of turn. He was tense. He had the most new lines to learn.

After lunch there's a rehearsal on stage which Sir John had insisted upon. Expensive but right and justified.

That evening the performance worked. A good audience. Full, for a Monday night. It must mean something – that people are not telling others to stay away, even positively saying, 'Go!' There was a quarter page advert in the *New York Sunday Times*. That means something also – that the producers *are* going ahead. Thank God it's a straight advert without eulogising quotes from the *Washington Post* which would have enraged New York critics, perverse creatures!

On Monday night, eating out with 'the crowd', there exploded an unpleasant scene as Gloria and Julie quarrelled, and Nick joined in to attack Gloria violently and crudely, shocking himself as much as us. She considered him her friend, and was hurt. I stayed out of it. Julie ended by fleeing.

It was over Joe's performance. Gloria had been criticising Joe – as everyone criticises everyone else. Julie told her she wasn't being fair and implied Gloria didn't know enough about the acting process. When Julie criticised Sir John, Gloria foolishly accused Julie of a Jewish bias. And anyway, why could Julie criticise Sir John and she not criticise Joe? What upset Gloria was that she greatly admired Joe, but not unreservedly. Nick's outburst was to tell her: 'Button your fat lip.' It shocked me. Gloria wept feeling an accumulation of resentments because she was the company's very junior actor and a friend of the author (nor did it help that Julie had to share a curtain call with her.) Worse, she had constantly been positive about the play when others had been negative and disruptive. And she possessed a quality of high spirits, a sunniness, that often attracts resentment. She's also possessed of opinions. About everything and everyone. And she offers them constantly in an abrasive, loud voice. It's as though she expects to be shut up and so feels driven to thrust her views upon a company. You don't feel an exchange takes place but a rape. I don't enjoy her insistence but I find that she's mostly perceptive about the play and people. Also generous. It was a miserable episode, one in which I felt uncomfortable and helpless. She should have walked away from the scene. She never does. She can't let go. Julie tried but Gloria lashed out again and again until Julie screamed like one oppressed. Gloria wanted to leave. I dissuaded her. Julie went to the toilet. When she returned Gloria still wouldn't let go, driven to defend her position again and again. Julie fled leaving Gloria to appear the guilty one.

PAUSE

[1977 *continued*]

Monday, 18 October

I went to London for twelve days. Before leaving I'd typed four sheets of notes for John as he requested.[199] In my absence great changes were made. Returned to Washington on 3 November to a tense and charged atmosphere.

Thursday, 3 November – Pan Am flight to Washington from London

Had two letters from John while in London to which I replied[200] enclosing a Walter Kerr[201] article about how audiences were being made to sit too long in the theatre. John saw this as a warning sign, adding that Richard Coe [*Washington Post*] who'd liked the play and reviewed it well – though complaining of its length – had seen it again and told Kerr (John had inside informants) that he'd seen no changes. How was that possible? The huge Scene 4 – apart from much else – had been drastically reconstructed. John wrote to say he had hoped my 'cutting mood' would have produced more cuts than those I'd left behind three weeks ago. I replied reminding him I'd cut a great deal and urging that we shouldn't be panicked. The play was coming down at 10.15, that was early enough by any standards. Now it was his and the actors' task to lighten up and stop swinging on those vowels. Anyway, it's absurd to be shaping plays to suit the tastes of bloody critics.

I wanted him to receive my reply before I arrived. Asked Dusty to ring Evelyn – his secretary – in NY to find where he'd be, and express it. In response Brent called. John wanted me to send the cuts to the theatre. What cuts? There was confusion. Told Brent there'd be no more cuts only that I'd look at one-line repetitions. A distressed John rang. Having received one message from Evelyn that I was sending him cuts he now had another from Brent that

---

[199] Appendix 5.

[200] Appendix 6.

[201] Theatre commentator for *The New York Times*.

I was not sending cuts. Had Dusty said to Evelyn 'Arnold has written a letter about the cuts' when she should have said simply 'Arnold has written a letter — where should it go?' Explained to John that my letter talked about one line repetitions — Brent had given him only half the message. He seemed pacified. 'I heard you'd adamantly refused to cut anything else, and we couldn't proceed that way ...' He sounded in good humour though. Told me exasperatedly he'd lost his *Rigoletto* — the replacement was having to learn it in twenty-four hours. Poor John! First Zero, now his *Rigoletto*.

Brent had also told me that in his view the courtroom, portrait and Antonio dinner scenes were a mess. Heard, too, that on one evening Roberta had walked off stage at the beginning of Act II because the audience were still coming noisily to their seats after the interval. And that Julie, in the court scene on another evening, had fainted into the arms of Gloria who had to take her off. Her period was on.

BETRAYAL

[1977 *continued*]

Friday, 4 November – Kennedy Centre

G. briefed me on arrival yesterday. She didn't know what to do or say first.

'The bad news first?' she asked.

'There are cuts?' I asked.

'Oh cuts! Cuts? I'm not saying.'

'Tell me.'

'They're not bad.'

'Tell me.'

'Everybody's morale is up and the curtain comes down at 10.10.'

'Tell me.'

'I shouldn't get involved. I rang my therapist and he said, "Stay away, it's not your affair, leave it to them."'

Finally she told me – at least about those cuts she could remember. When I saw it in the evening there were even more. The king leaves, the court betrays.

I arrived at the theatre a few minutes before curtain up. It had been pouring. I was soaked.

John was at the bar. 'You'll see changes.'

'I hope so.'

'You'll see big changes.'

'I hope so.' Not letting on I'd already been warned.

'You'll see it and then we'll talk.' As I was leaving he added: 'It's been savaged.'

'You mean,' I threw over my shoulder about to take my seat, 'you've cut without asking me?'

As I watched – and it was a great audience – I felt a mixture of anger and interest. The cuts *were* savage but mainly to do with what actors had been failing to handle: Jessica on '*Who owns a house*'; Moses' exchange about Coke; Antonio's piece about magistracy and the Lepanto story. But there's at least one section I want back – the Lorenzo/Shylock exchange in the dinner scene about '*Mine's not a university-trained mind*'.

Bernie Jacobs and Sam Cohn were there at curtain down. John

had fled. They were impressed by changes but anxious about two things: the wipe which ends both acts is flimsy; and the last scene which they feel should not end on the four least important characters. Sam felt that Shylock's last speech was too shrill. 'No intelligent resignation.'

Leib was waiting to tell me how unhappy he was to have his lines cut to only three. 'It was a small part but a nice vignette. Now there is no character at all.' He was right. Partly his own fault – he made such a meal of his words. I said I'd try to bring some of them back. 'It's only thirty-five seconds,' he complained. 'I timed it again and again. It saves only thirty-five seconds.'

This morning I rang John's hotel and left a message, one that didn't reflect the war in my heart. '*Well done. We must talk before rehearsal.*' He didn't ring back.

'He's afraid,' said G. 'I can't tell you how everyone was terrified of your wrath. Nick said, "When Arnold yells out in the middle of tonight's performance, 'STOP! it's not my play!' *you* can deal with it, I'll slither under the table." I tell you, *everyone* was worried. "What will Arnold say, what will Arnold do? Will he stop the play? Call the law?" And John kept talking about his fears that your friendship would end, and that you'd never speak or work with him again. But he kept urging us that *we* had to work harder and be clear with every word of "Arnold's beautiful play ...".'

Gloria works so hard to defend John. He owes her a great deal. I have all my quarrels with him with *her*! She reported that before beginning to work on the court scene he'd taken three Valium. He'd worked well!

I remember now, last night, Marvin was so solicitous, asking me did I want any money for expenses. Seems *every*one was anxious to see how I'd take it all. What do I feel? A mixture of many things. Humiliation to be so powerless, to have had it done behind my back before the company. Angry that lines are cut because actors can't deliver them. Depressed that a lot of what gave me pleasure in the play is now gone.

'For Christ's sake, Arnold!' G exploded. 'How can you say that when there's still two and half hours left of the play!?'

True, but I wanted to write an epic, now it's neat, a *Reader's Digest* version. And frustratingly I know that I can't really stop it.

The actors' work, John's work, the producers' money *are* to be considered. If it's a success I'll be earning a lot of money on something I don't really feel is mine – there's the humiliation. And a feeling of – rape. That's it! *That's* the nature of the humiliation. And some shame in suspecting myself of wanting to 'take the money and run' in order to pay income tax and the solicitor's fees for the RSC lawsuit. Although another part of me says, 'Let it go, just this time – to get a foothold in the States, let it go, and then you'll be in charge, dance to your own tune.' I console myself that the printed text will be fuller. And I look forward to directing *Love Letters On Blue Paper*.

I hear that Marian took John aside and warned him that now he must change his tactics and begin being a little more civil to the cast. The time was passed for rudeness. They couldn't take it.

John tells me he doesn't want to talk with me yet because he doesn't want to get into explanations about 'why I've done something I've never done before, which is cut while you weren't here'. Told him I didn't want to discuss that, only specifics. 'Well I do, because it's blazing inside me and it's all a mess and why I did it and what there was about your card[202] which made me rage, and I want to get it off my chest.'

Later

Tried to get John to say whether or not he'd do *The Wedding Feast* at the Court.

He said give him a week. He wanted to read it again and for us to have that talk. He hinted at his feelings. 'I find I'm inhibited in rehearsals when you're around in a way that I didn't use to be. I don't know if that's changed because I've changed or we've changed, but it's no good pretending it hasn't happened.' I said nothing. Partly because I was tired, partly because I didn't know what I felt, except at once depressed. For me the pleasure is gone from this production, and now, on top of that loss was the prospect of being squeezed out of the rehearsal process entirely. Do I say to John no, sorry, if I'm not there – no production? I'm not sure what I care about.

---

[202] I can't remember, nor have a record of, this card.

Monday, 7 November – New York

Friday and Saturday night – the last performances in the Kennedy Centre – were great houses, especially Saturday night when they seemed to be applauding every moment. Anthony Page[203] was in the audience to see it, and he was bowled over, prophesying it will be a great success.

But through Saturday night to Sunday the depression grew and gripped me as I've not been gripped in a long time. I wanted only to return to London and forget everything. The sensation of rape overwhelmed me, to have been violated, something done to me without my consent. Yes, I could have at once taken out an injunction and said put it all back and we'll start again, but that would have created an atmosphere to work in from which there might be no recovery. Throughout yesterday a murderous anger grew in me, and I quarrelled with G about the difference between interpreters and creators. Oh! This hunger of everyone to be thought 'creative', the immodesty of it. It was a most awful day.

Nor am I fully recovered. My heart is not in the production. And the more I realise it *will* be a success the more fraudulent I feel. I will have given birth to a neat, Broadway-tailored show. I think about Sir John's delight that what he wanted cut is cut, and what's left he renders crassly, screaming his words: *'Justice? For the people of VENICE?'* Even Joe, as his confidence grows, begins to sprawl over his speeches indulgently, that intelligent resignation – gone! I can't bring myself to talk about it. Susan wanted me to have interviews with *Soho News* and *Jewish Voice* but I cried off saying I'm not in the best frame of mind.

Of course John may be right. It may be that his is the real courage for having risked my fury and done what he guessed I might come to concede was right for the play. Perhaps. Certainly I'm not able to judge at this moment. I know only that the cuts have been made for the wrong reasons – to save restless Broadway bums being sat upon too long. On the other hand perhaps that's the nature of theatre; if you want to be expansive, discursive, if you

---

[203] Stage director.

want to be subtler, more complex — write prose. Perhaps. But I fear it's why serious writers don't write for the theatre, nor serious people attend. Diversion rather than experience is what's sought.

BROADWAY – HERE WE COME

[1977 *continued*]

Wednesday, 9 November – day of first preview, New York

On Monday there was a line read through. I didn't attend. John, my spy reported, very firmly told them they had to get back all the little lines and words they'd dropped, lost, got tangled back to front. Nothing, he said, was to be changed without his permission. And Pat, on the book, picked up everybody – much to the annoyance of Sir John and one or two others. But why did John need to tell them? Had he now realised that having cut the text without reference to me he'd set a precedent of contempt?

Yesterday, Tuesday, I came to the theatre for the first time. The outside looked handsome with the *Shylock* logo in red. The stage, thrust out at the expense of the two front rows, was tucked intimately into the auditorium, the blue of the backcloth echoing the blue of seating and box hangings. Here is the stage upon which *Chips With Everything* played fourteen years ago. Coincidence!

Blossom from wardrobe provides us with hot tea, honey and whisky. I watch changes which, to his credit, are based on my notes to John. He's worked out a tableau for opening the play: Portia and Nerissa in their arch, Lorenzo and Jessica in the centre arch, Shylock and Antonio in their arch, so that the last scene of Jessica, Antonio and Portia isolated in their separate arches echoes the beginning. 'Bookends' as he calls them. It's effective, but not as I'd do it. John wants symmetry, I prefer my orchestration to be less contained.[204] But he's brought Jessica into the first scene – a glowering daughter wordlessly bringing on drinks, impatient with her father's obsession for books – thus making more sense of Antonio's line '*Very haughty, your daughter*'. Nice touch. But I miss passages, the holes in the play gape at me.

Thursday, 10 November – day of second preview

Last night – the first preview before a New York audience. It went very well. The cast had energy and attack. The audience

---

[204] Not sure I'd agree with that now.

responded. Julie's friend, an actress, said she too felt the holes in the play. Sir John is still lugubrious in the court scene, making a meal of it; and Joe, now he's so close to his audience, seems cruder, unable to resist 'performing' for them. I hope he can tone himself down, or that John will be able to tone him down.

As I watch I'm struck, despairingly, with the realisation that, though they have energy and attack, most of them don't really understand what they're playing. Lorenzo doesn't, nor Jessica, Portia, Bassanio, even Shylock in places. Rebecca da Mendes does, and Usque, and Rivka. The phrasing is odd, nonsensical even. I shall never understand the virtue of an actor offering his own reading incorrectly rather than taking it from the author, which could make him more interesting, vivid.[205]

One person rose to her feet last night. Tonight it could be two. Friday four. Saturday matinée eight. Saturday evening sixteen. Sunday thirty-two. Monday evening sixty-four. By the first night two hundred and fifty could be on their feet. For a play full of holes! I am, as Sam Cohn says *Shylock* should be, full of intelligent resignation.

I buy a bottle of Courvoisier for Blossom's stock. He tells me Sir John, whom he dresses and looks after, gives him $5 a week. 'Oh yes, no one believes it. And I've worked for the best. Ralph[206] drops me $50.' Bought Jack Daniel's for the box office crew and one for Charlie and his prop man. And a bottle of Pouilly-Fumé for Andy, his assistant, Andrea, John and myself.

I give John a cup of wine – a peace offering at which he jumps. He says: 'Arnold, as we have a moment's pause, I've read your notes and I agree with them and I'm going through them as I come to each scene. But keep the notes coming after each run-through, even repeat yourself if things aren't happening as you've asked. And our little friend, Moses, can't you find just *one* exit line? You know he'll hold up everything if he has more. Oh go on. You'd do it for Rex Harrison. One of those funny Jewish lines.' The gesture of wine has touched him into good spirits. He throws jokes and tenderness all over the place. 'If you expect me to direct

---

[205] Twenty years on I'd phrase it differently. There is a spectrum of possible renderings of a line – an actor needs help not to go outside that spectrum.

[206] The late Sir Ralph Richardson.

this play on only half a glass of wine ...' I refill his cup.

He's refining the opening, attending to every detail, shifting a pile of books from one place to another, giving Jessica moves within the first scene silently to establish her character, bringing the lights on ping! ping! ping! one after the other under each arch, making the Androids glower at each other – Christians at Jews.

'If only I'd thought of all this in the first week of rehearsals I'd have saved us all a lot of trouble. Too lazy!' Portia had wanted to leave out '*idiot*' from '*and these caskets will find me an idiot husband for a partner*'. John, at my insistence, has made her put it back. Thank you! And it's better because she now reveals the mocking side of her nature. But he hasn't put back the line '*You are my friend and help, Nerissa*.' My first thought is to write it into the notes he's asked me to keep sending; but then I dare ask him on the spot – does he intend to return the line or not? He says yes, and instructs me to give the note to her.

He calls up: 'Robert, come down here and save my legs, Arnold has a new line for you.'

'A *new* one?'

'No,' I say, 'an old one in a new place.' I give it to her.

'Good,' she says, 'that'll help the Ethiopian princess bit.'

I wondered if Gloria heard that?

Giving Jessica all those silent moments in the first scene has made a new woman of Julie. She now thinks John a genius instead of hating him with a passion.[207] John says: 'I've not had lunch and I'm getting drunk. Must stop. Brian! Tell Blossom that neither Andy Phillips, I, nor Mr Wesker have eaten and if there's some cheese and celery ...' Half an hour later Blossom appears with a tray of celery, nuts, cheese, apples, tomatoes, small shredded wheat. It's fun time again.

Friday, 11 November – day of third preview

Everything begins to happen. I phone the Frankels' flat to check Dusty and kids have flown in safely from London. Susan Kindlund arrives with photos and cuttings of *Love Letters On Blue Paper* and

---

[207] My notes to John before leaving for London (Appendix 5) said: 'she needs attention and love'.

informs me that Arthur Storch, the director, has completely overturned my stage directions and had Sonia deliver *all* her letters live rather than a few as 'voice-over'. He may be right but my feeling is that the 'voice-over' helps create 'the other woman'.[208]

In the evening took the children to the second preview. Tanya and Daniel had to leave after interval, too exhausted to remain. They took a taxi to Judy Rossner's where they were staying. Dawna[209] fell asleep through half of it. LJ stayed awake and was very impressed. The audience response was tremendous, a great whoop. One woman stood up joyously at the end and said in a loud voice: 'Well thank God Broadway has a literate play at last!'

Applause came at very different moments − Antonio's line about the simple wisdom of the people being '*the ignorance we choose to keep them in*' received a batch of hear, hears as well as a round of applause. Roberta put in '***idiot husband***' and received a healthy laugh which in turn fed into, and improved her performance − livelier, truer. But, instead of saying to Nerissa as arranged '*you are not only my help but my friend*' she put it the other way round: '*you are not only my friend but my help ...*' quite different.

But the most fascinating moment of this entire production saga has manifested itself in the shape of Sir John. I've always suspected him of secretly resenting the intense − and positive − Jewish tone of the play, and had been waiting for something to happen. I wrote about it earlier on in this journal:

> ...' but something else he said made my antennae suspect his motives. He admired the writing but 'I don't agree with every-thing, you know!' There's something else in his head. Something, something ... It will emerge sooner or later, I feel it.

And here it was. I'll explain.

It had worried him that the three young Venetians were unsympathetically drawn, and I'd felt Shylock's cleverness intimi-

---

[208] Having since seen a production in Stockholm where *all* the letters were delivered live by the actress, and that was a disaster, I've since made it a contractual condition that the letters be delivered as voice-over.

[209] Lindsay Joe's black girlfriend.

dated – or at least irritated – him. And so, in the midst of this pro-Semitic hothouse, he found a moment to assert the Christian faith. It's a moment of the absurd. His big speech in the courtroom is a two-pronged attack on the handful of Venetian families who share power between them; and a defence of the Jew as usurer.

> ... The usurer's a Jew, and the Jew the people's favourite villain. Convenient! Easy! But usury *must* exist in our city. We have many poor, and our economy can't turn without it. The Jew practises what he hates because we have forbidden him rights to practise other professions. *He* relieves *us* of the sin. Do we condemn the Jew for doing what our system has *required* him to do? Then if we do, let's swear, upon the cross, that among us we know of no Christian, no patrician, no duke, bishop or merchant who, in his secret chambers, does not lend at interest, for that is what usury is. Swear it! On the cross! No one, we know no one ...

The absurd moment comes when he cries out, '*Swear it! On the cross!*' He turns to the audience, delivers the phrase with a melodramatic reverence in his voice, and, rolling his eyes to heaven, pauses before the words '*on the cross*'. In an instant he has turned the speech from a defence of the Jew into an assertion of the holiness of the cross. Struck a blow for Christianity!

Later – in Charlie's

Popped in and out of rehearsals today. John snapped at Graziano and Tubal in the Loggia scene. 'What are you two doing? You haven't arranged to cut lines between you, have you? I won't have any lines cut unless I say so!' Said for my benefit I'm sure. But it doesn't blind me to lines which *have* been cut. Character lines such as Tubal's distressed: '*You warned! I warned! Who didn't warn?*'

Sunday, 13 November.

All friends and family are here. Excitement grows, anticipation and expectations with it. Audiences at previews continue to be full, attentive, enthusiastic, and loud with bravos. The cast are proud, thrilled. Only I remain angry and ashamed that the praise and fortune will come for something that is not mine, and I don't know how to conduct myself graciously. On at least two occasions I was on the verge of confrontations.

Friday was the night Gloria exploded. When I met her after the performance she was like a firework gone berserk, cracking backwards and forwards in a rage along the street outside the Plymouth stage door, on the verge of tears, leaving me helpless and uncomprehending as to the cause. She wanted to rush away from the theatre district. Here's the story.

A cut of about nine lines had been made at the end of the play, just before Nerissa appears. To ensure I didn't hear about them the cut was given to all relevant actors except her. She was, rightly, furious. To bypass what they feared would be my objection they had risked her missing her cue. It was treacherous and unprofessional. Gloria has a way of being furious which places *every*one on the enemy's side, even me, so that she and I nearly quarrelled.

I determined to write John a note, which I did next morning as a follow-up to my last brief notes to him. Gloria picked me up and we took a taxi to the Saturday rehearsal. It was a particularly important rehearsal – the last chance to get the ending right, or at least nearer to my intention. I'd written out for John exactly how I saw the last moves for Nerissa, and he was going to try to make them work. My note was planned for him to read *after* the rehearsal. In the taxi I felt I ought to show it to Gloria since it affected her. As I suspected, she asked me not to give it to him. Frustrating, but I had to accede since it would be she who'd take the blunt of John's anger if he decided to turn vicious. My guess was that he wouldn't, instead he'd be hurt and ashamed. We couldn't risk it however. I tore off the 'letter'[210] part and just handed him the notes.

At the theatre two more things happened. John, who'd said the previous evening 'see you tomorrow' now said: 'You want me to

---

[210] Appendix 8.

direct this scene? Then I suggest you make yourself scarce this morning so that I don't become anxious ...' I hated the rejection but felt that, because he was going to make my specific request work, I should not be a presence. He was also going to have to direct Gloria. I went to look for her. She was in the basement, on her own in the makeshift costume room, reading a little art book, forcing herself to keep calm. I told her John wanted me to keep away but we both agreed it was probably *not* in order to cut more lines. We were, by now, the outsiders in the entire production.

The call came through. She went up one flight of stairs, I went up the other. I decided to linger to hear John's general notes to them. He said nothing special, except they were in good shape and he was going to work on the ending. Andy fiddled with last minute focusing. Everyone waited in their chosen corners backstage. I moved towards the stage door and into a furious row erupting between Gloria on the one hand, Nick and Roberta on the other. Gloria's full and confident anger was being unleashed upon the 'star' who'd tried to contain her, and the actor who'd been part of a betrayal. I've asked her to write her version of the exchange[211] but as I understood, it sounds as though, paradoxically, having discovered the treachery of the cut lines, Gloria had been so furious that she'd delivered her '*and heroes you are, sirs, true ...*' with just the right amount of outrage and scorn. Nick had asked her why she'd been so angry – she'd spat out the lines with such venom they'd withered. In replying she let him have it. Roberta was sitting nearby and butted in saying, 'Don't start trouble.' Gloria replied that Nick had begun the conversation and would she stay out of it, please.

'Fuck off,' said Roberta.

'You'd like me to do that wouldn't you?'

'Yes! I WOULD!'

'Well tough luck, because I have no intention of doing so at all.' And so it began. I was happy that she'd finally hit back, impressed at her controlled and dignified fury.

Instead of going back to the apartment I wandered around, bought her some books, and left them at the stage door with a

---

[211] She seems not to have done so. There's no record among my papers.

card saying I'd meet her at Downey's for lunch. Downey's was closed. We grabbed a taxi to the Greek restaurant where she told me the story of the clash, adding that Riggs had saved the day by getting her to calm down. John had heard the exchange but cannily stayed away. No one came to Roberta's side.

I asked how the new scene had gone, was she comfortable with my moves? Yes, and the scene had gone well. She'd rehearsed it four times but wouldn't know how they would really work until run in a few times before an audience.

I had to be with family and friends in Great Neck but returned to catch the second act of the evening performance. The matinée had gone well, particularly the scene between Gloria and Roberta. At the end of the first act Roberta had said, 'Perhaps we'd better have a fight every day.' At the end of the second act she apologised completely and said it was tension and that Sir John had been getting on to her and she was fed up to the teeth with him.

In the evening performance Gloria carried off the ending marvellously. Well – almost! She moved subtly from gentle irony into fury but her last turn on '*heroes*' was clumsy. Nor, once again, is it my ending. John has Shylock, Antonio, and Portia in their arches smiling and bowing to Nerissa. The script calls for melancholy tinged by Portia's defiance. John's staging is theatrical, I wanted a more lyrical sadness. Watching the knife raising in the court scene, Antonio baring his chest, listening to the silly moaning of the Jews,[212] and the Latin chanting of the Venetians I feel it's kitsch, cheap theatricality. The audience, and no doubt the critics, will love it, but it has no truth. It has no logic either, because Portia, knowing the judgment she has lined up, nevertheless sits and watches Shylock struggle to use the knife, and Antonio prepare to receive it. She watches up until the last minute before pouncing contemptuously to interpret the bond. That makes her, like Shakespeare's Portia, callous. And Shylock's contemptuous line '*here, you take it*' as he throws down the knife at the feet of the young Venetians, has been cut.

As I glance through the text and listen to more of the perform-ance I discover more that's been cut. My paranoia intensifies. I

---

212 I think the intention was to create Jewish lamentations.

imagine I hear a very trimmed 'contempt' speech. Stand at the back in anger swearing to myself that this is the last straw. Now I *will* take out an injunction. Rush backstage to check with Joe. No, I'd made a mistake. There'd been no trimming.

Wednesday, 16 November – opening night

Rang Merle yesterday to warn that I was unhappy with what was happening on stage and therefore, if the play was a success, I'd not be comfortable enough to speak with anyone he might line up for an interview. Told him I was angry with the producers for breaking their contract by insisting on cuts without my consent. Merle said he didn't think they had insisted. They'd simply said the play needed tightening. John did the cutting. I asked if anyone knew what Clive Barnes[213] thought. He said it wasn't his place to ask, more the place of Bernie Jacobs from whom Barnes is hoping for some sort of help. I asked what help? It seems that everyone is trying to get John Simon out of his job as theatre critic of *New York Magazine*, and put Barnes there. I said that must put some unpleasant pressure on Barnes to review *Shylock* well. Merle didn't think so. For example Barnes, although he praised Liza Minelli to the skies, had criticised the Shuberts' production of *The Act* in which she starred. I observed that John Simon was very intelligent. 'But so personally vitriolic,' Merle said, 'attacking the features of actors. I find him emotionally unbalanced which, coupled with an ambition for notoriety, results in an outburst of spleen that makes him a vicious prick!'

In the theatre are telegrams and a letter from a Rabbi Maza which the good rabbi had sent to Dexter saying it was contrary to Jewish teaching to have Shylock raise a knife to Antonio.[214] I left a note for John saying how relieved I was that someone else had seen it. 'Clements' knife-raising is a nonsense. A cheap theatrical trick.' I suppose that made John furious, but hell! It's my play and I hate unsubtleties imposed upon it. We're at the stage of avoiding one another. Gloria tells me he's giving a champagne

---

[213] Clive Barnes, now critic of WQXR Radio had attended the last preview.

[214] Appendix 9.

brunch to the cast on stage this morning before the last rehearsal, and presumably before he rushes off tomorrow for his holiday under an Arabian sun. I saw him struggling with a case of champagne; he looked at me, wasn't going to say anything, then grudgingly said, 'Good morning,' and scarpered. I've wrapped his presents – some Shakespeare prints and a signed copy of *The New Play*.[215] My note accompanying them said:

> DEAR JOHN: Thank you for dragging me struggling, screaming, and bleeding onto the Broadway stage, and helping me bring the Broadway stage screaming and struggling back into the orbit of serious theatre. ARNOLD.

Dusty and I have wrapped up about twenty other presents.

Last night's preview audience was galvanised. A hint of tonight's response? Kate Hepburn was there.

Later – 5.20 p.m.

Rushed to West 11th to pack the last presents and put all in a couple of boxes and carrier bag which we took in a taxi to the theatre. Laid each present outside the dressing room doors – one or two I was able to give personally.

Marian gave me her present – I knew it would be something her father had written.[216] When she saw me after she'd opened her's she collapsed into tears. Soft Nelly! I'd given her the original manuscript of the article I'd written for the Philadelphia programme, which she'd kindly edited, making helpful suggestions. She showed us a letter from Kate Hepburn saying how everyone was marvellous in a 'fascinating evening'.

Cast excited by what friends have said to them after seeing the show. Bumped into Henrik [Bering-Liisberg] and went to Charlie's for lunch with him and his girlfriend. The man at the door said he had no table. I shamelessly used my name with the owner who said of course there was a table. He added the play

---

215 See footnote 75.

216 *The Seven Lively Arts* by Gilbert Seldes, literary critic, essayist and chronicler of 1920s–30s popular arts.

would be a success because it was his birthday. Donald Howarth was there, too.

Dusty and Judith Rossner walked a long walk through Central Park yesterday and met a friend of Judy's who said the vibes for *Golda* had always been bad, but good for *Shylock*.

Strolled along Fifth Avenue with Dusty where, in Saks, she bought some shoes before finding somewhere to have her hair done. I continued on to Madison. Bumped into an actor who'd played Raymondo in the New York production of *The Kitchen*. Further up bumped into Peter Shaffer. Chatted about John's wilfulness. Peter said he needed to be stood up against as all bullies do.

Thursday, 17 November – the morning after

I'm in a state of shock. The reviews are negative. It was a brilliant first night but the reviews have murdered the play's life. None of us can believe it – cast, producers, friends. The bastards have done it again. Whatever may be said about the weaknesses of the play or the production I know in every bone of my body that the play carries a splendid audacity. But it's of the kind that induces discomfort in some who feel the need to shrug it off with feigned indifference, dismissed as though saying, 'I'm not going to show he's touched or impressed *me*.'

An interesting try, but one necessarily doomed. A '*try*'? A fatuous remark that bears no relationship to the work it ... but why do I waste words on them? Insensitivity cannot be countered. A description of last night will be more rewarding.

I'd had a suit specially made, and had bought a most beautiful coat of alpaca, grey,[217] with grey antelope boots to match, and a black silk scarf and handkerchief. Dusty bought a magnificent Venetian-type dress in black and gold. Daniel wore an old black suit of mine and bow tie. Lindsay Joe was in a grey velvet suit with black open-necked shirt. Tanya in a long, flowered very low cut frock. Dawna in a black dress of Dusty's.

---

[217] Remember vividly that I was driving down Savile Row when out of the corner of my eye I saw this stunning coat in the window. Stopped immediately. It was £150. I have never paid so much for anything, before nor since. But I was told I was going to be 'a rich young man'. I still possess the coat – it still looks like a million dollars. I just don't seem able to fit it any more.

Della and Ralph[218] came with Sylvia and Alex. LJ and Dawna came with Jerry,[219] Gloria's mother, and her son Adam. Tanya and Daniel arrived with Judy Rossner and her escort. Dusty and I shared a cab with Claire and William. We'd toyed with the idea of giving the children a treat ordering a limousine so that we could all arrive in style but it would have taken too much organisation, and I feared giving my kids false expectations – although God knows, this expensive trip is hardly calculated to establish sober perspectives for them.

Picked up more telegrams. And presents from cast: an old pre-Cassiodorus Venetian coin from Bill Roerick; a T-shirt from Gloria with SHYLOCK[220] on one side and HEROES INDEED on the other; a glass vase and flower from Joe Leon. Nothing from the English knight, not even a card saying 'good luck'. A sweet note from Riggs saying: *I lost respect for you both morally and professionally for not finishing the play*, which at least made him feel better. Drifted from dressing room to dressing-room wishing everyone luck, enjoying their praise for my new outfit – a relief from the small wardrobe they'd seen me in these past three months. Three months! Then back into the milling and excited crowds taking their seats.

Again, a sense that an audience was present mainly because it had heard the evening was going to be special. Family and friends a great support: Nathaniel Tarn with his girlfriend had come all the way from New Hope – I was particularly anxious that he, as a scholar and poet, should like it; Herbert Tarr, our new friend, rabbi and writer, so clever and funny; Bob and Nikky[221] from London; Joan Kahn and Charlotte Zolotow from Harpers; Burt Britton accompanied by Gina Belafonte; Henrik from Aarhus; Staphan Roos, who'd directed the world première in Stockholm … and so many others.

We'd occupied mainly the first and second rows of the circle. Despite it being considered *infra dig* in New York, we preferred it.

---

[218] Sister and brother-in-law.

[219] Gloria's therapist.

[220] THE MERCHANT, of course.

[221] Bob and Nikky Gavron. Now divorced Bob, semi-retired head of his printing group, St Ives, has been a loyal friend. Now chairman of the Guardian Media Group.

John Dexter was out of it all, getting drunk in Charlie's. My sense of elation and calm and sheer pleasure to have everyone there was high. It began.

There was a small change in the beginning, the Androids began with their backs to one another and *then* turned. Somehow it forced everyone to be quiet sooner. From then on nothing went wrong. On the contrary, they all performed with a confidence born of five appreciative preview audiences, and backstage praise from friends they could trust. Many elements remained which I didn't like − I still missed what had been cut, and was chilled by the holes in the play but − it was all exhilarating. The audience laughed, applauded in between speeches and − I looked at their faces − they were touchingly attentive, leaning forward in their seats, their faces poised in lovely concentration as though grateful to have their intelligence respected.

In the interval the buzz was high. Everyone was convinced they were witnessing 'an event', were in on a triumph. Tarn was full of compliments, impressed with what he felt to be an advance on previous work. Henrik was flushed with excitement. Daniel, Tanya, LJ and Dawna thrilled me with how proud they were of their father. The second act moved into the same gear of confidence and attack. I loved my '*I know, I know*' scene, but hated what was left of the Loggia scene, and Clements ridiculously rolling his eyes to heaven on '*Swear it! On the cross*', defending a Christianity that was not under attack. I wish that Shylock and Antonio had shown more that they were beneath a sword of Damocles in the court scene, and I regretted the fake happy ending with the *heroes* bowing to Nerissa. Still, it dazzled and held the audience who, at the end, gave an ovation more tumultuous than any yet given.

I was hugged and embraced. The producers were hugged and congratulated for having a winner. There was in the air a sense that Broadway had come home. I took Daniel and Tanya backstage with me, and asked Dusty and Lindsay Joe to shepherd friends back to the party at Sardi's.

About fifteen people were waiting in the wings to see Joe Leon whose dressing-room was at stage-door level. While I waited for him to get ready I kissed and thanked Pat de Rouse − stage manager and prompt. Joe was ecstatic. He knew, as they all did, that they'd pulled it off. The stairs up to the dressing rooms were jammed. Sam Cohn said 'Hug me!' Gerry Schoenfeld kissed me. There was love and admiration in people's eyes as the children and I struggled up to each one of the cast and finally to the dressing room of the three girls – Angela, Rebecca and Gloria – where we found Mary Ellen and Vibica. Gloria took flash photos. The room was filled with flowers and bottles of champagne. An air pervaded of excited wisecracks and triumph. The children were ecstatic, and their pleasure was crowned when, on entering Sardi's, the entire restaurant, filled with producers and their friends and members of the audience rose to their feet and gave me a tremendous – and it seemed to me – genuinely felt ovation as we walked through them to our table in the far right corner.

It was a brilliant occasion. My disappointments with the production, my fears that it was not *my* play, that the rapturous reception was fraudulent all disappeared in the certain knowledge that everyone's work of three months was to be rewarded. I went from table to table, greeting my guests and basking in their congratulations, and when finally I sat down next to Tanya she leaned into me and whispered: 'I'm so proud of you, to be your daughter and have you as a father.'

'As I'm proud to have you as my daughter,' I whispered back. 'Daughter, daughter, daughter.'

Gordon Wasserman, a Canadian friend in the British Civil Service, discovered that the wife of the critic of the *New York Times* (Richard Eder) was an old friend of his and he told me that in the interval she'd muttered to him: 'Dazzling! Just dazzling. I haven't seen anything like this for years.'

As the meal progressed I took Della to meet Joe Leon and Julie Garfield – Joe had his own party upstairs. Roberta came over to greet my friends whom she'd seen on and off during this long haul. Gloria's table was nearby with her family and friends. What gaiety was in the air! Judy was guest at our table, and witnessed one of those restaurant clashes cartoonists make jokes about. I ordered wine – red Mouton Cadet and white Mouton Cadet. The captain, with a dismissive sneer, said there was no such thing as a white Mouton Cadet, and though I was convinced I'd seen one, yet I blushed prepared as always to believe I was wrong. (But I wasn't! And some days later bought a bottle for Judy when I went to say my goodbyes.)

At around 11.30 Bob and Gordon said they were going off to find the *NY Times*. I told them not to bother, we'd get it before it was on the street. But they were eager, they wanted the New York theatre experience. The next minutes were a haze as I sat first with one friend then another until suddenly, out of that haze, I saw Eddie Kulukundis walk towards me. Eddie had originally bought the play in London and had offered it to Dexter who had set it up in New York. I'd hardly had a chance to speak with him all evening. Was he now coming to chat and catch up? I looked at his face expecting it to be relaxed, ready for conversation. Instead I saw a sad, uncertain smile.

At once I said – though not believing what I was saying: 'It's not good is it?'

'No it's not,' he replied. 'Can't you see them leaving?' I looked to where he inclined his head. Those who had stood to applaud us were now, with embarrassed glances back to me, emptying the restaurant. There was a queue to get out! 'It's incredible,' said Eddie, 'that no one's had the courtesy to come up and tell you.'

The shock grew in me, a slow burn. I felt myself smiling with helpless bravery across to Dusty and the kids. Gradually, like victims of a poison gas rising to catch the stragglers on a battle-field, my party in the farthest corner of the restaurant heard and became numbed by the news. A waiter came round giving out copies of the *Times*. We sat in groups, my sister reading aloud the review to one group, Bob Gavron to another. The most stricken were the youngsters who couldn't match what they'd experienced on stage, or experienced of the audience's response, to what they were now hearing.

'*It's dramatic structure is weak and it's dramatic impact fitful and uncertain* ...' What did *that* mean? The audience had been on the edge of its seat. The impact was not only certain but constant, the evening had been held up by applause after applause as it had been every preview night and every night in five weeks of a pre-run in Washington.

On the other hand Eder's review was not unintelligent. In

London it would command audiences. Here in New York it is the headline and the last line which are the killers.

Intelligent but weak
… The evening is stimulating but only sometimes successful

What sense did that make? If the evening was *stimulating* wasn't that an achievement? '*Successful*'? In the arrangement of these last eight words rested the decision whether years of work will be allowed to reach an audience or be censored for them. Why couldn't Eder have written: 'Though not always successful – for what is *always* successful – the evening is stimulating.' Would that have been dishonest? Consider, he had also written:

… A totally original play … provocative, generally intelligent … writing has moments of ferocious brilliance and wit … Joseph Leon plays the part with liveliness, humour and moments of real passion. He has his triumphs …

Of course Eder would have criticisms, we all have, but isn't he aware of his awesome responsibility? Doesn't he know that putting those four words at the end, '*the evening is stimulating*', is the difference between make or break?[222] Neither those actors, nor Dexter, nor I are flawless but we have track records, standards and achievement high enough to suggest we could produce a work for which an audience exists. '*The evening is stimulating*'. Four words which would have totally changed our lives and fortunes, and given both us and Broadway courage for the future.

I was told that, as the review was being telephoned through, one of the Shubert partners said: 'They're forcing us only to put on *The Act* and *Annie*.'

Shock, heavy-heartedness and a profound sense of demoralisation was what we all took from the restaurant to our beds.

Today the pattern takes shape. The reviews on TV were mostly silly – no minds at work there. But the *New York Post* and the *Daily News* with more time to make mistakes, made them!

---

[222] Eder, it transpired, was only a stop-gap critic. He was replaced after six months.

Wesker, in seeking to ennoble the harsh contract, has taken the malice, the very sting out of the play ...

says Mr. Watt in the *Daily News* imagining it was Shakespeare's play I'd reassembled. And why can't he see that the malice and sting remain, only not made of the same ingredients as Shakespeare's? Shylock's sting is in his intellectual contempt rather than fiscal contempt. His sin is hubris. It's his cleverness rather than his revengefulness makes the Jew hated. But no one has seen that. Or, who knows, perhaps they have, and through their hatred of Shylock hate the play.

Consider Mr Gotfried[223] saying it may be awful to have an anti-Semitic play from Shakespeare but 'we have to live with that'. What's that for criticism? Followed by an hosanna of praise for me as 'a proven major contemporary playwright ... stage imagination fertile ... a real writer ... ' Well why the hell doesn't he get out of the way and let a public see the work of 'a real writer'? Instead of apologising why doesn't he encourage? Or does my impudent Shylock embarrass the Jewish Gotfried and offend the Catholic Eder? God knows how the reviewer's mind works. Not in the ways of men, for sure.

And what are we to think of New York theatre audiences, those who will now obediently stay away, take no risks? The awful irony is that a play, supposedly 'subject to democratic scrutiny' – which God forbid anyone would want to block – lives or dies simply because of the tyrannical power of *one newspaper*. *Shylock* could have been reviewed by a new and entirely unknown reviewer, an ex-grocer, a taxi driver, a student off-campus, and the effect would have been the same, proof of which lies in the fact that Clive Barnes, terror of Broadway for the last ten years and relieved only a few months earlier of his post as drama critic for the *NY Times*, gave the play a rave review on radio[224] yet couldn't save it. His name and track record meant nothing. In that land of glorious individualism, take away the institution and the individual is bereft of authority. Long live democracy!

---

223 Martin Gotfried, theatre critic of the *New York Post*

224 And also in the London *Times*. '...perhaps Wesker's finest play...most of the writing is brilliant, with masterly sensibility ...The play raises issues and risks arguments and it teems with life as a consequence ...'

I'll survive. But poor Broadway! Poor American theatre! Poor American playwright!

Friday, 18 November

Dexter confronts a shattered cast an hour before the curtain goes up. Sam Cohn and Bernie Jacobs are present.

'Well, what do I say? You've obviously given the worst performances of your life, I've directed the worst in mine, and Arnold's written his lousiest play.' They laugh, warmed by him. He continues. 'I'm too shocked really to understand it all. There's no doubt in my mind you were all brilliant and that this is one of the most important plays to appear anywhere on the English speaking stage. Why they missed it, or most of them did, we'll never know. But someone will pick it up again, somewhere, and soon. Meanwhile you've got an audience out there tonight who've been told by their friends to come to an event. You have a responsibility not to lose your energy ...'

A great general's speech before a battle against unfair odds. He told them how he hoped to be doing *Pygmalion* and how he wanted to work with people he'd worked with before, and he felt he could cast it out of this company. A bait dangled to keep their spirits high.

Then came the cruellest blow. I had been leaning against a wall in the aisle by the prompt door, looking at the actors scattered in the front rows listening to John. When he'd finished he briskly picked up his briefcase, walked to the prompt door with the producers, said nothing to me, but to them – as he held the door open for them – he said, not without some perkiness: 'There's another little project I have to discuss with you. Got time for a drink at Charlie's? A spare hour?'[225]

I find it difficult to know how to conduct myself. Inwardly I know the value of the play. Outwardly my aura can be nothing but that of a failed writer. I remember the audience's responses, and comfort myself that but for the death of Zero and the fateful timing which lifted Clive Barnes from the columns of the *New York Times* the play would now be a raging success.

---

[225] I never saw him again.

I think also of the two days I had alone with the cast when Zero was alive, Dexter setting up the play in Philadelphia. I'd given them a little talk and tried to warn them how this play would attract a special kind of hostility, how my plays frequently had – evincing a parched and sour vocabulary. They'd smiled indulgently but ignored me, seeming more interested in the quotations which I read to them from the *Lexicon of Musical Invective*.

We find Beethoven's Ninth Symphony to be precisely one hour and five minutes long; a fearful period indeed ... The last movement, a chorus, is heterogeneous. What relation it bears to the symphony we could not make out ...

The Harmonicon, London, April 1825

Berlioz, musically speaking, is a lunatic ... His music is simply and undisguisedly nonsense ...

Dramatic and Musical Review, London, 7 January 1843

'The Sea' is persistently ugly ... Debussy fails to give any impression of the sea ... There is more of barnyard cackle in it than anything else ...

New York Times, 22 March 1907

The compositions of Richard Strauss do not even leave a clean taste in one's mouth ...

Henderson, *New York Times Supplement*, 26 December 1897

The finale of the Fourth Symphony of Tchaikovsky pained me by its vulgarity ...

Musical Review, New York, 26 February 1880

Rigoletto is the weakest work of Verdi. It lacks melody. This opera has hardly any chance to be kept in the repertoire.

Gazette Musicale de Paris, 22 May 1853

Sunday, 20 November

The family returned to London. I stayed behind. My heart is heavy. It's a crisp day with a blue sky. I still love this city, though we have crashed horrendously in it. In the morning went to have brunch with Merle and his friend, Perl. Liver, egg and onion, bagels with cream cheese and lox, fruit. I must have been sombre company for them. When I asked him did he think there was no hope the Shuberts might get behind the play he replied, sadly, no hope! We talked about the production. Both of them felt that Dexter had done a rotten job. I'll collect my own thoughts later.

They drove me to the Village where I dropped off Sylvia's keys. Being there, no one else in the apartment, I felt miserable. Here's where the odyssey had begun, in the heat of summer, three and a half months ago when Zero was alive. I can't write about it any more. What is there to say? This New York journal must have an end sooner or later. All that's left is to describe the last night.

I hung around for the matinée − a small but appreciative audience. Didn't watch it all. LJ and Dawna came back from the airport to see the ending − they were hanging on a few days to take in the city. The small audience was not embarrassed by its size and could still shout its bravos.

After her scene, I caught Roberta on the stairs. She talked to me. 'We're all a little down, of course, and it's been difficult to find energy. But curiously, I've given a more mellow performance, and you know, I find it works. Will you be there to watch it tonight? Watch it. You may find it's a pointer in a new direction for the next production.' I did. It nearly made me weep. She was so relaxed and deep, lifting words and phrases into their true meaning. It was almost a full house, the performance emotional, Joe delivering his lines with great subtext, '*I am so tired of men*'.

For much of the performance I was hanging around backstage in the wings, clinging to the actors, the carriers of my play, feeling great admiration for their courage. Idiot-like I found delight in watching Lorenzo, Bassanio, Jessica and Portia stand in the wings as people, and then squeeze between the curtains on to the stage to become characters in my play. Ghostlike I hovered among ghosts.

In the audience was someone from my past, Shifra (Rickless) Benattar − my first girlfriend who, I believed, had shaped the pattern of all my other relationships. She's a millionaire property dealer now, with an office in the building of General Motors 'which I built!' Ah, the scheme of things!

That evening two things happened which had not happened

before. One we'd been striving for, the other was eerie. This was an audience who'd come because they'd been urged to do so by friends. One sensed they'd come expecting an event, feeling privileged. They were also a 'dramatic' audience because they knew the play was sentenced, and therefore were manifesting profound respect. As they left the theatre many looked at me as though ashamed for their idiot guardians – the reviewers. Some came up to express their shock, almost too stunned to say anything. Do I exaggerate what I saw? I'd think so if it weren't for the fact that actors and acquaintances were bringing home the same stories from others who'd seen the play.

The eerie event was this: when the play ended the entire audience rose to their feet to applaud and, precisely at the moment when all the bows had been taken once, and Sir John, Roberta and Joe were lined up in front of the cast, the fire curtain swiftly fell narrowly missing the three actors. No one had touched it. The stage hands had to unleash the rope in order to raise it up – and it was then that the standing audience moved into thunderous applause.

God damn the critics. Little people who hate what intimidates them. No wonder David Storey[226] and John Osborne want to hit them!

After the performance we all went to Joe Allen's to drink together. Tony Harrison and Andy Phillips were there. I got into conversation with a stockbroker.

And John Pudney[227] is dead.

I am *so* sad.

All those debts accrued with such confidence. Why didn't I know? How couldn't I have guessed?

Five years' work!

---

[226] Novelist, dramatist.

[227] Second World War poet.

EPILOGUE

Assembled April 1997

Arnold and John [Osborne] supported me at a time when
I could not possibly support myself; mentally and financially.
The work was the only happy return, and were either of them
to ask me to direct a play which no one wanted to do,
I believe we would find a wooden hut somewhere.

John Dexter's notebook.
An entry dated 16 November 1985

On the plane back to London I wrote a three page letter to John which I never sent. A week later I attempted a shorter letter about the longer letter. That, too, I never sent. The one I did send was even shorter.

Munich 5 December 1977

DEAR JOHN

I don't know what, if anything, can be salvaged of *Shylock* in London. The Barnes review appeared in full glory in *The Times* last Saturday. But first to know in all discussions is do we want to work with each other again on the play?

Knowing all the love, energy and hopes you put into – and all the pleasure we got out of – the New York project, I can't bring myself to break the partnership. On the other hand there was much pain, and I do want to put back some of what was cut, restore the portrait scene to its original, and re-write a real warehouse scene anchoring it to a trading Venice. Nor, as you'd guess, could I not be at rehearsals.

It's important to know as soon as possible what your thinking is. I'm broke and am anxious to make immediate plans. Perhaps you'd let Michael Anderson[228] know (or me).

Ever.

ARNOLD

John replied on Met paper.

19 December 1977

DEAR ARNOLD

I think you know well enough that we do not wish to 'salvage' the play together. You, because you basically disliked the concept which Jocelyn and I drew from your text, requiring something more elaborate than we could provide. For myself, I do no wish to repeat an experience which I found professionally depressing. The night of the 17th August gave me a profound shock and, as I now realise, effectively ended our

---

[228] John's agent.

personal relationship. More than that, your consistent refusal to deal with one of the fundamental issues of the play brought to an end a professional relationship which, had we been a little less emotional, we might have recognised ended some time ago, or at least suffered from an irrevocable cultural gap.

You believe yourself to be a poetic writer. I believe you to be a superb writer of theatrical prose, who can invent or provoke poetic theatrical moments, but whose glutonous[229] poetics display neither your true voice nor a feeling for poetry itself. You must go on to find a director who shares your views, or direct your plays yourself.

Remember one thing, though, directing is a craft on its own requiring technical knowledge which you do not possess and an ability to let people grow and add something of themselves to your words. From auditions through rehearsals, you always press for results and demand readings which are alien to the actors you have cast or to whose casting you have agreed. Your manner of delivering notes to me is, God knows, patronising enough. To the actors it is more dangerous in the depression and confusion it produces. From *The Old Ones* to *Shylock*, I have been begged by actors not to let you give them notes. I am fully aware that actors can attempt these diverse activities in order to protect themselves, but not so many actors and actresses so often, and, moreover, people who were at that time devoted to you personally but who found your manner deadening and your language confusing.

I know of your immense success as a reader and a director in other countries, but you must remember that you speak and write in English, your audience does not. Even I have held a captive group of Dutch actors spellbound with my first reading of *The Kitchen*. Apart from the satisfaction it gave my ego, the day was wasted.

However, it is not the purpose of this letter to deliver a lecture on the director's craft or an analysis of your character (perhaps I should save this for the published text). The purpose of this letter is to answer yours which I received in Berlin, and

---

229 'Glutonous' is what was typed. I'm not sure if he meant my 'sticky' poetics, or a surfeit of it.

to give you my personal reasons for not wishing to continue the working relationship. To my agent, yourself and anyone else who asks, I shall be 'unavailable in the foreseeable future'. You will find another director who can share your view of your work and whom you will respect enough to trust, or you will direct the plays yourself. Of course, there is always the novel; there, the writer's control is absolute. His word is his word and also his responsibility. Maybe this is where your temperament is taking you. I don't pretend to know, nor do I pretend that the truth as I see it is the only truth, but I beseech you 'in the bowels of your God to consider that ye may be wrong'.

The only other people who will read this letter are Jocelyn and Riggs for obvious reasons, but I trust you will respect its privacy[230] to the same degree. Except for one necessary sentence, I have not discussed the pain and distress these past months have caused me nor do I wish to do so. Remember the good times, forget the bad, go on and make the play work your way.

With much sadness and regret and always, always love to Dusty.

Yours

JOHN

And that was nearly that.

The years passed. I reworked scenes, restored the old order and some of the cuts. At the end of 1978 Peter Farago, associate director of the Birmingham Rep, mounted the first UK production of the play using this new version. It received excellent notices from local and national press and so I didn't give up trying to get the play mounted in London. Three years after New York, on 16 April 1980, I wrote to John who was working at the National on a production of *Galileo*. An exchange ensued.

DEAR JOHN

Would you direct the new version of *Shylock* at the National?

I've started a new drive to persuade P. Hall to do it. His last words were 'It's too dense.' If you want to direct it I'm sure he'd say yes.

There would be no need for me to attend rehearsals. You

---

[230] The only person to whom it is 'private' is me, to whom the insults are directed!

know the play and know what I want from it.[231]

The 'new' version means: although I retained a number of the New York cuts I returned the play to its original scene structure, but with a completely rewritten warehouse scene, which in turn affected the Antonio dinner scene.

After Birmingham, Angela Down – who played Portia – suggested: why not leave the first Portia scene until the beginning of Act 2? In this way both Portia scenes come together, she's talked about but not seen for all of act one which whets appetites, and it makes act one shorter.

I personally think Chris Morley's sets[232] were brilliant, and was about to use them in my own production of the play in Montreal, but this was cancelled three weeks before rehearsals were due to start! Hence my initiating a new drive to get this play a proper production in London.

It needs it, and frankly – I need it. I think I'm asking you for help.

Love

ARNOLD

From John on Met paper.

24 April 1980

DEAR ARNOLD

Thank you for your letter of the 16th. It was good to hear from you again, but I wish my answer could be a little more positive than it is. *Shylock* has so many unhappy memories for me I do not at this time feel inclined to take it up again, nor do I feel I am in tune with the play as you see it. To be more specific, the observation you made to Zero, Jocelyn and myself when I pressed you to the point of the knife, your response was that if I were to be on the receiving end of the knife and you on the stabbing, you hoped you would have the courage to stab. For me, if friendship cannot transcend religious hostilities then there would be no point in continuing to work in the theatre or anywhere else.

---

[231] I must have felt very desperate!

[232] For Birmingham's production.

Secondly, I agree with Peter Hall the play is too dense and it still puzzles me how you who are capable of such finely honed writing could allow yourself to dissipate the drama in verbal and historical declaration. I hoped I could help for all the reasons that you well know, but frankly I feel I would be more of a hindrance.

Forgive the brevity of this letter; I have been flat on my back and suffering from shingles for the last three months and I am not yet fully back to work.

Sincerely,

JOHN

I replied.

2 May 1980

DEAR JOHN

Sorry you persist in holding that utterance against me which I withdrew five minutes later and which was uttered at a meeting where I felt everyone was on the verge of betraying me.

It's an absurd grudge and I can't think why you need to cling to it. I can't even step on a beetle let alone raise a knife. You know that and knew it then.

I'm the Jewish writer who wrote that Eichmann shouldn't be executed, for Christ's sake!

But your memory of it is wrong. It was not a case of 'transcending religious hostilities' — you can't seriously have imagined they existed between you and me any more than between Shylock and Antonio. It was a question of saving a community. Not the same thing.

More, there was so many instances of my proven loyalty through action that you shouldn't have given credence to a moment of wild words.

Still, that's your problem. I shall never ask for help again, and time will vindicate the play.

Love

ARNOLD

I hope you're fully recovered from shingles.

John replied on Met paper.

15 May 1980

DEAR ARNOLD

Thank you for your letter. Leaving to one side the question of whether a grudge is absurd, the point of my letter still remains. I do not believe in *Shylock* as you believe in *Shylock*, for reasons which I indicated in my last letter and which you obviously do not want to discuss. You use the phrase at the end of your letter, 'still, that's your problem'; Arnold dear, it's not my problem, it's yours. You do not see the play objectively nor do you discuss it intelligently. If the play is going to vindicate itself then for God's sake let it. Put it in a drawer and let the future discover it, in the mean time get on with your work.

Perhaps the most foolish sentence in your letter is the last one, in which you say you will never ask for help again. You will, we all do. Although you do not need my help you will need someone's.

Yours sincerely

JOHN

I reply.

23 May 1980

DEAR JOHN

You have a strange way of accounting life to yourself. You write: 'I do not believe in *Shylock* ... for reasons which I indicated in my letter and which you obviously do not want to discuss. '

What reasons did you indicate? You go on '... I'm not in tune with the play as you see it' then you write, 'to be specific ...', then you go on to make not a specific point about the play but about a personal hurt, and even that personal hurt you get muddled up as a conflict to do with 'friendship transcending religious hostilities'. Still, I *did* reply to it saying it was not a question of religious hostilities between friends (either you and me or Shylock and Antonio) but a question of 'saving a community'.

And when I say 'that's your problem' I don't refer to your interpretation of the play but to your evaluation of where true loyalty lies. Why are you making leaps between my sentences which distort their meaning rather than following the sequence as written?

Nor shall I ever understand the presumption that only you can see a work objectively. Once you have 'conceived' a production why do you imagine you are more able to be objective about your darlings than I about mine? Besides, there is so much evidence that I *was* 'objective' and did listen to your advice. *I* cut and restructured, *you* cut what you wanted without me knowing, we had a two-hour-ten-minute play. Didn't help. I listen to many people and change as a result. But only if I think it is right. You wouldn't have me change what I didn't think it was right to change any more than you could change what you didn't think it was right to change in your productions. (God *help* anyone who talks to you about what you're doing!) And if I go on to rethink the advice I've taken then that too is being objective.

I assume you *do* recognise yourself as human and therefore fallible? Sometimes you get it right sometimes you get it wrong. Or do you think the writer can only ever be wrong and the director only ever be right? And that God made us that way?

And to say I didn't discuss the play intelligently is to descend to insults, and doesn't deserve replying to. It is at least *possible* that your concept of the play in a stark Shakespearean setting was wrong and my wish for a bustling setting was right.

You are beginning to sound as school-masterish as Peter [Hall]: '… put it in a drawer and let the future discover it, in the meantime get on with your work.' And stop talking in class?! I don't *want* to put it in a drawer and let the future discover it. That play contains in craft, poetry and content what I treasure most about myself as a writer, as you once thought at a time when it looked like earning a lot of money. And I shall fight for it.

As for getting on with my work, well – I've written two plays since, a film script of *The Trilogy*, have directed, and am at work on a new play. I think you are impertinent.

Your last paragraph is again a haphazard reading of my letter.

You say a sentence is foolish. But when I wrote that sentence, 'I will never ask again for help', I was writing to *you*. It is obvious I would never ask *you* again. Of course I will need the help of others.

And how silly it sounds signing off 'Yours sincerely'.

Love

ARNOLD

John replied on National Theatre[233] paper.

18 June 1980

DEAR ARNOLD

I have received what I presume to be a photocopy of your letter of 22nd May.[244] The delay in answering is explained by the fact that I have been in England for the last four weeks, and my secretary has been on holiday.

I signed my letter 'sincerely' and I meant sincerely. Since I no longer read your letters accurately any more than you can read mine with understanding, I think the correspondence should come to an end. For reasons so complex that, lacking your facility with words, I find it impossible to explain them, I do not wish to direct *Shylock*. Please let us leave it at that.

Yours with as much sincerity as I can summon up.

JOHN

If this letter is the end of an arc then the arc begins twenty-two years earlier in a letter John wrote from HM Prison, Wormwood Scrubs, dated 16 December 1958.

... Now then, my return to life. Half of me wants and wants to come to you and Dusty for shelter, the other half thinks I ought to be strong. Give me a little more time (God how I get tears in my eyes if I remember those weeks in Coventry, your

---

[233] John was preparing his production of *Galileo* at the National Theatre which opened on 13 August 1980.

[234] His, or his secretary's, error.

cooking, the swimming, the arguments, the demented lady visitor and that perfect play ...) ... I love you very much, and in you – Dusty, your mother, Ralph and Della. For the first time in my life there are twenty-six people I love to a point just this side of distraction ...

A relationship spanning more than two decades was at an end. Our beginnings are recorded in my autobiography – *As Much As I Dare* (1994). When Riggs O'Hara assembled John's writings for his posthumous autobiography *The Honourable Beast*, I was astounded to read merely two mentions in passing of the *Shylock* experience.

Perhaps this story should end with a voice from the wings. Brent Peek, the stage manager, had worked on previous productions with John. He knew him at a different level. Shortly after my return to London from New York, Brent wrote to me.

6 January 1978

DEAR ARNOLD

Forgive the long delay. I had a lot of things to sort out, but, however belated, I did want to thank you for an extraordinary experience with *Shylock* ....

There are a number of things that I regret happening during the rehearsal period of *Shylock*, the most important of which was allowing John to get to me to such an extent that I didn't enjoy the experience. As the dust settles, however, I'm sure the play will stand the test of many years to come.

The reason I took the production (yes, I did have a choice in the matter!) was my firm belief that this was an important play, and one that would endure. I believed in the themes you were presenting and thought that you did it in an original way. That is certainly more than Broadway has had to offer in a number of years. That's essentially what I've written to the producers, lest they forget what attracted them to the project in the first place – which was you and your work.

I haven't been able quite to sort out what I think was wrong with the production as it was presented here. I hold John almost entirely at fault. But then I was taught in many years of school that the director is responsible for everything that is presented on stage. That would include poor performances, lack of focus, dramatic structure. I finally don't think that he served either you or your play well, and I'm fully prepared to go on record with that. While John raged through the theatre accusing everyone of not doing their jobs, he was not doing his. Those of us who recognised it and confronted him with it will no longer be in his employ, but I never had much respect for him as a man and now, not having any respect for him as an artist makes the loss not such a great one after all. I know he is a good friend of yours, Arnold, but people who treat other people as abysmally as John treated me and other members of the company should finally have to answer for their behaviour – something that I don't think John has had to do in his lifetime.

The two most disconcerting things that have happened since the production is that people are once again standing in line (even those in *Shylock*) to be in his new productions of *King Lear*[235] and *Romeo and Juliet*. God knows, members of the New York theatre are a hungry breed, but where is the integrity of the individual who finally says 'no'. I sincerely do not believe that anyone with any integrity can work with John.

I won't go on with this any more. Suffice it to say that the producers of *Shylock* would not hesitate in hiring him again, even after a loss of three quarters of a million dollars – almost a quarter of a million over budget.

I have had a couple of job offers, since *Shylock*, but neither the material nor the people connected with them have interested me too much. One of the wonderful things that has happened to me in my life is that I earned enough money with *Equus* that I don't have to accept any offer that is made to me. Being in the theatre is all about earning enough money that one can do only things that are interesting …

John is using a lot of people from *Shylock* in his productions of *King Lear* and *Romeo and Juliet*. The cast now stands – as I understand it – Richard Burton as Lear and Mercutio (yes, you

---

[235] Which seems never to have taken place.

read that right), Peter Firth as the Fool and Romeo, Roberta as Cordelia and Juliet, Marian as Goneril and the Nurse. I also know that all of the Androids have been contacted to play minor roles in both shows.

... I do so hope that John did not lead you to believe that I was some sort of villain in the piece – I think I would more aptly describe my role as fall-guy.

I hope this note finds you well and active ...

Love

BRENT

No, I can't end there. My autobiography not only recorded our beginnings it also carried a kind of valediction to him.

I can't believe John is dead. In a way it frightens me. If he is dead then it really means I am going to die. Don't ask me why the same conviction doesn't come into play remembering my parents are dead, it doesn't. To do with parents being part of an inevitable cycle, I think. John's death is different. He was an outrageous, cruel and opportunistic old queen who could switch his abrasive warmth on and off with alarming, confusing and unpredictable rapidity. Incomprehensible, too. And his most deplorable characteristic was his bullying. There was always a whipping boy (or girl) in the company whom he'd select to exercise his scorn upon, vaunt his reductive wit, vent his ill-temper for what had gone wrong the night before with his love life, annihilate with mockery for a foolish decision he had made that offended his sense of perfection and burned him with shame. But when he was high on his cleverness, his skill, his imagination, when he buzzed with elation from an inspired day's work, he was electrifying in a way that few other directors I know have been, and it communicated itself to the cast who would then give him their all. I despise bullying tantrums, I'm quick to detect the absurdity or petulance of ill-considered moments, and I can see through emotional blackmail. John went cold and silent with tangible fury at times, and it was best, then, to keep away. But something about both my ability to X-ray humbug, and our relationship rooted in shared beginnings, earned me his respect, caution, and, I think, a certain fear. John couldn't mess with me. I knew him. And so he listened to my notes on his production as carefully as I listened to his on my script.

Something about our family attracted him too. He loved my mother and Dusty, and admired Della and Ralph. Perhaps they echoed his background, or perhaps he felt comfortable in an atmosphere neither intimidatingly claustrophobic with university minds, nor sour with working-class resentments, nor judgemental with discontent. There was discontent, but my family maintained a generosity of spirit. Part of him hated theatrical camp. He was impatient with fools, weak, hesitant personalities and heartiness of any kind – especially that hearty intimacy which certain actors assume on first meeting. Having no education he warmed to intelligent wit, scholarship and brilliant spirits. When I arrived in New York for casting *Shylock* (he was director of the Metropolitan Opera House at the time) he was ablaze with his research into the history of Renaissance Italy ... He couldn't wait to begin rehearsals ...

In Conclusion

I'm troubled. Twenty-one years after having written *Shylock* I reflect upon why the major state theatres in London have resisted presenting the work. If no one had ever mounted it anywhere, or if it had been mounted and universally damned I would have retreated, bloodied, and considered that I had perhaps undergone a massive dramatic lapse, a sort of creative heart-attack! But I look back at the play's history.

Its world première, hailed as their success of the decade, took place in Stockholm's Royal Dramaten Theatre – no mean power-house, that; the English-speaking rights were bought by Eddie Kulukundis, no mean West End producer, he; Kulukundis offered the direction of the play to John Dexter – no mean authority, John; Zero Mostel accepted to play the lead – no mean actor that one; and to cap it all the Shuberts of New York took on the major role of producers for a Broadway production – no mean showbiz moguls, they. Then God stepped in, took Zero from us, and that *was* mean.

The New York reviews didn't help the play survive Broadway without a star but they were full of positive comments. Most were obviously stirred, many touched. And when the play was performed in Birmingham the national press was also full of positive comments. Take just one example from Ned Chaillet writing in *The Times*:

> ... a thoroughly original work ... elegant speeches that are typical of Mr Wesker ... a compelling play ... a passionate document ... a tract for intelligence and understanding ...

In 1989 I raised £20,000 to mount a workshop production over eight performances (16–22 October) bringing from Israel a brilliant actor, Oded Teomi, to play the lead. Commercial producers and the artistic directors of subsidised theatres were invited in the hope they would be enthused sufficiently to mount a full-scale production. Only Richard Eyre of the National Theatre attended the performances. He was not, I was informed, delighted. However, even for this workshop the critics were impressed. David Lemmon in the *Guardian*:

> ... a work of wit and intelligence which engages us intellectually and emotionally. It is a challenging play and it will be a travesty if it does not reach the West End stage.

The play has been tried, proven, well received. Its subject is an internationally notorious theatrical character; Shylock has a curiosity value, controversy encircles Shakespeare's portrait of this Jew; a British playwright of no mean international reputation has essayed an alternative portrait. Why is there such resistance? I am beginning to suspect it is other than artistic. 'Leave us the Jew,' the theatre establishment seems to be saying, 'we need to be allowed the pleasure of forgiving the Bard's Semitic villain whom we hate. Tamper with him not.'

In the *Guardian* of 1 April 1988 Melanie Phillips wrote an article ('A society that can laugh at the *Jew of Malta* by pretending anti-semitism is dead') about encroaching anti-Semitism in this country. She listed a number of examples. Two are illuminating.

> There was the theatre executive who told an astonished visiting playwright that the reason for the crucifixes and other

Christian icons on the wall of the office was to show the many visiting Jewish producers from New York that they couldn't have it all their own way. And there was the committee of great and good people who had gathered to make a senior arts appointment and who were startled to hear one of their number denounce a candidate as 'that bloody Jew', but who said nothing, leaving it to a Jewish participant to register a lonely protest.

'Shylock' has entered the language. To be called 'a Shylock' is to be insulted for being mean like a Jew. A director of Hungarian origin told me he had seen a production in wartime Hungary where the play's anti-Semitic aspects were, not surprisingly, exploited to the hilt. Jessica was portrayed as a whore. I cannot help feeling there is a certain honesty to such a production.

APPENDICES

APPENDIX 1

Chronology – Drafts and Performances

1974

24 June   First three pages of notes written in Boulder, Colorado, USA.

24 September   Main research begun in Wales. Three notebooks kept – 'Facts', 'Ideas' and 'Dialogue'.

1975

7 February   Handwritten draft begun in Wales.

10 May   Handwritten draft completed in London.

19 May   1st typed draft (second draft) begun.

30 May   1st typed draft completed, worked on and retyped into –

3 August   2nd typed draft (third draft) begun.

11 August   2nd typed draft completed, worked and roneoed into (from here on will drop the word 'typed' and give the draft its accurate number)

13 October   4th draft, worked on and roneoed into –

1976

22 May   5th draft.

8 October   WORLD PREMIÈRE (of 5th draft) at the Royal Dramaten Theatre, Stockholm, directed by Staphan Roos. Meanwhile 5th draft worked on in New York and roneoed into -

1977

22 June   6th draft.

1 August   Rehearsals of this draft directed by John Dexter began in Minskoff Studios, 1515 Broadway. Play cut, reshaped and reworked during rehearsals.

2 September   First preview (7th draft), Forrest Theatre, Philadelphia. Zero Mostel, actor playing Shylock, taken ill.

8 September	Zero Mostel died 7.47 in the evening, of an aneurysm of the heart.
11 September	Rehearsals began again in New York in ACT 48 Studios on West 48th, with Joseph Leon (who had played Tubal and understudied Mostel) taking over the role of Shylock.
28 September to 5 November	*Shylock* played at Kennedy Centre, Washington, during which more cuts were made and scenes merged and reshuffled.
10 November	First preview of five previews (still called 7th draft though in reality it was the 8th draft) in the Plymouth Theatre, New York.
16 November	NEW YORK PREMIÈRE. Opened to mixed reviews. Quote of last line of *New York Times*, 'The evening is stimulating but only sometimes successful.'
19 November	*Shylock* folds on Broadway after four performances.

1978

24 January	Between 22 October 1977 and 24 January 1978 old order of scenes returned, some cuts restored, scenes reworked and roneoed into 8th draft.
June	8th draft published in Miron Grindea's *Adam* magazine (nos. 401/403).
12 September	Rehearsals begun, directed by Peter Farago, at Birmingham Rep, during which changes were made resulting in 9th draft.
12 October	BRITISH PREMIÈRE opened to very good national and local reviews.

1980	9th draft published in June by Penguin books, Volume 4 of *Collected plays*.
1983	Changes constantly made. New 'student' edition published by Methuen.
1989	Further minor changes made and published in Italy in English/Italian edition (Guerni E Associati), translated by Esther Finz Menascé (who suggested some of the changes).

16 October	LONDON WORKSHOP, eight rehearsed readings performed at the Riverside Studios, directed by author with Israeli actor, Oded Teomi brought over specially to perform the role of Shylock.
1990	Version resulting from London workshop (10th draft) published October, Volume 4 of new Penguin edition of *Collected Plays*.

APPENDIX 2

Memo for John Dexter from Arnold Wesker

MY DEAR JOHN

Points to make to Zero

1   Too much of his performance is simply Zero Mostel strutting around the stage rather than an actor being a sixteenth-century Jew.

2   Too many lines are delivered in what sounds like a drunken drawl. One just can't hear or understand what he's saying. Some, which he appears to consider unimportant – or perhaps simply doesn't understand – are delivered in a perfunctory monotony, and the 'high drama' is saved for the fancy, spectacular passages, which any actor can do. A lot of lines he seems to consider not worth bothering with. The result is an absence of any subtlety.

3   He doesn't seem to hear the music, or see the overall shape of certain sections, so he delivers lines at a slow, ponderous speed when another actor is hanging on the edge of the cliff of his own lines. He doesn't *feel* the pace of certain parts. It's sometimes selfish acting.

4   When he gets lines wrong or when we can't hear word after word it's a sign he hasn't understood what he's saying, or has understood it only at a crude level. He lapses into American speech rhythms, somewhat lazily, because he hasn't understood the musical structure of his line. He can't relate certain line structures to the meaning and emotion that's in them.

5   An example that reveals how his performance is becoming self-centred is when he fails to show reverence and respect to Solomon Usque and Rebecca da Mendes. He behaves as if he is the 'star' of the house (the show), which he is, but through his ability to be deferential as well as through his steam-rollering appetites.

6   When he's being subtle and controlled, then he's breathtaking; but too often one watches and thinks, 'Oh, there goes Zero doing his *shtick*, the one he feels safest in.' How else can one explain his failure to carry off the 'creation of God'

speech; or his absurd laugh after what should be the utterly
sweet and simple and goose–pimple–making exchange:

> S: I love thee, Antonio.
> A: And I, thee, old man.

And even that he sometimes gets back to front!

And how else can one explain that he doesn't seem to
understand the portrait scene?

7   You're a great director because you conduct your entire
company including me as a team, you are big and confident
enough to listen. I would like to think that the fact I have
listened to people, and changed as a result, has helped make
my plays better. In the same way Zero has got to listen to
you, otherwise the audience will say: 'Yeah, Zero was good,
you know, like Zero. But he was really out of his class. He
should stick to musicals. '

I don't think he should – he has the talent, the genius to
give the performance of a life-time. I just hope his ego
doesn't get in the way.

Courage, my love.

PS   And 8.

You must stop him playing 'underneath the spreading,
chestnut tree ...' Pointing to the earth when he says 'earth',
to his head when he says 'brain', to himself when he says
'me'.

APPENDIX 3

Notes for John. Dated 1 October

1   Why is Antonio surly? We must know at once why he and Shylock love one another. They must be so relaxed and affectionate in each other's company. Need opening be *so* slow? More energy and warmth.

2   Portia. Too regal. She's not a queen, she's an eager young woman throbbing with 'pulses' of potentiality. The woman on the English throne should excite her – there's no sense of 'so beware, anything can happen!'
    '*What a mess my father's made of my childhood.*' She simply looks at a book, she should look around.
    And in the court scene – '*impartial, how?*' IS NOT ABOUT HER. Why does she move forward and speak out to the audience? Suddenly we're asked to listen to *her* self-pity when our pity should be for Shylock. She shouldn't take over. It just doesn't make sense.

3   Abtalion is playing King Lear! as one of our management said. Much too theatrical, slow.

4   Entry of Usque and da Mendes. Tubal and Abtalion must bow – even if they do it a second time when Shylock appears.

5   Exeter joke. Shylock mustn't pause to laugh. Let others laugh.

6   Tubal/Abtalion exchanges. Can't it be more interestingly staged? Tubal seems awkwardly turned back. Can't he be adding up columns in his account book?

7   Shylock. '*A bond, between you and me?*' Tender bewilderment. He needs more moments of tenderness, e.g., '*Your heart, dearheart, and I'd take that too if I could, I'm so fond of it.*'

8   Portia's scene with Bassanio. '*Now leave.*' She has no vulnerability, no trembling innocence. When she says '*now leave*' she means 'go, it's too exciting for me, and I'll lose control'. It's *this* quality of passion which is slapped in the face by an also (absurdly) excited Bassanio who says, '*I've no words.*'

9   Rivka/Shylock scene must be rehearsed because she becomes too frenetic due to panic that Joe is going to interrupt her in the wrong moments. It's got to build, needs shaping.

10   Lorenzo. Generally gabbles. In particular: '*Your pleasure in history is playful ...*', etc.

11   Portia. '*Your head, Bassanio? Not your heart?*' Where's her shrewd intelligence? Wit?

12   Shylock. Letter reading. Why *so* furious? His breakdown after Rivka scene much, much simpler. The lines are heart-breaking, we don't need to see his heart break until '*Oh daughter, daughter, daughter.*'

     '*Besides, honour would be accorded me if I pleaded such explanations. "He saved his people!" It would be grotesque.*' This needs to be spelt out because the audience should under-stand why later in the court scene he *is* so silent.

     'GRABBED BY AIR'. Not very happy about the way it happens. Slightly ridiculous.

13   Abtalion. '***Fleeing** the inquisition.*' Can't hear.

14   Nerissa. Can she walk [as though] with cannon balls on her shoulders?[236]

15   Renaissance speech. Technical movements must be rehearsed outside performance – fruit throwing, etc.

16   Problem of Leib?

17   Doge's entry. Why can't everyone bow/curtsey and remain like that till he seats Antonio and Shylock? After all, they bow when he leaves. This will give him dignity.

18   Melancholy of last scene? Lights must wait till curtain is half drawn? Can boys appear sooner with spread? What about my original idea of song starting at the end of court scene?

19   Portia. '*But ... strict adherence.*' Lost.

20   Bassanio. '*How can you make enquiry into silence?*' Lost.

21   Court scene. Jessica's leave-taking needs to be pointed. A gesture from Shylock?

22   Court scene. Where is the pain? Hate Shylock falling back on floor. And '*No, take my books*' is too energetic. He talks of having no appetites left but does so with great appetite!

---

[236] Nerissa: 'Have you watched the way a man walks? Careful that the width of him is seen? As though his shoulders balanced cannon-balls?'

23 Bassanio. '*What a pleasure to meet friends ...*' Too down. Can't they move forward?

24 Why can't Lorenzo *look* at Jessica?

25 Graziano. Before Antonio can say to Graziano, '*Read me the list*' Graziano must first have offered it to him.

26 Lights down too soon at end.

27 Nerissa is left talking to air as Lorenzo moves to Jessica.

28 '*Bubble, bubble, bubble*' should be given significance.

29 Portia. '*I hope, Signor Antonio, you've found a friend in me ...*' CAN'T HEAR!

APPENDIX 4

John's suggestions were:

1 To cut most of Antonio's speech in the dinner scene: '... *The most vital organs of our empire are warehouses, ships-holds, barges and pack horses* ...' down from twenty lines to seven which would wipe out references to the Sansovino statues '*now being carved in the Doge's palace*', and to Venetians not being even honest industrialists ... None of it *essential* but, to my mind, part of the tapestry of the times which I so much feel makes the play. John's reasoning was that he wanted to make space for Shylock's big speech. I agreed, reluctantly. Will keep it in the printed text, though.

2 He wanted to jump from '*Does any man have power to release a bond*' to '*Incredible! The man has even chained his victim to silence.*' It made sense but lost Graziano screaming about '*A Jewish plot!*', and Antonio telling his employee that he loved '*No one and nothing but a safe place in the multitude.*' Which is what I feel Graziano is about. Agreed to cut half the section.

3 A cut of four lines in Graziano's outburst in court: '*Where are your prophets now* ... ?'

He talked of cuts I couldn't agree to without reflection:

1 The list of Portia's tutors.

2 Shylock's request for a copy of 'Foxes Fables', and his sardonic joke about the expulsion of the Jews from England.

3 The exchange between Usque and da Mendes over '*I'm a woman with only a certain art of persuasion* ...'

4 Antonio's description of Graziano '*Now **he's** a happy man, no melancholy in him, and I don't know if I can stand him around* ...'

5 To begin act two with the casket speech, and cut the exchange between Bassanio and Portia.

6 To make what was now left of the warehouse scene into the beginning of the dinner scene – with Antonio and Shylock both out of the room.

APPENDIX 5

Last notes for John before leaving for London – 16/17 October 1977. (Not in order of sequence in the play.)

1   Would still like to see more youthful vibrancy in Portia. If she's regal from the start she has nowhere to go and *'something in me has died struggling to grow up'* has no weight.

2   I'm regretting the loss of the Portia/Nerissa relationship which went when we lost the line, *'Can I present my friend and help, Nerissa?'* In playing regal, Portia is making a mere maid of the black girl. Not my intention, or yours, and less interesting.

3   Antonio has lost his warmth in the first moments of the play.

4   Abtalion's King Lear!

5   Rivka less bent. She's always marvellous but her scene with Shylock is very frenetic and has lost its musical build. (Though it was good last night, Monday.)

6   The young men have great energy and make sense of their lines but too much shrillness makes them one dimensional and too easy as a target. I'd like to see them being simply more intelligent. They have the text.

7   Their exchange – after Shylock on his past – where they talk about nobility, is also intellectually interesting. It's there to show they can be intelligent, but about what *they* want to discuss, even though they're rude in ignoring Shylock.

8   Belmont to court to Belmont. You've done this one.

9   Antonio: In the court, must not make a meal of *'No special privilege?...'* He is not telling them something new, as a lecture, but impatiently reminding them of something they would prefer to forget.

10   Antonio and Shylock in court at beginning convey no sense of the doom hanging over them, the sense of being tragically trapped by their own, and the fates', whims. Example: *'I have our greatest doctors standing by.'* There should be some awareness of the horror of the prospect before them. As in, *'I refuse, and state no reason. Yes!'*

11   You are absolutely right to keep Joe down in the court. Even on the '*Jew, Jew, Jew*' speech. He should be up at the beginning but then low and biting and dangerous – building ...

12   After Portia's judgment what part does the Doge play? Shouldn't there be a moment when the court turns to him and asks 'is she right?' There's an extra moment of suspense to be found while we all wait for his nod.

13   I just don't understand Joe's rendering of '*No, take my books*'. There's no pain there. I see the ending, from this speech on, as the stretching of a long, melancholy note, as in the ending of Mahler's *Song of the Earth*. Or, if you want him to bite on '*No, take my books*' then it should slide into bitter melancholy halfway through (see 18).

14   Joe – hands and arms and the spreading chestnut tree???

15   I think you will find that many Jews will be shocked to see Shylock crawl on his knees. It is forbidden to Jews to go on their knees. It's all right to *bend* before Antonio, but Shylock would not *move* on his bended knee.

16   Why can't Nerissa take off Portia's cloak? An audience might be confused to see it buried beneath a picnic sheet. And why can't Graziano change Antonio's clothes on stage?

17   Portia now makes great sense of her '*I would not hold a sword ...*' speech, but she's *so* slow and deliberate with it. Where is the young woman raging with new and confident intelligence?

18   I *know* your reason for making Joe angry in the end of the court scene, but it not only doesn't make sense it is not what I would like to see happen. '*Give me Shylock's melancholy any time*', says Antonio. It doesn't have to be oppressive melancholy, but rich. Besides, we've heard so *much* anger from him already. *He* must not repeat himself, either!

19   I've told Joe I'm not enamoured of his *Shemah*,[237] on the raised knife. Too ethnic, sentimental.

20   I've talked to Everett about your new line to him in the courtroom – of huge munificent warmth, and have hinted of other places in the play where he could begin looking for it. It began to be very interesting but he was dropping his voice on the moments of being 'nicer'. I believe that will change.

---

237 Daily prayer – like the Lord's Prayer.

I've tried to tell him you were looking for a magnetism. He has to be attractive; an embracing giant whose embrace every so often threatens danger, is not to be trusted. But he doesn't phrase! God knows why he runs sentences one into the other. Perhaps Sir John should be deputed to tell him – that would make him feel wanted.

21 I spoke to Roberta and Joe about their tender moment which begins: '*I can't console you, Signor Shylock ...*' She understood and seemed excited by the idea. Joe said it went against your direction but he'd work with Roberta to show it to you.

22 Roberta seems now very thrilled by your new staging of the courtroom scene and her new found understanding of that last 'sword and scales' speech. She's ripe to have the regality taken from her in the beginning. An actor friend of hers who adored the play told her its great virtue was its 'domesticity': and he warned her not to play against it.

23 But Julie is incredibly unhappy. It's real, real wretchedness. She hates her work, what *she's* doing, her *own* performance. I think she needs attention and love. She won't ever be what we want, but if she's appreciated for what she's doing now I think she'll become better.

24 Change from court to Belmont – you know this one. Portia remaining and the song beginning earlier are both defeated if the lights go down. I'd love to see a cross-fade into an entire stage flooded with the shadows of leaves, the sound of crickets, a hot, richly-sad night, or an equivalent from your fertile imagination.

25 The Lorenzo/Jessica moment in the last Belmont scene doesn't make sense unless she turns away from him, which rejection finally throws him into his controlled rage.

26 Why, why, why, why don't people see, when they feel a scene goes on too long, that it's the actor who's dragging it not the writer? I believe that with less indulgence from the actors we can bring the curtain down at 10.15 and Jesus! that's early for *any* play, let alone this one!

27 Portia must tremble on '*I think you must embrace me after all*', and not get a laugh on '*Now leave.*' 'Now leave' means 'Go, go,

I can't take this excitement, it's too much.' She's passionate! And it's her passion that's being deflated by Bassanio's '*I have no words*' which makes her say, when he's gone: '*I'm touched.*' But her scene after the casket one is now becoming thrilling, and in this scene she's also beginning to have a relationship with Nerissa – a physical one! She's leaning back into Nerissa's arms and I think it ought to be encouraged.

28 Nerissa is losing the hard metallic ring to her voice on the last '*heroes, true*' lines. Better. It needs to go deeper still, and I think it would be a help if she's in the scene earlier. Bassanio's line could be, as she stands there holding the decanter (or whatever): 'Come, Nerissa, more wine for the heroes.' If she's there from the start then her lines won't seem such an appendage.

MY DEAR JOHN

Sorry these are so copious. Thank you for bearing with me and thank you.

Love X

ARNOLD

APPENDIX 6

Letter from John Dexter on Met paper

21 October 1977

DEAR ARNOLD

Thank you for your notes which I am digesting this week.

I note particularly your point about the actors being ponderous and slow but in my considered opinion when I have reflected this problem it will save not more than four minutes.

When you told me you were in a cutting mood, I relaxed considerably, but the cuts, when they came, though good were something short of what we need. I beg you, during the period when you have a little distance, look for the repetitions. It is still to me peppered with them and it only takes one noticeable repetition to make people think the whole play is repetitious.

There is a certain amount of confusion in Washington, apparently, about some of the notes you have given, but I shall be able to do nothing about that for a week or two. In the meantime, whatever practical common sense puts you in a cutting frame of mind, please let it keep you in it a little longer. Scenes, words. Not arms and legs.

Otherwise, things go well. The management is staying away until November 2nd, and the cuts that can be put in, i.e. those that do not affect moves, will be in by the end of this week.

Yours sincerely

JOHN

Letter from John Dexter on Met paper

26 October 1977

DEAR ARNOLD

I am enclosing this article rather quickly to follow-up my letter.

Our inside information via Jean Kerr and others is that Walter Kerr has been speaking to Richard Coe, who, although still enthusing for the play, is claiming that it's repetition and length have in no way been eliminated.

Kerr is up in the country at the moment and Sidney Grusson, editor of the New York Times, unavailable, but there is the strongest feeling that this is a kind of warning. Think on.

Best wishes.

JOHN

Letter from Arnold Wesker, 27 Bishop's Road, London N6

27 October, 1977

DEAR JOHN

Something about your two letters strikes anger and fear into me – not about the future of the play but that the wrong pressures are being brought to bear upon both of us. The play will come down at 10.15 for God's sake! What more could be expected of us? This is why the theatre is the laughing stock of the arts, and why Broadway has not produced any serious theatre for a long time. We should not be going into competition with television rhythms, it will be diminishing our work and my play. TEN–FIFTEEN! TEN–FIFTEEN! That's early out from the theatre by any standards.

When I said I was in a cutting mood I acted on it and cut everything *you* had been urging me to cut, plus a bit more of my own, plus I went back over Marian's long list of suggestions and found some more from her. Don't forget that there are some cuts which are still standing by to be given to them.

Now, I will make a bargain with you and the actors. They have been allowed to tell me where I must cut my work and I will only consider more cuts after I have been allowed to read them the court scene in order to show them the pace I think it can go thus cutting their time. It has all been, mostly been, one way – everyone telling me what's wrong with my text. As you said – what's the point of cutting if the actors fill in the cuts with their interminable pauses, and spreading of vowels?

But I *do* understand your point about even one line of repetition making it seem as if the entire play is repetitious, and since

I've missed some before, it's conceivable I've missed a few more. I will look, and if you find some I will listen, but I beg you not to be panicked by rumours of what this critic has said to that critic. It's not like you. Do we know *when* Coe saw the play? If he saw it while I was there it was being performed as draggy as hell. Maybe he saw it before the new court scene was put in. Maybe it's due to those cuts which have not yet been made.

God and any court of law would say I've done all I can but that now it was up to you and the actors. As for the notes I left in Washington [for the actors], I listed all those in my notes to you. They were only for Lorenzo, with whom I was trying to push *your* new direction into other areas, but they were only pointers; and for Joe and Roberta to whom I spoke about the tender moment in the court scene, and I told you about that also. Actors are in the mood to be confused by anything, I won't go into detail about confusions they've had up till now and how *they* came about. Be a kind boy, don't prepare me as the fall guy!

Love (or 'yours sincerely' if you like and as your last letter said!)

ARNOLD

APPENDIX 7

Notes for John (after third preview), 11 November

1   Last '*bubble bubble*'. Too much like an ending. Need Shylock
    stand there? Can't he embrace Antonio between 'bubbles' and
    then leave! Wouldn't Antonio rise anyway to bow his friend
    out?
2   Rivka's '*I've watched you wandering away from Jewish circles ...*'
    Why does Shylock smile at her and pat her hand? He should
    be so intensely gripped by gloom between his jokes. At least
    he should seem preoccupied. No sense of the sword of
    Damocles hangs over him.
3   Antonio keeps saying: '*I'm indebted to all Venice*' instead of '*I'm
    in debt to all Venice*'. The opposite!
4   The line you want clarified was clarified two weeks ago –
    you turned it down. Instead of '*I must not set a precedent*' try
    '*To break my bond with you would set a precedent to break a bond
    with Jews.*' That line has an extended rhythm to fit in with the
    previous short lines.
5   Other lines we discussed but which you may have forgotten
    to put back:

    A: *That's contempt, Shylock, unworthy of you.*

    S: *You must let my pride have its silence.*

    A: *If you show you think them incapable of understanding, they
         will mistake your silence for contempt.*

    S: *Perhaps they will be right. I am sometimes horrified by the
         passion of my contempt for men . . .* etc
6   Shylock: *Does **any** man have power to release a bond?* is much
    less crude than *Does the Doge have power to release a bond?* That
    seems rude to me. He should be more subtly arrogant.
7   Did you give Antonio these additional words (which I've
    underlined)?

    > *You will inflame the people's grievances <u>in order</u> to achieve
    > power, Lorenzo.*

APPENDIX 8

Letter to John *re* Nerissa

JOHN: I'm not only shocked by each new line I discover is cut, but that you have done it daily with *no* consultation, knowing that I will not rock the boat. But what was done to Gloria last night was so sneaky, humiliating and *irresponsible*! To let her go on stage without telling her of such a huge cut affecting her entrance – it's unbelievable. Especially since that production and *you* owe her more than you realise. All the big fights I wanted to have with you I had with her. *She* defended you, the need to cut, your methods, your everything. She talked me out of legal action and/or fleeing and leaving it all after Washington. She, in the midst of the depressing negativism of others who talked gloomily among themselves, was constantly positive.

The humiliation for me though, is the [company] joke: 'You don't like your line? Change it! Everybody does!'

In cutting without reference to me you lost me and my text respect before the company.

I had to write because I know we'll not meet to talk before opening night.

A

APPENDIX 9

From Rabbi Gabriel Maza, Suffolk Jewish Centre, New York

10 November 1977

DEAR MR DEXTER

I saw *Shylock* and enjoyed it greatly for its content and drama. It has been inevitable that the image of Shylock should eventually inspire a logical and brilliant correction.

All was going eminently well for me until Shylock raised the dagger over Antonio, and Portia had to save him from himself. At this climatic moment I was abruptly let down.

What we have always found most distasteful of Shakespeare's version was the portrayal of a Jew greedily ready to take a man's life. This image has now been corrected by eradicating the greed and replacing it with logic and reluctance. We are still left with the beleaguered Jew about to commit murder. Yet, Jewish law expressly forbids the taking of one life in order to save other lives and, most emphatically, a man may not commit murder even if a whole community is held in hostage. Shylock in your *Shylock*, portraying a character so enlightened and humane, could not possibly in this context have required Portia to save him from the deed. In the whole development of the play and at the climax, it is nowhere mentioned that the Jewish religious conscience here involves an unequivocal Jewish law. Shylock's sister's challengingly painful speech to him, though convincing and realistic, requires a subsequent development somewhere in the drama of the impossibility of Shylock stabbing a man who in this *Shylock* is a dear beloved friend. It's out of character in your version.

Perhaps in this *Shylock* it would be workable to have Portia save Shylock from the court while his friend Antonio pleads to be stabbed. The theatrical decision, of course, is yours. Religiously, however, all the work and brilliance that went into this play is contradicted by its climax. The play still offers much necessary edification and drama but religiously and dramatically it fails at the end.

I am aware of the great difficulty and hazards of achieving success on Broadway. I regret adding any problem to the frantic last week before the critics bring in their powerful verdicts. I and my colleagues to whom I have spoken and many other people wish Shylock great success. It is beautifully done and needs to be seen.

Best wishes and blessings.

Shalom